THE BODY, IN THEORY
Histories of Cultural Materialism

Editors
Dalia Judovitz, Emory University
James I. Porter, University of Michigan

Editorial Board
Malcolm Bowie, Francis Barker, Norman Bryson, Catherine Gallagher,
Alphonso Lingis, A. A. Long, Jean-François Lyotard, Elaine Scarry,
Jean Louis Schefer, Susan Stewart

The body constructed by theory and through social and cultural practices has provided the departure point for studies that broach new fields and styles of inquiry. The aim of the series The Body, in Theory: Histories of Cultural Materialism is to reconstruct a history of materialisms (aesthetic, linguistic, and philosophical) by locating the body at the intersection of speculative and cultural formations across a wide range of contexts.

Titles in the series
The Subject as Action: Transformation and Totality in Narrative Aesthetics
by Alan Singer

*Power and Knowledge: Astrology, Physiognomics, and
Medicine under the Roman Empire*
by Tamsyn S. Barton

Under the Sign: John Bargrave as Collector, Traveler, and Witness
by Stephen Bann

Simulacra and Simulation
by Jean Baudrillard, translated by Sheila Faria Glaser

The Deluge, the Plague: Paolo Uccello
by Jean Louis Schefer, translated by Tom Conley

Philodemus in Italy: The Books from Herculaneum
by Marcello Gigante, translated by Dirk Obbink

The Tremulous Private Body: Essays on Subjection
by Francis Barker

Picturing Silence: Emblem, Language, Counter-Reformation Materiality
by Karen Pinkus

The Gay Critic
by Hubert Fichte, translated by Kevin Gavin

THE GAY CRITIC

HUBERT FICHTE

TRANSLATED BY
KEVIN GAVIN

INTRODUCTION BY
JAMES W. JONES

Ann Arbor
The University
of Michigan
Press

Copyright © by the University of Michigan 1996
All rights reserved
Published in the United States of America by
The University of Michigan Press
Originally published as *Homosexualität und Literatur I* by S. Fischer Verlag,
Frankfurt am Main. © 1987, S. Fischer Verlag
Manufactured in the United States of America
⊚ Printed on acid-free paper
1999 1998 1997 1996   4 3 2 1
A CIP catalogue record for this
book is available from the
British Library.

No part of this publication may be reproduced,
stored in a retrieval system, or transmitted in any form
or by any means, electronic, mechanical, or otherwise,
without the written permission of the publisher.

Library of Congress Cataloging-in-Publication Data

Fichte, Hubert.
    [Homosexualität und Literatur. Band 1. English]
    The gay critic / Hubert Fichte : translated by Kevin Gavin.
      p.   cm. – (The body, in theory)
    ISBN 0-472-10501-9. – ISBN 0-472-08340-6 (pbk.)
    1. Homosexuality and literature. 2. Gays' writings – History and
criticism. I. Title. II. Series.
PN56.H57F5413   1996
809'.8920664 – dc20   95-49087
                                                                          CIP

The Gay Critic was originally published in 1987 by S. Fischer Verlag as *Homosexualität und Literatur I*. The publication of this work has been subsidized by Inter Nationes, Bonn. The editors also wish to acknowledge the assistance of Barbara Perlmutter and Gisela Podlech of S. Fischer Verlag.

CONTENTS

Hubert Fichte Warns His Readers	1
Eleven Exaggerations: Introduction to a Reader	3
The Bloody Man: Sade	15
Anyone Could Be Next: On Pier Paolo Pasolini's Film *Salò*	105
Voodoo Bloodbaths – Heroes of Mixed Religion: Remarks on Daniel Casper von Lohenstein's *Agrippina*	113
Woe of Woes! Remarks on Daniel Casper von Lohenstein's Turkish Tragedy *Ibrahim Bassa*	163
Revolution as Restoration: Jean-Nicholas-Arthur Rimbaud, Ethnologist	213
The Ewe Tribes of Jakob Spieth	251
The Land of Laughter: Polemical Remarks on the *Tristes tropiques* of Claude Lévi-Strauss	277
The Semblance of a Cure: *De Instauranda Aethiopum Salute* by Pater Alonso de Sandoval, Society of Jesus, 1627	307
My Friend Herodotus	333
Excursus: The Mediterranean and the Gulf of Benin: The Description of African and Afro-American Rites in Herodotus	359

Contents

A Petrified Magic City: Reflections on the Popular
Edition of the Monographs of Paul Wunderlich,
Edited by Jens Christian Jensen   373

The Objective and the Subjective Author:
Remarks on Henry James's *Washington Square*   381

INTRODUCTION
James W. Jones

You have already glanced at these essays. Pages filled with short paragraphs in different type styles, interrupted and surrounded by more white space than one expects in works of gay studies today. What is one to make of this postmodern, deconstructed amalgam? More importantly, who is Hubert Fichte?

That is the central question this introduction is intended to answer. This is difficult to do because Fichte himself was intent on questioning, even dissecting, individual identity, including his own. Let us gather the unraveled pieces like the thread Ariadne presented to Theseus and see where they lead.

Pick up almost any work on Fichte and you will find a one-sentence summation of the man as an "illegitimate child, half-Jew, homosexual who lives with a woman"[1] and a literary critic who had not finished school. Each points to a significant aspect of Fichte's life, but none tells enough. Hubert Fichte was born on March 21, 1935, in Perleberg (a city northwest of Berlin in the state of Brandenburg). He never met his father, who was Jewish and who fled the country that two years before Fichte's birth had become a National Socialist state. His parents had not married, and his illegitimate status along with his definition, according to Nazi law, as a "Mischling, I. Grades" ("half-breed of the first degree") became the first two points of orientation for the young boy's identity during the Third Reich. His Protestant mother had taken her baby to her parents' home in Hamburg. She found work as a secretary; her father was a customs inspector. The dangers of air raids put an end to these middle-class surroundings, and Fichte was sent in 1941 to a Catholic orphanage in upper Bavaria. After spending a year there as a half-Jewish, half-Protestant outsider, he returned to Hamburg, but soon he and his mother were evacuated to Liegnitz in West Prussia.[2]

Introduction

After the war, Fichte and his mother returned to Hamburg, where both found employment in the theater. Already as a teenager, Fichte was playing major roles – e.g., in Sartre's *Morts dans sépulture* and Saroyan's *My Heart's in the Highlands*. He studied acting and began learning French in the five years following the war, while he continued writing fiction, an activity he had begun as a boy of nine. In 1952, he published his first pieces of prose. His acting career died out after his voice had changed and Fichte turned to agricultural studies in the Provence region of France. Over the next few years, he continued his studies, both theoretical and practical in nature, in the North German province of Holstein and in Sweden. He also worked at times with young people, both at the Camp de la Pomponnette in Paris (a camp for working class children founded by the Abbé Pierre Grouès) and at a home for juvenile delinquents in Sweden.

All this time, Fichte was also writing works of fiction and publishing pieces of criticism. By 1962, he decided to pursue a career in literature. His first book, a collection of stories entitled *Aufbruch nach Turku* (*Departure for Turku*, 1963), brought him to the attention of the "Gruppe 47," a group of the most influential West German authors. His first novel, *The Orphanage* (1965), established Fichte as one of the new generation of West German authors.

These initial years of Fichte's literary career contain the seeds that the author nurtured and developed over the rest of his life. He created a prose style in fiction that was utterly unique in weaving autobiographical experience and fantasy with multiple points of view. He became friends with the photographer Leonore Mau, a somewhat older woman with whom he would share his life. He began to travel to countries around the world, especially to Africa, South America, and the Caribbean. He began to conduct interviews, which he would later publish as documentary interviews or would work into his fiction, and he trained himself to break through the barriers traditionally separating interviewer and interviewee. He did so by learning the language and living in the culture of the people whom he interviewed. Here, too, his personal experience shaped his writing.

Fichte wrote a series of novels that all reflected his own life experience and were narrated from various positions on the mar-

Introduction

gins of West German society: gay in particular, but also punk (beat), prostitute, and addict. These novels are: *Die Palette* (*The Palette*, 1968), *Detlevs Imitationen "Grünspan"* (*Detlev's Imitations*, 1971), and *Versuch über die Pubertät* (translated either as *Attempt at Puberty* or *Treatise on Puberty*, 1974). These novels trace the story of the boy "Detlev" as he moves through puberty into the young adult character of "Jäcki," following a path that mirrors the author's own development. Fichte was awarded several prizes, but he stopped publishing fiction in the mid-1970s. Except for *Die Palette*, his works never sold in great numbers and Fichte's name was never widely known, although esteemed literary critics such as Hans Mayer praised his novels. His stories remained too experimental for the taste of a large audience.

Instead, he intensely pursued his interests in African and Afro-American cultures, in particular the rituals and customs of rural tribes or voodoo religions. With these peoples who had resisted colonialism by maintaining their own practices and languages, Fichte felt a kinship. He described his experiences of living with them in works such as *Xango. Die afroamerikanischen Religionen: Bahia–Haiti–Trinidad* (*Xango: The Afro-American Religions*, 1976) and *Petersilie. Die afroamerikanischen Religionen: Santo Domingo–Venezuela–Miami–Grenada* (*Petersilie: The Afro-American Religions*, 1980). These books (in each case accompanied by a separate volume of photographs taken by Leonore Mau) form a part of a "poetic anthropology/ethnology" (his term) that Fichte wrote about non-European and European cultures and cultural phenomena. While *Xango* and *Petersilie* focus on the non-European, his collection of interviews with members of Hamburg's sexual underground, *Interviews aus dem Palais d'Amour* (*Interviews from the Palais d'Amour*, 1972) and the two volumes entitled *Homosexualität und Literatur* (*Homosexuality and Literature*, 1987, 1988) elaborate aspects of European cultures.

Hubert Fichte traveled to over twenty countries, not so much as a tourist but as one intent on participating in the new culture as fully as possible. He taught himself new languages; he lived abroad for extended periods of time. Yet, while seeking to enter new worlds, he always remained the outsider. Boundaries proved flexible but were never erased. From that perspective, within and

Introduction

without, Fichte created a body of work that reveals not only himself, the half insider / half outsider, but also the cultures whose borders he traversed and inhabited. Hubert Fichte died in Hamburg on March 8, 1986.

FICHTE AND GAY LITERATURE

Having followed the thread through the labyrinth of Fichte's life, we arrive now at the place where Fichte met gay studies. The meeting never went smoothly. Fichte created in his life and works a space between identities, but the very term "gay" seems to presume an identity whose position is fixed, at least long enough for close analysis. Certainly a volume entitled *Homosexuality and Literature* (as it is in German) or *The Gay Critic* (its English title) would seem to indicate that Fichte wrote from such a position. Leaving aside for the moment (we shall return to it at the end) the fact that these titles were chosen by editors, it is nonetheless true that Fichte did refer to himself as "homosexual" and made reference to "our movement," by which he meant the gay liberation movement. (He was never an activist in this multifaceted "movement" but more a sympathizer.) Fichte was not a joiner; yet, the eternal outsider searched for affiliations and affinities. Having found them, he could never integrate himself into the group because he continually questioned the basis of community and of individuality: identity.

It is precisely that questioning of how identity is constructed on a personal and communal level, however, that places Fichte at the heart of gay studies. In both his fiction and non-fiction, Fichte examines – perhaps "de-stabilizes" puts it more accurately – the social norms that construct identities for individuals. These social processes force an individual to conform to desires that are not his or her own. The expression of an individual's own nonconforming desires must then be defined as aberrant. They are either punished or channeled into avenues where deviance can be controlled. Thus, we find Fichte's fiction set in dive bars and on hustlers' streets, and his non-fiction is populated by the figures from the margin (Genet, voodoo priests, a leatherman). But, in capitalist societies, the margins can never unite. The critic Gert Mattenklott describes the way in which homosexuality functions in Fichte's works:

Introduction

Homosexuality, the way Fichte represents it and the way it drives his writing, does not build community, but rather just the opposite. That sets it apart from the movement politics of the Sixties and Seventies and at the same time supplies the foundation for its usefulness as an aesthetic metaphor for 'specialness.' The dynamic of coming out does not lead to reciprocal understanding, attachment and community but instead to increasing estrangement and solipsistic isolation.[3]

A reaction to that distancing is violence that can, seemingly paradoxically, also represent an attempt to span the abyss between desire and conformity, between individual and community. This theme of violence provides a very clear example of the way in which Fichte's fiction, interviews, essays, and radio plays all take up the same theme but deal with it in different ways. While he was writing the novel *Versuch über die Pubertät* (1974), he was conducting lengthy interviews with "Hans Eppendorfer" (pseudonym) about the latter's experiences in the Hamburg S/M scene.[4] Fichte reworked some of what Eppendorfer told him into sexual fantasies that appear in the novel. The fantasies that Jäcki, the narrator, has of mutual masturbation with his desired friend Klaus end in an orgasm of "blood and slime." As the critic Wolfgang Popp shows, the boy's fantasies center on the dissolving of one flesh, Jäcki's, into that of the other, Klaus.[5] This sex can only exist in the imagination, and that imagination is shaped by the real conditions in which the adolescent boys live. Those conditions forbade such sexual expression and directed sex into the violence of sport or into other avenues while they made love between boys impossible. Fichte juxtaposes these adolescent sexual fantasies with the realities described by another character in the novel, "Hans, the leatherman," who provides details of male S/M sex parties in the basement of a Hamburg bar.

The themes of identity and violence intersect in two other pieces Fichte worked on around the same time. In February 1975, he finished the essay on Sade (contained in this volume). Fichte used the same title, "The Bloody Man," for his radio play (written in 1975, broadcast in 1976), which is subtitled: "Larry Townsend, Friedrich Hölderlin, Marcel Proust and Others Talk about the Bloody Man."[6] Here Fichte connects his work with that of an

Introduction

array of gay (or in the case of Hölderlin, possibly gay) authors. The group is certainly a heterogenous one. The American author Townsend has written the bible of gay S/M, *The Leatherman's Handbook* (1980), and many pieces of fiction involving gay S/M sex. Friedrich Hölderlin (1770–1843) was an influential German poet of the late eighteenth and early nineteenth centuries whose sense of extreme alienation from the society around him fed his poetry but, perhaps, destroyed his mind. He spent the last thirty-six years of life under the care of a local carpenter in Tübingen. Whether he was actually mentally unstable or represented an unwelcome threat to the morés and morals of his society has never been completely clarified. Marcel Proust's great "novel" *A la recherche du temps perdu* (*Remembrance of Things Past*, 1913–27) became Fichte's model for his own writing from 1974 on, which he named the *Geschichte der Empfindlichkeit* (*The History of Sensitivity*, discussed in the next section).

What unites these authors with Fichte is the theme of violence within gay literature. In his article on "Violence" for the *Encyclopedia of Homosexuality* (1990), Gert Hekma lists eight categories of violence that relate to male homosexuality. At least five of them appear in Fichte's works, often as significant factors in the puberty of the main characters and the narrators: initiation, social repression of homosexuality, internalization of negative social norms by homosexuals, esthetization of cruelty by homosexual artists, and homosexual sado-masochism.[7] Hekma cites Fichte and several of those to whom Fichte felt a strong affinity (Rimbaud, Proust, Hans Henny Jahnn, Pasolini) in his overview of the literary treatment of this theme.[8] Hekma offers a tentative reason for the link between violence and male homosexuality, especially in Western cultures: "What cannot be dealt with openly and verbally becomes relegated to the furtive and physical, whether in favor or opposition."[9]

That is exactly what Fichte tried to uncover through his techniques of interweaving narrator and narrated in fiction and of combining his own commentary with citations from the authors he was critiquing in his essays. Fichte wanted to lay bare the social processes that shape homosexual desire and then try to find ways to set that desire free. Violence often became that path to freedom.

Introduction

A third theme that runs through Fichte's work and through many works of gay literature is that of leaving home and going out into a foreign culture in search of a new home. This is not so much "The Wizard of Oz" (although that is a version of this theme, perhaps the Ur-myth for the modern American gay man) as it is the need to escape the society that will not allow one to be gay. Perhaps the most well-known telling of this theme in German letters is Thomas Mann's *Death in Venice* (1912). The author Gustav Aschenbach, suffering from writer's block, leaves Munich for Venice where he is bewitched by the beauty of Tadzio, a Polish youth vacationing at the same hotel.[10] For many North Germans (Mann was born in Lübeck, a bit farther north than Fichte's Hamburg), the climate and culture of the southern parts of the Western world promised both recuperation and, more importantly, freedom from the constraints of bourgeois life at home. Fichte was drawn even farther south, to Africa, and west, to the Caribbean and South America. He seems to have been looking for the same thing so many before him had sought: "romance, companionship or sex," as Robert Aldrich puts it in his study of this theme in gay culture, *The Seduction of the Mediterranean* (1993).[11]

Traveling back and forth between Germany and over twenty foreign countries from the 1950s on, Fichte found many homes with cultures and with individual men in those cultures. Fichte also found homes in the works of other authors. Read the names of the cities where he wrote the essays that follow. On Christopher Street he is reminded of Herodotus; in the Caribbean, he writes about Henry James. Perhaps all homes proved temporary, but the desire to put down roots seems to be one desire Fichte did not feel. On the contrary, as he writes in the essay on Herodotus: "Travel is knowledge. Sex." Making the foreign familiar by means of sex, the most intimate form of knowledge, might be said to be one of the major themes not only of Fichte's life but also of gay literature.

A final theme that runs through Fichte's works, as it does through gay literature generally, is simply "sex." The importance of sex – of sex acts – has already been touched on in the discussion about violence. The split between act and emotion, between sex and love, defines the core of Fichte's representation of homo-

Introduction

sexuality in fiction. That division has been a major theme of gay literature from the ancient Greeks to E. M. Forster, to contemporary authors as different as Harvey Fierstein and Larry Kramer. Wolfgang Popp explains how Fichte moves this theme into a variety of areas within his fiction:

> [Fichte's protagonists] experience in their initial preadolescent or adolescent sexual contact with another person (with any other person) the separation of love from sexuality, the divergence of sexual fantasies whipped to a fever pitch from the triviality of sexual practices, the disintegration of homosexual desire and the loss of speech.[12]

Rituals serve as a way to express homosexuality, even though they may not be able to bridge that gap between fantasy and reality. Boys discover sex together and in each other's bodies by means of adolescent rites (such as mutual masturbation). These rites, in fiction and in Fichte's writings on Afro-American cultures, serve as a means of initiation into the community. This initiation does not always represent a positive step though, as Fichte wrote in his novel *Detlevs Imitationen Grünspan:*

> I think I have observed that early adolescent development and adolescent development proceed alternatively by means of imitating the world and identifying with the world – just like a magic ritual. On the one hand, the ego is hemmed in, in the imitation, I am trained, there is the danger that my ego will be consumed by the world; but then again I equate everything that I know about myself, everything I am feeling, with the world, I take the world inside myself.[13]

Rituals become paths of socialization that can dissolve identity. These concerns are raised in several of the essays that follow, in particular the essay on Sade.

If, as Fichte seemed to believe, each homosexual must find his or her own way through the world, then it is no surprise that Fichte developed a highly unique writing style. Moving between narration and association in his essays, the texts are for the most part composed of a collage of his own ideas and quotes from what Fichte has read. Hartmut Böhme explains Fichte's reason for developing this style: Fichte was trying to restore magical power

Introduction

to words (and thus to literature) by devising new ways to write about experience, by creating new words, by breaking the rules of organizing thought into logically developed and reasoned paragraphs.[14] In short, he sought to deconstruct in order to construct anew.

Further, he thoroughly mistrusted the language of "science" (including literary criticism), which he felt silenced those who became the objects of "scientific" scrutiny. Fichte wrote: "The language of the scientific view of the world has made itself in the image of the world and the mutilations in this language bear equal guilt for the mutilations within our world."[15] In his nonfiction works, Fichte searched for a language that would express "the dilemma of sensitivity and conformity, doubting and doing" and that would be "an essentially different kind of language."[16] In his essay on Henry James, which concludes this collection, Fichte expresses his mistrust of the very category of "homosexuality" since it is a construct of biology.

With his text collages, Fichte was pursuing a desire that motivates all his work. The critic Peter Laemmle described this as a need "to track himself down in other existences, to speak in other and his own voices until the point when they became inseparably one."[17] We see in the essays that follow how Hubert Fichte found himself in other writers and how he tried to speak with them.

There were certain gays in whom Fichte had little interest or to whom he even refused to talk. I myself am familiar with one such instance that took place approximately a year before his death. Wolfgang Popp had organized the first gay studies conference to be held in West Germany and had chosen as its theme the work of Hans Henny Jahnn. I presented a paper there on this author of intricate, lengthy novels and baroque, bloody dramas in which male homosexuality figures to a greater or lesser extent. Jahnn did not necessarily identify himself as gay, but the central relationship of his life was his love, erotic and emotional, for another man. He had also been a kind of mentor to Fichte, but their relationship has never been explained in depth.

Since Fichte had known Jahnn personally and was himself both a respected man of German letters and a gay author, Popp invited Fichte to give a major lecture. Fichte responded with one

Introduction

of his text collages. He had dissected Popp's letter of invitation and the accompanying call for papers and then arranged them so as to show "what I think of the language that talks about my language which is supposed to talk about Jahnn's language."[18] Fichte interwove such phrases from the call for papers as "maximum 20 minutes," "lunch," and "contact address" with "what role does homosexuality play," "exchange results of research," and "outsider problem." Jahnn followed this list of excerpts with a more precise explanation as to why he would not be coming:

> This language has nothing to do with Hans Henny Jahnn's language any more; it has nothing to do with my language.
> When I read something like that by committed, engaged friends, I would just like to hang myself.
> One banal, senseless empty word after another. We have worked for nothing.
> A language which does not camouflage oppression any longer.[19]

Popp, furious and personally insulted, responded with a long letter clarifying the conference's goals and his own philosophy as the only professor in West Germany at the time who was teaching gay literature. Fichte wrote back a note explaining that he had not intended to insult, but rather to bring out "a few indications of oppression, falsification through language." He also clarified his remark about "having worked in vain" by pointing to the present-day conflict in the Middle East and the reporting being done on AIDS as failures of "our" efforts to recreate language.[20]

Hubert Fichte was certainly a difficult homosexual. Difficult to categorize, difficult to comprehend, difficult to read. I must confess that I do not necessarily enjoy reading his works, but I am drawn to them. Perhaps here lies an affinity Fichte himself described in one of the novels published after his death, *A Happy Love:* "Irresistibly he was attracted by what he did not like." One ignores Fichte's works at the risk of losing a valuable perspective. Indeed, one is somehow drawn to him for that perspective – the one that puts all assumptions into question and exposes the compromises one has made in order to create a life for oneself.

Introduction

HOMOSEXUALITY AND LITERATURE 1 / THE GAY CRITIC

Our ball of thread has grown larger and larger. We have arrived at the end of a maze. Before us stands the labyrinth of connected rooms, the essays of this volume. You have already met your host, but it may be helpful to know something about the essays themselves. As this translation does not include the "Editorial Notes" and the "Afterword" that the volume's editor, Torsten Teichert, supplied for the German edition, much of what follows is a summary of that information.

In German, this volume of essays is entitled *Homosexuality and Literature 1: Polemics*. The subtitle gives you an indication of Fichte's intent. The essays are part of Fichte's magnum opus, *The History of Sensitivity*,[21] that he began writing in 1974. The "work" was to consist largely of novels (seven or nine, depending on what outline one reads), but several (four or five) were part of a new genre Fichte devised: "glosses." In these works, he combined edited versions of his diaries with other kinds of texts such as reports, interviews, commentaries, and feature articles. Fichte revised the outline of the *History* throughout his life, and by the time of his death in 1986 the work was to encompass between sixteen and nineteen volumes. Of those, twelve have since been published.

The two books of essays (*Homosexuality and Literature 1 and 2*) form the first volume of the "Paralipomena" to the *History*.[22] These addenda or postscripts (the meaning of the Greek word "paralipomena") extend over three other volumes: essays on his studies of religions and on his travels and a collection of his radio plays. Some of the essays on homosexuality and literature had been previously published. Many of these works were written for the radio, although Fichte probably read shortened versions of them. In Germany, radio has been a medium of much greater variety than it is in the United States. Many stations broadcast short plays written for the radio, lengthy pieces of cultural criticism, and in-depth interviews on topics that American listeners would for the most part find too intellectually challenging. Both Hartmut Böhme and Torsten Teichert point out that Fichte actually earned his living by writing for the radio because his novels never became bestsellers. Böhme also directs our attention to the

Introduction

influence of this medium on the linguistic style Fichte developed: "Radio is not only Fichte's economic basis but also the strongest determinant of the form of his literary language. It was not the literary market that carried Fichte but rather the limited public space of the medium of the radio."[23] Perhaps these texts would best be read aloud.

What I find fascinating in these essays are the dialogue Fichte creates, the selections he makes from his readings, and the themes he pursues. In his journey one can see that taken also by many gay men who leave their families of origin and create their family of choice. They choose among whom they will live and to whom they will turn for support. Through that network of elective affinities, they discover who they are.

And so we are back where we started, at community and identity. Is Fichte "the gay critic," as this English translation names him? Is he the essayist on "homosexuality and literature," as the German original is called? Does it matter? Yes, because the names reflect the values of the differing cultures. No book staking a claim to literary respectability in Germany would put the word "schwul" (the German equivalent of "gay") in its title. But no book aiming at a post-Stonewall, English-speaking readership and a gay studies/queer studies market would apply the polemical term "homosexuality" without at least an explanatory subtitle. Fichte's own questioning of identity remains unresolved; his search of community seems to continue.

With the information provided in this brief introduction to Fichte's life and work, I have guided you around the labyrinth. We return again to Hubert Fichte, that man of halves. The gay/homosexual critic/author invites you on a journey. If we are back where we started, are we trapped in the labyrinth (of language, of sex)? Follow the thread and see where it leads you. Bon voyage. Gute Reise.

NOTES

1. Gisela Lindemann, "Zärtlichkeit ordnen. Notizen zur Planung und Entstehung der *Geschichte der Empfindlichkeit*," a promotional pamphlet published by S. Fischer publishing company (Frankfurt am Main, 1987) to explain Fichte's series of works entitled *Die*

Introduction

Geschichte der Empfindlichkeit. (The pages are not numbered, but this quotation is taken from the second page.) All translations are my own.

2. Much of this information is taken from the chronology in Wolfgang von Wangenheim's *Hubert Fichte* (Munich: C. H. Beck and Verlag Edition Text und Kritik, 1980), 224.

3. Gert Mattenklott, "Erotologie als Form," *Forum: Homosexualität und Literatur* 9 (1990), 24.

4. The interviews were conducted at three different times: August 1970, September 1973, and March 1976. They were published under the title: *Der Ledermann spricht mit Hubert Fichte* (Frankfurt am Main: Suhrkamp, 1977).

5. Wolfgang Popp, *Männerliebe: Homosexualität und Literatur* (Stuttgart: J. B. Metzler, 1992), 175–76.

6. This can be found in the posthumously published collection of Fichte's radio plays, *Schulfunk,* 125–74.

7. Gert Hekma, "Violence" in *Encyclopedia of Homosexuality* (New York: Garland Press, 1990), 1373.

8. Hekma, 1374.

9. Hekma, 1375.

10. For an extended discussion of this work, see my *"We of the Third Sex": Literary Representations of Homosexuality in Wilhelmine Germany* (New York: Peter Lang, 1990), 276–90.

11. Robert Alrich, *The Seduction of the Mediterranean: Writing, Art and Homosexual Fantasy* (London, New York: Routledge, 1993), 4.

12. Popp, 255.

13. Quoted in Tomas Vollhaber, *Das Nichts. Die Angst. Die Erfahrung: Untersuchung zur zeitgenössischen schwulen Literatur* (Berlin: Verlag rosa Winkel, 1987), 171.

14. Hartmut Böhme, *Hubert Fichte: Riten des Autors und Leben der Literatur* (Stuttgart: Metzler, 1992), 31.

15. Böhme, 31, quoting from Fichte, *Petersilie,* 361.

16. Sabine Röhr, "Das exotische Selbst: Zur Beziehung von Sexualität, Erkenntnis und Reisen in Hubert Fichtes poetischer Wissenschaft," in: *Erkenntniswunsch und Diskretion: Erotik in biographischer und autobiographischer Literatur,* eds. Gerhard Härle, Maria Kalveram and Wolfgang Popp (Berlin: Verlag rosa Winkel, 1992), 406, quoting from Fichte's *Xango,* 119.

Introduction

17. Quoted in Böhme, 35.

18. Popp published the correspondence as an appendix to the conference proceedings, *Siegener Hans Henny Jahnn Kolloquium: Homosexualität und Literatur,* eds. Dietrich Molitor and Wolfgang Popp (Essen: Verlag Die Blaue Eule, 1986), 237.

19. Molitor and Popp, 238.

20. Molitor and Popp, 242.

21. Fichte originally called the series a "History of Tenderness" (Zärtlichkeit) and then a "History of Sentimentality" (Empfindsamkeit) before choosing the term "Sensitivity" (Empfindlichkeit).

22. Teichert points to the significance of Ezra Pound's *ABC of Reading* (1934), seeing it as the model Fichte took for the essays he wrote on homosexuality and literature. Torsten Teichert, "Nachwort," in *Homosexualität und Literatur 1,* Hubert Fichte (Frankfurt am Main: S. Fischer, 1987), 497–98.

23. Böhme, 42.

TRANSLATOR'S NOTE
Kevin Gavin

The essays in this volume were originally conceived as part of a larger series, "The History of Sensibility," a nineteen-volume opus that was left unfinished at the time of the author's death in 1986. This title offers us, perhaps, as good a place as any to begin tracing some of the vectors in the work of this brilliant, if sometimes baffling, literary critic. The writings of Hubert Fichte are a play of/on (the) senses. Of words and their meanings, and of the body. Across borders, and across cultures. And across historical periods. To get a sense of Fichte's work, to be sensitive to its effects, one must first of all know that the author is himself a translator – he crosses borders. And, more importantly, he carries something across. He gets his point across.

And what is Fichte's point? Can we find a common thread in essays whose subject matter is as diverse as German Baroque drama, the African slave trade, voodoo, Herodotean historiography – and of course, homosexuality? Statements as lucid and concise as "secularization – that is, bisexuality," with which he closes his essay on Homer, are rare. That is, he rarely makes such a clear point. More often he offers us vectors, trajectories. Or passages – both textual and figurative. Places where meaning might be glimpsed, or pursued. As in the essay on Herodotus, where he comments on the author's penchant for making subtle connections over large expanses of text:

> *Croesus, burning at the stake, will cry out into the stillness three times the name of Solon, as every student knows. He does so in the first book, chapter 86, recalling, some fifty chapters earlier (I, 32). Solon's advice to the king: no one may be called truly happy before his death.*
> *Herodotus likes to build these kinds of arches, and he must have expected his readers and listeners to be able to reconstruct them.*

Translator's Note

The same could surely be said of Hubert Fichte. Which might also help us account for his peculiar style. Can we label it? It looks aphoristic but often lacks pointedness. His favorite rhetorical device is the catalogue – or better, the (secular) litany, its spoken form, a kind of verbal inventory. Things to be noted, itemized, as if one were putting them in order prior to taking a journey. What types of exotica does he offer us? "Travel is knowledge. . . . Travel is a sexual need," he notes in the same essay on Herodotus.

Fichte has a keen ear for poetic effects, including those that frustrate semantic sense (above all in Sade and Rimbaud). The long work on Sade, in which many of the book's major themes are sounded for the first time, is actually a radio play and should be read accordingly, acoustically. Fichte's is a poetic prose style. But loose, syncopated, and jazz-like. Or like the notes of an ethnographer. Which he was.

As well as a gifted linguist. He is fond of citing Ernst Robert Curtius's requirement that every literary scholar should master at least two European dialects as a minimum standard for entering into the literary dialogue. Fichte had little trouble meeting such a standard. He moves with relative ease between ancient Greek and Latin, he reads (and scans) medieval French poetry, and he spoke Spanish, Portuguese, French, English, and Italian. He comments on the inadequacies of various translations, makes emendations, sharply criticizes German scholarship for ignoring the works of Lohenstein, the great baroque dramatist. And then offers his own, newly edited version of several of the poet's works.

The poetics of translation: the word is itself a trans-lation, the Latin version of the Greek *metaphor*—in either case a process of carrying things, and meanings, across borders. As opposed to a transgression, which would be a crossing without carrying, without caring—senseless, and insensitive. The poetics of translation are the poetics of metaphor. Hubert Fichte crosses borders—linguistic, literal, and sexual. That is, he's a poet. His insights facilitate free exchange, and his criticism, at its best, is a liberation.

HUBERT FICHTE WARNS HIS READERS

My dear friends and colleagues.

I must warn you.
As you may perhaps already know, I am an author who has, throughout his life, associated more often with prostitutes, male and female, and with voodoo priests, than with those important figures with whom one should, as an author, associate.
And I believe, moreover, that prostitutes and voodoo priests – upon whom, in recent times, in a pogrom of vast proportions, the blame is laid for every evil, in order thereby to divert attention from the real evils of our time – I believe that prostitutes and voodoo priests perform crucial and self-sacrificing acts, artistic acts, if one considers them aright, as well as hygienic, psychoanalytic, and poetic ones – I mean to say that they belong to the last great benefactors on earth.
I would like, ladies and gentlemen, by my words neither to shock you any further, nor apologize.
I mean only that association with prostitutes and voodoo priests is not the sole precondition for quoting Goethe or Opitz reliably. Thus it may happen that in the pedagogic and erotic rush, in which, in this and the following week, we will hopefully find ourselves, it may happen that I should not know something, or misquote someone, or lose my thread.
At that point I would beg your assistance.
For you see, if all these figures with whom one should, being an author, associate, who are more at home sitting on boards, on juries, and in editor's chambers than in red-light districts, bathhouses, and parks, had done their work more carefully and not neglected Daniel Casper von Lohenstein on his 350th birthday in so scandalous a fashion – then you would not need to simply make do, at present, with the author of *On Puberty*.

Department of Poetics!
The word *poetic* comes from *poiein,* to make.
I know something about *poiein.*
Would you like to work more closely toward an understanding of Lohenstein's poetics?[1]

---

1. Speech delivered as part of a series of lectures on Daniel Casper von Lohenstein in Vienna, 1986. (Except as noted, all footnotes are the translator's.)

ELEVEN EXAGGERATIONS
Introduction to a Reader

Dakar, June 1976

1.

Guilleaumin: For God's sake – an anthology!
Lockstedter: Do you think in collected works?
                              Conversations III, 1975

2.

My reader:
Homer.
Sophocles.
Petronius.
Nizami.
Villon.
Rabelais.
Quevedo.
Marlowe.
Defoe.
Casanova.
Stendhal.
Flaubert.
Strindberg.
Lagerlöf.
Proust.
Euclides da Cunha.
Genet.
Borges.

3.

German Literature – is there such a thing?
As a relational network – *Correspondances*?
(Genet alludes to Proust, Proust alludes to Racine, Racine alludes to Seneca, Seneca alludes to Euripides.) As a relational network consisting of language – on the inner world and the world at large?
German world literature in a double sense:
Within/without the world?
What German author is known and read like Dante, Shakespeare, Cervantes, Molière, Dostoyevsky?
Hegel. Even in Senegal. In French. Kant. Marx. Freud. And *Mein Kampf*.
But is that German literature?
Freud, Marx, and Hegel are not regarded as German literature in the world at large, but as scholarship, imported from Germany. And Goethe? Hardly. More like an institution.
Kafka? Likewise.
Nietzsche? Not these days.
Broch? Because he's mentioned in *La Notte*?
Thomas Mann? In Venezuela?
Grass? Since *The Tin Drum* is on Liz Taylor's bookshelf?
Brecht? How long has it been? And how long can it last?
Hesse? Sure, like a Swiss guru.
Who in the world learns German in order to read Adorno in the original, like one learns Greek to read Sappho, or Spanish to read Calderón, Swedish for Strindberg?
Perhaps the problem lies as well in a lack of representation.
What German author would be so honored by German expatriates as the queer Genet by the French, or the Maoist Sartre?
What German cultural reviewer even notices the name of Gabriele Wohmann?
A German politician referred to all German writers as conceited asses – at a time when de Gaulle addressed Sartre as *Cher Maître* (which Sartre declined; he forgot that de Gaulle had asked, coming out of exile: *And how is M. Gide doing?* – just as Napoleon, returning from his Russian campaign: *And how goes it for Herr Goethe?*) What German politician has even flipped through the

pages of Peter Weiss's last novel? Which has seen more than a *Spiegel* review on Ilse Aichinger?
But do we really want to scold politicians?
Could one out of ten specialists extemporize on the work of Daniel Casper von Lohenstein?
One of the representatives of a large publishing house, who was working assiduously on an edition of the complete works of Günter Grass, asked the author of *The Tin Drum*: Where did you spend your childhood?
In no other country is there such a fear of bookstores as in the German Republic. Hundreds of thousands of workers and staff in the modern settlements not only don't own any books but have never in their lives even entered a bookstore. There were more bookstores in Santiago, Chile, at the time of Allende, than in West Berlin – though this may no longer be the case.
Economically:
In the land of poets and thinkers, poetry and thought are burdened with income taxes and capital gains taxes.
Bazon Brock makes and sells books like the auto industry makes and sells mud flaps.

German literature as a world literature without the world?
What German literati, lecturing on Artmann, would refer to the work of Borrows; or, lecturing on Burroughs, to the work of Swift; in a recension of a piece of nonfiction to the work of Euclides da Cunha?
What German literati have fulfilled Curtius's requirement to master at least two European dialects, without which one cannot even, as it were, enter the literary dialogue?
(Even the word *pederast* is wrongly used, *psychic* and *psychological* are mistaken one for the other.)
What German literati have read through, even in translation, the *Recherche du temps perdu*?
German literature – is there such a thing?
In itself, or for itself?
In no country is the writer, author, literary scholar, or poet held in so little esteem as in Germany – and least of all in the Federal Republic.

In no country do the literati square accounts with one another so mercilessly, in a manner so unritualized, so unsheltered by conventions, tradition, forms of play and social mores, so unrelentingly middle class in their transactions – even those said to be the most progressive.
Not only Heine with Platen.
But also Harich with Raddatz.
One does not lecture so much on a writer's work, its particularities and flaws, as pronounce one's own ideas. A writer is scourged for not having a sufficiently class-based orientation, or for poor behavior, a wrongly accusatory disposition.
Writing is transgression, not work.
In no other country does one praise so irresponsibly:
The most significant work of the postwar period . . .
One of the most important . . .
The most important . . .
In no other are the reputations of those once favored and celebrated so ruthlessly trashed, once the affections of the media, the publishing community, or the public in general have waned; how quickly is yesterday's darling denounced as an onanist, a sex offender, thief, fool, or fascist – by his own colleagues, no less, and this in a tone of one giving gymnastic instructions, or talking of final solutions, or pronouncing death sentences:
Out of the game . . .
He's out of steam . . .
Definitely peaked out . . .
Nothing more to say . . .
He's sick . . .
He's at his end . . .
He's dead . . .
I look back and see him fading . . . !
Little self-restraint, lots of straw man bravado.
Is the cause linguistic?
Is there a German language, which might have developed its own word playfulness, dignity, and respect?
Friedrich II, that most German of Prussian kings, had his complete works bound as *Oeuvres complètes*. His German was monstrous, as mangled as a battlefield.

Isn't our language, and with it our consciousness, increasingly disintegrating into bureaucratic documentese, mandarin scholasticism, and clubhouse jargon? What language brought forth expressionism and the *Dictionary of Inhumanity,* Heidegger and the jingle: *Good morning, Mr. Marmalade*?

4.

Klaus Hennies writes me from prison, where he awaits trial for attempted murder, saying that he is innocent. I send him a copy of the *Simplicius Simplicissimus.*
When I visit, I bring along a volume of Thomas Mann's selected stories. He says that he has been able to read the *Simplicissimus* in its entirety for the first time.
An anthology has to be more than just eclectic:
What should I give my friend Klaus Hennies, who hasn't mastered any foreign tongue, to read in prison where he awaits his trial?

5.

At forty-one one should possess an overview of the literature of one's own language, as well as the literatures of the world. Have I an overview merely of myself, and my time spent reading in the Babylonian library?
Suddenly, since I must somehow arrange them, books become heaps of various types of paper, handmade from before two world wars, ligneous from before the time of the currency reforms, parchment – dusty, yellowed, black with printer's ink.
I pull out volumes bequeathed to me by my grandparents, my mother, neighbors, and friends, and my own first acquisitions, the school editions that I bought for twenty marks at Dulu Krucks for a class in agriculture.
Gaps.
Typeface from the *Jugendstil* period, or the thousand-year Reich, the time of the economic miracle, the decline of the West.
Readings in the shade, in bomb shelters, temporary housing, youth hostels, and hotels – by candlelight and orgasm, neon, rubble and *ergo sum.*
What's left after the great reading impressions of the previous years?

After *Le Rouge et le noir*?
After the *Sertoes* of Euclides da Cunha?
After reading of Lamarca's murder in the *Jornal da Bahia*?
Or having read Martha Mitchell's obituary in *Newsweek*?
Few recent things have any claim to excellence.
Much that was truly cherished has grown stale.

6.

Hrosvitha of Gandersheim didn't make much of an impression – nor Walther von der Vogelweide's *leg with leg together, both like keys fitting*, in spite of Ezra Pound's emphatic reference: more and more mildewy little island stacks of books – peripheral investigations.
And Luther?
And the Bible?
I know: Samuel, the Song of Solomon, the Book of Revelation – but I don't wander in the Torah. Five books full of zealotry, foreskins, and genocide.
I know: *And the king was much moved, and went up to the chamber over the gate, and wept: and as he went, thus, he said, O my son Absalom, my son, my son Absalom! would God I had died for thee, O Absalom, my son, my son!*
But even the singer David forced the people of Rabbah to toil with iron saws and pick axes, and scorched them at the brick ovens. I see all this complacent, self-accusing petite bourgeoisie in a context of mass deportation out of Africa – a movement in which the Luther Bible merchants of Frankfurt have an interest.
The Bible – not for me!

7.

German literature is, for me, baroque literature.
Orthographic spirit, grammatical turbulence, a frenzy for learning and a mania for rules – it soars over the greater part of the literature of its epoch.
And it speaks to the nonexistence of German literature that this period is known neither in the German-speaking countries nor in the world at large – and can't be known, since only the smallest portion has been edited and is often reproduced only in obscure or inaccessible editions.

This is especially true of Daniel Casper, who takes up where his predecessors Marlowe, Shakespeare, and Calderón left off and looks as well to his contemporaries Corneille and Racine.
Lohenstein!
Forgotten.
Even by the literary journals.
Bombast.
At best.
Daniel Casper von Lohenstein was a Silesian diplomat who held various important posts at the court of Vienna during the time of the Turkish invasions, and who composed for noble patrons dramatic works possessing all the melopoeia of a Genet, the phainopoeia of an Arrabal.
Bombast?
Bullshit!
A lapse in judgment, babbled down through the centuries, sanctioned by the mild-mannered publican Tieck.
The world of intrigue surrounding the royal court, which Lohenstein knew, is reconstructed with economy, vividly, often in a single sentence – Kleistian tempo, Kafkaesque infamy.
Daniel Casper builds a consonantal and vocalic microstructure, his task lightened by baroque license, in which *Purpur* and *Purper*[1] can, from time to time, coexist; metrical regularity is introduced into a verse form consistently punctuated by end rhymes.
Daniel Casper exposes psychological complexes next to which Freud seems merely derivative.
Lohenstein, who dates his dramatic works with meticulous care, writes the first German *Psychopathologia Sexualis*.
He conflates the dramas of both Oedipus and Orestes in the figure of Nero, who, as Lohenstein knew, once played Oedipus.
If Hölderlin and Hans Henry Jahnn had referred to him, German literature might exist.

8.

The sun is, in German, feminine – as Malaparte correctly observed.
Hölderlin's stranger, masculine – the moon.

1. Both meaning "purple."

The Gay Critic

The Oedipal environment – a compulsion to speak?

The German language is, to the point of nonsense and even madness, dark; dark in the works of Wittgenstein and Rosenberg (to whom the ethnologist, voodoo priest, and dictator François Duvalier referred); its poetry is dark, now and then uncannily quaint, to the point of being amenable to sophomoric witticisms – in the works of Günther, or Lenz, initially in Busch, and also in Wedekind.

The carnivalesque descends to clubhouse jargon – and attains an oracular intensity, Zen-like and "conceited":

Whosoever has sorrows also has spirits.

Moments of dazzling reason, Saint-Simon, Saint-Just, Stendhal, are lacking; comedies are rare – *Don Juan; or, The Passion for Geometry* being no proof to the contrary.

The history of German literature is a history of infelicitous designations: The Group, Storm and Stress, Twilight of Humanity, A Stormer, a Clean Sweep, Movens, the book series with the bright red band on the cover.

Oedipal:

Following Luther's fire-and-brimstone fury against incest and what is, in the Bible at any rate, related to it – homosexuality – we see mother and son joking in Hofmannswaldau, copulating in Daniel Casper.

Kuhlmann makes use of a collage technique in his poetry and interweaves portions of three translated texts from San Juan de la Cruz – a luxurious, threefold pleating.

In the *Don Carlos* of Schiller, the translator of Racine, once again hatred of the father, love for the mother, a son's sacrifice, reminiscent of the Old Testament, or the Inquisition. In Goethe there is no sleeping with the mother, but rather – in that work praised by Gottfried Benn *(I wear you like a wound upon my brow)*, the *Iphigenia* – a matricide is presented in incomparably beautiful German verse. (Another contrast to the theme of Oedipus and Orestes – not lust for the mother, or matricide – is offered us by the *Medea*, Grillparzer's *Medea*, Hans Henry Jahnn's *Medea*, and finally that of the Oedipus *regisseur* Pasolini: A mother murders her sons.) In Hölderlin, then, the clearest rendition: the black noonday light of tragedy.

Hamlet, the son, given greater significance by Schlegel, knows no pleasure with a woman or a man.
Heine, who denounced the queer outsider Platen, esteemed the queer outsider Adelbert von Chamisso.
Peter Schlemihl is a marvel, a romantic veil cast over novelistic convention.
Here all is shadow play, parable, around a lost shadow. The mother sun, the father of shadows. A sublated (*aufgehobene*) doubling.
The secret, which shuns the light of day and prevents marriage, pursues him endlessly – just as today it drives homosexuals to Tunisia, to the Philippines – Neckermann makes it possible – one reads astonishment where it is experienced.
Chamisso, the strange wanderer among symbols and plant species, abandons seventy pages and launches onto the South Sea to visit his friend Kadu, dreams of taming the whale to harness its productive power for a world economy.
Döblin's *Hamlet*, psychoanalysis in novel form, calm classification, graceful science.
Once again a detective piece, this time with English tea, as it was in the beginning, Oedipus, Maigret, and M all in one, the most refined with the most primitive: man's self-transformation.
An Oedipal environment.
The sun.
The stranger, the moon.
Freud's Oedipus complex – a compulsion to speak?
Alas! if only Chamisso had written *The Theory of Sexuality*, and Döblin *The Joke and Its Relation to the Unconscious* – the psychiatric clinics in the Third World might look quite different. In France today there are more and more publications devoted to the work of Freud – and Döblin's *Hamlet* remains untranslated.

9.

In no other land do the literati square accounts with one another so ruthlessly as in the GDR, the Federal Republic, Switzerland, Austria, Luxembourg.
Few colleagues who have not been slandered by other colleagues,

who have not themselves slandered others, and who have not complained of it, bitterly.

Nowhere is the song of wailing over the poet's life, one's own, or that of a contemporary so vigorously seconded, for consolation, and justification.

Arnold laments Kuhlmann at the furnace.

Bobrowski mourns for Jahnn, Jahnn for Lessing and Klopstock. Jahnn, whose many-thousand-paged corpus has been wrongly cast aside under the heading "baroque" – the term should be laudatory, in reality is simply cause for neglect: When was the last time anyone worked through the *Notes of Gustav Anias Horn*? The elder Jahnn, in one of his briefest and most disturbing texts, mourns the fate of the brilliant young Chatterton, as does Ernst Pezoldt in his unjustly forgotten novel, which Hans Henry Jahnn knew.

Büchner for Lenz.

Affinities over generations, and with one's own neighbor.

Goethe on Winckelmann.

Thomas Mann on Platen.

Hans Mayer on Thomas Mann, Platen, and Büchner.

One's own existence is always here implied, the highest concentration directed toward a colleague forever transformed into an analysis of the writer's own ego.

One could recount like stories indefinitely.

Mourning – razor sharp.

Raddatz rightly refers, in his *Life of Mühsam*, to Arnold and Kuhlmann: the style is feature writing in any case.

There, Kuhlmann's crisis of faith, here, Mühsam's death in a prison camp.

Fear.

Colleagues.

10.

And yet – *Correspondances*?

Could there still be a German literature, a German world in literature, a German literature in the world?

In spite of all the game-show-host-lobotomized types, the smooth talking so much in fashion these days?

Eleven Exaggerations

After the demise of the Group 47, it seemed that a consensus, hardly twenty years old, an admittedly provincial, yet German, literary world, had totally collapsed.
Once again, the death of a nonexistent German literature?

Peter Michel Ladiges looks into geophagy. He strips anthropology of its ideological husk and reduces it to bare facticity; his is a secularized litany that works.

Oswald Wiener has mastered several African languages as well as the language of symbolic logic.

Gabriele Wohmann rouses Johann Christian Günther with a kiss.

Bengta Bischoff makes a fuss about a Rabelais speaking in mixed-German dialect. And Ulrich Krause has a manneristic vitality. Through his lips speak the voices of Morgenstern, Sigmund von Birken, Abraham a Santa Clara, and Góngora.

Helmut Heissenbüttel's diary from 1976 takes up the chronicle of the missing Hugo Ball – at once baroque, ascetic, and inflammatory.

Astel's couplets are as Martialian as Martial's are gay.

Hans Eppendorfer follows the instructions of Genet and Sartre to the letter.
He outlines a new chapter of *Murder as a Fine Art* – with glass fragments and bits of scrap.
He writes, not out of the Café Flore, but from a prison for youths in Kiel.
A secret message.
He is no *poète maudit*.
He ruins reputations.

II.

Good morning, Mr. Marmalade!
If logopoieia, phainopoieia, and melopoieia cease to be furthered as the very criteria of thought and language, thought and lan-

guage shall themselves cease to exist and, with them, any truly human existence.

The postwar period, under the influence of American authors, the BBC, and the Affaires Culturelles Françaises, has produced two new literary genres:

The feature (compulsory lack of constraint) and the interview (confession, interrogation, psychoanalysis, conversation) – *Oedipus Rex* and *The Symposium*.

My German reader: a feature work made up of poems, plays, articles, and prose – a reader conceived as symposium.

THE BLOODY MAN: Sade

Venezuela, February 1975

Sade, the Satan.
Sade, the Divine Marquis.
Sade, the liberator, the psychopathologist.
Sade, our nearest and dearest.
Judgments and prejudices.

Donatien-Alphonse-François de Sade was born Louis-Aldonse-Donatien, on June 2, 1740, in Paris.
His twenty-eight-year-old mother was a lady-of-the-court to her relative, Princess de Condé; his father, thirty-eight, held the position of king's envoy at Cologne.
Sade was raised together with Louis-Joseph de Bourbon at the Hotel de Condé.
The abbé de Sade d'Ebreuil, an epicurean friend of Voltaire, takes the five-year-old marquis with him to Provence.
At ten the young man enters the Jesuit college of St. Louis le Grand.
  5:30 Wake up.
  6:00 Pray.
  6:15 Study the Scriptures.
  7:45 Breakfast and recess.
  8:15 Study.
 10:30 Mass.
 11:00 Study.
 12:00 Lunch and recess.
 13:15 Study.
 16:50 Vespers and recess.
 17:00 Study.
 19:45 Evening meal and recess.

20:45 Prayers.
21:00 Sleep.
Not so terrible.
Sade remains here for four years. He becomes acquainted with the Jesuit theater through productions of *Justinian, The Czar from Constantinople,* tragedies by J. B. Geoffroy, and others.
Sade begins his military career as a fourteen-year-old cadet in the Ecole des Chevaux Legers. At fifteen he is a second lieutenant, adjutant to the king. At seventeen he serves in the war against Prussia.

The psychosocial systems to which Sade was subject for the first seventeen years of his life seem sufficiently unambiguous:
The system of the French high nobility, the royal court with all its easy freedoms and exalted etiquettes;
the system of a liberal, libertine clergy;
the system of mild Jesuit brainwashing, and their pop theater;
the system of French militarism.
Nothing, then, could be easier than to derive the Sadean personality – or whatever one postulates as the Sadean personality – from truly legitimate, and analogous, conclusions concerning other figures subject to similar circumstances.
Proximity to the king, a soft uncle, the Jesuitical influence, and voluntary military service – all these made an impression on another French writer and led to a completely different working out of aggression and frustration – I refer to Marcel Proust.
In all honesty, one must admit that nothing is known of the marquis's early childhood experiences.
The nineteen-year-old, newly promoted captain leads a robust life and comments upon it in the conventional style of a well-bred French intellectual:
. . . *in the morning I arose, and pursued some trivial enjoyment or other.*
. . . *in the evening I was despairing.*
. . . *ah, is the happiness that one buys a real pleasure, and can a love without consideration and respect be truly tender?*
The father requests a confession, the son resolves to give one honestly:

The Bloody Man

I know . . . one has to treat a girl kindly, be charming, to achieve any degree of intimacy. But I don't like doing it. I'm grieved when I hear someone coax and fawn upon another, saying things that they don't at all feel. Courteous, upright, proud without being arrogant, obliging but not dull – these are my virtues, these the virtues to which I aspire. I ask that my petty desires be fulfilled only on the condition that they be harmful to no one – myself, you, or anyone else. I would like to live well, amuse myself, without becoming depraved or dissipate; a few friends – perhaps none at all.

. . . an even temperament . . .

. . . trusting in no one . . .

. . . to speak only the best of those who have spoken ill of another . . .

. . . that is my entire confession. I open my heart to you not as a father whom one fears without loving but as if I were speaking to my truest and best friend, the dearest I have on earth.

. . . please respond promptly. You cannot imagine how much joy your letters give me. Please do not send me just a few words, however, as you usually do.

No *Oedipus*? Or rather explicitly? Uninterpretable from every angle. The short, tender reproach at the end, referring to the brevity of the father's letters, seems to me an unusual flourish, a light touch unspoiled by convention.

In any case, the father writes his brother the abbé, the latter having recently been confined for a few days due to his excessive habits, expressing indignancy that his twenty-three-year-old son does not go to balls or public functions but rather diverts himself backstage with theater types and hangs around in bordellos.

The father-son relationship starts to become brittle. The father wants him to seek out a rich woman, and thus to free himself of him, and suggests Renée-Pélagie de Montreuil. In March 1763 Sade becomes engaged with her, though he is, at the same time, engaged with Laure Victoire Adeline de Lauris, one of his lovers, whom he prefers to Pélagie. Father Sade, for his part, has nothing against Laure, but the de Lauris raise objections, and fourteen days prior to his marriage to Pélagie, Sade junior is still trying to bring the de Lauris round – he who, four months after his wedding, was confined for the first time, on charges of moral turpitude, in the dungeon at Vincennes.

Double-crossing out of an inclination for Mademoiselle de Lauris? Out of abhorrence for Mademoiselle de Montreuil? Double-crossing out an inclination to double-cross?

On April 6 he writes to Laure, referring to a *petite histoire de la c . . .* , which one perhaps can decipher as gonorrhea, or *chaude pisse*.

The threat of suicide – conventional, but no less base thereby – is followed by a second, more stark:

. . . guard yourself against inconstancy; I don't deserve it. I admit, I would become mad with anger, and there is no act of cruelty that wouldn't tempt me. The minor episode with the c. . . . should move you to have some consideration for me. I admit that I would not conceal it from a rival, nor would I leave off with a single notice.

Between threats of suicide, the clap, blackmail, paternal authority, monetary considerations, visits to the whorehouse and prison, there begins, then, this most touching, tender, and boldest of love stories in world literature – the marriage of the Marquis de Sade with Renée-Pélagie de Montreuil. It was celebrated on May 1, 1763, at Versailles, under royal auspices.

The first years of the marriage seem not to have been particularly "divine" or "sadistic." Sade writes from jail to a police lieutenant Sartine:

I beg you, inform my wife of my wretched fate. She is undoubtedly in the greatest distress because she hasn't received any word from me. I deserve God's punishment. I mourn my own shortcoming, detest the error of my ways.

And finally at this point the later so oft repeated request for a walk in the fresh air:

I believe it is absolutely essential to my health.

What precisely had happened?

Only the father expresses himself in any detail:

[He] rented a house, bought some furniture on credit, and gave himself right over to the most extreme prodigality and depravity, indulging in the most horrifying godlessness, and to such a degree that several women saw themselves compelled to speak out against him.

By 1763 the police inspector Marais already shadowed him day and night, would never again let him go about freely.

Through Marais one knows how often Sade slept with Mademoiselle Colette of the Comédie Italienne, the fact that

Mademoiselle Beauvoisin is kept by him, that he has some bad luck with Mademoiselle Le Roux at the opera, and that he openly holds hands with Mlle. Beauvoisin.

Sade travels with Beauvoisin in 1765 to his chateau at La Coste, most likely presenting her as his wife. A theater hall is constructed and all the nobility of Vaucluse appear regularly at balls, parties, and dramatic presentations.

Sade writes to Mademoiselle C. . . . :

My days are full of thorns, through that unhappy bond to which I gave myself merely out of convenience. They once brought me eternal roses of spring . . .

In Paris Mlle. D. and Mlle. M. now play a role. M. seems to spurn him and Sade writes:

If you wish, I will assume all responsibility for your son; I would let him be brought up on one of my estates; there he would be cared for and watched over like my own – he shall want for nothing in the world. . . . His progress would be my sole concern . . . if I at least saw some mark of gratitude in his eyes: a sign that I had given rise to some higher sentiment.

Even if one draws the conclusion, to my mind untenable, that the violent family episodes, the dismembering of parents and children in Sade's work are in fact substitute gratifications for actions the author himself would gladly have undertaken, and thus that he wished to bring up his lover's or his own illegitimate son only to pervert him, one must nonetheless also account for the verbal, poetic ambivalence that in Sade's work speaks out beside every poetic and unrealized sadocomic scene.

On January 24, 1767, the twenty-seven-year-old Sade loses his father.

On August 27 of the same year Sade's first legitimate son, Louis Marie, is born.

Marais reports on October 16 that Mademoiselle Rivière of the opera has also spurned Sade's offer of money.

Since 1766, reports Lieutenant de la Bernardière, the Marquis takes *persons of either sex* into a rented house in Arceuil, *day and night, with whom he engages in perverted and unnatural sex acts.*

On February 1, 1768, he brings four women to this location, whom he whips; afterward he has them served dinner and instructs a servant to give them each a louis d'or.

We hope that the witness Jean-François Vallier spoke precisely – this would be the marquis's only attested flagellation scene that was carried through to the end without interruption.

On Easter Sunday, April 3, 1768, Sade speaks with a beggar woman, Rose Keller, at the Place des Victoires, and promises her a domestic position. He takes her to his rented house in Arceuil. The marquis and Rose Keller give different accounts of what followed.

She claims she was bound and thrown facedown onto a bed.

Sade contests the claim of bondage.

She: I was beaten with switches and a cane.

He: with a whip made of knotted rope.

She: I was stabbed with a small knife. Melted wax was put into the wounds.

Sade denies any stabbing.

Afterward she was cleaned up, bandaged, and generally attended to.

She flees before things can go any further.

The question of stabbing is decisive. The answers are contradictory.

Surely not everyone takes pleasure in being bound and beaten, and one can hardly comprehend Sade's admiring biographers when they attempt to ironize the figure of Keller, making her abduction, the mocking of her beliefs, and the brutalities committed against her person seem ludicrous; to the moral credit of a hitherto little more than vulgar aristocrat who, seen in the light of a few abysmal letters and an admittedly ingenious theatrical audition, personified nothing but a particularly reckless traitor to his class.

Shocks like Keller's may, however, have been commonplace in the *siècle de la lumière*.

If in any case the stabbings did occur – which Sade contests, which the court doctor Le Comte proves, which the court disputes, charging Le Comte with perjury – perhaps the work of

Sade's powerful mother-in-law, the *présidente* de Montreuil – if Sade did in fact cut into the body of Rose Keller, then another phase of the marquis's sadism is thereby documented, a magical, man-eating phase and, moreover, one that suggests a progression from sexual rites involving maidservants and whips to sacrificial bloodlettings, and a further approximation to the monstrous myths of his works would become all the more conceivable.
And yet no real clarity prevails.
His mother-in-law's influence seems to have been sufficiently powerful – on November 16, Sade is released after a six-month confinement.
A handwritten copy of the marquis's can be found in *Oeuvres diverses 1763 à 1769;* contained therein are several charming *chansons,* a dull battle description written by the eighteen-year-old soldier, letters of a more substantial content, a prelude for the theater that – for the first time? – in 1764 anticipates the illusion of the destruction of the illusion of the peep-show stage, as in Anouilh's *Antigone,* or Wilder's *The Skin of Our Teeth,* not excepting that requirement practiced by the playwrights Shakespeare, Strindberg, Pirandello, and Brecht to replace falseness with false authenticity, to substitute one ritual with another, seemingly nonritualistic, element – to secure the fictional at the same time that one claims to overcome it.
Discontinuities in the relationship of reality and representation, breaks that his novelistic works display in another form, like the production marked by gala attire.

In a piece he later discarded, *Le Philosophe soi-disant,* the not yet thirty-year-old, in youthful, enlightenment fashion, mocks the money-grubbing hypocrite, the dull-witted ideologue, and lovers' sweet talk, in the figure of an alleged philosopher who has "procured" the personae of the comedy for his own amusement, like puppets – a philosopher whose behavior he will later present with feigned admiration; sweet talk that he only too often used. The *Journey to Holland,* composed one year after *The Sentimental Journey,* is a wasteland of ill-inspired reflections, narrow-mindedness, and boredom. It seems hard to believe that the same young man here writing and traveling once opened the theater

at Evry Chateau with his prelude, and who in his *Philosopher* penned such scathing remarks, à la Wolfgang Bauer, against the society in which he played a role – a piece in which the president remarks:
For twenty years I haven't read anything except my list of wines and the dinner menu! – If nothing else, a French noble on the state of other French nobles grown flatulent from culinary arts and cultural refinements.

Even the events on or around June 27, 1772, do not prove conclusively that the marquis was involved in anything more than extensive flagellation, with switches and whips full of curved needles. Flagellation both actively given and passively received, extended arousal rather than incision, or some irreversible intervention, the destruction of a sexual "object."
(Sade himself seems now and then, unconsciously, to have distinguished between a "minor" and a "major" sadism – in the *Statutes of the Friends of Crime* the use of any instrument other than switches, on any part of the body, is strongly prohibited; is this an objective distinction between different types of sexual behavior or a subjective one between an experienced, actively pursued "minor sadism" and a literary, fantasized "major sadism"?)
The so-called masochistic component is more pronounced in Marseille, with the four women and the maidservant. Sade strikes and is struck, counts the number of blows by writing on the wall. Neither he nor his servants eat the mock candies of anise seed and Spanish fly that he serves to the women and that subsequently bring on symptoms of poisoning.
Does this mean that he did not see the candy as part of a sadomasochistic ritual, and that he had therefore no intention of poisoning anyone, wishing only that the substance might act as an aphrodisiac and carminative – or does it mean that he only displayed masochistic traits in less harmful rituals, that he – whose books are full of poison fantasies – knew very well its effects and simply didn't wish to expose himself to them, masochistically?
It is impossible to reach a decision.

The Bloody Man

As for administering an aphrodisiac, the thirty-two-year-old proceeds in an astonishingly careless fashion. The effects are intense vomiting, gastritis, and irritation of the urinary tract. Still a fairly harmless result, at any rate, for a ritual poisoning.

The punishment for these crimes is surprisingly sadistic and would surely have brought great satisfaction to a masochist. Sade would suffer it for the remainder of his life. Nor did he, it seems, enjoy it.

Sade and his servant Latour are condemned to death on September 3, 1772, for the crimes of sodomy and poisoning. Sade is to be beheaded, Latour hanged and choked *until a natural death ensues*. On September 12, in Aix, both are executed and burned in effigy. Sade has fled with his sister-in-law de Launay from La Coste.

On October 27 Sade, traveling incognito with Mademoiselle de Launay, reaches Chambery, where he is, at his mother-in-law's insistence and by command of the king of Sardinia, imprisoned on December 8 and brought to the fortress at Miolans.

His servant Latour is allowed to sleep in the same room. During their confinement the servant elicits from the marquis the following fatherly sentiment, apropos of a gambling quarrel:

I declare that I am totally prepared to give up the twelve louis that I lost; I have in fact already given them over to the baron. But I beg your excellency to return the promissory note for one hundred louis to the young man [Latour]. The meager fortune that he might one day hope to acquire shall never allow him to match this sum without ruining his family. Moreover, he has been in my care since childhood. What reproaches would I bring upon myself were I to allow him to be so utterly neglected, and that at a time when he has given himself up for me in prison? I would forever hold it against myself.

On March 6, 1773, his wife, dressed as a man, travels to Chambery from Paris to see her husband.

Sade:

I lost my father and that was my undoing, for I would not be here if he were still alive.

On April 30 Sade flees Miolans and writes back on May 1:

The tempestuousness of my blood resists punishments of this sort.

Sade flees to Grenoble, through Bordeaux to Cadiz; he stops in La Coste and hides himself within the shelter of his castle, in a state of extreme alarm.

In January 1774, the castle is thoroughly searched by the police. In June Sade writes to his custodian Gaufridy:

For God's sake let [my wife] know that she must do whatever is necessary so that I might not be forced to wander and live like a vagabond any longer. I feel that I am not born for adventure, and the necessity of taking on this role is one of the greatest torments of my situation.

From obsessive boldness Sade nevertheless arranges an orgy shortly thereafter with five "young women"; Madame Sade seems to have taken part in it.

The tradition refers to a certain "buttonhole game" and insinuates, on scanty evidence, that it involved bodily incisions. A macabre game involving human remains is also held to be cannibalistic – Sade consistently denied both. The young women were hidden away with relatives and in convents.

Sade in May 1775 to Gaufridy:

People here think I'm a werewolf.

On July 26, 1775, Sade flees to Italy, and his complaints to Gaufridy increase. He speaks no Italian; he suffers under the increasing egocentrism of his environment and from its lack of generosity and finally writes:

They have the flaw common to all who have never traveled: they are unable to put themselves in another's situation.

The notes and excerpts from *Voyage d'Italie ou Dissertations critiques, historiques, politiques et philosophiques sur les villes de Florence, Rome et Naples* arise, for the most part, from the trip itself. The title aims high. He promises an entirely new type of travel writing, *voyage ou dissertations* – actually a kind of travel feature. This promise is not kept. The dreariness of the marquis's first descriptions is still easily perceptible to modern readers. This voyage takes place, however, at the major turning point in Sade's existence. The rather insipid beginnings of the man of letters and a few brief flashes of poetic genius have already been realized, fatherhood, love's tenderness, the great perversions and their sadistic punishments: the death sentence and a long confinement – six months is a long time – all lay behind him. The axiomatic experiences of this life have occurred, they are simply not yet

habituated, not yet systematized. Not until ten years later does the astounding, literarily unprecedented *120 Days of Sodom* appear. The metamorphosis of the Sadean personality can be carefully observed in the *Voyage d'Italie:*
The tie between the atheist and the church, and between the church and the agonies of its martyrs – three-quarters of the text is filled with descriptions, taken mostly out of handbooks.
It is not the travelogue of a Malaparte or a Burroughs – how could it be, really. And yet on several pages something larger seems to rumble beneath the surface, and the descriptions of Naples are in no way inferior to those of *La Pelle*.
Here lies some indication of what might otherwise have become of Sade – a modern Petronius or an early Proust? – had the dismantling of conventions not been followed by a loss of freedom, but rather intensified by such an extraordinary assimilation of the world and its ways, not so much through masturbation as surrender.
The prude, the hypocrite already speaks out, and henceforth:
with a large handkerchief, which they tie around their neck like women, they seem every bit as ridiculous as they are unseemly, a fact that proves, in my opinion, if one may assess custom and intellect on the basis of outward demeanor, how spoiled the one, and how little comprehending the other is.
The man, one reads on the next page, *owns a collection of natural-colored terra cottas that depict the various stages of childbirth, and he has a nine-month-old girl made of wax that can be taken apart to let one carefully observe the anatomical detail.*
The considerable aesthetic charm of anatomic representations – here heightened by the wax material and the figure's detachability – fascinated Sade as it did Goethe and pop art. Might his later fantasies of vivisection find their source in this manneristic lifelikeness?
In the Palazzo Vecchio, which he named Vieux Palais, he notes the hermaphrodites: *Roman licentiousness dared to seek its pleasure even in these freaks of nature.*
The Drusilla and Caligula group *demonstrates a greater truthfulness of expression.*
The Priapus is *wondrously massive.*

A garish depiction of castrati in an opera house:
... *who originally owe their debasement to the most shameless refinements of pleasure, and whom musical taste has retained in spite of an all-deploring humanism.*
... can you imagine, Countess ...
for naturally the letters are addressed, just like the lines in the song by Gustaf Gründgens, to a countess:
that these manikins arouse fervent passions? ...
Their capacities, claim les femmes débauchées, *are so prized because they can hang on for so long; their fires are never quenched. But do not the most tender pleasures lie in shared passions? And how despicable in my eyes is that woman so little concerned over her lover's desires that she values him only for his duration, that he should, most importantly of all, satisfy her own desires.*
A hypocritical system, no doubt – but equally a sublimating one. There follows a lucid analysis of the Florentine dramatic art. A true specialist, like Brecht or Strindberg, writes:
It is the practice here not to learn the role. An actor has the nerve to put himself before the public without knowing a single word of the character he is supposed to play – many times he doesn't even know the piece that he enters. The prompter does all the work. He dictates to each one his part, and the actors have such a hard time following him that they repeat, word for word, everything he says and in this way bring on various appropriate and inappropriate gestures, right as well as wrong intonations. The work proceeds, miraculously, from beginning to end, the one drawback being that the voice of the prompter, which one always hears first, is echoed by that of the actor who repeats, word for word, everything the former says.

Here as well the voice of Sade seems to be supported by what will follow – does he not already at this point hint at his novels' many ingenious devices, is he not already prompting his mannequin Justine, and mustn't we, if we take exception to the babbling virtuousness of his victims and the eloquent satanism of his sadosupermen, perhaps consider that he intended this quite consciously, as an artistic effect, that his novels might aim, exclusively, at reproducing an evening at the opera in Florence?

The Bloody Man

In Florence eight-year-olds often perish in palace orgies.
Half of the noble class prostitutes itself with the help of two procuresses, *who, instead of being hanged, chatters the opponent of the death penalty and one who had once, we recall, been condemned to death, as they had deserved, were paraded through the streets on asses.*
Or does the clown once hung in absentia mean here, exposing himself, to elicit the insipid laughter of the gracious countess?
Ten pages later: *This prince, so gentle and humane, and who knew the value – the value – of a human life, felt that the crime was not eradicated by the death of the one who committed it, and that the example of a punishment that in any case delivers him over to the state is, rather, carried out to lead one back to virtue who by predisposition disregards it, as an example of a needless death, which nonetheless only conjures up despair and often accomplishes nothing other than helping someone think up more clever ways of avoiding a like punishment.*
Death sentences, vestal virgins buried alive, *the sorrowful curiosity, which this heathen cruelty arouses?*
The martyrdom of Saint Cecilia:
There prevails in this divine work such a striking truthfulness that one cannot view it without being deeply moved.
In Saint Agnes he visits the catacombs, where the Roman *lupanares*, or brothels, were located and where the saint was supposed to have been raped:
But if I have failed to sufficiently abbreviate my consideration of such matters, Countess, which are all too risqué for your delicate sensibilities, I confess it to be merely the product of my overheated imaginative faculties.
A Spaniard, he reports, shot poisoned arrows into a crowd merely for amusement.
This bizarre mania of committing evil deeds for their own sake, for the pleasures they yield, is one of the least understood and consequently too-little analyzed of all the human passions – and I would for all that think it possible to rank it among the usual class of pleasures of the imagination. Fortunately one sees it so seldom that I can spare myself the trouble of describing it.

The mendacity of this statement determines its philosophical absurdity. Trouble? Seldom? Spare? His novels clearly, lustfully, demonstrate the contrary.

Nonetheless a truly iridescent statement: To do evil for its own sake is a habitual pleasure of the imagination.

Does he really, however, and in so credulous a fashion, think to debunk the hypothesis that between fantasy and crime a certain boundary exists that is only transgressed in unusual cases – and surely not in his own?

In Naples he sees a crucifix said to embody a *horrifying truth*.

Titian's maidservant, a type of living furniture, which an artist and man of letters can scarcely do without. It is good to have them at one's disposal. Nature's needs can be seen to without disturbing the mind. Love is not the thing for a man who works. When his desires flare up and he has no available means of extinguishing them, the fire of the senses devours the fire of composition, and the work consequently suffers.

Sade describes five thousand poor being fed at Shrovetide.

A school for plunderers, hardly a festival.

Two men scuffle over a side of beef . . . One of them pulls a knife. The other falls and swims in his own blood. The victor, however, does not celebrate for long. He goes up some steps to claim his prize, these give way under his feet and he falls like a lump of flesh upon his rival.

Sade here anticipates some of Melville's more sadistic scenes.

I felt that the sublime horror of this scene lacked only one thing. The bodies of the dead and the wounded man should have been allowed to lie where they had fallen, before everyone's eyes, on top of the remaining decorations.

In a manner not unlike Malaparte, Sade relates the following:

I have seen young girls in Naples, four or five years old, who made themselves available for the most extreme sexual depravities, and who, when someone accepted their invitations, would inform them that because of their tender age they were unable to perform in the natural way, could not yet put their bodies to the uses for which the Creator had intended them.

As this work begins, so it ends, amidst veils and sleight-of-hand trickery.

The Bloody Man

At the end of October Sade, in La Coste, hires the twenty-two-year-old and *very pretty* Cathérine Trillet, as a cook. In mid-December he takes on a secretary, Rolland, a wigmaker from Paris, a chambermaid, and a foreign kitchen maid.
At night the marquis makes his way to their rooms and tries to seduce them with promises of money. All but the kitchen maid are horrified and leave the castle on the following morning. Someone informs Trillet's father in Montpelier.
On January 14 Sade's mother dies in Paris. The marquis will first learn of it upon his arrival in the metropolis three weeks later.
On January 17 Trillet gains entrance to La Coste and tries to murder the marquis.
At the end of January 1777, Sade writes:
in a country like this one, where it is important to keep one's vassals in a state of guilty respect, a state from which they are at every moment inclined to escape.
I have recognized the fact that the residents of La Coste are a worthless lot, whom one has to discipline constantly and severely.
Today some stranger walks in, firing a pistol and demanding his daughter back, tomorrow some farmer will demand his day's wages under an exchange of rifle fire. Don't they already show enough independence by virtue of the fact that they can hunt and hike up into the mountains?
Madame de Montreuil refuses to vouch for the marquis any longer:
From now on let him defend his own reputation and his own head!
Sade travels to Paris, learns of the death of his mother, and in the beginning of February writes to a Parisian clergyman:
My mother's death has brought me here.
Which isn't true.
The services that I requested of you in Provence can now be carried out here. I admit, moreover, that I require these services with the greatest urgency, for I could never find anyone who, like you, would carry them out; furthermore, they can be mutual, if you so desire.
Anality at the mother's grave. Orestes and Pylades?
From the dungeon at Vincennes, in a letter to his mother-in-law, the translation reads as follows:
Following the care that my mother required, my second concern was

to improve her spirits and to calm her. My own condition was dreadful. My blood and head could never – you know this – be kept within precise limits. . . .

From within her grave my wretched mother calls out to me, it seems to me that she opens her womb a second time and beckons me to return there, as to the only asylum yet left to me.

Tomb, womb, anal sex, and the threat of suicide thus all become one; Eros and Thanatos; lie, confession, bombast.

In Parisian slang there is an ambivalent expression one uses to decline a homosexual's advances: *Ma pièce de dix sous est pour les croque-morts.*

Whereby one understands *anus* for *pièce de dix sous* and *homosexual* for *croque-morts*, which nonetheless doesn't cancel out the expression's various levels of meaning.

It would be a blessing to follow her so soon, and I must beg of you a final favor, Madame – to bury me next to her.

Madame de Montreuil, the despised persecutress as a *croque-mort*, the mother-in-law as gravedigger for the reunion with a second party, the primal womb.

On February 13 Sade is imprisoned by the relentless Inspector Marais and taken to the dungeon at Vincennes.

Madame de Montreuil forsakes all responsibility and writes on March 4:

Things could not be proceeding any better, or more promisingly.

Sade to his wife on March 4:

My dear, you are the sole thing left to me on this earth: father, mother, sister, wife, friend. You are all these to me. I have only you. Do not abandon me. I implore you. . . .

For seven nights I have not slept a wink, and at night I vomit what I have eaten during the day.

To his mother-in-law on March 13:

For too long I have been your victim. But don't think for a minute that I am a fool. It is, now and then, rather interesting to be a victim, but it is always degrading to be held a fool.

From which we can infer that, if one equates *victim* with *degrading*, it may be interesting to be degraded, or degrading to be a victim. In either case the accent lies on rejecting masochism.

You have enough intelligence to understand that some minor offense, usually brought on by intense passions, is not lessened by denying these passions all release, an act that only serves to incite the mind through seclusion and fire the imagination through loneliness. For me the only result can be a disturbance of my organs. . . . I cannot endure this fearful loneliness, I feel it too keenly. You, on the other hand, think that you derive no advantage from letting my soul become increasingly savage, my heart accustomed to insensitivity. Only give me the time to make good my errors, lest you become complicit in all the deeds toward which this dreadful confusion so violently draws me, and which I feel now rising up inside of me.

On March 18, to his wife:

I have decided to become as false as everyone else, and to precisely the same degree.

On June 20, 1778, Sade arrives in Aix-en-Provence, accompanied by Inspector Marais.

On July 14 the death sentence of 1772 is revoked and changed to a fine of fifty livres.

On the way back, on July 16, Sade flees while passing through Valence and reaches La Coste on July 18.

After a period of thirty-nine days, on August 26, at about four in the morning, Sade is once again apprehended by Marais and ten others who shower him with threats and beatings.

After a trip of thirteen days Marais places Sade once again in the prison at Vincennes.

On October 4, to Madame de Sade:

And bear in mind, that so long as I have a drop of blood in my veins I shall never forgive you. I shall dissemble and present myself falsely, as I have been taught, but I shall always think of you as a woman without any heart or sensitivity, as one who is turned about by the slightest breeze, toppled by the slightest push.

On October 21, again to Madame de Sade:

Here is a brief letter for the poor little angels . . .

Choux, his children –

whom I love more than you can ever imagine.

Give your mother my warmest and most affectionate regards. Assure her of my constant devotion and respect.

On February 8, to Madame de Sade:
Madame de Montreuil is a whore![1]
On February 17, to Madame de Sade:
I was once looked after more attentively than I am now. Earlier I was often taken for walks. I never ate alone. I was in a good room, where I could make a good fire. Now: No one eats with me; far fewer walks and cramped up in the dampest chamber in the whole prison.
Shall I say nothing of this upon my release? One would have to destroy me a thousand times, since it is the truth, what I say. My only solace here is Petrarch. Laura has truly turned my head. I have become like a child. I read about her each day, each night I dream of her:
"Why do you torment yourself so," she says to me. "Come, give yourself over to me. No more ills, no worries, there is no unease in the wide spaces where I dwell. Take heart and follow me."
Upon these words I threw myself before her knees and cried:
"O, my mother."
Womb and tomb once again.
On March 22, 1779, to Mademoiselle de Rousset, his *dear Saint*, à la Kafka:
My time is predetermined, the day, the hour, the moment are all irrevocably fixed, and there is no uncle, no aunt, no Saint Rousset who can possibly lengthen or shorten a single minute. . . .
. . . what reason do you expect from a man who is treated as if he had none. . . .
. . . why are we, so tender, so delicate, and so charming, yet more cruel than Tiberius?
. . . I am now an animal in the menagerie of Vincennes.
And on the same day, to his wife:
Lovely gifts. And a nice little something extra. And then the mirror shattered into a thousand pieces, which doubtless meant that the following year would not go well for me, since there is nothing more foreboding than a broken mirror.
My little dove, I kiss you on the . . . and then on the . . . and then on . . .
March 22. Still eleven months to endure.
It would be almost eleven years.

1. *Puffmutter*, i.e., madame.

In March or April to Madame de Sade:
with what deep gratification have I been informed of my son's achievements.
In April or May to Mademoiselle de Rousset:
I once said to you at La Coste that the greatest pain one can ever inflict is to give an unfortunate person occasion to cherish hopes that are then left unfulfilled. I repeat, there is no torture on earth quite like it, and if one were to look into the causes of suicide, surely twenty-nine out of thirty cases would be seen to depend upon it.
A torture that Sade nowhere in his work describes.
On May 16, 1779, to Madame de Sade:
I must, for my health, get some fresh air, at least an hour a day.
. . . In the next package please: Biscuits, as I said, six regular, six glazed and two small tubs of butter from Bretagne, but the good kind, high quality. I believe there's a small shop in Paris that carries it.
May 1779, to Madame de Sade:
He who laughs last, laughs best. In my spare time I amuse myself with various plans. I have the most unequaled kind. . . . I'll discover nothing new, I'll rest content with imitations. What I need are pen and paper, ready accomplices, a few reminiscences – touched up, of course – and the print shops of The Hague.
He laments that he can no longer keep up with the marquise.
Not even a little fling with the inmates.
He reports that Monsieur de Rougemont, his cell master, has taken a foul and disgusting prisoner into his confidence as lover, reader, and correspondent.
A homosexual's contempt for one like himself?
The desire for foul and disgusting types becomes a recurring topos in his work.
As a devil's advocate, then, hate for de Rougemont, or, as prisoner, a secret admiration. Or both at the same time.
The ambivalence felt with regard to one's captor finds a correspondence in Hans Peter Reichelt.
May 1779 to Mademoiselle de Rousset:
My wife and children should throw themselves at the king's feet?! But don't you know, Madame, how I love these children, and that I would prefer a lifelong blotch upon my honor rather than that they should be defiled by such an act?

On October 29, to Madame de Montreuil, the president, his mother-in-law:
the air of this place, Madame, and the manner of living to which it has befallen the commandant to subject me, so disturb my health and afflict my chest that I spit blood.
. . . the rooms here are untiled, and one cannot move about in them without kicking up a cloud of dust from the plaster and saltpeter.
. . . I seize the opportunity to assure Monsieur de Montreuil of my highest esteem and to thank him for the books that he so kindly sent me last summer.
On December 2, to Madame de Sade:
O, I shall expose everything to you, all the disgraceful intrigues, the conspiracies waged from ambition and greed!
After April 21, to Madame de Sade:
I know of nothing that more plainly demonstrates the poverty and barrenness of your imagination than the unbearable monotony of your insipid "signs."
And there follows a lecture on the protocols of the secret message.
The signal must not only be honnête, *it must also distinguish itself wholly and clearly from the ordinary objects with which it is surrounded, otherwise it is only a loathsome mark, something black and common, for which one ought to be chastised.*
On June 25, 1780, to Madame de Sade:
I have always thoroughly hated and feared the sea.
Might one here interpret Sade's words psychoanalytically and translate *la mer* with *mother*?
The prince's court lady, recently deceased, who never hindered him from the pursuit of his anal pleasures – or perhaps caused them, the one who called him out of the grave back into her womb, Laura finally, Petrarch's Laura, who arose out of the book of his uncle and educator, whom he tried to blackmail and with whom he has ever since been on bad terms?
Sade cannot sleep. The doctor finds his appearance remarkably healthy.
July 27 to Madame de Sade:
This man looks at me like some doctor during the Inquisition who takes a pulse during a torture session, to determine whether or not one ought to continue, and who says each time: Keep going!

Sade here cites a commonplace of torture technique, and one that is still used in Brazil in 1970, two hundred years later.
Gold and the asshole are the gods of my fatherland.
And the pillars of a Viennese science.
No more illusions. I have reached the ripe old age of forty, at which I have always sworn that I would renounce Satan and all his pomp. . . . That my cherished lover, who alone can make the remainder of my days more pleasant, does not do me the additional harm of dying before me . . . and that the unfortunate creatures who owe their existence to me will someday be happier than ourselves – these are the only wishes that I dare to put to the Infinite, and the only ones whose fulfillment might allow a few roses to bloom upon my life's thorns.
Sade's blabbering rhetoric here commits a fairly heartrending lapse. Roses and thorns make up the image he used to betray Madame Sade with Mademoiselle C. . . . The extraordinary love affair with his wife then takes its course. Madame de Sade reciprocates with heartfelt passion and nevertheless, for reasons unknown, waits to see him again after eleven years in prison – only to take her leave of him permanently.
On September 17, to Madame de Sade:
The king once again permits me my walks.
On December 14 he sends the marquise a jealous song: How she wanted for nothing, during his confinement, not even a fat prick.
On December 24 he begins some sketches for his comedy *L'Inconstant.*
On December 30, to Madame de Sade:
That you and your detestable family might be stuffed into a sack and tossed into the sea, and that someone should quickly report it to me, this would be the happiest moment that I have ever experienced in my life. These are my New Year's wishes, Madame, which include that slut de Rousset from head to toe.
On February 10, 1781, he writes *a very significant letter* to his wife: *to put someone into prison for four or five years for a little fling with some women, such as takes place a hundred times on any given day in Paris. . . . Human bones in my garden! They had been brought to me by a woman named Du Plan. She's still alive, anyone could ask her. We were making a good or bad joke, that is, using them to deco-*

rate a room, for which purpose they were originally required, and they were then buried in the garden when this rather banal jest was ended. . . .

Granted, I'm a libertine, and I have considered everything that can be considered by a person having such a disposition, but I have hardly carried out everything I have considered, nor shall I ever do so.

I am a libertine, but I am no criminal, nor am I a murderer.

I am a libertine, but I have never endangered my family's well-being. . . .

Have I not loved what I was supposed to love and what should have been dear to me?!

Have I not loved my father?! Alas, not a day goes by that I don't mourn his loss!

Have I treated my mother poorly?

How then can people think that I, having had such an innocent childhood and youth, should have suddenly brought myself to perform the most extreme and elaborate cruelties?

On May 21, to his wife:

How do you all expect me to respond to such things? I shall lose my good character, my temperament and become like the rest of you — servile, mean, and thievish.

On July 13, 1781, Madame de Sade is allowed to visit her husband accompanied by a third party.

Sade breaks out in a jealous rage, he accuses her of the worst kinds of perversities, berates her for dressing like a prostitute.

If you had the slightest sense of honor, you would wish to please me exclusively, and you shall do so only by conducting yourself, in all your actions, with the highest degree of decency and modesty.

I demand therefore that you visit me dressed in what one refers to as a robe de chambre, *wearing a very large cap, no coiffure, your hair should be combed-out and down, not a single false lock, tied but not plaited, no bodice and the breasts fully covered, not open in an unseemly manner, like the last time, the color of the dress as subdued as possible. . . .*

Man's natural tendency is to imitate — the tendency of sensible people, to assimilate the ways of the person one loves.

The idea that one could think of another while lying in my arms has often irritated me, and I have yet to see a woman a second time without suspecting that she has deceived me.

The Bloody Man

The rules of a monastery are precisely those which the various "friends of crime" shall prescribe in their writings.
Did Madame de Sade furnish the grounds for such a statement? The marquis goes so far as to stick pins into the portrait of a supposed rival, an execution carried out "in effigy," just as he himself underwent almost ten years earlier, and just as it has been, and continues to be done, in magical rites.
In August 1781 Madame de Sade enters a convent to soothe her husband.
In October his former domestic servant, Gothon, dies.
She was corrupt, and had her hands in the most crooked affairs, I suspect, but she was cheerful and quick-witted (omparlée).
If Gothon left any last will and testament, or if any children of hers exist, let the former be carried out to the letter and the children attended to.
Half a year later he composes a sort of dirge and writes:
Gothon had, so they say, a most beautiful behind. . . .
I have made it clear that I despise a certain significant proverb:
In the house of a hanged man one shouldn't talk about rope.
Nor should I occupy myself with such shameful topics, since they say that my surrender to them is the source of all my misery.
The anal and a scaffold. Underworld Eros and Thanatos of the underworld.
On July 12, 1782, he finishes the rather measured – at least in comparison to the bold passages of the *Voyage d'Italie* – *Dialogue entre un prêtre et un moribund*.
On August 6 his books are taken away from him, the claim being that they incite him to write on improper subjects.
And in August as well he begins the first drafts of the *120 Days of Sodom*, on which he will work for the next three years.
On October 21, to Madame de Sade:
The indignities to which I am subjected have become so outrageous that I am now denied any medical attention. That proves only too well that my eyesight has been forfeited.
On February 4, 1783:
I am so weak that I cannot even relieve myself.
Might this be the source of the coprophilic undertone of the *120 Days*?

After February 4:
I have completely lost my sight in one eye. I would rather die than live on in such a state. I can neither read your letters nor anything else. I embrace you and suffer terribly.

The president, his mother-in-law, Madame de Montreuil – Sade would like to skin her alive, drag her over thistles, and plunge her into vinegar.

On February 13 to Madame de Sade:
My sufferings are indescribable.

In reference to his comedy *La Folle epreuve ou le mari crédule*, Sade writes to his wife on March 26:
It is entirely unnecessary that a dénoument should be effected by punishing vice and rewarding virtue. That is an old misconception, and as evidence I would cite Aristotle, Horace, Boileau, and, the model for us all, Molière. . . .

The art consists not in condemning vice but in depicting it in such a manner as to discourage its imitation; then one need no longer condemn it. The judgment takes place naturally and with ease, in the heart of each spectator.

Here one sees an anticipation of the alienation effect, and of the introduction to August Strindberg's *Miss Julie*. Might it also serve as an instruction for reading the then-nascent *120 Days*?

On April 20, to Madame de Sade:
Go then and nibble on your dear little god and murder your own family. For my part, I'll jack off, and I assure you that I will have done less harm than you.

On June 24, while cleaning his cell, one of the prison attendants breaks Sade's copy of the "Venus with the beautiful ass," from the collection at Farnese.

In July 1783 to Madame de Sade:
You have put fantasies into my head that I must now realize.

That he therefore hasn't yet realized? And that he surely no longer can, in the following years of custody, revolution, and poverty.
. . . the dangerous deviations of an overheated imagination, which forever pursues happiness and, never finding it, puts in its place a chimera instead of reality, strange irregularities in the place of a healthy enjoyment.

At the close of this letter he requests a container, specifying the precise measurements and overemphasizing the fact that he requires it for some harmless use.

On September 2 he begs Madame de Montreuil for his freedom, writing nevertheless that he could never live in freedom without his wife:

I would be thrown back into prison. But that is dearer to me, a thousand times dearer, than to live freely without her.

On December 23–24 Sade writes to his wife:

Enchanting creature! You ask for my soiled laundry, my used clothing. Do you realize what an extreme act of tenderness that is?! You see, I know how to judge the true worth of things. I shall do anything in the world to satisfy you, for I respect every whim and every fantasy.

Alas, righteous heaven, if it were only possible for me, for however short a time, to enjoy your many gifts. They would be devoured as soon as I held them in my hands. How I would fall upon them, I would fly, I would try to match their worth with gold and declare: Give it over, give it over, king, it belongs to the one I adore! I would breathe your life's scent; you would set fire to the vital sap that courses through my body, you would bear some part of your gifts into the very center of my existence, and I would judge that I was happy. . . .

. . . send me the container, I beg you, I must have it; if I don't receive it, I must force my plans –

dessins, desseins, "drawings" and "intentions" sound alike –

into objects that will tear them asunder, though they are of the same size.

In the beginning of January 1784, Sade writes to his wife that he does not wish to see his son Louis Marie de Sade in any other uniform than the one that he himself wore in 1757.

The end of February 1784, to Madame de Sade:

However great the desire may be to see you, my love, I must implore you not to set out in such inclement weather.

. . . if someone said to me: Sir, there is nothing more natural than your perversities, please feel free to do them as much as you like, no one has anything against it; he would thereby rouse such an aversion against my deviant practices that I would never again take them up. However, as it is on account of these that I am held in prison, I shall

spend my whole life speaking affectionately of them. If I ever get out of here, there's no need to clean out my room, since it won't be long before I return.

On February 29, 1784, Sade is transferred to the Bastille. He is imprisoned for another five and a half years.

On April 29 he receives his belongings from the dungeon at Vincennes.

These include: *Aventures de J. Andrews,*
Les Voyages de Monsieur Bouquinville [sic]
La Maria Anne de Marivaux [sic]
La Logique de Nicole,
Le Petit Carême de Massillon,
Les Ceremonies religieuses,
Les Mille et une nuits,
L'Iliade,
Marivaux,
Jonatan Wild [sic].

On May 24 Madame de Sade visits for two and a half hours, on June 7 for two hours.

On June 8 he writes to her:

The reason for your overheatedness, for the frightful condition in which you find yourself each time you visit me, is now revealed: you come on foot! Like someone hawking wares, or a streetwalker . . . and your parents allow it, your servants, the rogues, don't try to oppose you. . . . I can only say one thing to you: If you ever visit me in such a state again, I'll not so much as look at you, I'll immediately withdraw to my room, and I shall never again come down to see you for as long as I live.

And why do you commit such an outrageous act anyway? Why do you want to destroy the one cherished hope of my existence, exposing yourself to the danger of being killed? A woman, alone, walking on the street! Some drunk . . . a stone, thrown by a bum . . . a falling tile . . .

Examples of displaced anxieties. The world is so closed off that the only escape leads into phobias. The outside world, except when it is loaded down with terrors, no longer penetrates isolation.

I'm returning to you the book, which cost twelve livres. No one shall be able to say that I buy twelve-livre books while my wife goes without necessities.

Not only rhetoric, then, but also deeds, and truly severe, performed under considerable hardship.

At the end of 1784 Sade furnishes his wife with a detailed analysis of his masturbation habits; it seems that he could ejaculate only with considerable difficulties. He would typically spend an hour each morning, a half hour each evening.

On October 22 he begins the final draft of the *120 Journées de Sodome, ou l'école du libertinage*. It takes him about a month, until November 28.

When the prisoner is brought to Charenton on July 4, 1789, all the drafts, as well as the final version, are left in his cell in the Bastille.

For the rest of his life, Sade must have believed that his masterpiece was destroyed during the storming of the Bastille, on July 14, 1789, although it was actually found in his cell, in perfect condition, by Aroux de Saint Maxim; it was first published in 1904 by Eugen Dühren, alias Ivan Bloch, in Berlin.

The work was originally to be comprised of four parts.

Only a sixty-seven-page introduction and part I are complete.

The major wars into which Louis XIV was forced to lead France during his reign exhausted the state's finances as well as the people's spirits, yet those bloodsuckers were, in some mysterious fashion, enriched, among whom are numbered the four libertines, who prepare themselves for the Polanski party described in the text. *The third dinner was prepared for the dirtiest, most vile creatures one could ever encounter . . . it's a real turn-on to mingle with filth. 120 Journées de Sodome* (5)[2]

Then, dare we say it, if immortality does not possess the tenderness that one finds in virtue, does it not have something more sublime, something great and sublime that raises it over the effeminate – effeminate

– advantages of virtue and, moreover, always will? (7).

2. The following citations and page references are taken from volume 13 of the *Oeuvres complètes du Marquis de Sade,* 16 vols., Edition Définitive, Cercle du Livre précieux (Paris, 1966).

Sade develops a quasi-hydraulic theory of sensitivity:
He remarked that a violent motion in the body of an adversary exercises an effect upon the mass of our nerves that, insofar as it rouses the animal sensibilities that run in the hollows of these nerves, compels them to exert a force upon the erection nerves, which then achieve the shudder we call a pleasant sensation (10).

The expression is as stilted as it is unclear.

Here Sade's rhetoric, and one could cite thousands of pages containing like passages, babbles on for its own sake. Nothing is elucidated, nothing declared other than a layman's half-baked notions puffing themselves up into quasi-syntactic expressions that, moreover, one could scarcely judge "divine" or "satanic."

No real contribution to a psychopathology of sex.

The connection between sex and money is offered, as well as between murder and rape, cowardice and perversion (12), perversion and dementia and gluttony (16).

Auditory impressions are more pleasant and are among the most vivid of sensations (27).

There's also plenty of obscenity to go around.

To this end, four elderly bawds are hired. The libertines' daughters are all brought forth, virgins, young boys, fornicators.

Besides, beauty is actually common, whereas true ugliness is something extraordinary.

The party withdraws to a remote chateau – the one, recalled from early childhood, belonging to Sade's uncle, the abbé?

The rules are explained; these are monastic rules, the rules of a cadet academy, of a prison, of initiation rites, the rules of the leather crowd.

The slightest laughter . . . is the worst possible transgression and will be severely punished (55).

At the close of the introduction a quick sketch of the major personae and a few critical remarks from the marquis:

4. *Give a description* en détail *of the servant-girls' breasts, and of Fauchon's cancerous ulcer. Flesh out the portraits of the children's faces.*

The first completed part is entitled:

150 Simple Passions; or, The Passions of the First Order, *which lasted the thirty days of November; the stories of Duclos, combined with the scandalous events at the chateau, in the form of a diary.*

The Bloody Man

Pissing.
The lecherous Father Laurent desires very young girls, yet never wishes to see them a second time (77).
Father Henri likes the taste of children's snot (84).
Ejaculating into someone's hair (105).
Sade anticipates leathermen's fist-fucking (107).
He made use of a fresh young wet nurse; he sodomized her and discharged on her thighs.
In Sade an uninhibited and innocent audience naively and promptly imitates the things that it finds in Duclos.
Thus is represented people's inability to resist the influence of evil books and corrupting films.
Does it correspond to human behavior in general – a behavior to which, supposedly, that of the sexual automatons of the *120 Journées* doesn't correspond?
Or does it correspond merely to the conduct of a writer-onanist?
Colored ribbons, as in initiation rites (117).
Sniffing at someone's ass (125).
Powder and paint (127).
One fellow wants to swallow his semen as soon as he's expelled it (129).
We're tired of ordinary things. Our trifling means and a general depravity of spirit draw us back into atrocities (133).
Yet another vulgar-scientific notion.
An orator delivers a speech consisting of belches (139).
Another swallows what his companion has vomited (140).
Anise seeds are eaten to spice up everyone's farts (143).
The anise seed that once brought him a death sentence.
One person eats *faux germes* and *faux couches* (150). Premature births and – what are *faux germes*? A verbal monstrosity. A false seed.
Eating something that another has chewed first (152).
Tenderness only with a repulsive old woman (159).
Durcet says, like Proust: *Happiness does not lie in enjoyment so much as in wishing. It consists in overcoming the shackles that have been laid upon one's desires.* Proust does not say the latter – or should the sadomasochistic scenes from *Sodom and Gomorrah* be read in such a manner?

I get a hard-on when I do something mean (164).
Did Sade get a hard-on from describing evil deeds?
One can only commit two or three crimes in this world. Once these are done, there is nothing more to say [sic] (164).
It is thus a question of the narration of crimes, should one accept that this passage is actually a Freudian slip.
Rest is an inferior state, and while in it one experiences no more sensations. How many times, the devil take it, have I not wished that I could attack the sun, remove it from out of the sky and the universe altogether, and use it to set fire to the earth?
This is the moon that Camus's Caligula desires – not to mention the Ptolemaic universe, four years before the storming of the Bastille.
That which is here wished for in vain, to bring about a harm greater than the destruction of the earth, to leave a scar on God's own consciousness, is then described in the *Histoire de Juliette*.
Someone insists that the hookers shit their pants (168).
Shit is equated with riches (169).
Shit is eaten (170).
Another lets his whole body be smeared with shit (183).
Stealing is eroticized:
It is my deep conviction that all the goods of the earth ought to be divided equally, and that it is only violence and injustice that hinder this equality, the first law of nature. I undertook to correct this fortuitous state of affairs (187).
Erection muscles (196) – on page 10 they're still erection nerves.
One of the king's brigadiers is diapered like a baby, bursts out in uninterrupted sobbing, and eats shit (208).
Snow as a symbol of isolation. *Only God and one's own conscience still exist* (207).
Eating one's own shit out of another's mouth (210).
Defecating into a cunt (215).
Having an orgasm while someone is murdered (218).
When one has not done all the good that one owes to another, there is a certain pleasure in doing him harm (286).
Anal sex, performed frequently, is referred to as *Socratization* (238).
Someone lets himself be whipped to the point of bleeding, after which urine is rubbed into the sores (238).

The Bloody Man

Another lets himself be bound to a ladder and has his testicles, anus, and thighs pierced with a golden needle (250).
Someone's anus is burned with a red-hot spade (256).
Another wished that I might put a knotted stick, which he carried around in his briefcase for just such a reason, into his urinary tract (268).
A ceremony that one sees in African initiatory rites, as well as in *Leatherman*.
Also the item known in any German bordello, that a prostitute has to screw a client in the ass with a rubber dick (272).
Choking off the nuts with a cord (273).
Everyone knows the story of the marquis de. . . , who, when informed that he had been burned in effigy, whipped out his cock and cried: My God, I've finally got what I've always wanted – to be covered with infamy and disgrace! Stand back! Stand back, let me come on it!
And someone was then moved to remark that he would rather be screwed than understood (279).
I pray to the asshole and want to die while kissing one (287).
Someone lets his asshole be sewn up (289).
Another wants to be taken for a donkey.
Someone is burned with a candle (295).
Another is treated like a horse.
Another has his penis bitten (296).
Another is hung like Saint Andreas upon a cross, whereupon someone pretends to break all his limbs with a cardboard stick (297).
On Formosa, women who become pregnant before they reach the age of thirty are crushed to death (302).
Topos: cruel Asia!
Scalding with hot water (302).
Singeing with hot metal. Evaporating semen on a heated shovel (303).
Someone is brought to a deathwatch and then urinates on the coffin (304).
Shitting on a cadaver (305).
Coming toward the wall clock (305) – taken from *Tristram Shandy*?

Coming on the occasion of an execution or torture (311). It was actually a practice of the time. Casanova did it. Did Sade?
Having sex with someone condemned to death (313).
Nothing is criminal if it makes you hot.
Masturbating while a woman gives birth (322).
Voyeurism, as a man makes love with a woman and her daughter (340).
Part 1 as well closes with another of Sade's self-critical reflections: *I have spoken of active and passive sodomy too often.*

The remaining three parts exist only as drafts.
Part 2. The 150 Passions of the Second Order; or, The Twofold Passions, *during the thirty-one days of December, the story of Champville, to which the precise diary of the scandalous events at the chateau has been added.*
Why didn't he carry this out?
The execution and final draft of the first part were completed by November 28, 1785; Sade remained in the Bastille until July 4, 1789. During these four years he wrote *Aline et Valcour, Les Infortunes de la vertu,* and *Les Crimes de l'amour.*
Did he simply lose interest in the *120 Days*?
Did he conclude that the sketch, as a form, was sufficient for a schematic representation of the construction of an extended cruelty-fantasy?
Was a certain quantity of psychic and physical arousal exhausted by the writing of outlines, just as a pornographic magazine can be exhausted, for many onanists, simply by flipping through the pages a single time?
Did he feel that he had created something unprecedented in all of literature, something unusual and strangely powerful, unique with respect to both form and content? That the singularity of a mythic power of discovery had been realized in a much more measured fashion – that is, by outlines – than in the golden fragments of the classical French novel form?
The 150 Passions of the Second Order, the "Twofold" Passions, then:
One man screws three young women, all born to him by his mother (351).

He marries one of the daughters to his son.
There's a joke in French: *Mon père est maire à Mamaire et mon frère est masseur.*[3]
61. A woman mounts a crucifix used at the same time to penetrate another. She masturbates with Christ's head.
64. Two women defecate on a crucifix. Communion wafers are shoved into a cunt during sex (356).
86. Some are whipped by coachmen while others fart into each other's mouths.
107. The idea of hormonal treatment:
He brings her menstrual flow to a halt by the use of a potion that can bring her serious illness.

Part 3. The Passions of the Third Order; or The Criminal Passions.
19. *Want only to fuck monsters in the ass, or Negroes, or counterfeit humans.*
31. He fucks a she-goat, while another whips him. The she-goat bears him a child, which he fucks, even though it's a monster.
37. *In a basket expressly designed for such a purpose, he lets a woman copulate with a bull.*
44. *He screws a monkey, locked up in a basket, in the ass; the monkey, meanwhile, is tormented.*
66. *She falls through a trap door and into a darkly decorated room, where there is a confessional, and a coffin; severed heads are set out as objets d'arts. There she sees six armed ghosts.*
A tunnel of horrors.
75. *He sticks large needles into the woman's breasts and body and, once she is totally covered, comes on her.*
A practice that when performed in magical rites makes use of a substitute doll is here carried out during an actual sacrifice.
92. *He sticks a red-hot iron into her anus and cunt, after he has whipped her at length.*
Sophie's blood is drawn. The duke uses it to have blood sausage prepared for his breakfast (382).

3. *My father is mayor in Mamaire and my brother is a masseur,* which sounds the same in French as *Mon père est mère à Mamaire et mon frère est ma soeur,* or *My father is a mother to my mother and my brother is my sister* – TRANS.

103. He is bound like an animal by the four extremities. He is covered with a tiger skin. In this state he is pierced with needles, whipped, beaten, his ass left bruised and bleeding. Opposite him a naked woman is bound so that she can't move. As soon as he is thoroughly worked up, he's released and falls upon the woman like a wild animal. He howls and cries like a beast and bites into her clitoris and nipples. He comes on her, howling.
Teeth are knocked out.
Limbs broken.
113. He cuts off one of her ears.
116. He pulls off her finger- and toenails.
119. He cuts off a piece of her tongue.
121. He turns a young boy of about fifteen into a eunuch.
132. He takes out an eye.
138. *He puts out both eyes and swallows them.*
144. He cuts off the legs and arms of a small boy, fucks him in the ass, and keeps him well nourished. The boy lives for about a year.

Part 4. The 150 Deadly Passions; or The Passions of the Fourth Order.
12. He lets a virgin be deflowered by a stallion. She dies in the process.
21. . . . *he sews up the girl in a newly cut donkey-skin. Her head sticks out. She is fed and left inside until the skin shrinks and she is asphyxiated.*
Someone makes use of a powder that induces a deathlike state, just like in *Romeo and Juliet,* and, it is said, like Haitian voodoo priests. He buries his unconscious sacrificial victim and listens for her cries when she comes to (402).
A catamite *(bougre)* burns (just as in Haiti) poor people's houses and expresses the wish that children in particular might perish in large numbers as a result of his actions.
61. The stomach of a woman far into her pregnancy is opened, the fetus is removed and, before her eyes, burned.
Suffocating someone in a shit-filled pit (408).
The heart is removed from a living body and the hole that is left by its absence is fucked (408).
Hacking a woman into small pieces with a machine.

The Bloody Man

It's a Chinese torture.
Roasting someone on a spit (410).
97. A catamite rips out the bowels of a girl and a young boy, puts hers into him and his into her.
106. A mother is locked up with her four children, while someone observes which of her children the starved mother will be the first to eat.
111. He removes his testicles and lets him eat them, unawares.
Tantalus and Leatherman.
115. He strips back the skin of a young boy, covers him with honey, and lets the flies devour him.
118. A stallion, trained for this purpose, is brought in to a young boy; he screws the boy in the ass. The boy dies. He is covered with the skin of a mare, and his ass is smeared with juice from the mare's cunt.
122. *After he had completely severed his penis, he fashions for the boy a makeshift cunt, using a machine of red-hot iron.*
He reaches into her cunt with a scalpel and slices open the wall separating her anus and vagina. She is then forced to shit through her cunt (419).
A second is hung by her breasts.

Nothing similar had ever been written.
The *120 Days* are unprecedented in the history of world literature, unprecedented in the history of Sade's work and the Sadean persona.
The curiosities and unusual details of the Italian journey, the timid epicureanism and ambivalent atheism of the *Dialogue entre un prêtre et un moribund* give no hint of such a direction.
The myths of Hesiod and Homer, the slaughters and crucifixions of the Old and New Testaments, the initiatory rites of travelogues, torture manuals, all the cruelty of the Elizabethan and Jesuit theaters are here synthesized and surpassed, Freud and Kafka, Artaud and Genet, Polanski and Warhol, marionette theaters and spaghetti westerns anticipated and outdone.
It is, within the enchanted frame of a journey toward self-discovery – like *Robinson Crusoe, Nils Holgersson, Moby Dick* – a schematic outline of a number of dismemberment fantasies: a blueprint, not a confession.

More precisely: a schematization of the principles of dismemberment, and just how purely verbal such a project can be is attested to by maxim 116 from part 3: *He pulls several nails off of his fingers, hands, and feet* (384).

Once again a quasi-syntactical expression, a gruesome word facade, like the joke about the butcher who accidentally cut off his left hand and was so distraught that he cut off the right as well. Was Sade a poetizing verbal sadist?

Immediately after completing the final draft of the first part, he takes up *Aline et Valcour,* finishing this philosophical novel three years later, on October 1, 1788.

In between he completes *La Vérité,* in 1787, and *Pièce trouvée dans les papiers de La Mettrie,* in the same year; from June 25 to July 8 of 1787 he composes the first of three versions of his *Justine, Les Infortunes de la vertu.* During 1787 Madame de Sade is allowed to visit the marquis regularly, for two and a half hours every fourteen days.

Might the more tender impulses of *Aline et Valcour* be traced back to these visits?

On September 22, 1788, he changes cells in the Bastille.

On July 2 he yells from a prison window that the inmates are being executed and should be liberated.

On July 4, around one in the morning, Sade is unexpectedly taken to the mental hospital at Charenton.

The manuscript of *Les 120 Journées de Sodome* is left in his cell, and Sade spends the rest of his life believing that it was burned during the storming of the Bastille on July 14.

Aline et Valcour is a masterful work. The sole one, in fact, that assures him a place among the great authors of France, if one judges it according to the classical standards of phainopoieia, melopoieia, and logopoieia and not, as was hitherto never the case, according to a standard that admits the discovery of situations, the content itself, as a literary category. Following the rules of a classical literary criticism, to which, in practice, we all adhere, right down to our judgment of Artaud, Beckett, Burroughs, and Genet, *Aline et Valcour* is, with the exception of two poems and a few small novellas, Sade's only "successful" work. Not for nothing was it selected for the Bibliothèque de la Pléiade.

The Bloody Man

Sade, whose fate and temperament so resisted sublimation, who was not so much formed as broken, could finally, in a single medium, one unmarked by any hurried activity, truly perfect his skills – in letter writing; is it then so surprising that he found so much more success in the epistolary novel than in any other genre? The boil seems as if drained. After such monstrous figures, the book-length depiction of dismemberment, a refined artistic osmosis of horror and benevolence, positive and negative utopia.
Consider this, that beggars are also men like yourself, upon whom the same sun shines, and that they too have a right to bread and shelter. You don't want any beggars? Stop pumping money from the provinces into the capital city. Let the money freely circulate, and as soon as this fortune has been evenly distributed among the citizenry, you will no longer see it so unevenly divided between the pinnacles of success and the tatters of poverty (I, 62).
What can that mean except the overcoming of capitalism?
Righteous Heaven, if men knew what sorrows awaited them as they came into life, would a single one venture forth, once given the opportunity to turn back?! (81).
Lessing at his son's grave!
A human sacrifice among the Jagas:
The tree that they had torn out of the ground was again set upright . . . upon it was bound one of the unfortunate captives; they then began to dance around him; at each beat . . . they skillfully ripped a piece of flesh from his body with an iron tool . . . and killed him by continuous lacerations. Each piece of flesh was consumed as soon as it was taken; but before placing it in the mouth, one had to smear one's face with the blood that ran from it, for it was a mark of triumph (186).
Fontenelle is cited:
There is a solitary pleasure that does not require communion and that is quite precious, though never purchased (213).
Onanism?
Writing on onanism?
Describing immorality?
Writing with no intent to publish?
One tends to recognize the war god Ogun in Sade's description of a bloodthirsty African god, and he might just as easily have been speaking of the still-existing snake temple in Ouidah (222, 233).

Again, one of Sade's *leitmotivs:*
It is just that the weak should suffer (241).
One of the few depictions of masturbation in world literature:
Seduced by this bittersweet illusion, I dared for the first time to satisfy myself without Leonore (247).
Upon the negative utopia – in Africa, naturally – there follows the positive, the Asiatic.
Already the European conceived of Asia as a realm of enlightenment, Africa as a pool from which one might at best hope to acquire raw materials and manpower.
More curiously, the hideous, self-righteous, homespun and vain, paternalistic Zamé – the lucid counterpoint to the bogies of the *120 Days*, through whom Sade makes known his own conceptions – places homosexuality and incest under penalty. A self-flagellating degree of difference purchased by the *décadent* who, when he opts to move in society, works against himself and his own kind. A mode of conduct not limited to the age of the French Revolution.
I have only one enemy to fear, continued Zamé, the inconstant European, the vagabond, who renounces his own pleasures to disturb those of another, who always supposes that riches greater than his own lie elsewhere, who constantly demands better government . . . turbulent, cruel, restless, a bane to the outlying reaches of the globe, bringing catechism to the Asian and, to the African, chains; he annihilates the inhabitants of the new world and seeks out unfortunate isles even in the middle of the sea, that he might put them under the yoke (284).
And as for moral crimes, their perpetrators will be required to wear a mark on their clothing (300).
The pink triangle of the concentration camp.
There is, says Marmontel, a type of excessive sensitivity that borders on insensitivity (255).
The antinomy:
Certain unheard-of and outrageous crimes must, for the sake of the larger moral climate, be carried out (256).
In the midst of this journalistic babble, the – as it seems to me – campy prose that more and more threatens to spread itself cancerously over the multileveled body of the novel, suddenly an image of poetic savagery and archaic severity:

She lay upon the earth . . . drowned in her own blood, before her mother's (severed) tresses, in which she had placed the sole portrait that she possessed of her dear mother.

The *Crimes de l'amour* and the *Historiëttes, contes et fabliaux,* written during the same period, deserve comparison with Boccaccio, The *1001 Nights*, Stendhal's novellas, and Kleist, his contemporary, who, like Sade, obsessively places the sexual act, defloration, at the center of his fictional work.

These novellas occupied Sade until 1804. In 1800 the gloomier of these appear, prefaced comically with an introduction: *An Idea concerning the Novels.*

The historical novellas are the weakest, the short ones the most successful. The grisly note is scarcely sounded throughout without being answered by a tremolo seemingly marked by some extraliterary nervousness. The repetitions, the ever-similar rationale concerning similar things is here overcome – with one exception: a good joke about anal sex is recounted twice in slightly different garb.

(*Soit fait ainsi qu'il est requis; Le Mari complaisant*) (XIV, 117 and 169 f.)

La Double Epreuve is, in a more serene fashion, both imaginative and horrifying, although a certain incongruence is detectable in the main narrative line.

The influence of the *1001 Nights* gives rise to a hall of mirrors, doublings, and disappearances of the highest manneristic luster, anticipating even Benn's formulation on the simple and the refined:

even the singular and precious is formed from the simple (X, 84).

Even Genet's risky undertaking, to produce from a stone something artistic, which will still, afterward, look like a stone, is already here described. Lemons are made into ice that is then hung from a tree as a lemon.

Faxelange uses Buñuel's method, the quick cut from the amorous to the chilling. In *Ernestine*, Casanova meets the Marquise of O as Oxtiern deflowers the unconscious girl at the moment of her lover's execution.

Insofar as Sade takes a relatively benign revenge, in *Président mystifié,* upon his judges in Aix-en-Provence, does he not ironize himself? Does he not, after ten years in prison, and while still in prison, resolve his complexes in a literary manner? Does he not here make fun of his own considerable literary bombast?

The first of three versions of *Justine* could with respect to length and technique be classed among the novellas.

Any attempt at a binding intrigue is, nevertheless, just as in the *120 Days*, given up; we see numbers, travel descriptions.

Sophie already possesses all the characteristics of her reincarnation, Justine – bluntness, stupidity, cowardice, hypocrisy, a tendency to weep and prudishness.

What was Sade's intention in setting forth such a heroine?

Did he really believe her to be a true portrait of virtue?

Was that the virtue of his day?

The effect is rather that he wished to make fun of false virtue. And yet the idea of lashing out against false virtue is incompatible with the dedication of Justine to the clever, human companion of his later years, the dedication to Constance:

Have I accomplished it, Constance? Does a tear from your eye acclaim my triumph? In short, will you, after you have read Justine, say: O, how these images of crime make me proud to love virtue?! How sublime she is in her tears?! How beautiful misfortune renders her?!

Here tears, there tears. Is Constance being compared to Justine? Is he making fun of them both?

The homosexual episode, which is retained in all three versions, and which the virtuous Sophie/Justine eavesdrops upon, that she might be thoroughly scandalized, is presented in the *Infortunes de la vertu* in the following fashion:[4]

One of the two men, the active partner, was twenty-four years old. He wore a green overcoat and was well dressed, and seemed to me a man of some standing. The other appeared to be one of his domestics, about seventeen years old and very attractive. The whole scene was as prolonged as it was outrageous, the time I spent there seeming all the more hideous in that I was afraid to move for fear of being perceived (XIV, 358).

4. In these and the following passages Fichte quotes at length from the French text. I have simply reproduced his translations, altering them only slightly when it seemed necessary. TRANS.

The monsieur is the passive participant. Sophie is discovered, whipped, and brought to Le Chateau Bressac, where she is taken on by the count's mother. Monsieur de Bressac resolves to convince Sophie into poisoning his mother; Sophie apparently concedes, confesses the plan to Madame de Bressac; the son discovers her betrayal, Sophie is once again whipped.

The same scene in *Justine ou les malheurs de la vertu:*
One of the two men, the passive partner, was twenty-four years old, well dressed so that he gave the impression of having considerable social status; the other, about the same age, seemed to be one of his domestics. The act was scandalous and prolonged. The young master supported himself with his hands upon a small elevation opposite the bushes where I was sitting, and offered to his companion in debauchery the naked sacrificial altar of his depravity; this one, overcome with passion at the spectacle, caressed that altar's idol, and was on the verge of felling it with a dagger more awe-inspiring and larger than the one with which I had once been threatened by the leader of a band of brigands in Bondy. The young master, however, was intrepid, and welcomed that fearful bolt hovering before him; he plays with it, excites it, covers it with kisses, takes hold of it and puts it into place, engulfing it with obvious pleasure (III, 103 f.).
Madame de Bressac is in this instance the aunt of the effeminate count, once again is the intended victim of a poisoning attempt to be carried out by Justine, again betrayal and again discovery of the betrayal. Justine is again thoroughly whipped, and the count's three English mastiffs are set upon her.
The New Justine:
Then the master, about twenty-four years old, undressed the other, no more than twenty, stroked him, sucked him and quickly brought him to the heat of passion. The scene is prolonged . . . scandalous . . . full of various activities . . . the voluptuous and the filthy, and in exactly the right measure to shock one still groaning under more or less similar outrages. But what precisely were these infamies? We understand that many readers, hungrier for the details of these obscenities than for observations on the noteworthy character of Justine, beg us to supply a clearer picture. Alright then, let us gratify them and say that the young master, in no wise fearful before the monstrous sword

that threatens him, excites it, covers it with kisses, seizes it, thrusts it into himself, and is overcome by sighs (V, 168).

As the prose becomes more bare, the marks of insincerity become more frequent.

Madame de Bressac is once again the count's mother. Before he has her disposed of, he enters with two servants and performs the homosexual acts for her, which she condemns; she is, at his command, outraged from front and behind at the same time; she is mistreated further.

Finally the count, hitherto depicted only as passive, declares:

Oh! foutre, qu'il est divin d'enculer sa mère! (VI, 199).[5]

Justine's punishments for betrayal, sodomy, the English mastiffs, and matricide are here conflated in a single episode.

Once again, then, gravediggers and "gravediggers" (*croque-morts*).

On Good Friday, April 2, 1790, Sade is released from Charenton by a decree of the Constituent Assembly.

He writes that henceforth, on every Good Friday, he shall fall to his knees and give thanks.

On April 3 Madame de Sade, in the Convent of St. Anne, refuses to receive her husband.

What has moved her to do so?

What has put an end to this most extraordinary of love stories?

Sade interrogates his mother-in-law, Madame de Montreuil.

On April 22, to his aunt:

[The Montreuil family] wants to keep me from my wife. Not a single one of these common rogues, with the exception of my children, whom I can only praise, even extended a hand to me as I came out of prison, not one I tell you. I found myself in the middle of Paris, a single louis in my pocket, not knowing where I should eat, or sleep.

On April 28 Madame de Sade files for divorce.

In the first days of May, to Gaufridy:

I have lost my eyes, my lungs; I have become so obese from my sedentary life that I can hardly stir; all sensation has been extinguished. I take no joy in anything. I love nothing. The world, which I was

5. O, fuck! what rapture, to screw one's own mother in the ass!

foolish enough to miss, seems to me full of boredom and sorrow. There are moments when I consider becoming a Trappist. Why didn't my wife do everything in her power to retrieve my belongings from the Bastille? My manuscripts. . . ? My manuscripts, whose loss makes me shed tears of blood. One can recover a bed, a table, and small necessities, but ideas, once gone, are lost forever.

By the end of May he is living with an actress recently abandoned by her husband. She has a child. Is it already the tender Constance?

On June 9 the separation from Madame de Sade is formally declared.

On July 1 Sade registers himself publicly as Citoyen actif de la Section de la Place Vendôme, the later Place des Piques.

On August 25 he is engaged to the not yet thirty-year-old actress, Marie Constance Renelle, who has recently been left by her husband, Quesnet. She is raising a child by Quesnet.

On September 16, a play entitled *Le Misanthrope par amour on Sophie et Desfrancs, comédie en cinq actes et en vers libres* is accepted unanimously by the Comédie Française.

On June 12, 1791, to Reinaud:

buried in my study under volumes of Molière, Destouches, Marivaux, Boissy, Regnard, whom I consider, analyze, admire, and never reach.

In 1791 *Justine; or, The Sorrows of Virtue* appears.

In 1791 the marquis begins his career as a political writer.

In an *Addresse d'un citoyen de Paris au Roi des Français* he writes:[6]

You take me, perhaps, due to my strong language, for an enemy of monarchy and the monarch: no, sir, I assure you that this is not the case; no one in the world is as convinced as I that the French Empire can be governed only by a monarch: but this monarch must be elected by a free people, and subject to the law (XI, 74).

In October to Gaufridy:

I eat only once every twenty-four hours.

One of many letters to his estate manager requesting money.

On October 22 the play *Count Oxtiern ou les effets du libertinage* is staged in the Théâtre Molière and repeated on November 4. The crowd calls out for the author to make an appearance onstage. Sade takes a bow.

6. See footnote 4, above.

On December 5, to Gaufridy:
My way of thinking cannot wholly support any of the political parties. I'm anti-Jacobin. I detest them. I worship the king, but I abhor his old blunders; I love many articles of the constitution, others raise my ire; I wish that the nobility might recover its former luster, since it seems to me hardly progressive to strip it of it; I wish that the king would be the nation's head; I don't want a national assembly, but two houses, as in England, in which system the king's authority is divided and checked by requiring him to work with a nation necessarily split into two classes.

In August of 1792 Sade is once again endangered because of his children. These are abroad and find themselves declared émigrés. On September 3 Sade functions for the first time as secretary of the Section des Piques.

On September 17 Chateau La Coste is plundered.

On September 28 Sade, in a work entitled *Observations présentées à l'Assemblée* (i.e., the one charged with overseeing the operation of hospitals), makes reasoned suggestions concerning hospital administration.

On November 2 he presents his *Idée sur le mode de la sanction: cette liberté qui ne s'acquiert que par des flots de sang* . . . (XI, 85).[7] Private blood-hallucinations jibe with political reality. But good God, when hasn't the idea as to how laws should be ratified by the people been the dream wish of every political writer? The effect achieved is touchingly utopian, humanitarian, and honorable.

A letter shall inform the mayors of the major cities in each canton of the French territory, who will then summon the primary assemblies to convene in the capital of each canton. As soon as they are assembled, the text of the suggested law shall be brought to them by a second courier, having been prepared in advance by our prudent legislators. The people's magistrates shall declare the law before the assemblies; this law, once examined, discussed, and given greater depth by the mass of people whose interests it is supposed to serve, shall be then either accepted or rejected. In the former case, the courier who has just delivered it carries it back out immediately: the majority exercises its prerogative, and the law is from that point on enforced. Has it only received the approval of the minority? At that

7. this freedom realized only through streams of blood . . .

time your deputies touch it up, discard it, or start anew; if then they happen to truly improve it, it is once again taken before the entire French nation, which is once again assembled in like fashion in the cantons of the various regions (XI, 89).

... while it may be true that elected officials are necessary for the proposal of laws, this is not all the case in the matter of their sanctioning (XI, 90).

I love the people; my works attest to the fact that I developed the present system long before the cannon shots that overturned the Bastille announced them to the world at large. The most beautiful day of my life was when I believed I had seen the sweet equality of the Golden Age reborn, when I saw the tree of liberty cover with its benevolent branches the debris of scepter and throne (XI, 91).

Skillfully expressed and perhaps, as far as his books go, in some subtle way even true. Freedom, figured as a growing tree!

On April 13, 1793, Sade functions as a judge.

On May 7 he is received by the minister of the interior.

On July 12 he writes, in the *Extracts*, the clever neologism *liberticide* (XI, 107).

On August 3, to Gaufridy:

I'm spitting blood. I mentioned to you that I was president of my section. . . . They wanted to let me vote concerning some atrocious act, a bit of inhumanity. I didn't want to. Thank God! As far as such things are concerned, the word is out on me!

While I was president I saw to it that the Montreuils were put on a list that guaranteed them a measure of safety; had I but said one word, it would have gone ill for them. You see how I take my revenge.

On September 29 Sade composes a speech addressed to the shades of Marat and Le Pelletier:

Marat's barbarous assassin, not unlike those mixed beings to whom one cannot assign a definite sex, vomited forth from hell, belonging rightfully to neither and a curse to both . . . (XI, 121).

As in any popular revolution, those who remain between the sexes must surely believe that what is involved is not so much a change in the relations of production as a change of underwear. For Sade it was naturally the latter, which makes him not only an example of bisexuality within revolutionary movements, but equally an example of a bisexual fear within revolutionary movements, of bisexuality itself, as well as of homosexuality and hermaphrodism.

He demonstrates how those who have the most to repress can be the most oppressive of others who don't subject themselves to the same repressive mechanisms.

The fact that the Sadean repressive and oppressive mechanisms remain strictly verbal accords with his characteristic ambivalence.

The verses written to the bust of Marat are some of the most meager products of French lyric.

Sade is to be held in check no longer. In a petition of November 15 he suggests the founding of a temple of virtue, the establishment of its cult – St. Sulpice, for revolutionaries:

that filial piety, magnanimity, courage, equality, faith, love of country, beneficence, etc., that all the virtues, I say, should be set up, one in each of our ancient temples, and should become the sole objects of our worship (XI, 130).

Was he serious?

Or driving cynicism to its extreme?

On December 1, 1793, to Gaufridy:

Henceforth, write comrade *in your letters.*

On December 8 he is detained for allegedly seeking enlistment in the king's Garde Constitutionelle in 1791.

On January 8 the thirty-six-year-old publisher Jacques Girouard is beheaded, most likely on account of his royalist convictions. The printing of *Aline et Valcour* remains unfinished.

By some bit of luck Sade cannot be found on July 27, 1794, and in this way he avoids a sure death sentence, one that the guillotine enforces upon all of his codefendants.

On October 15 he is released.

On October 19 to Gaufridy:

In ten months I was held in four prisons. The fourth was a heaven on earth, a fine house, with a lovely garden, exquisite company, charming women – and suddenly a place of execution is set up directly under our window, a cemetery for the executed in the middle of our garden. In 35 days, my friend, we buried 1800 victims, a fourth of these from our own unfortunate house.

The Bloody Man

Sade suddenly sees himself confronted by the same corpse worms that he had imaginatively conjured up in *Justine*.

On January 21, 1795, to Gaufridy:

My time spent in confinement with the guillotine under my eyes has harmed me a hundred times more than all the Bastilles you could imagine.

On February 26 he asks Rabaut Pommier for a position. He is wholly without means.

In 1795 both *Aline et Valcour* and a novel in dialogue form, *La Philosophie dans le boudoir*, appear, although the latter actually stems from the period between the *120 Days* and the versions of *Justine*.

A school for libertinism into which a quasi-revolutionary passage has been inserted – *Français encore un effort* . . . (III, 478 ff.).[8]

An idea later taken up a second time in the *Histoire de Juliette*:

with this system you shall even show how the extermination of the human race would be an act done solely in the service of nature.

The dialogues end with the schoolgirl's mother being screwed from the front and behind by a syphilitic servant, after which both orifices are stitched together.

The Story of Juliette, Justine's wicked sister, comes from about the same time. Vice's prosperity is better demonstrated than virtue's misery. *Juliette* may perhaps be read as Sade's attempt to replace the text of the *120 Days*, which he believed lost. If the plot of the *120 Days* involves the relatively limited dismemberment of a group of people, in *Juliette* the destruction and desecration extend over Friedrich II of Prussia, the pope and the Holy Family, and finally into the cosmic.

Sade observes, with sharp psychological insight:

I worship gold to the point of having often found myself aroused before the sheer immensity of the louis that I have accumulated – a clear adaptation of the famous scene from Molière's *Miser*, from Molière, so often the object of Sade's admiration (VIII, 275).

A motiv of the younger Sade is heard again:

Je ne suis l'ami de personne (VIII, 235).[9]

---

8. French people, a great effort still [is required of you, if you want a republic].

9. I am no one's friend.

... *je frémis; personne n'est plus poltron que moi* (237).[10]
... *ô divin destructeur de l'espèce humaine!* (300).[11]
... *l'art d'aiguiser ses passions par une abstinence industrieuse* (303).[12]
C'est au grelot de la Folie à sonner les heures de Vénus (304).[13]
L'homme du peuple n'est que l'espèce qui forme le premier échelon après le singe des bois (311).[14]

Buttocks are sawn off and hung on hooks, crucifixions performed. One of Himmler's experiments is anticipated, in which victims cooled to the point of hypothermia are then forced to copulate.

The torments shall be prolonged into the Beyond:

She must be forced to sign, in blood drawn from around her heart, a statement giving her soul over to the devil, after which a penis will shove the contract into her ass (357).

Neither life after death nor Hell, then, is abolished, but rather everything is done to make them serve the general scheme of cosmic destruction and desecration.

Oh, Juliette, quel beau godemiché que le vit de ce bougre-là! (442).[15]

In principle, once again Genet's "artificial stone out of a stone": A dildo that will work like a penis, made from a penis that has been severed and specially prepared; the substitute becomes the real thing, the real substitutes for the substitute that is supposed to replace the real.

Afterward Saint Fond entertained us with a plan that he had conceived for the devastation of all of France (458).

The priestess Durand is the all-destroyer:

The life of man is in my hands. I can spread plagues, poison rivers (519).

---

10. I shudder; no one is more cowardly than I.
11. O divine destroyer of the human race!
12. The art of intensifying one's passions by persistent abstinence.
13. The bell of madness shall sound the hours of Venus.
14. The "man of the people" is merely the species that in the scale of evolution follows directly upon that of the monkey.
15. Oh, Juliette, what a lovely dildo this sodomite's penis makes!

The puppet theater and Punch and Judy find their highest expression in the orgy at St. Peter's:
Sodomized by the pope, the body of Christ in my ass, my friends, what bliss! (IX, 206).
Sade doubtless wishes here to profane God's symbol, the eucharistic Host, as well as his representative, the pope. He wants to debase God himself, and in searching for the means of representing this desecration he is blessed by a stroke of genius:
Juliette visits a mental institution in Naples, where she finds schizophrenics who take themselves for the Father, Son, and the Virgin Mary. These are no surrogates: in portraying their sufferings and the outrages done them he paints the sufferings and outrages of an authentic divine consciousness.
On March 14, 1796, Louis-Aldonce Sade visits Clichy-la-Garenne with Constance Renelle. The double meaning extends right down to the usage of the marquis's forenames.
On June 24, to Gaufridy:
Money . . . money . . . or I ask that the doctors might put an end to me!
On October 13 he sells La Coste. In the same year he acquires the properties of Granvillier, Eure-et-Loire, Malmaison, and Seine-et-Oise.
On January 29, 1798, Sade offers his services as an actor to a theater troupe.
On April 15 an attack upon Sade and his novel *Justine* is published in the *Journal de Paris*.
On April 18, in the *Journal de Paris:*
It is false, totally false, that I am the author of Justine ou les malheurs de la vertu.
Sade once again experiences difficulties with the emigration laws for, among other reasons, having occasionally changed his forenames.
On January 24, 1799, to Gaufridy:
Madame Quesnet will stay on with her friends for a while longer, and I shall spend the winter near Versailles, where one can live on the least amount of money of any place in Paris or its surroundings. There, with my lady friend's son and a servant-girl, we'll live on carrots and beans.

Sade, the relative of Prince Condé, had in his youth known another Versailles.

On February 13 to François Gaufridy:
Our household has been thoroughly depleted since September 10. Madame Quesnet is surviving as best she can with some friends, and I am currently employed with the theater where I earn 40 sous per day, as long as that holds out, and which I use to support the child (Madame Quesnet's son).

On December 13 the *Oxtiern* is performed once again by the Société Dramatique de Versailles; Sade himself plays the role of Fabrice.

On January 3, 1800, the nearly sixty-year-old Sade writes to Gaufridy:
I must be satisfied with the fact that the public-welfare system has stuck me in a hospital.

On January 26 to Gaufridy:
I have been wasting away for three months from cold and hunger in the Versailles hospital.

On February 20 Sade is taken into custody on account of his crimes.

On August 18 the police raid a bookbinder's shop where fourteen-year-old female workers have been inserting the obscene illustrations to *Justine* into a published edition.

While Sade repeats his denial of the book's authorship, its publication continues unabated.

On October 22 several extremely hostile articles appear denouncing the recently published collection of novellas, *Les Crimes de l'amour.*

On March 6, 1801, the police clean out the publishing house of Nicolas Massé; more of Sade's manuscripts, including *L'Histoire de Juliette,* are discovered. The marquis is arrested. It is possible that the publisher himself denounced the book's author.

On March 7 Sade is tried and admits to being the "copyist" of *Juliette.*

On April 7 Sade is "deposited" into the Sainte Pélagie prison.

Marie Constance Quesnet obtains permission to visit him every three days.

The Bloody Man

On August 20, 1802, Sade writes Fouché, again denies authorship of the infamous *Juliette*, and demands that he either be judged or released.

In the spring of 1803 several actors are jailed in the Sainte Pélagie following a scene of unrest at the Théatre Français. Sade tries to seduce some of the youths, is found out, and on March 14 is transferred to the prison at Bicetre.

The marquis's family attains information that he has been moved, on April 27, to the mental institution at Charenton.

In 1803 he writes to Charles Quesnet, his lover's son:

Consider, my friend, that your mother's existence divided its own self in order to bring forth yours. . . .

I have often said to you that a mother is a friend that nature gives us only once, and one that, should we suffer the misfortune of losing it, nothing in the world can ever replace.

On April 14, 1806, the Marquis de Sade serves the evening meal in the parish church of Charenton, St. Maurice.

On January 30, 1806, he pens – at sixty-six, eight years before his death – his last will and testament:

In conclusion: I expressly forbid that my body ever be opened under any pretense whatsoever. I urgently request that it be left to lie in state, in a wooden coffin, for forty-eight hours in the room where I pass away, and that the coffin be nailed shut only after the prescribed hour. . . .

I want it to be buried without ceremony in the thicket, near the right of the above-mentioned forest. Once the hole has been refilled, oak trees should be planted above it . . . that the traces of my grave might disappear from the earth's surface, just as I wish that my memory might be erased from people's minds (II, 631f.).

He feared then, that even after death his body might be dismembered, and he therefore gave up the idea of trying to cause any posthumous disturbance through his work; and could he really hope for the latter with a clear conscience? And even were his name erased from human memory, many of his works would appear anonymously. His hope, from the perspective of eternity, would absolve him only of the responsibility of the author Sade, not from whatever harm his published works might cause – that is, if he was truly in the end convinced of the dangerous as opposed to enlightening effects of his writings, there being admittedly only a few weak signals to suggest this. On April 25, 1807, he completes the *Journées de Florbelle*, a last reminiscence of the *120 Journées de Sodome*, believed lost, and of *Justine*, which was seized by the authorities.

Two months later the manuscript is confiscated in Charenton. From 1807 to 1812 the seventy-year-old works on the novel *La Marquise de Gange*.

Everything serves to impress upon the imagination that species of religious horror which seems to warn us, and which gives us to understand that true happiness is – alas! – humanly possible only in the lap of God, the creator of all the objects of our wonder (XI, 201).

In this novel the clergy step all over each other's feet.

The abbé of Ganges is the familiar Sadean villain – at his side, however, stands Father Eusebius, *far removed from the failings of his habit, dwelling in the shade of the Gospels' sublime truths* (205). Protestants and Catholics alike pay heed to his sermons. Sade has praise for the sacrament of confession and the once-so-profaned communal Host:

A great and stirring precept of our holy religion, which hinders or even annuls the repercussions of a crime by rendering even one who plans a criminal deed worthy of forgiveness – a sacred emblem of that sacrifice made by him who was both God and man, for we recover, in this sublime sacrament, some portion of that grace that his death granted us (IX, 233).

Sublime was once Ornan's epithet for torture and immorality.

Surely Christ's crucifixion was also a torture, a torture that a father allows to be performed upon his son, in the presence of the wife-mother, in the presence also of the more-than-friend John – there is no more sadistic configuration; the same God the Father of this Agnus Dei, who once requested of another father, Abraham, the sacrifice of his son Isaac, and who only at the last moment, once the son had experienced a near death at his father's hand, and the father had been proven capable of filicide, relented, and substituted a ram. In 1808 Sade directs several theatrical presentations at Charenton, a fact that aroused a fashionable interest not only from a Dutch queen's lady-in-waiting, but even all the way down to Peter Weiss and Peter Brook.

On July 7, 1810, the long-since-blind Marquise de Sade passes away.
The seventy-year-old Sade requests the following from the prison head:
1. *That I might have control over the key to my room . . .*
2. *That I be allowed to go for a walk without being followed . . .*
3. *That I be allowed to speak freely with the three persons named below, by which I mean: I agree in effect to speak with no one other than Madame Blotfière, my neighbor, Monsieur de Savines, who is my relative, and Monsieur de Léon* (II, 576).
On July 9 and 10, 1811, and on April 19 and May 3, 1812, Napoleon signs decrees ordering Sade to be kept in confinement.
From September 1, 1812 until December 4, Sade writes the novel *Adélaide de Brunswick*.
Here the sorrows are not the sorrows of virtue but of vice, although Adélaide's vice is admittedly subdued, and rather tame; Mersbourg, a twilight specter that looms behind the suffering, seems almost like some envoy of a higher power, about to call those souls back to the fold who now wander, lost in a Manichaean fate, through the imitation sacraments of the Albigenses, the Bogomils, or Rosicrucians.
In the figure of the servant Bathilde a wholly new type of woman is introduced into the Sadean corpus, a rather plain, yet clever and charming persona, in whom one might perhaps see the outline of his companion Constance.
The knights weep less boldly and swoon – the age of sentimentality forces itself upon the aged Sade at the mental hospital in Charenton, romanticism with a touch of necromancy, cemetery scenes and almost Hugoesque carnival.
I sentence you to the following torture: you will twist together a rope forty feet in length that, when finished, shall be halved and used to hang you both within this dome. You will be transported into the Beyond, one just like the other, only when this rope is finished. Work on it as long as you wish. We have as our revenge the consoling knowledge that every moment of your life serves only to lead you into death. . . .
From this moment on the tender and quivering hands of the princess labored on that most gloomy of works that can ever be taken up.

Slowness doubled her life's pains, haste brought death on all the more quickly. Ah, me, said the princess, is this torture not the torture of all men? The labors and the pleasures in which they pass their days. . . . Don't they only quicken death's step?! (XIV, 124).

Sacred tower, sacred isle, sacred cave, here the evil side – is it still the evil of childhood, in Provence with his epicurean uncle, the abbé, or out of the *120 Days,* or *Justine,* or has it been metaphorically purified?

There is a second abbey, seen in the usual eerie panorama:

Adélaide wishes to fulfill the duties of the house and submit herself to all the rules that have made this holy community into the most severe in all of Christian Europe.

. . . such compulsion . . .

. . . such severity . . .

. . . such violence . . .

I have come into your house to learn how to die.

My hands have dug my grave beneath one of the willows in the garden.

Like the sacrifices in the *120 Days* and the *Justine* novels.

Sade drives the rules of monastic life, one last time, to their sharpest extremes, to their alliance with death and the grave, and in so doing sublimates his own sexual fantasies into these same ascetic structures.

On March 3, 1813, Sade writes to Monsieur de Coulmier:

I beg you in all earnest to give the room above me, which you promised to my son, to Madame Quesnet. My health and well-being depend upon your response.

On May 6 the theater evenings at Charenton are forbidden by administrative decree.

On May 19 Sade begins writing the final draft of *Isabelle de Bavière.*

In 1813 *La Marquise de Gange* appears.

In October 1814 to Monsieur de Coulmier:

I have the honor of greeting M. Coulmier and urgently request that he allow me to retain the nurse whom he gave me, and not expose me to the unpleasantness of seeing a new face each day.

Sade worked on his historical novel *Isabelle de Bavière* up to thirty days before his death.

The Bloody Man

The title itself is both a program and a psychogram.

The secret story of Isabelle of Bavaria, queen of France, in which one can find deeds seldom seen, unknown or forgotten to the present day, and which have been carefully substantiated through reference to authentic German, English, and Latin documents.

Arrogant pretension, lies, crypticisms, and authenticity mania. In the foreword Sade sets himself the task of exonerating the *interesting* Isabelle, a task that is not fulfilled in the least – no one has accused Isabelle of so many crimes as does Sade in his novel. His expressed purpose is thus either a mere *façon de parler*, or he admires Isabelle's actions. Of what or from whom then, does he wish to exonerate her? No one has accused her of lacking heinous qualities. Or, perhaps the change in style, the more frequently observed gaps in logic and the way the narrative spills over into the unnecessary and improbable, may all answer to an ambiguity of intention that can find its justification only in Sade's personality, in his identification with his heroine.

The introduction is forceful, well-paced, and brief.

The book's compilations are often stated in brief outline, a clever montage of quotations or of material presented as quotations.

One is reminded of a successful radio feature.

The villains have plundered enough, Isabelle says to the Duke of Touraine. *Now it's our turn!*

And this written under Napoleon!

The virtuous Laura and the aura of love surrounding her are contrasted with Isabelle's vices – just as, later, the young woman of Orléans.

He would have loved to go into detail, but he has understated everything that might have been deemed morally offensive – with good reason, since the inmate didn't want to see his manuscript confiscated once again. He wants to see it published.

Not only in the portrait of Isabelle, surely, but also in that of Heinrich V, one can discern a need for self-justification, self-aggrandizement.

Did not Sade, as a youth, live a dissipate, sinful life?

Did he not, just as this figure, sublimate a desire for cruelty?

Every now and then, though more seldomly, he reaches too high, moves into the ridiculous:

The mother finds that the milk in her breasts has frozen.
Sade, who wished to exonerate Isabelle, writes at the end:
It pleased God to spare her life's ephemeral sorrows, that she might know those that have no end.
Was Sade afraid of Hell?
In his will and testament of 1806 he requests that he be buried without ceremony – eight years later, thirty days before his death, he finishes his novel with the statement that Isabelle was buried without ceremony.
The earth's bowels would tremble; they would have refused that criminal who with such haughtiness tried to settle herself into its bosom.
Did he fear that he would have to wander, become a ghost, if he were properly buried?
It's hard to say. *Isabelle de Bavière* is a novel of dissimulation like no other, in a body of works replete with dissemblance novels. The mention of Laura, her predecessor, Petrarch's beloved, works like a sure signal – in reality she is nothing but one of the many objects disguised as warning lights, of the kind that isle dwellers use to try to seduce boats laden with treasure toward their sandy shores.
He praises Laura's love aura; he scorns that of Isabelle and thus truly scorns her. The one he wants to exonerate? By blackening her name? How ambivalent the figure of Laura is, she who already appears in the book, written in prison, in the ambivalent figure of Sade's uncle. As his mother, his ambivalent mother, who calls him back to her womb-tomb, the tomb of the "gravediggers."
Falsity,
dissemblance,
intrigue,
disguise,
feigning,
nursing one's wounds in silence,
cunning actions,
faithless,
adroit,
counterfeit,
deceived,
untrusting – these are the key words, the sparks that set off the larger narrative conflagration.

There are times when the perseverance with which one sees to the punishment of some guilty party is more harmful than the crime, at which time, for a moment at least, justice must yield to caution (XIV, 426).
Everyone acts as if they truly believe in their own suffering (XIV, 358).
A hall of distorted mirrors:
Isabelle is grieving, everyone believes her.
Isabelle feigns grief, everyone believes it is genuine.
Isabelle feigns grief, everyone feigns sympathy.
And Sade hints at how it actually was: Isabelle knew full well that no one was taken in by her false grief, while the court knew that Isabelle did not believe that it was on to her.
A ritual, an artistic design is being fulfilled.
And yet the hypocrisy is not only societal, the ritual is a global, biological one:
Certain plants, which conceal the most beautiful properties beneath the most unattractive exterior . . . (XIV, 384).
Not only the painting but the painter himself is caught up in the flood of perspectives.
How painful it is to always have to contradict oneself in simply trying to tell a story (XIV, 382).
The man whom we saw engaged in such false pretenses is one in whom one could, at the same time, invest a great deal of trust. One must be blind to have so lost all understanding. . . . As if such a man could feel obligated by religious oaths, he upon whom not even the holiest laws of nature could put a single bond.
These laws, in Sade's youth, once condemned the sodomite to death. Did the revolution and Napoleonic rule actually change so little, or did these changes simply escape Sade's notice, since they had, for him, become meaningless?
Is, then, in a work on dissimulation, the story of one who dissembles, the condemnation of pretense itself mere pretense – or, by the same mathematical computation – self-criticism? Does Sade pose the question of distortion as simply the reader's distortion, and thus as one that no longer holds any interest for himself as author, since in fact he lays bare the mechanism of his distortions right from the beginning, claiming that the enlightened

reader sees through him – does he, therefore, shortly before his death denounce his own dissimulating arts in the figure of Isabelle, in effect exonerating her by a form of catharsis, not unlike the cathartic effect of *Adélaide de Brunswick*?
On December 2, 1814, Sade dies at the age of seventy-four; his testamentary instructions, which he must have expressed in earnest, are held to be of little importance by his son.
Sade is given a Christian burial in the cemetery at Charenton.

If I might pull a few threads together:
SADE, THE SATAN, THE SADIST. Was Sade unfairly labeled?
Was Sade a sadist?
In a more than superficial sense?
Was he a potential leatherman seeking out willing masochists?
Seeking out sacrificial victims?
Whether aggression and sadistic tendencies in general are inherited is a point of contention still debated by the popular scientific publications, like those of Lorenz and Fromm.
Such questions can never be answered decisively.
Sadism as the result of specific psychic and social influences, as "conditioning" in the ethnological sense, seems likely, but such a hypothesis explains nothing, really, and in a pinch one can still fall back on an alleged crossing over of instinct and environment, the Oedipus complex, malignant anality or necrophilia.
The conditioning to which Sade was subject up to his seventeenth year – high nobility, life at the king's court, libertine clergy, a Jesuit education, the military – lets the empiricist ascribe a sadistic component on the grounds of, among others, frustration, shock, and imitation.
That these elements made any lasting impression upon the marquis, however, cannot be proven with any certainty.
The twenty-three-year-old visits brothels and blackmails Laure de Lauris:
there is no act of cruelty that wouldn't tempt me.
What lover hasn't used such terms?
In the year of his wedding, and first incarceration, *he rented a house, bought some furniture, and gave himself right over to the most extreme depravity, living in a frightful state of godlessness, and to*

such a degree that several women saw themselves compelled to speak out against him.

On February 1, 1768, he brings four women to this location, whom he whips; afterward he has them served dinner and instructs a servant to give them each a louis d'or.

The incisions he allegedly made in the body of Rose Keller have never been substantiated, and it seems incredible that he could actually have wanted to "sadistically" poison, kill, or sacrifice those women in Marseille in 1772, using anise seeds and Spanish fly.

Did he want to revel in their sufferings, these being, for the most part, cramps?

There were at that time less complicated medications available that could have served his purposes, and ones possessing no aphrodisiac or carminative properties. Inexperience seems more likely.

In 1774 he arranges for an orgy with five young women, in which Madame de Sade supposedly takes part; there are rumors of a "button game," that is, bodily incisions, and of cannibalism. Both are unproven. Sade admits to a rather macabre jest involving human bones. Fromm would rejoice and claim that he was demonstrating the most malignant of anal-aggressive tendencies; if Fromm had taken the trouble of analyzing his works, he would place Sade on a par with Hitler – by which nothing more is proven than that psychoanalytic doctrine is more aggressive and inhumane than the modern judicial system, where judgments are at least rendered on the basis of evidence, which evidence, further, shown to be doubtful or circumstantial, benefits the accused, and not the state.

From what source does psychoanalysis derive the moral justification to overturn this principle, what sort of sophistry tosses necrophilia, the cleansing of corpses, and sadism into the same pot – in a publication, by the way, that calls itself *Anatomy,* even though it professes to make use of psychoanalytic terminology?

The reader troubling him- or herself over the proper determination of sadism, however, needs to be more circumspect.

In October 1776 Sade tries once again to arrange an orgy at La Coste with some domestics. His plan fails. Nearly all of his victims depart, appalled, on the very next day.

And that's it.

The rest – a prisoner's masturbatory fantasies.

As a sixty-three-year-old, he tries once again to seduce several young members of the Théatre Français who are locked up with him in Sainte Pélagie. In vain.

From his testament of 1806:

I expressly forbid that my body be opened under any pretense whatsoever.

More than this cannot be proven.

The question remains: would Sade have let himself be drawn into more serious perversions if an occasion had presented itself?

Did he in fact do more serious things, which simply haven't become a matter of record?

Nor does he seem to have shown much evidence of the masochistic component, usually set forth, untested and unproven, as a parallel phenomenon to sadism, both by psychoanalysts and *Leatherman:*

He lets himself be beaten as much as he beats others; in Marseille he expresses the desire to be struck with whips on which curved needles have been fastened. The women refuse. He counts, by marking on the wall, blows administered him by another.

He lets himself be "Socratized" by a servant, a practice that at the time implied extreme dishonor and disgrace, as it still does today, in all the Romance-language-speaking countries.

In 1783 Sade asks his wife to bring him containers, whose exact dimensions he provides; in the description of his masturbatory habits, further, he again mentions their use. He seems to have required them for anal practices, a hypothesis which is further supported by a letter written on December 23–24, 1783:

if I don't receive the container, I must force my plans into objects that will tear them asunder, though they are of the same size.

Truly a masochistic act, if not a very far-reaching one.

His relationship to his mother-in-law, a figure whom Sade both detested and, by turns, flattered, would seem most likely to yield a masochistic underpinning; nevertheless, must it not also be understood as a nonmasochistic tendency, that he truly hated her, and simply had no other recourse than to flatter the one upon whom his fate so often depended?

In any case, when he was released from prison after eleven years, he had no qualms about borrowing money from her.

On March 13, 1777, he writes to her:

For a long time I have been your victim. But do not take me for a fool. It is, now and then, not uninteresting to be a victim, but it is always degrading to be held for a fool.

Victim – gladly, degraded – never! A further step is taken toward true masochism.

Yet the question remains:

Would Sade have gone further if the opportunity had arisen? Did he in fact practice more extreme perversions that simply haven't become a matter of record?

Sade himself again and again denies this, both in his works and in his letters, but he also had good reason for doing so:

Granted, I am a libertine, and I have considered everything that can be considered by a person having such a disposition, but I have clearly not carried out everything that I have considered, nor will I ever do so. In the *very significant letter* to his wife written on February 10, 1781.

In *La Philosophie dans le boudoir* he claims that, in a state of arousal, people often attribute to themselves acts of cruelty that they have never committed.

Yet there are other expressions and statements that point toward a more flexible sexual behavior on the part of the marquis:

Ce qui n'avait d'abord l'air que de badinage devint peu à peu un tourment réel. L'Epoux corrigé (XIV, 256).[16]

Si, contenu par le remords qui se fait sentir au brisement du premier frein, on avait la force d'en rester là, jamais les droits de la vertu s'anéantiraient totalement. Dorgeville (X, 399).[17]

Are we to infer then, that he had the will at that time? And afterward?

Eugénie: Ne voudriez-vous pas me persuader, mes chers instituteurs, que vous n'avez jamais faits ce que vous avez conçu?

16. What in the beginning seemed to be mere flirtation became increasingly torturous.

17. If, checked by the remorse one feels at the breaking of the first restraint, one had the will to leave off, then virtue had not been so utterly destroyed.

Madame de Saint-Ange: Il m'est quelquefois arrivé de la faire. La Philosophie dans le boudoir (III, 419).[18]

Self-avowal, or the satanic self-importance of an *homme de lettres*?

The examples of the marquis's genuine goodness and tenderness in matters of the heart are every bit as substantial as the proofs of his sadistic practices are tenuous, a striking paradox viewed in relation to his work, not at all paradoxical in relation to his fate. *Alas, is that happiness which one purchases a real pleasure,* exclaims the nineteen-year-old, *and can love without mutual consideration be truly tender?*

At age twenty-four he writes to Mademoiselle Collet:

An object that has once given me pleasure remains forever honored in my eyes.

And he begs Mademoiselle M. to allow him to raise her son.

. . . he would want for nothing in the world . . . his progress would be my sole occupation . . . if I could at least see in his eyes some sign of gratitude: that I had given rise to some noble sentiment.

In 1772, concerning his servant Latour:

But I beg your excellency to return the promissory note for one hundred louis to the young man [Latour]. *The meager fortune that he might one day hope to acquire shall never allow him to match this sum without ruining his family. Moreover, he has been in my care since childhood. What reproaches would I bring upon myself were I to allow him to be so utterly neglected, and that at a time when he has given himself up for me in prison? I would forever hold it against myself.*

During the Italian journey:

But do not the most tender pleasures lie in shared passions? And how despicable in my eyes is that woman so little concerned over her lover's desires that she values him only for his duration, that he should most importantly of all satisfy her own desires.

This prince, who was so gentle and humane, and who knew the value – *the* value – of a human life, felt that the crime was not

18. Eugénie: Do you not then wish to convince me, my dear teachers, that you have never done the things that you have thought out?
Madame de Saint-Ange: It has happened, now and then, that I have carried them out.

eradicated by the death of the one who committed it, and that the example of a punishment that in any case delivers him over to the state is, rather, carried out to lead one back to virtue who by predisposition disregards it, as an example of a needless death, which nonetheless only conjures up despair and often accomplishes nothing other than helping someone think up more clever ways of avoiding a like punishment.

On October 21, 1778, from the prison at Vincennes to Madame de Sade:

Here is a brief letter for the poor little angels – his children – *whom I love more than you can ever imagine.*

On March 22, 1779, to Madame de Sade:

My little dove, I kiss you on the . . . and then on the . . . and then on . . .

Around the same time, again to Madame de Sade:

With profound gratification have I heard the news of my son's triumphs.

In May, to Mademoiselle de Rousset:

My wife and children should throw themselves at the king's feet?! But don't you know, Madame, how I love these children, and that I would prefer a lifelong blotch upon my honor rather than that they should be defiled by such an act?

On February 10, 1781, to Madame de Sade:

I am a libertine, but I have never endangered my family's wellbeing. . . . Have I not loved what I was supposed to love and what should have been dear to me?! Have I not loved my father?! Alas, not a day goes by that I don't mourn his loss! Have I treated my mother poorly?

On September 2, 1783, he begs Madame de Montreuil for his freedom, writing nevertheless that he could never live in freedom without his wife.

Christmas Eve, to his wife:

Enchanting creature! You ask for my soiled laundry, my used clothing. Do you realize what an extreme act of tenderness that is?!

On June 8, 1784, to his wife:

I'm returning to you the book, which cost twelve livres. No one shall be able to say that I buy twelve-livre books while my wife goes without necessities.

Once freed, and acting as president of the Section des Piques, in 1793 he writes the names of his wife's family upon a list and thereby saves their lives.

On January 21, 1795, to Gaufridy:

My time spent in confinement with the guillotine under my eyes has harmed me a hundred times more than all the Bastilles you could imagine.

In 1803 he writes to Charles Quesnet, his lover's son:

Consider, my friend, that your mother's existence divided its own self in order to bring forth yours. . . .

I have often said to you that a mother is a friend that nature gives us only once, and one that, should we suffer the misfortune of losing it, nothing in the world could ever replace.

And finally, in his testament of 1806, the phrase, fraught with significance:

In conclusion: I expressly forbid that my body ever be opened under any pretense whatsoever.

Benign sadism, benign masochism, a choleric temperament, an extreme sensibility, a complicated libido, an openly espoused atheism, an ambivalent conversion experience, the prejudices of three French regimes and his own prejudices, voiced for reasons of self-defense and survival – who would claim for himself that he could withstand thirty years of confinement with less psychic disturbance, or could undergo such a radical sublimation process?

But the work! Is it not an extreme mark of sadism when a man of letters writes such an extremely aggressive and sadistic work? Sadism as verbal construct, a sadism of the word, the effect of which would lie in the dismemberment and violation of fantasy, in the corruption of future generations?

Sade, who said everything that could be said on this topic, said the following only once:[19]

In addition, he cites other motives for his literary productivity. And the realization of these motives is clearly discernible.

---

19. The German edition notes that the citation that should follow this remark is missing.

If this constitutes literary sadism, pain through the operation of language, then one must also charge Racine, Corneille, Molière, Rimbaud, and Claudel with the same crime, and with them all of world literature.

This strange fascination with doing evil for its own sake, which Sade describes in the account of his travels in Italy, never seems to have held the marquis very strongly, or for any length of time, if we judge the matter on the basis of the solid evidence at our disposal; and even when he himself refers to some sadistic "conditioning," nothing seems entirely clear:

In July 1783 to Madame de Sade:

You believe, for example, that some miracle has been accomplished by the mere fact that you've compelled me to live in cruel abstinence from the sins of the flesh. You are deceived. You have, on the contrary, encouraged a growth of fantasy images that I must now see realized.

The realization of fantasy images meaning, for Sade, as far as we can judge, not becoming a sadist but describing sadists.

Two final observations opposing the hypothesis of Sade's sadism: A sadist would, in fantasy, be most interested in the reaction of the victims, and not in those of their tormentor – yet in the Sadean work the center and focus of the events described is without exception the sadist, and not his or her victims.

This might suggest a preponderance of masochistic tendencies in the act of writing as the marquis understood and practiced it.

And a last index:

Sade repeatedly informs us, in his letters, that the greatest pain he ever endured stemmed from the manner in which he was led to believe, under false pretenses, in his imminent release – and the subsequent, repeated denial of these pretenses.

This greatest pain, the most extreme intensification of suffering that Sade ever underwent, is never brought up in the literary work.

We are thus directed away from the marquis's supposedly pure sadism, or pure masochism, and thrown back upon the work, the work of a moderately perverted nobleman, of an eighteenth-century French man of letters.

Sadistic – in the sense of the Sadean literary figuration – the marquis was not. He bears his name unjustly.

THE DIVINE MARQUIS,
LIBERATOR,
ENLIGHTENER!

We all, surely, recognize in Sade the enemy of the divine order of the universe, of feudalism and early industrial capitalism, of totem and taboo, a writer who anticipates Darwin, Pavlov, Freud, and Lorenz as well as the linguistic critique of Viennese positivism. And yet what a wrinkle in the larger fabric of Sade's genius. Signs of the times. Times of confinement.

The question must be asked as to whether this explosion into extremity would have even taken place in the absence of certain contemporary events, and without the period of confinement, if in the absence of these Sade had not merely chastised his conscience, as did so many of his peers.

Surely Sade had a notion of evolutionary theory prior to Darwin, but the journal of the *Beagle* was written by Darwin – in the year of Sade's death.

Sade had an idea of dream interpretation, described the ego and the id – nevertheless Freud became the father of the Oedipus complex.

The great legal code that, for example, guaranteed homosexuals relative immunity from persecution – until it was threatened by Madame de Gaulle – was put into effect by that tormentor of Sade, Napoleon.

Capital punishment, polemicized with a vengeance by Sade, has to this day not been abolished in France.

Thus Sade polemicized in vain, wrongly, remaining unheard. He is an enlightener who not only wished for clarity and change in the relations of production, but who also took steps to realize them.

Sade's methods and philosophemes did not influence modern literature so much as those of Lautréamont, Kafka, Artaud, Genet, Schwitters, Peter Handke, and Oswald Wiener, all of whom Sade preceded, anticipated without directly influencing.

His works present themselves as far too contradictory, far too abstruse and distorted, and as a result those who have read him the least seem most inclined either to condemnation or to worship – a fate he shares with Proust and Joyce.

The Bloody Man

Like no other, Sade dared to give vent to the crudest atheism, to the most outrageous expressions of scorn for the family, the state, the church, and the legal system. He discovered allegories powerful enough to obliterate the European cosmos and contributed useful, rational suggestions on the subject of hospital management. Like none before or after he discovered archetypal myths and rituals – if there really are archetypal myths and rituals.

As one sees in details like:

Ejaculate is the vital element of philosophy (Nouvelle Justine, VI, 154).

. . . if there really were a God, there would not be so much evil on earth; I believe, then, that since this evil exists, it must either be divinely ordained, in which case God is a savage, or that he is not capable of acting against it, in which case he is very feeble – in either instance a hideous being whose thunder I have to withstand and whose laws I can well afford to scorn (Justine, III, 300).

Gide will say something quite similar.

The social critic remarks, half justifiably:

I love the people; my works attest to the fact that I developed the present system long before the muzzle fire that overturned the Bastille announced them to the world at large (XI, 91).

The falsely written plural could suggest a revealing identification with the revolution and the flames:

His books were made known to the world at large by the flames of July 14; in reality he must have assumed that his masterwork *Les 120 Journées de Sodome* was destroyed during the storming of the Bastille.

In the *120 Days*, long before the maxims of the French Revolution and of Marxism became commonplace, in a book regarded as the satanist Bible, he wrote:

I am thoroughly convinced that all of the earth's riches should be equally divided, and that only violence and crime prohibit this, the first law of nature, from taking place (XII, 187).

He observed, in the *Nouvelle Justine*, what his class for the most part failed to regard:

Gorging oneself before the eyes of the starved (VIII, 139).

His sharpest argument against capital punishment:

One is already a criminal if the only deterrent is the scaffold (Nouvelle Justine, VII, 292).

. . . there is no inclination, however bizarre or criminal it might be, that doesn't ultimately depend upon the type of organization that we have been given by nature (III, 199).
Inherited qualities, then, are instinctive qualities. But didn't he himself know better, wasn't his own life proof to the contrary? And conditioning:
Habit is all, Madame, there is nothing to which one can't become accustomed (Faxelange, X, 201).
Did he conceive of a blurring of instinct and conditioning in a specific mode of behavior?
In a word, the one was brutal by predisposition, the other, by refinement (Justine, III, 164).
He formulates a theory of psychosomatic disorder:
the madness that attacks the moral faculties is able to do so only because the latter are physical; for everything that disturbs one's moral center also harms one's organism, and vice versa, madness being a disease that attacks both body and soul, and that is infectious as well as curable, or better said, is infectious because it is able to be cured (Isabelle, XV, 293).
His most astonishing remarks involve Freudian psychoanalysis.
We are all members of the family of Oedipus (Nouvelle Justine, VII, 181).
Like Freud, he knew how to invoke the opponents of his theories as those theories' clearest examples, an inhumane exercise that accords well with the marquis's conventional image, the fascistic and masochistic implications of which have never been analyzed by Freud:
If you are painfully struck by the colors that I have used to paint the image of crime, and if they make you groan, your cure is not far off, and I have brought forth in you the desired effect. But if their truth offends you, and you curse their author . . . unfortunate one! you have recognized yourself and will never change (Crimes de l'amour, epilogue, X, 493).
Id, ego, superego:
Cruelty is nothing other than the energy of a man that civilization has not yet corrupted (La Philosophie dans le boudoir, III, 437).
Around 1787–88, Sade writes, in a footnote to the novella *Faxelange*:

Dreams are secret movements to which one too seldomly assigns a proper status; some simply ignore them, while an equal number of others trust in them. There would be little lost, however, in examining them, in submitting oneself to their logic, even in the following case. When we await the outcome of any event and have cause to wonder how that outcome shall effect us, such that it occupies us the entire day, we shall, no doubt, dream of it. Our mind, uniquely occupied with its object, will almost always show us a side of it that we have never consciously considered, and in this case, would it be superstitious, erroneous, or an offense against philosophy if we were to number among the event's possible results that one offered us by the dream, and to conduct ourselves in accordance with that possibility? (X, 187).

In *Florville et Courval*:
Mademoiselle, you came to me in a dream, where I stood, surrounded by horrors (X, 243).

In the *Literary Notes* of 1803–4:
It takes only one bad dream to dull all the ideas of the following day (XV, 31).

In the *Marquise de Gange* (1806 to 1807) Sade picks up the line of thought pursued twenty years earlier in *Faxelange*:
Man's nature is such that he will forever attach perhaps too much importance to dreams and premonitions. This weakness results from the state of misery into which we are all born, some less, some more, than others.

It seems that these secret inspirations make their way to us from a source more pure than life's ordinary happenings; and the penchant for religion, which is weakened by the passions, but never extinguished, leads us constantly to the idea that, everything supernatural coming from God, we shall, in spite of ourselves, be forever drawn to that species of superstition which philosophy condemns, and which our unhappiness, in tears, takes up. But in fact, what would be so ridiculous in believing that nature, which gives us notice of our needs, which consoles us for our wrongs, and which gives us the courage necessary to support them, should not also possess a voice that might warn us of their approach? You object? – that the force forever active in us, which always points out to us the things that either aid or harm us, should not equally well prevent us from that which tends or contributes to our destruction?!

The mythic-magical character of dreams is taken up once again in the following:
One must here recall the words that she uttered, in that dream she had the first night she spent in Ganges, wounded in that same shoulder where the sword would soon pierce her (XI, 383).
Depth psychology's recognition of the mechanisms of the dream is here touched upon, but not elaborated, and once again a veil of occultish mystification is draped over it.
In the *Histoire de Juliette* he succeeds in presenting a critique of atavism as a critique of language:
It is strange indeed that the Jacobins wished to overturn the altars of a God who spoke precisely their own language. And what is even more bizarre is that those who hate the Jacobins, and wish to destroy them, would do it in the name of a God who speaks like a Jacobin.
In the late *Adélaide de Brunswick* finally a declaration espousing enlightenment and humanity:
it is true that the passions corrupt men's souls, but I believe as well that reflection leads them to goodness, and that once a man wishes only to be himself he will again become virtuous (XV, 182).
And yet what a mass of bigotry, superstition, absurdity, and class conceit could be set against it:
The pornographic writer, whose work abounds in sexual detail, nonetheless becomes angered in a letter over the words *foutre* and *bougre*, the revolutionary threatens to have his son transferred into a lesser regiment because of his unworthy attitude.
The libertine prescribes, for his wife, a more subdued dress and modest headwear.
The observer of nature utters the most obscure biological insights.
Divine – and afraid that he might one day wander, become a ghost?
Such contradictions as are expressed in the following:
To Madame de Sade on March 22, 1779:
the coming year does not bode well for me, there being nothing so unlucky as a broken mirror . . .
A mother's seeing her milk frozen in a withered breast (*Isabelle*, XIV, 462) is wrong, but comical, if not intentionally; his prescribed methods of abortion are either false, out of cynicism, or cynical, out of narrow-mindedness:

with two lovers there is much less risk of becoming pregnant than with one, she said, possessing a good knowledge of anatomy, in that the two seeds will cancel each other out.

The "macho man" fixates on the idea of virginity in a manner not unlike Kleist:

Traces of sincerity exist even in the soul of a scoundrel, and virtue is of such a worth in the eyes of the world that even the most corrupt of men are obliged to pay it homage in a thousand different occasions of their lives (Faxelange, X, 197).

That someone could think of another while lying in my arms is an idea that has always angered me, and I have never seen a woman a second time whom I have suspected of having deceived me (XII, 330).

A lesbian speaks:

Leave off, I renounce with pleasure, for your sake, those errors to which vanity leads us as often as our own inclinations. I sense that nature has got the upper hand, that nature whom I tried to suffocate with petty indulgences, which I now abhor with all my soul. Her empire is irresistible, she has created us for you alone, and has formed you only for us. Let us obey her laws; it is she who now reminds me of these by means of that organ made for love, through which they only become all the more sacred (Augustine de Villeblanche, XII, 167).

A text that would doubtless meet with the approval of American feminists, various *internationales,* as well as the Vatican.

Yet the marquis's babbling rhetoric betrays itself still further:

The presiding judge in *Le Président mystifié* condemns someone to death as a sodomite, even though the latter is married and has many children . . . all things giving the lie to his offense.

I've mentioned that in Thamé's positive utopia homosexuality would be punishable by exile.

Asiatics are inhumanly cruel – the marquis has no qualms about repeating this commonplace – and the Africans?

The unfortunate Negress escaped and howled like a bitch who has lost her puppies (Le Président mystifié, 190).

Naturally, then:

Compassion is the virtue of fools (120 Journées, XIII, 187).

The strong sacrifice the weak, the weak are the victims of the strong – and there you have it: nature (Justine, 209).

Was he opposed to the idea of monarchy?
No one in the world is as convinced as I that the French Empire can be governed only by a monarch (XI, 74), writes Sade as late as June 1791, and yet such a comment bears an almost carnivalistic trait. In *Adélaide* the pious Sade goes even further:
A government, good or bad, is the work and image of heaven, and thus no one subject to it may overthrow it without committing a crime (195).
In the same book:
Feelings of sincerity and loyalty are steadfast in the heart of a soldier (176).
With such a statement Sade assumes a tone that is not at all foreign to him, and that one can already perceive in the first *Justine*, where beggars were to be hanged and:
The poor man is part of the order of nature (291).
One is reminded of the unattractive statement in the letter to Gaufridy from the end of January 1777:
Today some stranger comes in, firing a pistol and demanding his daughter back, tomorrow some farmer will demand his day's wages under an exchange of rifle fire. Don't they already show enough independence by virtue of the fact that they are allowed to hunt and hike up into the mountains?
In *Juliette* (VIII, 311):
The so-called man of the people is, on the evolutionary scale, only one notch above the ape.
Had Sade's contempt for the masses not kept him from considering the implications of his *bon mot*, he would, perhaps, have more significance for us as a natural philosopher than as a novelist.
Is Sade's atheism at all substantive?
The young freethinker's fascination with churches begins with the trip to Italy.
Prayers and appeals to both God and the devil occur throughout the thirty-year confinement.
In *Adélaide* he translates the De Profundis:
From the deepest depths we raise our voices to God.
And finally the precise wording of his own testament, in which he requests internment without ceremony, and the concluding passage from *Isabelle de Bavière*:

. . . tearing it away at last from life's transient sorrows, and delivering it over to those which never end . . .

. . . the ceremony was completed without pomp: the bowels of the earth would have trembled, and pushed from their breast the crime of burying such a one in splendor.

Verbal monstrosity: the breast of the earth's bowels, and the legitimate supposition that Sade underwent a deathbed conversion, fearing Hell and the fate of having to wander as a ghost.

Sade's significance, therefore, as liberator and enlightener, or as psychologist, does not bear up under a close reading of the details, nor does it derive from any particular ingenious revelation, of which there are many, and all of which he nevertheless contradicts – but rather outside of the realm of literature, as being the first, however monstrous, to play out the meaning of a world without God, or limitations – a world of uninhibited aggression. In this he was clearly prophetic; the sadistic world, one of unlimited annihilation, has been realized in Himmler's human experiments; we read of it daily as well in reports of torture in Chile and Brazil.

The evaluation of literature must begin with the premise that the writer either means what he says or clearly lets the reader know when he doesn't.

Kant and Schiller were confident as to the veracity of the convictions expressed in their writings, and even Swift, in *A Modest Proposal*, clearly indicates his position: that of the satirist who out of irony assumes the role of the murderer of children.

Two examples, of Sade's day, where clarity of conviction becomes indeterminable, and, astonishingly enough, both are revolutionaries: Kleist and Büchner. Which beliefs may be said to be Kleist's own in *The Prince of Homburg*, or *Käthchen of Heilbronn*? What does Büchner think of Danton or St. Just?

Psychic reality not only reduces, for the reader, the clarity of the author's expression – such clarity no longer exists.

In the case of Sade it is doubly, triply impossible to know what his standpoint was, the intention that informed his works.

A clearly expressed intention of duplicity can present itself as the opposite of any possible tendency, position, or philosophical opinion.

The singular audacity of his imagination may have led him to certain considerations of respect, and so forth, but not necessarily – and finally, there is in Sade a certain tangledness or vertigo that, intentional or not, occasionally requires the reader to shift perspective, and often within a single sentence.

On April 18, 1777, Sade writes to his wife:

From this moment on I resolve to be as false as everyone else, and I shall conduct myself so that only those having the keenest of perception may be able to read the content of my feelings from my countenance.

Sade is thirty-seven years old at the time. He has been imprisoned for the fourth time and will remain another eleven years. Later, he will do another fourteen-year stretch.

We can assume that the tendency to dissimulation increased under such conditions.

At thirty-seven none of the great works had been completed. All of the texts that concern us can thus be considered only under the aspect of their intentional distortedness – and must be read, as it were, against the grain.

The motif of falsity, hypocrisy, and distortion is present in all of the marquis's works.

In the *Nouvelle Justine* (VII, 31):

To increase my vices under the imposing mask of religion.

In the *Notes littéraires* of 1803–4 (17):

It has become so much the fashion of our day to judge the morals of a writer by his writing, this misleading notion finds such partisans, that very few dare any longer to even attempt a bold idea.

The testing of bold ideas would thus fall under the domain of literature, charged with introducing other ideas than those that are held to determine private modes of conduct.

Does this render invalid both the satanistic philosophemes of the *Nouvelle Justine,* as well as the social maxims of his political writings?

In *Adélaide de Brunswick:*

Is it not permitted to deceive others when it is a question of saving oneself? (171).

Isabelle de Bavière, Sade's last work, is an orgy of intrigue, hypocrisy, falseness, and dissimulation:

Everyone assumed an air of having sympathy for her grief.
How bothersome it is to always be forced to contradict oneself when one wishes only to tell a story (XIV, 382).
And this man, whom we have just seen indulging in such an outrageous lie, is the very one in whom so many place such an exorbitant good faith! Let us agree, then, that only the most willful blindness is able to be fooled on this point . . . as if such a man could feel bound by religious sentiment, having no regard for the holiest laws of nature (445).
Hypocrisy, distortion, double-dealing, can be observed throughout the life of the marquis – and not, at all times, in his writing. The nineteen-year-old writes to his father:
I know . . . one has to flatter to get anywhere. But I don't like doing it. . . . to speak only the best of those who have spoken ill of another.
The twenty-three-year-old becomes engaged to two women at the same time.
During his first confinement, he writes to police lieutenant Sartine:
I deserve God's punishment. I bear it.
Two years later, while staying at Chateau La Coste, he very likely presents his lover Beauvoisin as his wife.
The married marquis writes to Mademoiselle C.
My days are full of thorns, through that unhappy bond to which I gave myself merely out of convenience.
And even his first truly masterful work, the prologue written for the opening of the theater at Evry Chateau, is duplicitous, with its instructions to raise the curtain "accidentally" over a stage full of unprepared props and players.
In Marseille, make-believe is couched in a sexual ritual: He calls his servant "Monsieur le Marquis," and Latour, in turn, calls him "Lafleur."
In the *Voyage d'Italie* the figures are comparably simple, easily seen through:
At best one immediately tears oneself away from these objects that are impossible to consider without shuddering.
And then, in 1777, the line written from prison:
From this moment on I resolve to be as false as everyone else.
Is it really from a definite moment on, however?

The Gay Critic

Is it not rather an inclination, whether from instinct or conditioning, toward duplicity and disguise?
One thing is clear: he always wanted to be a writer, a man of letters, dramatist, novelist, and philosopher, and in a rather naive fashion, ever since, at the age of eighteen, he delivered his drab battle description.

And occasionally, in the course of his life, he expressed himself on the subject of literature and the literary mind without any masking or masturbatory undersighs, without drooling:
In the *Journey to Italy*:
Titian's maid-servant, a type of living furniture, which an artist and man of letters can scarcely do without. It is good to have them at one's disposal. Nature's needs can be seen to without disturbing the mind. Love is not the thing for a man who works. When his desires flare up and he has no available means of extinguishing them, the fire of the senses devours the fire of composition, and the work suffers.
In the plan for the work *Séide, conte moral et philosophique*, one reads:
The philosophy of the projected work would be . . .
The moral aim shall be . . .
(treatise on alms and the feeling of pity) . . .
His works could thus have a philosophical tendency and were written for the realization of a moral purpose.
He drives the analysis of the literary down to the level of the verbal material:
Everything barbaric has preserved a barbaric idiom. It seems that we all must of necessity speak the language of our cruel ancestors each time we imitate their atrocious customs. Consider the style of the language of judgments, warnings, summonses, arrest warrants; fortunately, it is quite impossible to kill or confine a man, in good French (Aline et Valcour, V, 2).
A dazzling, if unproven, thought, and one that is reiterated, following the Second World War *(Dictionary of Inhumanity)*, and especially by the Vienna school.
In 1791 Sade finds himself a free man, and writing: *buried in my study under volumes of Molière, Destouches, Marivaux, Boissy, Regnard, whom I consider, analyze, marvel at, and never reach.*

Might then perhaps some type of hurt-injured authorial pride play a role in the Sadean fixation on myths of destruction?
During this learned disquisition Madame de Noirceuil and the catamites had fallen asleep (VIII, 147).
The self-critical fear that his own formal inquiry might also be sleep inducing?
Above all, however, one sees again and again in Sade's work the idea of alienation, of distancing and the distance that is created by language.
Opposed to these notions there stands the unmasker, doer of harm, the torturer-through-literature who conceives of language not as obeying only its own laws, but as an immediate, unalienated, and undistancing continuation of deeds, torment, and pain:
To Madame de Sade, on December 2, 1779:
O, I'll lay it all bare, all the horror, the shameful intrigues, the conspiracies plotted out of ambition and greed!
To Monsieur le Noir on April 12, 1781:
I'll denounce and disgrace her [Madame de Montreuil] *in my works!*
And, already during the Italian journey:
But let us abbreviate my consideration of such things, countess, which are all-too-risqué for your delicate sensibilities, but which are not, I confess, extensive enough for my imaginative faculties.
. . . the sad curiosity that this heathen cruelty rouses . . .
And from prison:
You have enough intelligence to understand that some indulgence or other, which has as its source the blood's surges, is not helped by spoiling the blood further, overheating the brain by restraint, and enflaming the fantasy by loneliness.
In July of 1783 to Madame de Sade:
You have put fantasies into my head that I must now realize . . . the dangerous deviations of an overheated imagination, which forever pursues happiness and, never finding it, puts in its place a chimera instead of reality, strange irregularities in the place of a healthy enjoyment.
In the *120 Journées de Sodome* we read the programmatic line:
Besides, beauty is actually common, whereas true ugliness is something extraordinary.

As a motto for *Philosophie dans le boudoir*, which climaxes in the heroine's mother contracting syphilis, as well as the stitching together of both her anus and vagina, there stands:
Mothers shall make this book mandatory reading for their daughters.
Sadistic with regard to the mother, for the daughter compulsively masochistic and corrupting.
In the same book:
To shock is a very sweet thing (434).
My pleasures would be twofold: to indulge thoroughly my passion for these voluptuous atrocities; and to teach others, that they too might develop a taste for them (376).
I address myself only to those capable of understanding me, and only these shall read me without danger to themselves or others (494).
In the *Idée sur les romans*:
Thus it was necessary to call Hell itself to my aid, in order to discover some interesting titles (15).
And the ingenious allusion to the aggressive Oedipus:
the novelist is a man of nature; she has created him to be her painter; if he does not become his mother's lover from the time of his birth on, he may write whatever he wishes, and we will not read him (X, 16).
Oedipus is the first occidental detective, uncovering the perpetrator of the crime to his own ill, and eventual destruction, and thereby feeding speculation on the nature of man, from Sophocles through Sade, to Freud, Chandler, and Simenon, on the example of crime and sex, incestuous crime and sex.
In the *Justine*, we read:
these perverted authors, whose corruption is so menacing, so productive, have as their goal, in their dreadful systems, little else than the extension of the sum of their crimes beyond the terminus of their lives; they themselves can then do no more, but their accursed writings shall inspire many others, and this sweet notion that they carry to the grave consoles them for having been forced, under death's compulsion, to renounce evil (III, 211).
Introducing a mannequin, he walks and talks and writes books and is called Sade.
A young man from the best of families, highly educated, extraordinarily restless, and very sexy, driven by an ambition to become

The Bloody Man

a writer, a rather baffling tendency to lie, a love for the theater both in front of as well as behind the scenes, into floggings and anal sex.

His perversions land him in jail, where he composes – that he might make his sorrows known to the world, and take his revenge – a monstrous literary universe full of pain and injustice: mirror worlds with their own peculiar blind spots, and filled with lewd panting. Literature and the composition of literature oftentimes have an onanistic counterpoint.

Writing with a feather, the left hand is unoccupied; both during pauses with a machine.

An interesting investigation – the writing process and masturbation.

Sade states the case clearly enough as early as the *Voyage d'Italie*:
Love is not the thing for a man who works. When his desires flare up and he has no available means of extinguishing them, the fire of the senses devours the fire of composition, and the work suffers.

As did Sade's work, often enough.

Not only did he, like any other writer, often interrupt his work for some idle sexual pursuit, but he was forced as well to reckon with extreme sexual frustration while in prison:

Not even a little fling between cell mates!

On top of this he was clearly aroused by his own stories of cruelty, the artistic elaboration of criminal injustices, rape, and dismemberment.

This erotic problem of Sadean poetology is frequently expressed in the works themselves:

In *Juliette*:
I told you that I am aroused only by my own imagination (VIII, 283).

In the *Nouvelle Justine*:
religious enthusiasm is a passion like any other and only perturbs the spirit (VI, 306).

In *Philosophie dans le boudoir*:
When aroused, you love to speak of certain horrors, and perhaps now you will present such things as true that are merely showy exaggerations, the product of your overheated imagination (III, 463).

In *La Double Epreuve*:
there are moments in everyone's life when one will admit to, or say, most anything (X, 122).

His own predisposition, his exposure, and his revenge conditioned him, slowly, and through years of confinement, to find a masturbatory pleasure in his own literature of outrage, rape, and dismemberment, and perhaps even to find the same pleasure in any, even imaginary, discourse on outrage, rape, dismemberment. Inclination and conditioning thus drive him, in a painfully slow circuit, to exposure and revenge, and from exposure and revenge to inclination and conditioning.

Literature's least ideal nodal point, the presentation of masturbatory impulses, spurs Sade on to develop a bureaucracy of terror capable of exposing hypocrisy, and of even prophetic proportions.

On December 2, 1779, to Madame de Sade:

Oh, I shall expose them all, all the atrocious misdeeds, the conspiratorial plot-hatchers, weaving designs out of greed and thievishness! For now I know them all, I have made their acquaintance at my own expense: and now all of France shall know of them as well (XII, 227).

On March 22, 1783 – the first sketches for the *120 Days* are already completed:

And here then lies art, in its essence: it consists not in punishing vice, through comic means, but rather in depicting it in such a manner that none shall wish to resemble it; this being the case, there should be no need to punish it. Vice's condemnation is uttered deep in the soul of each spectator (XIII, 381).

In the *Idée sur les romans*:

What function do novels serve?

Can you tell me what function they serve, you deviants, marred by hypocrisy? For you alone pose this ridiculous question – a ridiculous question that he himself had to pose, otherwise he couldn't have written his essay – *they serve to show you as you truly are* (XI, 15).

Never, I repeat, never will I present the criminal deed in any other light than in that of Hell; for I wish that my readers might see it in its bare essence, fear it, despise it, and I know of no other way to accomplish this than to simply demonstrate it in all its characteristic horror (XI, 22).

Eugénie de Franval, the novel of incest, begins:

The Bloody Man

The instruction of man and his moral correction: this is the sole end to which we direct ourselves by means of this small tale (XI, 425). And finally, the touchingly iridescent dedication to his longtime companion, Constance:
you will exclaim: O, how these tableaux du crime *inspire in me a love of virtue. And these sorrows, how they only make it more beautiful. O, Constance, should these words escape from your lips, my works shall have found their crowning achievement!*
One writing in the throes of a masturbatory fantasy defers, even in fantasy, its realization. Such fantasies, and not only their Sadean version, may be thought to be similar to horror stories in that they arouse one without, at the same time, arousing even a hopeful need for their realization.
Each, once used, is used up – we are, as it were, dulled to them, without being dulled in general.
All are familiar with the vicarious thrill one experiences at hearing someone speak of a traffic accident, of surgeries, details that engage us a single time, are boring the second, yet we do not become cruel fathers because of it, or sadistic nurses.
It's only a story! and *I've heard this one* are impulses similar to those of the onanist who quickly goes from one sex shop to another.
I've heard this one could perhaps be the motive force behind Sade's variations on what amount to the same sexual, sadistic, and intellectual acts.
A suffering writer, not a masturbating sadist.
The masturbating sadist would get a kick out of the pain of the tormented, would show them and their reactions, not the actions of the tormentor.
Sade, however, portrays the tormentor. He doesn't show us the agonies of those who have been murdered for pleasure, or their souls that have been eternally corrupted, but rather how a pleasure-murderer might think, were he trying to ruin the soul of his victim for eternity.
And further:
For Sade it was the most extreme cruelty to be promised release, month after month, year after year.
This most dreadful of all his pains appears in none of his works.

Would he not have inserted it there at some point, if his works had really been a substitute gratification for some supposed *Grand Sadique*?

Sade was into horror stories.

These masturbatory fantasies are fantasies in a double sense: the very stuff of the stories, the photographs and hectographic pages, which otherwise, for an onanist, come from outside, from an alien source, as if from an intimate "you" – Sade produces these as well, it is his own reflection – the self-analysis of his own capacity for arousal and powers of imagination – the relevance of such notions beginning for the leatherman at this point.

How are these psychisms, these poetologies transformed into words?

There are more vehement bits of prose from the eighteen-year-old than the following:

on the night of the fifteenth we camped in the plain of Brauweiler, where earlier we had fought, and kept watch. We stayed until the twenty-fourth at Brauweiler. On the twenty-third, the enemy broke camp; we did the same on the twenty-fourth (Campagne de 1758, XVI, 47).

And the other extreme, kitsch and treacle:

She is no longer a woman, but an angel, who but for a moment called down the anger of the heavens and was, at the last, forgiven (Adélaide, XV, 215).

A sugary kitsch not at all far from naked hypocrisy.

"Franval voulait consommer son crime. Frémissons . . . Il le fit!"[20]

And a sour kitsch:

He pulled several nails from his fingers, hands, and feet (120 Journées de Sodome, XIII, 384).

A rhetorical figure that blurs into the unreal, verbal sadism, a monstrosity of the word.

The convert places his figures at the disposal of the revolution:

Marat's barbarous assassin not unlike those mixed beings to whom one cannot assign a definite sex, vomited forth from hell, belonging rightfully to neither and a curse to both (Manes de Marat, XI, 121).

20. Franval wished to carry out his crime to the end. We shudder at the thought . . . he did it.

Unintentionally comic:
he promptly gave up his pure and unblemished soul to God (Marquise de Gange, X, 236).
Unintentionally comic?
. . . he penetrated her, suddenly, leaving her no time to defend herself. "Oh, Monsieur, what are you doing?" cried the chaste young girl, "what place have you chosen to carry out such things? Good God, do you know where you are?" (Nouvelle Justine, VII, 101).
No, he can't be serious!
And yet how perfectly the classical rhetorical shell can sometimes fit the thought:
For a long time now, Madame, I have been your victim; but do not take me for a fool. It is sometimes interesting to be the one, but always humiliating to be the other, and I flatter myself with possessing the same measure of insight, as you deem yourself as possessing, of falseness (Lettres, XII, 117).
The aphoristic, condensed from a mixture of slang and formality:
And this it was that moved a man of great intellect to remark that he would rather be screwed than understood (120 Journées de Sodome, XIII, 218).
The language of the *siècle galant*:
Ah, I tell you, if any of these good souls blessed by God should possess the means of unlocking . . . the door to divine beatitude, it would certainly be Monsieur the vicar, for I have never seen such a large key (Le Talion, XIV, 240).
Sade, the satirist:
and suddenly there appeared forty or fifty provincial magistrates, their flies open, cocks in hand, proving thus like the sailor that not a single one of them was any less a Christian than Saint Christopher.
The parodying of his own horror pieces takes on, in *Le Président mystifié*, almost [Wilhelm] Buschean traits:
Tell me then how you think that a man who, having spent the night with a Negress, is treated like a heretic the next morning, and is then forced into an ice-cold bath for lunch, and shortly thereafter falls into the river, who finds himself stuck on the commode like a bird in glue, his ass burned while he defecates, and whom one dares to tell, to his face, that the judges responsible for uncovering such crimes are measly little cheats, and that the whores with colic weren't poisoned –

how, I ask you, can such a man ever think again of deflowering a virgin?

Untoppably carnivalesque:

Sodomized by the pope, the body of Christ in my ass, O, my friends, what bliss! (*Juliette*, IX, 206).

And ironic, as in the *120 Days*, when he has someone belching into the mouth of a speaker.

Phainopoieia, the art of writing with pictorial vividness, is in Sade for the most part rather mildly expressed, if one leaves aside his almost mythic powers, a subject to which I shall return.

And yet in the novellas several of his scene paintings succeed in conveying an unsettling beauty:

There, in a decorated room, naked on a pedestal, stood Eugénie, representing a young savage, wearied by the hunt and leaning against the trunk of a palm; its lofty branches concealed an infinity of lights that seemed only to shine with favor on the young girl, playing upon her features to the best effect. This living statue stood in the midst of a small theater and was surrounded by a canal, six feet across, which served as a barrier to the young savage and denied access to her from all sides. Beyond this moat, as it were, a chair had been placed; a silken cord led from the pedestal to this chair, by which one could, in turning, perceive the object of cult from all sides, and however it was turned, the view was always very pleasing (Eugénie de Franval, X, 468f.).

Hard and simple:

Go then and nibble on your dear little God and murder your own family. For my part, I'll jack off, and I assure you that I will have done less harm than you (April 20, 1783, to Madame de Sade).

As a lyric poet, the ostracized Sade composed many works of timeless beauty; these belong to the finest examples of French lyric.

Their timbre is akin to that of Villon, Rutebeuf, or Ronsard:

Chanson, chanson
Il vous faut, dites-vous, poulette
Pour vous rendre plus grassouillette
Un mandat? – Fi!

Ah! bon dieu, comme elle me flanque!

Je sais bien que rien ne vous manque,
Même un gros v[it] (XII, 259).[21]

And, sung to the tune of *Carillon de Vincennes:*

je te plains – je te plains
il n'est plus pour toi de fins
qu'en poudre – qu'en poudre

et j'ai dit
de plaisir, de jouir
il faut donc vous désaisir
mon âme, mon âme

Capucin, capucin
rencontre au moins, un main
qui b[ranle] – qui b[ranle]

mais ici – quel souci
pour tout bien j'ai dieu merci
la mienne, la mienne

venés donc – venés donc
soulager par votre c[on]
ma peine, ma peine

ma moitié, ma moitié
me rend sans nulle pitié
tantale, tantale

ah quel sort! ah quel sort
oh, par ma foi c'est trop fort
j'en crève, j'en crève

le sainfoin, meurt sans soin

21. Chanson, chanson / Must I, you say, my pet, / To make you even plumper yet / Send money? – Ha!
Good God! how she pushes me! / How well I know you lack for nothing / Not even a fat [prick].

*venés en chercher au moins
la graine – la graine*

*Quel martir – quel martir
je vois bien qu'il faut souffrir
sans cesse, sans cesse* (XIII, 388).[22]

These are the lilting syncopes of Renaissance poetry, combined with a verbal and aural audacity worthy of Verlaine.
We also find the absolute metaphor of a *Bateau ivre,* by Rimbaud, already in *Aline et Valcour:*
On the way we saw this extraordinary animal, about the size of a cat, and a face like that of a man, with a very attractive white beard. Its voice was like that of someone crying. It lives in the trees and can be tamed only with great difficulty; blessed with a love of liberty as intense as man's own, it withers and dies as soon as it is deprived of it (V, 60).

There are three levels at which the poetic event may be said to occur: Sade depicts an – imaginary – animal and compares it with men in general; the depiction, and the comparison of this depiction, in turn comprise an absolute metaphor for his own situation.
Next to which stand rather rustic provincialisms:
A man, in his later years, wished to marry (*L'Epoux corrigé*, XIV, 255).
In the remarks written to the lost work, *Journées de Florbelle,* we come unexpectedly upon the author as he speaks, to himself, of his characters:
And thereby the hermit shall be done in; Eudoxie worked over, but still in one piece.

22. I mourn for you / nothing shall be left of you / but dust
and I have told you / from pleasure and from lust / you must refrain / my soul
a Capuchin / can find a hand, at least / to stroke him
but here – such worries / have I only, thanks to God / my own
come then / and soothe, with your crotch / my pain
my wife / pitiless, has made me into a / Tantalus
What a fate! / oh, I feel it is too great / I am undone
The flower dies without care / come then and seek out, at least / the seed
what martyrdom / I see well that one must suffer / without end

The Bloody Man

The mythic economy of a cookbook:
He strips back the skin of a young boy, covers him with honey, and lets the flies devour him (120 Journées de Sodome, XIII, 416).
Joyce – or: an inner monologue, written out.
To Carteron, called La Jeunesse, called Martin Quiros,
Martin Quiros . . . you make bold, my son, if I were there I'd let you have it. . . . I'd tear off your toupee, that false one that you reconstruct every year out of horsetail hairs taken from the road leading from Courtheson to Paris what could you do so late in the morning to mend it? Tell me what would you do?
And Schwitters:
Cat chu kri cacambos (La Double Epreuve, X, 82).[23]
And in the letters (XII, 196):
let him be called what he will: Chivarucmarbarbarmarocsacrominecpanti
A power of creating words that occasionally exceeds his powers of expression:
I don't understand it any longer, and have stopped trying!
(On March 4, 1781, to Madame de Sade.)

Marlitt and Homer, Kafka and *"him, the magazine with the man."* A writer blessed with an extraordinary wealth of linguistic skill, who anticipated many of the important discoveries of modern literature, and who extended the breadth of "high" literature by legitimizing the role of its masturbatory underpinnings.
Should we invoke Pound's parameters once again: logopoieia, melopoieia, and phainopoieia – and there are no better ones – we would have no difficulties with melopoieia, the audible and rhythmic quality of the Sadean art being easily recognizable and amenable to analysis; seen on the whole, however, the melopoieia comes up short, if we measure the verbal melodics of the Provençal poet, say, by his forefather, Arnaut Daniel, or his descendant Aubanel, the shepherd of Vaucluse.
Logopoieia, the art of implementing specific linguistic registers, or of setting them in counterpoint against one another – Thomas Mann's polished archaicisms and his oft-cited irony in the *Selected Stories*, for example – Sadean logopoieia is remarkable,

---

23. A wholly nonsensical expression.

uniquely multifaceted; phainopoieia, the art of making visually striking images, falls far short; it is a picture world constructed out of pasteboard, where stages designed for Corneille often seem out of place and outdated set to works by Molière.

And yet, in measuring Sade's work by such a standard, it seems that something decisive evades us.

For is not any significant literary phenomenon only truly significant insofar as it finds these traditional parameters too constricting? And in the case of Sade, the immeasurable isn't some arbitrary imponderable *x* – rather the immeasurable belongs to the very essence of Sadean literature, going so far as to become a new literary category:

There are only two types of literary critique that invoke the artistic object itself as a standard of judgment – the Catholic, and the Marxist; by doing so, they explode the very concept of literature, which can't survive this explosion, since Genet is obviously better than Claudel, Wedekind than Brecht, whatever Trotsky and the Vatican may say to the contrary.

The object makes no difference; the quality of the representation is all that matters, a quality best measured in terms of melopoieia, logopoieia, and phainopoieia – Burroughs, Genet, Artaud, Proust, Joyce, Kafka, Lautréamont are clearly all best evaluated and understood in these terms.

A grandmother who suffers a stroke in a public nursing home no longer interests today's news reader – its representation, in *Recherche du temps perdu*, is one of the greatest tragedies in the history of mankind.

In Sade the object itself is what strikes the reader – and not only for the specialized, masturbating kind.

The literary interest of his work does not, then, rest upon two or three remarkable poems, or a series of smoothly polished novellas – it rests rather upon his fearful myths, unique in all of world literature, which aren't always even particularly well written, are often in fact very poorly written – to include Sade's mythic, magical genius we must broaden our critical parameters, we must recognize a primal literary stratum of the fantastic-factical, camp and pop, but not as figure, or calculated effect, but rather something immediate, literature being conceived in this

The Bloody Man

instance as reportage, just as an onanist might label a work of pornography "hot," even if rather clinically rendered, and whether it comes from Genet or is called *Mutzenbacher*.

The Oedipus myth has literary force whether it's translated by Hölderlin, Freud, or Gustav Schwab.

Sade's scandalous and destructive cosmic retribution reaches its highest point in the *Histoire de Juliette*, as the heroine describes anal intercourse with the Virgin Mary, Jesus Christ, and God the Father himself. The quality of the representation at this point counts for nothing. Sade, to attain his ends, discovers an ingenious trick that is neither melodic, topical, or imagistic:

The scene takes place in an insane asylum outside of Naples. There, several inmates are abused and violated, specifically a group who think themselves to *be* the Holy Family and not merely to represent them – for were the latter the case, Sade might equally have abused a theater troupe or a communion wafer; nor would a series of conventional literary tricks, an allegory, say, in which the libertines ascend to heaven and exercise their bestial natures above the clouds, have fulfilled Sade's purposes; the reader would have refused to accept the divine consciousness as anything except Sade's own; in that he shows the paranoiacs to the reader, however, and depicts the violation and abuse of this Virgin Mary, this Jesus Christ, and this God the Father, he makes the abuse of the divine consciousness credible, and only in this way would it be possible to do so.

The *what*, therefore, is the point of interest, and not the *how* – as in a work of pornography. The fact that it is words that relate the sexually evocative stories is, for the onanist, the decisive factor, the fact that it is words that convey this *what* is, for the man of letters Sade, decisive.

Is not then the *what* in literature the phainopoetic element? And therefore phainopoieia the elaboration of reality toward a literary ideal of imagistic vividness, and the representation of reality sans literary reworking, pristine reportage?

Insofar as we wish to consider the extraliterary as a literary topos, an extraliterary problem checks our advance, and in a threatening way.

Is Sade's mythic-magic mountain image or material?

Are brutally violent television films image or material?

In their effect, as image or material?

Has some change at the (arguably) secondary level, that of the phainopoetic, occurred or not, or do these films simply reproduce behaviors and condition further behaviors, affecting the criminal in a criminal way, offering instruction in aggression?

Or not at all?

Are they, rather, rites having a substitutive and cathartic function, like dolls pierced in the place of an enemy – the latter is indeed met, but the question remains as to whether he succumbs; he can for example exert a counterspell, but the aggressions of the one piercing are nonetheless diverted onto the doll, and not the person. Sade pierces the image of the alleged rival, not the rival himself, or even his wife.

Sade's myths are like the doll's wounds. They make up, in turn, the truly extraordinary literature of a man who, due to a minor episode of sexual deviancy, was imprisoned for thirty out of his seventy years; and just as, in my opinion, every magical procedure relieves aggression and is thus therapeutic, Sade's writings are not the monologue of a psychotic but of one who guarded himself against psychosis.

Can this work then contribute anything to an analysis of the sadomasochism of a leather fetishist?

Only under the condition that one adopt untested and popular opinions, as when we revel in terms like the *arché* and the collective unconscious, or when we bestow scientific credibility upon analogous inferences, at the same time conjuring away the proof of their applicability.

For me then there remains the conviction that, in Sade's work, acts are represented that possess certain affinities with African initiation rites, as well as with the rituals of the leather culture.

ANYONE COULD BE NEXT
On Pier Paolo Pasolini's Film *Salò*

Hamburg, February 1976

The subject matter involves human waste, semen, blood, shit, decay. A rather intimate catastrophe gets, due to its surroundings, and with the help of the media, projected over the face of the entire earth.
The entire gay community felt shocked at the news of the murder of the poet and filmmaker Pier Paolo Pasolini; all of its members had, at one time or another, foreseen their own murder – all will continue to do so time and again.
Neither fame, nor wisdom, nor wealth offers any real protection. Anyone could be next – in New York, in Eimsbüttel, in Cotonou. Practically speaking, there are two possibilities: he was either already dead when his body was put in his car, the victim, perhaps, of a political murder, a vehmic murder carried out by some queer Cosa Nostra – this seems, however, by all appearances false – or – and everything seems to support such a thesis – Pasolini picked up one or more male prostitutes at the Stazione Termini and drove to Ostia in his Alfa Romeo, a familiar, recognizable pattern, and was murdered there, at night, in some desolate place, by one or more persons. Every fifty-three-year-old bearing the status symbols of the queer culture: fame, perfume, flashy or expensive dress, sports cars – and who drives to Ostia after midnight with one or more street boys, risks being jumped or killed. Every gay knows it, and the streetboys know that their clientele knows it. To go there in the face of such knowledge expresses a weariness

with behavioral strictures, or a conscious or unconscious flirtation with violence, a death wish.

When Gustaf Gründgens was found murdered in Manila on October 7, 1963, his death was camouflaged as accidental.

Not Pasolini's. The Italian press gave it frontpage coverage for weeks. The word *homosexual* was carefully avoided, however, by the Catholic Church and the Communist Party – the two organizations that laid claim upon the corpses.

They who, together in Italy, wept on their wreathes, and who together in Portugal successfully choked off a sexual revolution, would have denied him any opportunities for employment, or happiness, in Spain, Ecuador, Cuba, or the Soviet Union. Publicly, no friend or police officer referred to the possibility of a masochistic component in regard to his murder.

A few days after his burial, Pasolini's final film, *Salò*, was shown to Italian censors and banned.

It was quite clear: like no other poet or filmmaker, Pasolini was both repulsed and fascinated by violence, confronted it both in the studio and in his private life, dressing up his own inclinations in sentimentality and artistic frillery.

Like the Sadean disciple and resistance fighter Jean Desbordes, who was tortured to death by the Nazis, Pasolini had to suffer the consequences of his imagistic fantasy in a black passion.

At the threshold of the pseudoliberal, pseudopacifist postwar epoch stand several elegant murderers: Jean Genet, an admirer of Hitler and the concentration camps – who never himself committed a murder, however; the militaristic Orestes from Sartre's *The Flies,* wanting to cloak himself in the city-state of Argos, as if in a blanket, and who surpasses, in guilt, an entire nation through one cold-blooded and monstrous deed – presented at the crest of the absurdist movement, in 1947, as Gustaf Gründgens, the Göring protégé, celebrated on stage the murder of his kin.

At its close stand the assassination of Allende, the murders carried out by the Manson family, the acts of terrorist revolutionaries; the fourteenth amendment to the federal penal code concerning the unconstitutional advocacy of violence, the atomic energy treaty between the Federal Republic and Brazil; the latter state's many reported acts of torture; the rise of the leather culture, the sadoculture, Pasolini's murder, Pasolini's film *Salò*.

Anyone Could Be Next

Ritual reenactments of violent acts, bureaucratized rituals, cover-ups, violence various and sundry, poeticized, imagized, a philosophy of violence.

Shortly after the completion of his last film, shortly before his murder, Pasolini remarked that the proletarian violence of Italy's slums had changed its focus, that it had lost its revolutionary impetus and was now intent upon nothing more than the acquisition of consumer goods, and that it must therefore be punished like the violence of the neofascists.

Jean Genet, I recall, denied this notion, in a conversation we once had. The murder of the Genetian character takes place according to strict ritual necessity, just like murders in the films of Pasolini. Genet quickly replied that his own murderous impulses were in effect diverted by his poetic activity, he who as a younger man often robbed older homosexual men, and who as an older man was himself in danger of dying under circumstances similar to those surrounding the murder of Pasolini — Genet denied any thoroughgoing change in the nature of proletarian violence.

For him Pasolini is a lira-billionaire who might very well be perceived by the young baker Pelosi as a traitor to the proletarian class. Genet understood the violent deeds of the oppressed as a panic-stricken means of intoxication, a type of potlatch that uses consumer goods as a mere pretense and in reality is subordinate to the rules of carnival, of jacquerie, of revolts, of revolutions in general.

A pattern is discernible in homosexual behavior, a frequent, and frequently irreversible, sliding from a desire for attachments to an urge to break all bonds, and from this desire into fetishism and sadism. It seems as if archaic modes of behavior find expression within marginal forms of sexual practice.

The flagellations of S-M episodes, their fecal and urinary rites, their fetishes, mutilations, and heavy scenes[1] are not only anticipated in the works of Proust, Genet, and Sartre — they have their exact counterparts in the initiation rituals of the entire world, and above all in African secret societies.

It is a question of rites of passage, according to Genet, rites of passage that he himself underwent as a young man, while in

---

1. In English in the original.

prison, through constructing his novels, and that demonstrate the same syndrome: torment, iron, leather, feces, murder.

Which means: Certain sexual practices bring about a regression, and not only to earlier periods of childhood, but to earlier phases of social formations – ritualistic, magical even? Or which could mean, in a totally opposite sense: religious, magical rites, within a secularized, consumer society, degenerate into marginal behaviors, neuroses, symptoms of psychic imbalance?

In almost every Pasolini film, one finds the most alluring erotic environments juxtaposed with images of horrendous violence: human sacrifice, castration, executions. They are shown in such a way as to take the spectator's breath away, to let each one hear, and feel, the sound of their own heartbeat.

This throughout his work – not only from *Salò*.

Should one lend credence only to the director's sense of horror, or to his synaesthetic pleasure as well?

In *Medea* one finds human sacrifice, there are execution scenes in the *Canterbury Tales*, castration episodes in the *1001 Nights*, all straightforwardly presented, and seen with an eye as if sharpened by the view to its own aesthetic gratification – nor are they inserted into any dialectical context. And surely Pasolini must have been sensitive to the dreadful impact of human sacrifice, an impact made palpable by his own cinematic excursions into the enchanted realms of magical societies, the all-too-clearly presented metamorphosis of a handsome young man into chunks of flesh.

Why would Pasolini, as if shrugging his shoulders, let such a scene continue?

Why, in *Salò*, does he use Sade's *120 Days of Sodom* as a vehicle of protest against an admittedly changed, secularized, yet still essentially fascist authority? Or is this protest only superficial – just as the poeticized, magical world of the *Medea* could be invoked only superficially?

Who was Sade, the figure to whom *Salò* refers?

Sade was hardly a sex offender of the same magnitude as those he portrays in the *120 Days*, or those whom Pasolini lends artistic form in *Salò*. Sade was a libertine, noble by birth, who took advantage of the prerogatives of his social standing, as well as a false

Anyone Could Be Next

revolutionary whom the revolution brought down. He engaged in acts that were typical of his day and that are a far cry from those engaged in today by a gay bank clerk in Anvil, the Bronx, or in Knolle. Sade's problem was that he wanted to write and that he – compelled by decades-long confinement – could only conceive of his metaphysical tractatus as a grand masturbatory project.

In Pasolini the effect is mirror inverted: Did he not finally disguise his own masturbatory project, driven to its existential limits, in the form of the "philosophical" film *Salò*? Sade's *120 Days of Sodom*, which must always figure as his masterpiece, unfinished due to unfortunate circumstances, was not kept from completion by external forces.

Sade's ideology and Sade's poetology are self-contradictory. On the one side, a piteous virtue that Sade both gives over to ridicule and that he takes seriously – and on the other: word fetishes, word diabolics that he puts forth as accusations against sadistic social formations and their representatives – under monarchy and revolution alike – and from which he seems to derive real gratification.

Likewise for Pasolini. *Salò* is by turns, in both letter and spirit, an exact filming of the Sadean project – right down to its hapless virtue – and, just as often, it distances itself from the novel, outdoes it, and has nothing more to do with it.

In the first place: Sade's *Sodom* is made up of word scraps and conceptual settings – black phantasmata foregrounded against a white backdrop; Pasolini's *Salò* consists of arresting images. *Salò* is thus, with respect to aesthetic-imagistic technique, a legacy. As opposed to the verbal facade, however, which claims to corrupt the reader for all time, it is safe to say that Pasolini's soft and cinematically embellished tortures do the spectator even more harm.

Memories, which we have been forever ashamed to relate, is the caption, as it were, that Pasolini places over *Salò* in the film's opening credits. It is therefore untrue to simplify the work as a critique of Italian fascism. In a much larger sense, Pasolini refers, in alluring images, to the fascistic and inhuman character of a good deal of traditional Western aesthetics.

Klossowski and Nietzsche, Paul of Tarsus, Baudelaire and Dada and Benn are included, the whole pictorial splendor of our civilization, not to mention the Renaissance church music used to accompany the concentration camp scenes of the film's conclusion – an apt choice, since it also accompanied the atrocities of the Inquisition.

The victim's cry: My God, why have you forsaken me? calls the spectator back to an ancient, sadistic paradigm: God the Father, who wishes to save the world through some shocking deed, like that of Sartre's Orestes, and in so doing exposes his son to one of the most dreadful sufferings imaginable, the Crucifixion – an event that has lived on ever since, from the *matapanus* (a medieval Venetian coin bearing the figure of Christ), to everyday decorative wall hangings.

Fascist tormentors no longer treat their victims like dear God did his only-begotten, human son. Or at any rate Pasolini doesn't show us any crucifixions.

Memories which we have been forever ashamed to relate; which we shouldn't, then, be ashamed of? To which Pasolini wishes to confess?

In *Hell's Circle of Blood* we reencounter the archaic masks of an *Edipo Re,* a *Medea,* or the *1001 Nights.*

All give expression to a single impulse, from prehistory to the consumer society, to the commodification of sex: aggression, mutilation.

And it fascinated him.

Hatred and desire collapse into a single entity. Pasolini goes further than Sade, Freud, or Genet. His film is a hitherto unknown species: an aesthetic phenomenology of violence. Was there for Pasolini, after his film's completion, only one remaining gratification? His own demise?

Did Pasolini provoke the seventeen-year-old baker to commit the deed? By picking up the young man, Giuseppe Pelosi – and here I take the latter at his word – arousing him, by striking him, to return blows upon him – and thus poisoning the young man's life well beyond the director's own death?

Sade, admittedly, spun out several like scenarios, but shunned their mise-en-scène. Pasolini was not only a victim – Pelosi's ruin was instigated by Pasolini's suicide wish.

The one's violent act is identical to the other's revenge.

Anyone Could Be Next

The victims in *Salò* are placed entirely at the mercy of their tormentors. They return no blows upon them.

Does a film like *Salò* evoke, in the mind of the spectator, the very forms of cruelty that the latter thinks to denounce? And corrupt us irrevocably thereby, just as Sade, supposedly, wished to damage his reader?

One thing's for sure: *Salò* is a product of the brutal consumer-world, which the film's creator damns. When do certain images begin to condition an audience? When do they begin to determine the character of an individual or a society?

Aristotle's idea of catharsis, as well as Artaud's Theater of Cruelty, equally presuppose that shudder-inducing images of mutilation should, ideally, liberate people from their anxieties and fears.

The correctness of this can, in fact, be demonstrated, with reference to certain theatrical rites performed in Wolof or in voodoo ceremonies. In *Salò* the viewer experiences an absurd reversal: this cunningly cruel film on cruelty descends to its most inhumane levels at precisely those points where it seeks to spare the viewer some unpleasantness.

The concentration camp scenes of its conclusion are seen through the voyeur's opera glasses – the voyeur Pasolini uses a second filter, that he might by this double negation make the impossible-to-swallow once again aesthetically consumable.

Quite logically, in fact: since to Pasolini everything aesthetic appears as fascistic, why shouldn't the concentration camp be aestheticized?

The apparent softening, however, deprives the viewer of the possibility of resistance, of a cathartic reversal.

The Theater of Cruelty is transformed into a silent death camp opera. *Salò* offers its spectator no redemption.

The young baker's cruelty hasn't changed – only the media in whose service it has been enlisted.

VOODOO BLOODBATHS – HEROES OF MIXED RELIGION
Remarks on
Daniel Casper von Lohenstein's
Agrippina

Caracas, May 1977

1.

Few figures in world history have been so frequently portrayed, imitated, praised, and dismissed as Nero – few poets so harshly repressed as Daniel Casper.
I don't find Lohenstein's work bombastic; bombast suggests an arbitrary, extravagant profusion.
Lohenstein has Nero say before Poppaea:
My child / Time's course
Leads us out from spring and into fall.
The tree, at last, bears fruit when once it's blossomed.
Agrippina, however, seeking to draw Nero into incest:
In fact, we ought to use the circle to describe the nature of things.
For if her path did not turn back, to its point of origin
Her works would soon become confused, and all motion would eventually cease.
Heaven's cause must once again look eastward
To where its orbital motion finds its source.
Spring must to Lent, the river to its source again return.
The sun, leaving the crimson Dawn behind
Takes its rest at last, again, in its mother's lap.
How then can this deed be cursed, reviled

When such a glorious son seeks out his own sweet parent's breast?
The well from which he's daily born? Because he desires that precious fruit,
Renewal from life's tedium.
By the corpse of Agrippina, Anicetus again takes up the fight between norm and regression:
Now the proud animal lies, that boldest of women,
Who thought the clockwork of her brain
Powerful enough to change the movements of the stars.
Bombast?
We find ourselves in Nero and Nero in us – Lohenstein, however, unsettles us more than Sade and Freud, since he offers us neither the absolutions of science nor the consolations of a mechanical worldview.

2.

By *voodoo* one designates a Haitian folk religion, a mixed form arising both from African rituals – above all those of the Fon tribe – and Catholicism; the word itself comes from *Vodun*, meaning, in the Fon language, god.
Antonin Artaud, traveling to Mexico, came into contact with the Afro-American culture in Havana.
Aristotle's catharsis – the transformation of tragic cruelty and fear into compassion and serenity – takes place as well in voodoo.
In the trance, the poor and the mystic encounter one another; the possessed are transformed, and become Vodun.
Voodoo arose during the age of slavery; it survived kings and kaisers, American occupation, tourism, and neocolonialism.
The strata of Haitian history are revealed in every ceremony; the instruments and songs of Africa, the slave master's whistles and whips, the machetes of the sugarcane harvests, the nasalizing gods of America.
In the trance, the faithful come to terms with their compulsions. Artaud's Theater of Cruelty promised Parisian audiences something similar.
In voodoo, too, one observes an accumulation of cruelty: goat sacrifices, various other rituals involving animal slaughter, initiatory trials, hierarchical oppression.

Voodoo Bloodbaths – Heroes of Mixed Religion

Primal scream,[1] affect therapy, dream interpretation – all attempt something similar, though their means, like the couch, are relatively disinfected, their fees higher.
In the voodoo temples, as in the poorest districts of a modern city, every available object is put to use.
A religion of bricolage, a patchwork mythology:
costumes from the French Revolution,
the president-for-life's propaganda photo,
a plastic bucket,
ancient African figurines of the gods, smuggled in the stomachs of those dragged off to the New World.
Pop. Underground. Landscape art[2] – realized daily by the starving.
Hills and valleys transformed into Afro-American versions of Chartres and Ephesus.
Shrewd and merciless ideologues itemize voodoo's links with fascism – like the Baptists with the devil.
The shrewd forget that the revolution that took place in 1804 and led to the independence of the New World's first black state was made possible only by the existence of voodoo; they forget that the type of agricultural settlement, traditional to Dahomey and known as the *koumbite*, fosters a communal-type existence, and to this day keeps millions of Haitians alive; they forget that the Haitian people have survived four hundred years of hunger, poverty, and repression only through the effectiveness and beauty of voodoo.

3.

One would hardly refer to Lohenstein – even after extracting the magical element in his work – as a reactionary:
In *Epicharis* and *Cleopatra* he scorns the powerful and discusses republican ideas; not *Miss Sara Sampson* – in 1755 – but *Epicharis* puts, for the first time, a bourgeois woman upon the German stage; in 1665, against Opitz's demands and before *Nathan the Wise*, he pleads the case for religious tolerance; close to 150 years after the beginning of the transoceanic slave trade he defends, in

1. In English in the original.
2. All in English in the original.

Cleopatra and *Sophonisbe*, the rights of the "Moors," the rights of Africans in the face of a rising imperialism.

Lohenstein knew what was what. He had read around in Arabian medical practices, in Herodotus, in the African Corippus, in Leo Africanus.

In the *Epicharis,* he gets information for a learned dispute from John Milton's *Pro populo anglicano:*

Seneca: *The leader of the Moors has become almost like a god.*
Natalis: *If he were their priest, he'd have to kill himself.*

Masanissa exclaims in *Sophonisbe* (302):

Rise! Noble Moors, turn back force with force.

Sophonisbe (339):

Do you prefer to see Africa become the prey of nations,
The noble Moors become the earth's discarded race
And drawn in chains?

1665 (347):

Unmerciful Gods!
What storms of rage do you not cast down upon us?
Now all of Africa bloodies itself with its own steel.

As a counter to racial and moral prejudice he cites the legend that Asdrubal and Scipio slept in the same bed (284):

that greatest pair of heroes
Of Romans, Scipio and Hasdrubal of the Moors.

And, everywhere in Lohenstein, one sees the all-encompassing presence of magic.

Agrippina plays in eschatological time, frozen time, tragic time – a mishmash.

Lohenstein's atmosphere is pagan. Christianity appears in his work as a religious variant, almost as an alibi, and is never spoken of effusively or manneristically, as in the works of Quirinus Kuhlmann.

Lohenstein's heroes are, with respect to religion, mixed:

Ibrahim Bassa stands midway between Christianity and Islam – like many blacks in the New World.

Cleopatra invokes whatever gods are at hand.

Antony, that representative of Roman state religion, prays to Isis.

Agrippina gives audience to Chaldeans, Nero to the voodoo priest Zarathustra.

Epicharis practices pagan blood-rituals (181):
> *The blood of the grim prince*
> *Shall for our pleasure mix with sweet wine*
> *His skull*
> > *will be our drink- and tableware.*

Epicharis: *May mine, and the same blood that hates the tyrant, be a foretaste of pleasures to come.*

Rites of the leopard men, Africa's revolutionary outlaws – *Pacte du Sang au Dahomey* and *Cochons sans Poils*; the revolution in Haiti began with a voodoo priestess's bloody toast.

Sophonisbe, too, performs a syncretic ceremony.

Ibrahim Sultan's base pagan manner is referred to; his son converses with Maltesians.

Lohenstein gives one of the rare, anthropologically precise descriptions of a syncretistic trance:

The Mooress Sophonisbe exclaims, during an invocation scene (335):

The urge to sleep presses me; my body is covered with sweat.

Cleopatra is transformed – Shakespeare uses the same method in *Romeo and Juliet* – into a zombie.

She is brought into a deathlike state – one Haitian priests are said to induce with a specific remedy – out of which she can, after a certain amount of time, again be retrieved.

In nearly all of Lohenstein's works there are one or more ghostly apparitions.

Talking wax statues carry a special significance:

Piso (*Epicharis* 241):

Hell's black spirits are by Heaven given great sway.
A waxen image was seen by me to prophesy: and falsely.

Lohenstein notes an account from Pierre Matthieu: *He will not admit that he made it seem to me as if the wax were speaking, and that it said these three Latin words: Rex impie peribis.*[3]

And another time (261):

Natal has with magic put me in her spell
An angel-seeming waxen figure spoke to me.

Haiti too has its oracle-uttering images – perhaps they got their start there.

3. You shall perish, unholy king.

Columbus's son, in a biography of his father, tells of Indian priests who by means of pipes brought their clay-formed gods into states of prophetic utterance. And still today, in voodoo temples, the dead express themselves through pipes and similar contrivances, speaking out of urnlike clay vessels.

In Lohenstein one sees not only voodoo bloodbaths, but also herbs and other plants put to use in cultic practices, African nail-fetishes, Haitian flower-augurs, and a political example:

Nero punishes one of Epicharis's coconspirators (269):

The dwelling of Scevinius must be torn down to the ground.

This too was long the custom on Haiti: the homes of fallen political figures were plundered and destroyed, both by their victorious enemies and by the populace at large.

When the young Jean-Claude Duvalier brought down Cambronne, the powerful minister of the interior who was also his mother's lover, it was held in the West to be a mark of progress that there was no subsequent plunder or razing.

4.

The word for a voodoo priest – *houngan* – is often used as a synonym for "homosexual," while the word for a voodoo priestess – *mambo* – may also refer to a lesbian.

(In Afro-Brazilian syncretism the word for the male priest is *entendido,* that is, complicit, "in the know," and for the female, *uma forte pessoalidade* – a formidable personality.)

Voodoo is one of the few religions to espouse a homosexual divinity, the god of the dead Guédé Nibo, and on Dead Sunday the believers chant, throughout the city and in the countryside: Guédé Nibo Massissi! Guédé Nibo Massissi! – gay Guédé Nibo! gay Guédé Nibo!

Entendido, queer, priest-leader Nero – and *forte pessoalidade,* brash Epicharis are also the antagonists of both of Lohenstein's Roman tragedies.

Almost all of Lohenstein's heroes have androgynistic characteristics; almost all of his female figures are formidable personalities. Soliman says to Ibrahim Bassa (22):

*Does Ossman seem too mean to you, does Ossman seem too petty
To love, who loves you in return? . . .*

*Was the hand too heavy that with tender fingers
Lulled you so softly into sleep?*
Irreproachably strong in her virtue, Isabelle; strong in her malice and, for the wavering Soliman surely a source of great anxiety, Roxelane, his first wife.
Mark Antony was a lover of Gaius Julius Caesar – who was, according to the reliable Suetonius, a man to every woman and a woman to every man.
Cleopatra a *forte pessoalidade*, who didn't tremble before the specter of apparent death, nor, deceitful, before the prospect of turning the head of a third conqueror.
The traditionally recorded account of erotic relations between Nero and Otho is guardedly referred to by Lohenstein:
Otho (23): *And I had thought myself to be the thunder god
If only Ganymede, and not a Venus
Had given me this surge of vital sap.*
To which Nero responds:
But where is the Venus star that shines upon us?
The conversations between Agrippina and Octavia have something of the air of a predominantly lesbian ladies' tea party. All the women of the first Roman tragedy are strong figures, even when they fail: Agrippina, Octavia, Poppaea, Acte the envious gossip, and Sosia the staunch refugee.
Incredibly prudish, Octavia lashes out at her husband Nero (28):
*That he, in pederasty, a loathesome act
That our modesty rightfully contemns, yet which is sweet to him
Has intercourse with men, and takes some eunuch for his bride.*
A passage noted by Lohenstein in his commentary (118 ff.):
Nero himself carried out this outrage on the person of Britannicus. Immediately afterward murdered him by poison.... How he married Sporus as his wife, however, is described by Suetonius ... as well as the fact that he gave himself as a wife to Dryphoro, or Pythagone.
Sardanapalus was even more base; he very much wanted to play the role of an unchaste woman. He let his hair be completely shorn and married a servant from Caria by the name of Hierocles: he frequently wished to be openly caught in the act, as when he carried on his sexual depravities with other men; and for this reason he willingly

endured abuse and severe beatings from the hand of Hierocles and eventually decided to make him emperor. This emperor had a young man by the name of Aurelius Zoticus of Smyrna . . . brought to Rome, in the greatest splendor, made him treasurer prior to meeting him, bathed him and indulged in unspeakable vices with him, slept and ate on his lap.

Chaste Epicharis, impertinent, a transvestite with an unavowedly lesbian disposition – or perhaps not so unavowed:

Jean Desmarets de Saint Sorlin, in his novel *Ariane*, which Lohenstein knew, had already surrounded the figure of Epicharis with a transsexual ambience.

Bernard Asmuth writes (*Lohenstein and Tacitus*, 80):

a married woman, who in book 6 falls in love with Epicharis disguised as a man named Eurylas, and pursues her . . .

Epicharis herself says:

And now the heavens seem more precious
Since Ariane, the earth's most wondrous being
And my master's niece, first returned my love.
The clouds gave way before the brightest sun,
And I became her own.
By her my once embittered life was filled with joys.
By her face I was consoled, her actions were my instruction.
My servitude was not, to me, servile.
She lived and loved, and I with pleasure saw her every need fulfilled.
. . . My truer mind, however, drove me
To follow on those men of deeds, dressed as a man.

And again (168):

But I that I might more safely flee
Took on the dead sentries' helm and garb.

Lohenstein has Epicharis write, in cryptically pornographic fashion (240):

 I wish to know this pleasure still:
That Nero's tongue might lick these bloody shackles.

And Sophonisbe finds pleasure even in her misery. Before her, the strong, man-crushing female, stands her husband Syphax, who through most of the play goes around in chains. She introduces her travesty in the following manner (270):

 Fetch me a helmet! Cut the

Hair from my brow, and let it
Be stretched upon the bow.
One of the play's recurring themes is King Masanissa's wavering between homo- and heterosexual love.
Scipio, who lay in the same bed with the Moor Asdrubal, says to the king (321):
and he came into my tent
When we had made a pact of friendship between us
And:
Have you never seen Scipio kiss a woman?
Masanissa leaves Sophonisbe for Scipio, and with the same amoral grin as Sophonisbe, when she leaves her husband for Masanissa.
A shamanistic quality informs the androgyne's character.
Syphax, speaking of Sophonisbe in her priestly attire (285):
I hear my love yet see a man.
Two pages later Sophonisbe says of the same Syphax:
Strange – has Syphax changed himself into a woman?
And threatens him:
That Masanissa's sword might tear into his insides.
It is said of the Sikhs of the Himalaya region that, once having conquered an enemy, they butt-fuck him.
Young men in the Gabès Oasis, in order to demonstrate their willingness to comply with a friend's wishes, say:
Tu es le couteau, je suis le viande.[4]
Jean Genet, in *Enfant criminel*, speaks of an identity between the knife and the phallus.
Lohenstein writes of Ibrahim Sultan (176):
Who hourly disgraces himself, like a common woman
. . . and burns and rages all the more wildly
When some Sardanapalus . . .
The modest Ambre is thereby recalled in a note that Lohenstein had written eight years earlier. Ibrahim Sultan succeeds neither in winning over the aging widow Sisigambis, nor can he, without the aid of his Achmet, overpower the younger Ambre. His powerful mother has him murder the cherished giantess.

4. You are the knife, and I am the meat.

Love for the mother, and the anal phase, often appear close to one another (121):
Kiosem: For it is your mother's wish
As well to feel the drawn sword tear into her middle.
Lohenstein shows us an outspoken lesbian, and *forte pessoalidade*, in the figure of Sekierpera. She says, of the not-yet-fifteen-year-old Ambre (123):
Passion's spark is set aglow in me
Since I saw her in the bath, and only twice.
The chaste Ambre promises the immodest Sekierpera:
I cannot and wish not and shall not love Ibrahim.
But if you, my sweet, should wish to use the mercy
That, enraptured, clings to your neck and plays about your feet,
Keeps you in the Sultan's heart and holds you for her angel,
If you are able and you are to move the Sultan from this all-too-ardent longing
And still, with reasoned speech, recall to him the outline of my credit,
So shall this gentle hand be always open to you (151).
A formula that Lohenstein has already used in reference to a homosexual relationship – that of Ibrahim and Soliman – and a very concrete one at that!
Lohenstein's representation of sexual behavior includes incest, the seduction of youths, male and female homosexuality, necrophilia, sadism, and masochism.
Representations that attain to an amoral serenity:
How matter-of-factly Cleopatra deceives two men, how naturally the partners in *Sophonisbe* are exchanged, how calmly the girl Ambre offers herself to Sekierpera.
All a part of Lohenstein's utopian vision? A republic without racial discrimination, equality for women, and without sexual repression – before Sade and Freud?
This sexual liberality seems to have allied him with the Moors, and with Africa – it is the jovial amorality of voodoo. For Lohenstein, a utopia of reason:
The gay Scipio, to the bisexual Masanissa (349):
When the light of reason shall drive away this mist.

5.

Lohenstein's outlook is skeptical.

Voodoo Bloodbaths – Heroes of Mixed Religion

In contrast to Freud, he emphasizes the predominance of Thanatos over Eros.

Ambition, lust for power, torture, murder – all loom larger than love. Lohenstein already has a notion of trauma:

(*Epicharis* 172) *Rome feels the soul wounds*
That Nero carved into her.

Octavia (28) would have let the emperor's perversions pass, but:
The fact that he brings young slave girls into our bed
Gnaws at my woman's heart, bites through bone and marrow.

Nero to Poppaea (41):
How's that? Or are you plagued by doubt? Whether those flames
Are fed by the heat of our mutual desire? Just as a crime's secret admission
Wakens long-dead feelings of guilt, which are quickly brushed aside,
Just so does my heart surge, my blood begin to rage
In your presence. And all my wounds are renewed and rest
Upon my face, in my mouth, and in my heart.

Paris says of Agrippina (65):
That perversion might serve her as a set of wings won in honor.

A notion for which Daniel Casper might have cited Tacitus, who remarks in the *Annals*, book 12, 7:
Her house was without shamelessness, unless it furthered her ambitious designs.

Lohenstein, however, neglects this passage in his commentary. A fuller representation of virtue, Puritanism, and repression occurs in the *Epicharis* (227):

and when I fold these bloody limbs
Around the stake or on the rack, I'll take great joy
In knowing that these acts will prey upon the kaiser's mind.

The wholly virtuous Kessmus becomes a totally depraved queer; Daniel Casper lets Nero remark, in moderate, ironic tones:

Epicharis: *Ah! bring it closer, then, and let me kiss that face;*
That its fresh and fragrant blood might mix with mine;
And that my tears of joy might wash away the dirt and sand!
Nero: *Bring it to the mad one, that she see what madness does.*
Epicharis: *My yearning mouth is refreshed by such strong blood.*

The sadist Nero does the masochistic Epicharis a service, that she, by vainly turning sadistic, might heighten the pleasure of the true, calculated sadist.

Each for the moment plays the role of the other.
Epicharis (269): *Can't you, in your bloodlust, stand to watch the torture anymore?*
He himself gives in:
that it might hurt him worse.
The slaughterer, it seems, is conquered by the sacrificial animal.

6.

Excursus: On Milk, Breast, and Breasts

The manner in which parents take care of their offspring – runs a certain behavioral theory – is hereditary and determines the sensuality, erotic capacity, and sexuality of those growing up.
Ibrahim Bassa, a work Daniel Casper wrote at the age of fourteen, begins with a monologue (16):
Asia, in the figure of a woman, has been set upon the stage, and bound by the vices:
The speech runs:
The withered breast
On which the Father put his Son, in sucking,
Gives hunger, war, and plagues, Leeches, lizards, and snakes,
A poison well-spring.
...
Archfiend! Alas, have I suckled you,
You tiger, you worm, with mother's milk,
Raised you up to eat me, you dragon,
You child-killer?
Isabelle says (27):
   come, stab me in the breast
Till blood and soul gush forth, and I die like a Christ.
Soliman (33):
It isn't safe at all to try to fool poisonous snakes
And stroke them with the fingers.
No indeed; even if one, while feeding them sweet milk,
Should put them on one's lap and drape them on the neck.
Isabelle again (45):
With what fear did I endure upon my breast the angry waves
That mightier than I, a helpless woman, did assail?

Soliman falsely swears that he shall take back Ibrahim in friendship, and no longer lust after Isabelle (52):
Not the marble breasts . . .
Never in the work of the young Lohenstein have I encountered such a proliferation of breasts, breast metaphors, and milk metaphors – five in 72 pages.

More still in the *Cleopatra*. I've counted eleven in 130 pages. The queen says of the snake that shall kill her (135):
It scorned my arm and thirsts after my breast.
Come, then. Since I bring down death by my lusty flesh.
Now bite! And suck poison where rosy mouths once
Drew milk and honey. He bites! I'm stricken.
I feel sleep and powerlessness descending.

In the thirty-year-old's *Agrippina*:
(20) *Otho: That the lamprey's milk and Scarus's liver should adorn the kaiser's table; . . .*
Is nothing out of the ordinary.

(22) *Otho: Breasts like snow*
Where over the sealike milk no milder wind can blow
Around two rocky island masses.

(23) Otho, attempting to fix up Nero with his wife Poppaea, out of ambition:
From her breast there flows such a strong and heavenly stream,
Such a nectar-sea.

(24) Nero, of his mother Agrippina:
And her mother's-breast not only holds, but also hatches,
Such a deadly poison, which, bitter, tastes like that of snakes and vipers.

(30) Agrippina, to absolve herself, lies:
In my mother's-breast
No coldness lets me lust for new and strange desires.

(34) Agrippina pleads with her son to come to her defense:
Who would let that mother's-milk of love go sour:
The wise? That what more sweet might flow from him than this,
From his mother's breast?

(40) Nero lies, in order to seduce Poppaea:
> *I wish to give up my dutiful life, in sacrifice*
> *Upon the altar of your breasts.*
> *Now, bare for me that holy sanctuary of the soul – your breasts.*

(41) To which Poppaea, flirtatious:
> *The kiss upon the mouth and play upon the cheek*
> *And fondling of the breasts are flowers / that a woman*
> *Lets be taken, when she wills. . . .*
> *Behold my naked, heaving breast!*

Nero replies:
> *My dear, all too rare have been the moments*
> *Spent before these lovely forms, and too soon was I deprived of*
> *The breast, unemptied, that almond milk's voluptuous flow.*

(42) Poppaea in the same scene:
> *His devotion will fade*
> *As soon as some young maid's perfume enflames him*
> *And profanes, with vile lust, his passion's present, sacred flame*
> *Which flame he'll spend on Acte's lap and breast that's known a servant's hand.*

And later:
> *And I hardly got to know*
> *(And after a maid had known it fully) the foam, even*
> *Of his milky grace.*

(57) Acte, as she reports how Agrippina in her lust for power arouses her son:
> *her breast, revealed,*
> *Served her as a snare in her lechery. . . .*
> *Her breasts swelled, and heaved*
> *From broken, quickened breathing. As if he could take nourishment from this sea*
> *The sweetened milk of her charms and feed it to a heart already wasted from desire.*
> *This poison forced its way through the kaiser's eye and pierced his very soul.*

(58) Burrhus acts as mediator:
> the lewd lily adorns
> No mother's breast. And evil, ashamed
> Binds mad passion to this marble fountain
> Where the tongue once sucked.

(60) Agrippina tries to seduce her son:
> The love that still exerts its force upon your eyes
> Can, if it wishes, glut itself again on the lukewarm milk of kisses.

(61) The breasts that you have often kissed once also fed you.
> What difference is there between this breast and the lap of my thighs?
> . . . Should a mother feel shame
> In loving her own son? Who once held forth
> To him the loving stream of milk. . . .
> Who could love a mother's breast more than her child?

(63) My light, come, then, and from these marble breasts,
> As earlier you took milk, take pleasure in love's feel and scent:
> Taste, whether something more than milk now flows here;
> Because these mountains are the gallows of Ida
> Where beauty fells both majesty and mind.

(64) Nero is overcome:
> I burn you breast, I burn, now I have tasted for the first time
> And know: within those snowy peaks a fiery Aetna burns.

(65) Paris:
> I worry, great prince, that he will come too late
> To know the vipers we let play within our hearts.
> Anicetus: Ninus's hand pierced through that lewd mother's breast.

(68) Nero feigns desire for his mother that he might more easily murder her:
> So from now on our pleasure blooms twofold,
> Even if envy's bite draws milk and growth therefrom.

(69) And as he puts her on a death ship:
> Yet bid her come a final time to me:
> That I might kiss her eyes, her hand and breasts.

(73) The spirit of Nero's half-brother Britannicus, whom he murdered:
   A hound cries in the breast
   Whenever the heart beats and wakes that one from sleep
   Whom spilt blood more than royal purple charms.
   . . .
   Your mind is all too savage, your heart too wild . . .
(82) Love sings in the round:
   My seed first enters the souls
   Before the breast milk flows into them.
(87) Agrippina, troubled:
   My surging heart rages beneath these marble cliffs!
(88) *Behold! how she points at the bloodied breasts of my guilt.*
(91) Agrippina before her murderers:
   The bloodhound himself who sent you here, comes not
   That he might suck blood where once he tasted milk?
   Slash through the milk of my breasts!
   That such a child tasted . . .
(92) Nero regards his mother's corpse:
   That such breasts once nurtured me so sweetly.
   . . . that this lily breast . . .
   Could hide such a coal-black heart within.
   . . .
   Milk turns vermillion, ivory into ruby.
(97) Poppaea pursues her ambitious goals still further:
   if the breast, like love and passion, burns.
(96) *is this mouth, this breast, worthy of love?*
(99) Agrippina's vengeful spirit:
   My life-giving springs, these breasts, never gave forth blood
   That wasn't mixed with milk; they gave you suck
   In your helpless infancy
   As well as purple, your royal rank.
   Yet in the end they must have poured a sweet chilled wine
   Of power lust and vengeance.
   No vulture doesn't drink of vulture's blood;
   But you have sucked your mother dry.
(102) Anicetus, of Agrippina's remains:
   Because you still see poison milk within her ashes?

(107) Zoroaster during the voodoo ceremony:
*For Hecate arises. You must bring me milk
Drawn from a black cow, that you might soon see
What both in heaven and on earth shall come to pass!*
. . .

*The pits have all been dug in which the spirits
Will find honey, milk, and blood, and juice from the grape
If they should bless our ceremony by their presence.*
. . .

*As this knife pierces Mnester's icy breast
So let your soul pass through this abyss
To this altar of sons.*

In many African-American religions honey, milk, blood, and wine are also sacrificed; in Haiti they are put into pits and given up to the dead.

A priest by the name of Dieusifort, in Croix de Mission, once allowed me to observe a milk bath, something I had never seen before; it is thought to bring both health and luck.

On the west coast of Africa, in Senegal, in a psychotherapeutic rite known as *n'deup*, the initiates have milk spit upon them.

Over forty references to milk and breasts in the *Agrippina* – much fewer in the less oppressive *Epicharis*, in *Sophonisbe* about thirty, likewise in *Ibrahim Sultan*.

The breast, breasts, milk and
annihilating thunderbolts,
ruptured arteries,
sharp cuts,
revenge and zealotry,
a lovely sword,
sighs,
vipers,
purple,
sacrifice of the heart,
arrow,
poison,
filthy, voluptuous sex,
a drawn dagger,

bitter from sweet,
a greatest enemy,
a love-sickening sweetness,
poison and blood,
haze,
disgust,
blaze,
snakes,
exuberance,
smoke of desiring passions,
lizards,
curse,
sabre,
stigma,
glow of rebellion.
The breast, breasts, and milk to infanticide, matricide, rape, betrayal, lies, perjury, seduction, ambition, the end of the world, greed, suicide, unease, debasement, repentance, terror, illegitimate birth.
In the *Agrippina* the breast, breasts, and milk of prodigality, pandering, and power lust are set against those of incest, matricide, fratricide, revenge, necrophilia, and the conjuring of dead spirits. There is only one citation of a fruitful breast, when love sings in the round (82):
My seed will have entered the souls
Before the breast milk flows into their mouths.
A qualified assertion, implying that the rearing of young has nothing to do with Eros; for Lohenstein love doesn't pass through the stomach.
The instinctive care and preservation of the newborn is, for Lohenstein, nothing more than suppression, an urge to destroy. (And is it not?)
The image of the aggressive *mamma dentata*, the sinister nurturer, is known to me – outside of Lohenstein – only through an archaic, magical culture. In the eight-thousand-year-old settlement of Çatal Hüyük, in Anatolia, female cult figures, presumably of goddesses, often had the jaws of wild animals, or the beaks of sacrificed birds, attached to their breasts.

7.

Lohenstein's theatrical work has an axiomatic quality.

He places similes for human conduct into fresh contexts and combinations that allow them to shimmer beneath the traditional rhetorical codes.

Displacements achieved through multidimensionally displaced words.

This is the method of his earliest work, written after the end of the Thirty Years War, at the age of fourteen:

Soliman, in the young student's tragedy, becomes infatuated with the wholly inaccessible Isabelle, the lover of his friend Ibrahim – fifteen years later this constellation is reversed in the pair Nero-Otho: Otho doesn't flee, like Ibrahim, with his lover but rather offers Poppaea to his lover Nero.

Isabelle, who, pursued by the kaiser, defers his advances, not like Poppaea, who only playfully defers, nevertheless takes refuge in the image of the Roman courtesan:

Isabelle (45):
With what fear did I endure upon my breast the angry waves
That mightier than I, a helpless woman, did assail?

Poppaea (41):
The kiss upon the mouth and play upon the cheek
And fondling of the breasts are flowers that a woman
Lets be taken, when she wills.

The love relationship of Nero and Agrippina is that of a homosexual with a *femme impossible*.

In *Ibrahim Bassa* Roxolane, a European in the Turkish court, plays a mother figure to the homosexual Suleiman.

Is there not some resemblance between the rhetorically skilled preceptor, the Mufti, who defends himself against the murder of his lover, and the rhetorically skilled Seneca, the preceptor who conceals Nero's matricide?

(Both held the Christians to be dangerous.)

Just as in *Agrippina*, prior to the murder of the mother, there also appears in *Ibrahim Bassa*, this time prior to the murder of the lover, a younger rival who has been murdered outside of the play's main line of action, in the latter case the son, Mustafa, in the former the half-brother Britannicus – in *Agrippina* the murder attempt fails, while in *Ibrahim Bassa* Soliman tries to call it off.

(The putting to death of Britannici, that is, any haughty pretender to the throne, took on, in Turkey, cultic forms – just as in many African cultures.)

In Isabelle's attitude with respect to Soliman one can see, pre-formed, the attitude of Epicharis.

Isabelle receives from Soliman the lover's head, as a gloomy consolation, Epicharis from Nero the head of Senecio.

(The worldly Stendhal as well ends *Le Rouge et le noir* with the hero's severed head resting on his lover's lap; and in Haiti high priests have been rumored to keep the heads of their former enemies under refrigeration, taking them out for special occasions, and setting them on their writing tables.

After 1829 Goethe kept, in his home, the skull of his friend Schiller: *Once, in a solemn grave . . .*)

Lohenstein wrote his second tragedy, *Cleopatra*, at around twenty, and later revised it at forty-five, three years before his death.

Cleopatra, fallen to Mark Antony by the hand of a bisexual friend, Gaius Julius Caesar, greets her latest lover effusively, already scheming:

My prince! My lord! My heart!

just as Poppaea says, flirting with Nero, to whom she has fallen by the hand of her husband Otho (40):

My prince, my king, my lord.

Cleopatra, about to die for Antony (68):

My naked breast heaves; where is poison, sword, or fire?
My warm mouth longs to kiss the dagger.

Poppaea, seeking to lure Nero (41):

Behold my mouth, smiling in desire for you
And my bare breast, heaving.

Thyrsus sets a trap for Cleopatra. Feeling her way in, she remarks (60):

How she trembles! and grows pale; now she stares like a stone.
She sighs, says nothing, all her limbs are quaking.
She laughs, her heart is pounding, now her color returns.

Agrippina in the incest scene (63):

How he trembles and grows pale; all his limbs are quaking
Now he sighs, now laughs; now his color returns!

Cleopatra cleverly tries to bring Augustus around (122):
He sighs, he grows pale!
Augustus replies:
What stone shall not here turn to wax, or frozen mass to fire?
just as Nero encounters his mother:
Who feels no strong desire here
Nor wishes to stay and taste must have a soul of stone.
He cannot be the child of Agrippina nor have her blood.
Cleopatra is to go to Rome, to be disgraced (131):
And the ship, that dog, stands ready, its sails hoisted.
Nero summons his mother to her drowning (69):
The ship, my light, stands ready, its sails hoisted.
Cleopatra wishes to be murdered by her own son (132):
Here are my naked breasts, and here, a sharpened blade! Now stab.
In the incest scene Agrippina offers her breasts to her son; in the murder scene, to her murderers (91):
Slash through the milk of my breasts!
Cleopatra addresses the snake (135):
Now bite! And suck poison, where rosy mouths once sucked milk and honey.
Agrippina dies (91):
The bloodhound himself who sent you here, comes not?
That he might suck blood where once he tasted milk?
Lohenstein probably wrote *Agrippina* and *Epicharis* at about the same time, around thirty years of age.
Just as Nero lusts after Otho's wife, Epicharis lusts after Ariana, ignoring the latter's fiancé, Melint.
The republican revolutionaries, like Nero, their nemesis, are the source of a mother's pain.
The poet Marcus Annaeus Lucanus, cited appreciatively by Tacitus, and the nephew of Lucius Annaeus Seneca, is said, following the exposure of the so-called Pisonian Conspiracy, to have denounced his mother, Acilia.
Lucan is executed and dies like a soldier in one of his poems, reciting before his death some appropriate lines from his own work (– and thereby not dying like a soldier in his poems).
His mother, Acilia, writes Tacitus in *Annales*, 6, 71 *sine absolutione, sine supplicio dissimulata* – was passed over in silence and

forgotten, without absolution or punishment, left unscathed. This word *supplicium* stirred Lohenstein, and he constructed a scene around it.

In the play's summary he writes: *Attilla [Acilia], because she does not wish to confess / is beaten with whips . . . in the presence of her son, the poet Lucan.*

Epicharis sees herself as the lover of Nero, her tormentor (227):
  and when I fold my bloody limbs
Around the stake, or on the rack, I'll take more pleasure
Than Acte, she who now lies upon the kaiser's breast.

Not only Epicharis and Lucan, however, are brought before Nero the matricide, but also his uncle, the Stoic philosopher Seneca (225):
  Whoever will read my writings
Shall also judge: That death was the midpoint
In which my thought and writing wandered, and were lost,
Having been drawn there by vanity alone.

And indeed, whoever knows Seneca's tragedies, or the letters to Lucilius, must come to the conclusion that torture, destruction, and death exercised a fascination upon the statesman that is discernible on many pages.

Nero, on the other hand, makes himself out to be a mother, using a well-known formula (237):
We suckle a snake upon our mother's breasts,
Which no milk of comfort has tamed or softened
Nor stilled their thirst for blood.

He speaks here of his favorite, Subrius Flavus, just as Agrippina speaks of him.

In the end, Epicharis sings the empreror's dirge (268):
The spirit, though, shall find its home among the stars.

Mnester on Agrippina (101):
She rose to the stars, whence she came.

Sophonisbe – performed for the first time in 1666 or 1669 – is a transvestite like Epicharis (270):
  Fetch me a helmet! and shear
This unused hair from off my brow and temples
To strain upon the bow.

Voodoo Bloodbaths – Heroes of Mixed Religion

(In this she is perhaps sadomasochistic as well: shearing rites have a function in the leather culture, in Sade, and in *Le Rouge et le noir*.)

The priest Bogudes, a Moor, strikes up Sophonisbe's wedding song (297):

Let heaven itself bless this, our holy temple.

And the priest Zoroaster, the sacred song for the spirit of Agrippina (104):

Let heaven itself bless my temple of death.

In a complex arrangement, Sophonisbe attempts to commit suicide, matricide, and to carry out the sacrifice of a child, all at once.

So drive this lovely sword (and let me cease my longing!)
Through the body of my children, and Sophonisbe's breast.

Later, she again expresses the wish to die (290):

I sacrifice my heart and dedicate, to the temple, my breast.

Nero attempts to seduce Poppaea (40):

My steadfast life
I'll yield, a sacrifice upon the altar of your breast.

Sophonisbe, just prior to the child sacrifice (272):

Still, receive my kiss.

And Nero, before the murder of his mother (69):

take one last kiss!

Sophonisbe, as she kills herself (344):

Come, bless me, too, with your kiss.

Nero to Poppaea (44):

Come, bless me with a kiss.

And prior to the catastrophic ending, once again a ghostly apparition.

Masanissa, the androgyne king, before the corpse of Sophonisbe (348):

And still it glows, within her chilly breast, alone
That unquenchable flame, the heat of my desire.

Nero, the androgyne kaiser, before the corpse of his mother (92):

The heat that rises yet from her bloody wound
Has such force that my mouth and tongue are parched.
Bring me a glass of wine.

Masanissa:

Yes, and I'll fulfill my carnal needs – with her shade.
With *Ibrahim Sultan*, Lohenstein returns to the Turkish scenes of his earliest, preadolescent work.
Ibrahim tries to live off the recently widowed, aging figure of Sisigambis.
The mother, Kiosem, locks up her son Ibrahim like a rare bird and eventually murders the beloved, Felliniesque giantess.
Sekierpera, the lesbian bawd, greets the sultan as Poppaea greets the emperor (122):
My prince, my lord, my king.
Of Ibrahim it is said (176):

> *who hourly disgraces himself*

Like a common woman.
Eight years earlier, in his comments to *Agrippina*, Lohenstein had written (119):
Sardanapalus was still worse; he very much wished to be a sluttish woman.
At the scene of Ibrahim's filicide (166):
You raven-father you, what animal devours its own young?
What snake even, its own offspring? Since you've swallowed your child
Let your mother be your next victim.
Nero cries, while receiving a blow from his mother (24):
What dragon eats its own young? What worm gnaws its child?
Ambre (144):
Thus the tyrant plunges his fist, fat from blood, into the very vein;
And may God bless these breasts
Before that bloodhound chooses them for sacrifice
For his own lusts, and to our ill.
Anicetus advises Nero (65):
The fist of Ninus pierces through that wanton mother's breast.
Ibrahim, as he attempts to seduce Ambre (170):
She sighs, she pales, she looks down!
That all-purpose phrase.
Another spirit, that of Ibrahim's murdered brother (185):
The ghost of Amurath:
Flee! mother, take flight, before you're forced to bloody your son's sword.

Kiosem:
My child! my Amurath! stay! where are you going, with such haste?
Nero to the spirit of Agrippina (100):
Ah, mother! Please, forgive me! forgive your wicked son!
. . .

You flee? Have mercy!
In the figure of Kiosem as grandmother, this kaleidoscope of cruelty comes to a halt, ten years before Lohenstein's death (212):
Bewildering play! Strange midnight!
That I should lose a son and watch his offspring grow.
Is there anyone alive who doesn't shudder before this sweetness
Of power, which, in the end, tastes of bile and vinegar?
And how the lust to rule infects most every soul?
Lohenstein's axiomatics function like dreams, madness, and psychoanalysis:
Sultan Soliman is transformed into the figure of Nero,
chaste Isabelle into the courtesan Poppaea,
the wife and intriguer Roxolane into the mother and intriguer Agrippina,
chaste Isabelle into chaste Epicharis,
power-driven Cleopatra into power-driven Poppaea,
a trembling Cleopatra into a trembling Nero into a trembling Augustus,
the mother Cleopatra into the mother Agrippina,
Nero into Epicharis,
the Stoic Seneca into the wildly raging Epicharis,
Nero into his mother,
his mother into his father,
Epicharis into Agrippina,
Sophonisbe into Epicharis,
Sophonisbe into Cleopatra,
Sophonisbe into Nero,
King Masanissa into Emperor Nero,
Sophonisbe into Agrippina,
the mother Kiosem into Nero's mother,
the lesbian Sekierpera into the gay Otho,
Ibrahim into Nero,
Ibrahim into Agrippina,

virginal Ambre into the courtesan Poppaea,
virginal Ambre into virginal Ninus,
Ambre into Nero,
the mother Kiosem into the son Nero.
Seduction is transformed into rape,
flight into pandering,
deprivation into concession,
vice into virtue,
power intrigue remains power intrigue,
the murder of a loved one is transformed into matricide,
filicide into fratricide,
the death of a loved one into seduction by means of a loved one,
traps remain traps,
the humiliation of a loved one into matricide,
filicide into incest with the son,
torture into the throes of passion,
breast into male member,
member into vagina,
love for the mother into anal intercourse,
marriage song into funeral dirge,
suicide into devotion,
filicide into matricide,
matricide into coquetry,
necrophilia remains necrophilia,
maternal power lust remains maternal power lust,
pandering remains pandering,
the queer stays queer,
the queer becomes brash,
incest turns into the seduction of minors,
loss of power remains loss of power,
filicide becomes incest,
ghostly apparitions remain ghostly apparitions.

Agrippina says, dying (91):
Stab, murderer, through the guilty member.
Slip of the tongue. Slip of the pen. Slip of the mask.
Nero's homosexual acts – or so the historians seem to think – came before his incestuousness; Lohenstein presents and legitimates this chronology.

Just as in the story of Oedipus, where Laius's death at his son's hand and Oedipus's incestuous deeds serve as punishment for the homosexual experiences of Laius's youth. Teachers, playmates, the younger half-brother, the mother's intrigues which allow him to become emperor – all drive the young man away from the norm.

He is suspected in the murder of his stepfather Claudius, and perhaps he was involved in it, at any rate he clearly benefited from it and therefore appears to have let it happen. And Nero's murder of his younger stepbrother Britannicus, whom he killed in a disgraceful manner, stabbing him from behind, partakes of certain Theban motifs, as well as psychoanalytic ones.

The threat of castration by the stepfather and the competitor for the mother's love both fall away.

According to Suetonius, Nero's incest was carried out publicly, casually, and repeatedly.

Not according to Lohenstein, who shows Nero's involvement only as a result of provocation, spurred by Agrippina's political motives: either to wrest him away from his own independence, or away from Poppaea and toward Agrippina's cohort and half-sister Octavia, or simply away from the mother and back to the mother.

– If you don't sleep with your mother, you'll be stripped of power for murdering your father and brother.

– If you do sleep with your mother, you'll lose power by castration.

– If you sleep with Jocasta, you'll lose both eyes, as if they were your genitals.

Nero avoids these alternatives, instead at a certain point feigning an interest that he might have a good opportunity to murder his mother.

Stab, murderer, through the guilty member.

With this sentence Agrippina takes on the character of an androgynous shaman, as certain bicontinental voodoo practices attest.

Her vulva becomes a member.

She bore Nero through this member.

She engendered him with her vulva.

The member and the knife are one, the knife and the sheath/vagina *(Scheide)*.

She castrates the son in his father's place.
She kills the father in the Oedipal substitute.
But Nero has Agrippina stab the knife into her vagina.
Member meets member.
Incest with father and mother, castration of father and son, patricide and matricide blur.
Stab, murderer, through the guilty member/ – the *coincidentia oppositorum* of voodoo and the baroque.

8.
Excursus on the pleasant aura surrounding the corpse of the enemy.

All comparisons are lame. Some manage to get about, through usefulness or grace, while others are simply orthopedically flawed.
Should Lucius Annaeus Seneca be compared with Henry Kissinger?
Counsel, secretary, ghostwriter[5] in a world empire at the point of its furthest extension, who both covers and makes good his superior's psychopathological tendencies – an intellectual as the most powerful figure in the world?
A scholarly industriousness renders Seneca comparable to Goethe. I realize that it's foolish to try and deny Goethe all cultural and poetic influence, in spite of a Romantic movement that seems, at times, to absorb him; yet this influence hardly smacks of the classical tradition.
We know Homer through Voß, Sophocles through Hölderlin, many of the tales of classical antiquity through Gustav Schwab; the *Iphigenia* is regarded – unjustly – as a secondary work. And how many have read the *Achilleis*?
The Olympian's influence is a romantic one. Faust belongs squarely in the romantic-gothic tradition, not the Roman-Hellenistic.
The ground of Greek tragedy – between magic and secularization – was in the desperate *die / become / become / die*. *Die* and *become* are romantic invitations, poetically a minimalization, politically the watchword of an approaching knighthood of

5. In English in the original.

Voodoo Bloodbaths – Heroes of Mixed Religion

industry, and a division of labor: the one must die that something might be gotten out of another.

By casting a vote on the condemnation of a child murderer, Gretchen's composer said: *And I as well, Goethe.*

(And Seneca's pupil Nero, in a similar circumstance: *Alas, if only I could not write!*

German haughty provincialism and the classical world.)

As a poet one cannot compare the author of *The Wanderer's Night Song* with the hack Seneca; as a mediating figure of the classical tradition and Roman intellectualism, and of a Stoicism often close to early Christianity, for his influence on the Renaissance, the baroque, on Shakespeare, Corneille, Racine, Lohenstein, Goethe himself, as well as Nietzsche, Rilke, and Benn, his is a figure that straddles millennia.

No tradition begins with Goethe, with Goethe rather it is recuperated and ends. In short: Weimar is no Rome.

Daniel Casper, at the age of thirty-five given the title *von Lohenstein*, was compared to Seneca by his colleague Zesen, and the younger Gryphius.

It was meant as a compliment. It was, if one compares Breslau with Rome, rather ridiculous, and even insensitive, unthinking, when one considers Seneca's endless to-and-fro next to Lohenstein's brief period of intense productivity. At best a horror-filled insensitivity that will continue to be passed down within German literary history. Lohenstein and Seneca – doubly neat and doubly false.

And yet!

Seneca says (92), in the fourth act of *Agrippina:*

The enemies' corpse gives off a pleasant aura.

A rather shady statement; shady for the figure who utters it, shady for the poet who puts it in his colleague's mouth.

The corpse is Agrippina's.

Pleasant is pleasant.

Aura is aura.

Seneca is a Stoic.

Lohenstein is our German Seneca.

The statement of an unabashed sadist, a necrophile, of an intellectual in a period of decline, who puts himself within shouting range of the archaic gods, a decadent cannibal.

How did this expression occur to Lohenstein? How was he moved, or on what evidence? In his complex and nuanced play *Agrippina* Lohenstein gives us a fairly uncomplex and unnuanced picture of the philosopher-poet Seneca:

In the first act he talks full-blown trash – particularly in one sarcastic remark (48): *Our slaves should be held accountable for fires and storms.*

In the fourth act he takes part in the fatal intrigue plotted against his "Maecenas," Agrippina, the teacher of young lords there arguing like a pimp.

Seneca looks silently on the torture and murder of Agerinus.

He who, together with Burrhus, holds the reins of power, lets the matricide occur, looks on the corpse with Nero, establishes the fact that it is rather pleasant, aids the emperor in the cover-up, and convinces his student to bury it without distinction or ceremony, in disgrace.

Seneca forgets how Agrippina retrieved him from exile, made him the tutor to the heir to the throne, and thus cleared the philosopher's path to power.

Earlier, Lohenstein has Agrippina herself express scorn for their actions, and thus also for Seneca (88): *Seneca's goodwill is easily bought with sexual favors.*

In his remarks Lohenstein further casts a negative light on this exemplary figure (129):

Of this world-famous, worldly wise man, Xiphilinos writes in Nero, *p.m. 161: He was involved with Agrippina, and in every circumstance he both acted and professed otherwise. He expresses contempt for tyranny and became a tyrant's teacher: cursing those who move in princes' circles, he seldom left the palace. Launching tirades against hypocrites, he wrote polished laudatory speeches of queens and freed slaves. He helped to punish the rich and himself amassed a fortune of three million sesterces. He damned the excesses of others while compounding his own. He had five hundred cedar tables with ivory chairs.*

Yet Lohenstein adds a qualifying sentence:

And on p. 162 he says of Seneca that he spurred Nero on to matricide: . . . That gods and men might all the more quickly fall upon him.

A Machiavellian justification.

So schizophrenic during the baroque period was the evaluation of the honored preceptor.

The poet Busenello, who wrote the text of *The Incoronation of Poppaea* for Monteverdi around 1642, has the courtesan remark:

Seneca il tuo Maestro
Quello stoico sagace
Quel filosofo astuto
Che sempre tenta persuader altrui
Che il tuo scettro dipenda sol da lui

To which Nero replies:

Ché? Quel decrepito pazzo ha tanto ardire.[6]

And Monteverdi further sharpens his librettist's judgment, by simply leaving out Busenello's apotheosis of the philosopher, written for the second act.

The Seneca of historical writing, above all that of Tacitus, is quite different.

Tacitus, *Annales*, 13, 2:

And the murdering would surely have continued without the efforts of Afranius Burrus and Annaeus Seneca. Both were advisors of the young emperor and, moreover – what is seldom seen in shared power arrangements – were kindly disposed toward one another, having a comparable influence in diverse matters. Burrus, with his military interests and severity of bearing, Seneca the rhetorician and sincere companion, helped one another that they might the more easily keep the young man's indulgences within generally conceded bounds, even if he rejected virtue on the whole. Each had to struggle with the ferocity of Agrippina, who, aflame with all the lusts of abusive power . . .

18: *He now (after the murder of Britannicus) rewarded the closest of his friends. Nor was there any lack of persons ready to denounce those men of pretended dignity (like Seneca and Burrus), who at such a time had divided up homes and villas like booty. Others believed that this had been done out of compulsion by the emperor, stricken by remorse and hoping for pardon* . . .

42: *At this point a man, deservedly hated for a number of offenses, was condemned, though not without rousing ill will against Seneca.*

6. Seneca, your teacher / that wise stoic / that shrewd philosopher / always tries to convince others / that your power depends on him alone. And Nero: How's that? That stumbling madman has such courage?

His name was Publius Sullius, a feared and venal figure, powerful during the reign of Claudius. . . .
He tore into Seneca as the worst enemy of the friends of Claudius . . . under whom he endured a just exile. At the same time, used only to sedentary studies and inexperienced youths, claiming that he was envious of those who exercised their worthy eloquence in the defense of their fellow citizens. Further, that he himself was a quaestor of Germanicus, while Seneca was just an adulterer who lived in the latter's house. And was it to be esteemed more offensive, then, to receive a voluntary reward for effective litigation than to spoil the beds of royal princesses? By what wisdom, or by what philosophical precepts had he managed to amass, in four years of imperial friendship, a fortune of three hundred million sesterces? In Rome, the bereaved and their inheritances are caught up as if in his net, while Italy and the provinces were sucked dry by his outrageous usury. And that he, on the other hand, possessed only modest means, won by his own labor.
XIV, 7: *Unless, perhaps, Brutus and Seneca might devise some means. He called them immediately, it being uncertain whether they were already in the know. Both were long silent, either unwilling to vainly try and dissuade him, or believing that matters had come to such a pass that Agrippina would have to be stopped if Nero were not to perish. After a moment, Seneca responded first and, glancing at Burrus, inquired whether the order of execution [of Agrippina] should be given to the military.*
The tragedies' subsequent torture scene, with Seneca looking dumbly on, is Lohenstein's invention.
11: *He [Nero] even spoke of a shipwreck. But none could be so naive as to believe that this was a mere coincidence. . . .*
After which Nero, whose inhumanity rose above the mournful cries of all, was no longer held in such contempt as Seneca, who had, in writing the oration, penned his confession.
52: *The death of Burrus undermined the power of Seneca, since there was no longer the same force for good with one of its heads removed, and Nero was inclining toward worse advisors. These assailed Seneca with various accusations.*
53: *Seneca was not unaware of his slanderers, for those who had retained a concern for the good told him, and, since the emperor*

increasingly avoided his company, Seneca requested a private interview.

. . . you, however, have granted me a large measure of influence, and boundless wealth, and to such an extent that I often wonder: could I, born a provincial knight, truly be one of this state's highest leaders? Have I really arrived at a station equal to these noblemen, with their long and decorous pasts? Where has that mind fled that was content with modest things? Does it construct such gardens? or such suburban mansions? rejoicing in these broad spaces, this wide usury? Only one defense comes to mind: it was not right of me to have struggled against your beneficence.

54: *But each of us has filled the measure.*

XV, 45: *It was said that Seneca, attempting to free himself from public ill will (having plundered a temple, on Nero's orders), had asked permission to retire to a far-off estate. When it was not given, he feigned sickness, some disease of the nerves, and did not leave his bed for some time. Some say that by Nero's orders one of his freedmen, a certain Cleonicus, had prepared a poison. Seneca, however, managed to avoid the betrayal, either by the freedman's open avowal or by his own caution.*

He maintained himself at that time on an extremely simple diet of wild fruits and spring water.

65: *The story was that Subrius Flavus, in secret council with the centurions, had, not without Seneca's knowledge, planned to give imperial power to Seneca after the murder of Nero by Piso, and after the latter was, in turn, despatched; the philosopher would thus appear to have been chosen for the highest power by innocent men, and on account of his eminent worthiness.*

Regarding sadism, necrophilia, and shamanism nothing, and nothing in Suetonius either; that Proustian prototype Pliny the Younger, who both arranged and attended torture sessions, himself an advisor to the emperor and bon vivant, refuses, in his letters, to even mention his great-grandfather Seneca's name.

In the *Epicharis*, Lohenstein has Seneca appear in two major scenes, neither of which, however, belong to the work's main plot line.

In the first he defends the divine sanction of Nero's rule, plays a reactionary (176): *Vices will remain / because people are going to* live as they choose – while rejecting fascism (175): *Romans don't render judgments according to the blood laws of Argos* – a wise man of almost Ghandian principle (176): *It's better to perish than to stain oneself with blood* – the seasoned statesman (177): *I'll stand neither by you nor by Nero* – a diplomat who, though he supports the revolution, still expresses himself in veiled understatements (177): *And Seneca would have meant this, too, were he Natal* – and who in the final sentence reveals himself as an *advocatus diaboli*, putting himself into question, as well as his doctrines, his pupil, the Roman constitution, and the divine emperor (177): *My wish is your triumph, and my precept: don't delay.*

The advice given by the reactionary convert was precise. Had the revolutionaries only followed it.

By the beginning of the second act the old man is already moving himself toward the virtuous sadomasochist Epicharis – and as a result, once again toward Nero:

(248): *A wise man can feel these, and the slightest pains*

(249): *No situation is so bleak that a wise man can't draw some solace from it.*

> *and this is so because the wise are gods upon the earth.*

Like kings!

Here Seneca's apotheosis, which Monteverdi, a generation earlier, had repressed, is recovered – but with severe counterarguments

(248): *How can one, reasonably, be both wise / and a tyrant's servant?*

Seneca defends himself against Xiphilinos's slanderous accusations (250): *That Seneca could disclose these trifles and the nonexistent bribe by which he was supposedly swayed.*

And by contrast (251):

> *Whoever doesn't save his fatherland, given the chance,*
> *Gives to the Furies a lighted passage and to tyrants, the smoke of consecration,*
> *Throws peoples into ruin, helps friends onto the bier,*
> *And builds more murderous altars to the gods than Busir.*

Seneca deftly parries with ubiquitous slander –

> *More evil must have attached itself*
> *To Seneca than he ever wrote, or ascribed to another.*
> *Now he must have advised a fratricide and now on*

Agrippina's lewd breast dishonored himself.
The powerlessness of a powerful *écrivain engagé*, of a Machiavelli, a Gorky, a Brecht, a Malraux, a Marquez.
De Gaulle: *Mais laissez-donc les intellectuels!*
   Let all this be a warning:
That whoever works only to keep himself within a tyrant's favor
Will get no thanks from him and only scorn from others.
Posterity, rest assured, shall still praise Nero
And will cover the shame of his sin under your guilt,
Paint the mother-killing dagger into your hand.
Lohenstein – rejecting the better judgment of Tacitus – had done just that only a few months earlier.
In the very next sentence the playwright castigates himself:
And yet no strange delusion can separate the gleam from virtue,
Even when its beauty fails to please dull eyes.
In a remarkable phrase, the thirty-year-old lets the seventy-year-old come to an acceptance of the threat of death (252):
   I don't long
For fear, or for life and its petty seasons of grief.
Seneca rejects the praise and success of his political career, instead presenting himself as one who tried to control, both on the field of battle and in the endless scenes of domestic intrigue, a dangerous personality who happened to be emperor, and who most likely suffered from some sort of hereditary defect (253):
   The suspicious will no doubt conclude:
I restrained him far too little;
When in fact: that he might not squeeze more tears from Rome
I let him play his harp.
And finally, with a stylized necrophilia (255):
I once received, while dining in Egypt, as a gift
A skeleton, stripped of flesh and wearing the latest fashion,
For a public execution; and I was delighted by the pots I saw
Filled with ashes of the dead. Whoever reads my work
Shall judge: that death was the midpoint
Toward which my thought and work were drawn
From their circle, out of vanity, and were lost.
The German Captain Cotuald, sent by the emperor, mocks Seneca's attempted suicide (258):

Who wouldn't laugh at these tender wounds?
If you have, as you claim, such a wish to die
Then thrust the cold steel through your chest, into your heart,
Put an end to your pain and meet death.
Seneca is metaphorically evasive; perhaps he is already planning on drinking hemlock.
Lohenstein doesn't spare Seneca the following, extravagant phrase (259):
I see Socrates drink this cup before me . . .
Enough: that Seneca should die like Socrates.
And two times, something not mentioned in historical accounts, like the skeleton at the dinner table. Tacitus says expressly, *Annales* XV, 63: *After which they [Seneca and his wife] cut into their wrists with a single stroke. Seneca, since his body was old and had been weakened by his meager diet, and was bleeding slowly, severed as well the arteries of the knees and legs.*
Tender wounds?
What compelled Lohenstein to insert a lie into Seneca's death? How collegial, by contrast, is Tacitus's remark:
And since, at the moment of death, he was still in full possession of his faculties, he let his scribes be admitted and dictated to them a longer speech.

Tacitus – we are informed by Bernhard Asmuth – is Lohenstein's source for the tragedies *Agrippina* and *Epicharis*, and for his notions of the art of statescraft and deception.
In the commentary, Seneca is represented only by the *De beneficiis*, *Hercules Furens*, *Thyestes*, and the second epistle.
Lohenstein suppresses something worked out by Asmuth, namely that the Zoroaster scene at the end of the *Agrippina* is modeled after a scene in Seneca's *Medea*, in which the heroine prepares a poison.
The primary source for the distorted image of Seneca seems to have been that obscure exploiter of Dion Cassius, Xiphilinos. No source is given for the sentence *The enemies corpse gives off a pleasant aura*, in a commentary where everyone seems to be cited at one point or another.

The remarks appended to the *Epicharis* cite Tacitus above all else, up to the fourth act. Of Seneca, mention is made of *De beneficiis, De ira, Hercules Furens, De clementia, Troades, Octavia.*

In the fourth act one sees increasing references to Seneca; *De mundi gubernatione et divina providentia* is introduced as well as several of the letters to Lucilius, including 75, 104, and 118. In the fifth act letters 69, 60, 36, 55, 24, 93, and lastly *De tranquilitate vitae ad Serenum.*

Eventually Lohenstein discredits himself and the image of Seneca he presents in the *Agrippina:*

The loathesome vices ascribed to Seneca by P. Suillius are described by Tacitus.

His primary witness against Seneca is then revealed: He is even more mercilessly abused in Xiphilinos's *Nero.*

As if to absolve himself Lohenstein picks up Seneca's aura remark again in the *Epicharis* and develops it further (197):

Sulpitius Asper, one of the republican coconspirators, remarks,
    From the lifeless bones
that gave voice to a tyrant and that an executioner broke,
There rises an agreeable odor of future glory into the world,
Keeping the dispirited yet alive.

Did the Seneca of the *Agrippina* also, from republican sentiment, wish to imply: this is the pleasant aura and scent of a tyrant's death, which will assure Agrippina a lasting glory?

A diplomatic and sincere expression, which nevertheless wouldn't condemn him to death?

So might Lohenstein have talked and interpreted himself out of his dilemma.

Both of the Roman tragedies appeared in the year 1665 – exactly sixteen hundred years after Seneca's suicide. The effect is one of simultaneous conception and completion.

Did Daniel Casper conceive of them as the halves of some dialectical whole? On the one side the queer, diabolic Nero, and on the other the virtuous effrontery of Epicharis? Here Seneca the toady, with cadaverous aspirations, there the torn intellectual? The commentaries speak against it.

Xiphilinos, in the *Agrippina,* is introduced as a wholly trustworthy source – in the *Epicharis* he is devalued.

Did Lohenstein finish the Seneca of the *Agrippina*, as well as its commentary, before finishing the Seneca of the *Epicharis* and, having overstepped himself blindly in a given direction, sought to correct his own conception in the later play?

Lohenstein was clearly unclear with himself as regards this figure.

The Stoic Mnester, who in a secularizing fashion rejects, in the *Agrippina,* all magical and atavistic funereal rites, insists on retaining one:

The blood sacrifice for the dead empress, thereby aligning himself with certain voodoo practices – just as in Dahomey, where many voodoo rites have their origin, at the death of a king from Abomey, various friends and relatives, servants and women, of their own free will, of course, buried themselves along with their ruler.

The Seneca of the *Epicharis* is also fascinated by blood. His final statement (260):

My life has an end.
Jupiter the redeemer, accept my sacrifice,
My hand full of blood, since I have nothing else to give.
Seneca – a Roman Lohenstein?

Is it necessary to read Lohenstein's work as the creation of a purely utopian, depth psychology revolutionary?

Daniel Casper's formative years fall during the Thirty Years War; in 1649, at the age of fourteen, he wrote his first play, *Ibrahim Bassa.*

The remainder of his brief life, he was only two years older than Schiller when he died, stands in sharp contrast with his youth, it being on the whole more peaceful, one might even say leisurely, and upper middle class.

There are fewer occasions for incest, homosexual behavior, and sadomasochism in this later period than in the years of war, education in the gymnasium, and wandering.

After twenty-two everything has boiled down to marriage, petty squabbles, socializing, political activity, and a legal practice.

In 1675 he traveled to the Viennese court on a political mission. Klaus Günther Just, to whom we owe the edition of Lohenstein's complete tragedies, writes: *He won the seneschal and Hofrat over to* his views, even managing to acquire a chest full of salmon by courier from Breslau, the largest of which was given to the emperor as a gift, and the remainder of which fell to the three chancellors.

The student already shows himself capable of systematically combining a divine destiny, state power, and sadism (*Ibrahim Bassa* 32):

God aids the suffering
Yet strikes not at tyrants,
Though they put thorns in his eyes
And draw and suck from us our blood,
Not until they might fulfill their role
And not until he, when we have often sinned,
Makes them the servants of his revenge,
The messengers of his unfailing vigilance,
And so reveals his zealous fury, his heated rage.

Might one also read Lohenstein's theatrical work – superficially – as a drum-and-trumpet cry of stock moral outrages, "Turks get out," "Off with their pricks," "Off with their heads"!?

In the dichotomies virtue/luxury and progress/assimilation, Lohenstein demonstrates a susceptibility, an inclination toward both salmon and sympathy with the oppressed.

Is the figure of Seneca then one of sheer fakery, virtue's mere aping, a tactician – did Lohenstein unfairly insert the Egyptian skeleton and the necrophiliac aura?

In the epistles written to the young Lucilius, three years before his death, Seneca combines, for a final time, his convictions with his more stylized figures.

In epistle number 50, he writes:

You know Harpaste, my wife's feeble-minded servant, has remained in this house as its rather burdensome inheritance. I lay no real worth upon such strange creatures; if I want to have some fun at a fool's expense, I don't have to look far: I laugh at myself. This simple woman suddenly became blind. Now, this may sound incredible, but it's true: she doesn't know that she's blind. She repeatedly asks the steward for permission to move out, that the house is too dark. We laugh about it, but rest assured, none of us is any different.

Number 66:

Without hesitation, I can say that I value the gnarled and useless hand of Mucius more than that one, uninjured, of the most illustrious hero.
Filled with scorn for both the enemy and the flame, he stood before the foreign hearth-flame, watching his hand smolder, until Posenna, who had allowed this punishment, moved by jealousy lest he outstrip him in glory, bid him remove it. . . .
Or should I rather stretch my limbs out before one of these amorous young men, that he might make them more supple? Or wish rather, for some woman, or some lad turned woman, to come and do the same to my fingers? Wherefore shouldn't I hold Mucius to be more fortunate, who held his hand out to the fire as if it were a masseur?
Number 78:
Replenish your memories upon the objects of your greatest admiration: some hero or some conqueror will then occur to you over your pain; for example, the man who reads calmly from his book, while being deveined; or another, who laughs unmoved, while his extremely animated tormentors try every conceivable tool or torture upon him.
Number 94. Letter to Lucilius:
The wretched Alexander drove his rage for destruction to unprecedented heights. Or do you consider a man who began his career by defeating all of Greece, the country where he had received his education, to be mentally sound?
Seneca/Lohenstein/Lohenstein/Kissinger – what a cute combination:
Salmon and alexandrines.
Torture and the White House.
Cairo and the Oedipus complex.
Sadat and Mark Antony.
Let me stop this kaleidoscope by a little phrase:
As in Lohenstein, there are ruthless words in Seneca:
In the first letter:
One part of our life is taken forcibly from us, a second without our noticing it, and a third dissolves of itself.
In the seventh letter:
More greedy, more ambitious and hedonistic, I return home: also more cruel, more inhuman – simply because I was among other people.

In number 14:
An instrument of torture will have a larger effect if it is shown with a large variety of other such instruments.
Brecht remembered this and had Galileo prove it.
Number 22:
No one is so cowardly as to prefer eternal hanging to a single fall.
Lohenstein has Agrippina utter this sentence before her death, without acknowledging his debt in the commentary.
Number 23:
Many people live for the first time when they are no longer able. If you think this strange, I might add something stranger still: many cease to live before they have even begun.
Number 43:
Flattery – alas, how close it is to friendship.
Number 44:
You will scarcely find a single Roman capable of living with an open door. It is our bad conscience, and not our pride, that has made door guards necessary; we live in such a manner that our sudden glance is perceived as a prelude to a surprise attack.
Number 91:
The expressions of the uneducated strike me as a consequence of gas. Whether they release it through the mouth or bottom is a matter of indifference.
Official tone and slang – a table of laws and stylistic incongruity. There is in Lohenstein, as well, that element which Caligula referred to in Seneca's speech as:
Sand without chalk.
Illustrious, Noble Duchess, Gracious Princess and Lady.
Agrippina, whom Rome adores, the kaiser honors, and whom the people must serve would consider it her highest mark of distinction if she might lay herself before your princely, gracious feet. For her sins know no other place where they might find refuge than in the company of the virtues of a great and noble duchess, her country's mother, being at present unable to escape the murderous sword of her son.
Well, never without at least a little chalk.
Seneca, too, is moved by ambition, a drive for power, a lust for torture and destruction. Whereas Seneca, however, brings the disjunct whole together –

in the second letter: *that man is not poor who possesses little, but who craves more.*

in the fourth letter: *Poverty, if necessitated by laws of nature, is itself a great wealth.*

in the fifth letter: *That one is great who eats out of clay pots, as well as silver; great is that one, too, who treats the silver pots as if they were of clay. It is not a sign of magnanimity not to be able to deal with wealth.*

number 20:

It is an accomplishment in itself to mingle constantly with the wealthy and not let oneself be corrupted; great is the man who remains poor in the midst of his wealth.

number 55: *It takes a real effort to allow oneself to be constantly carried.*

number 94: *Nature creates us all with pure hearts, without vices* – Lohenstein rips open the tactical screen.

Daniel Casper did not, while at the court, turn a philosophical system into a source of income. He dared to put his poetic analyses on the stage without any concessions. *The enemy's corpse gives off a pleasant aura* is the expression of a thinker who had submitted himself to a system of repression; not to signal some elective affinity does it stand there, abruptly – but to make clear a certain, reversed path, to knowledge.

Seneca gives off an aura.

Not of a *penseé sauvage,* but rather of domestication.

9.

There is in voodoo – as in many magical societies – an ambivalent posturing vis-à-vis power and aggression, an aggression-inhibiting recognition of power structures.

Believers, cult assistants, and novices are, for many years, exposed to a discreet terror, which they pass on to the lower ranks while rising, until eventually they arrive at the peak, becoming powerful voodoo priests and priestesses themselves.

The highest peak is the magical function of the *président à vie.* The appraisal of power and aggression remains, in Lohenstein, as in Busenello and Monteverdi, opaque – condemnation is mixed with excuse. Nero is princeps *à vie,* a priest, divine. More is at

Voodoo Bloodbaths – Heroes of Mixed Religion

stake than dramatic function; Lohenstein presents the fate of the gods, archetypes, complexes.

Sexual ambivalence, rhetorical perversions, and sexual myths stand opposite ghastly, fleshless ritualizations.

Religion and sex seem – despite all presented evidence to the contrary – to cancel each other out.

Otho and Nero joke around together – they don't go into a clinch; Poppaea turns Nero on, on the stage she keeps him at arm's length; Agrippina and her son want to get undressed – Acte cuts in between.

Courtly impossibility of the baroque?

But there's Suetonius's sedan.

No. Voodoo unsexuality, oversexuality.

One isn't invited to sex – instead, sex is carved up, ritualized, typified – as in Fellini.

Magic creates the possibility of an avoidance of aggression, as well as an avoidance of sexual aggression through carnivalesque exaggeration.

The enemy isn't pierced with a sword, but a puppet, a thousand times with needles.

Metamorphosis.

Catharsis – whose functions Lohenstein knew via Seneca.

Lohenstein's analysis of aggressive behaviors seems to go far beyond any example drawn from voodoo.

One sees in Haitian voodoo, as in every other Afro-American religion, cruel rites of sacrifice – human sacrifices, with ritualized incisions, are rare, while torture and death by torture simply don't exist.

The tales told by the faithful of the *cochons sans poils,* the two-headed boxer, or the loups-garous, however, mirror the deeds of their African forebears.

Therefore ought we to think that such things never happened? A resounding no!

People whose limbs are severed from their bodies, crushed infants, Hansels and Gretels garnished with cultic herbs, human heads under refrigeration, drinking blood – just like out of Tacitus and Xiphilinos.

How about political reality?

Isn't there something late-Roman, something Neroesque about the kings and emperors of Haiti, about the revolutionaries and oppressors, about the son-in-law of the consul Napoleon?

These black Othos and Agrippinas, Senecas and Epicharises live on as heroes in the clay vessels of voodoo, next to cannibalistic leathermen and leatherwomen like Erzulie Zé Rouge, Ti Jean Pied Fin, Guédé Nibo, Guédé Journaille.

The faithful are transformed into these figures while in trance, of which the baroque theater is only a late, secularized, and distant echo.

What this trance means – next to the Christian litanies and the mixed-religious Masses – is the reversed path of morality: not the imitation of the good, naturalism, classicism, but rather the expulsion of evil, concepts,[7] Asianism.

Lohenstein refers often to the Asiatic tales of Candaules, of Medea, and to the Attic tales of Oedipus and Orestes.

He takes his examples from Turkey, Rome, and Africa.

He constructs his own syncretistic mythology.

10.

Whoever misreads Lohenstein's posturings as bombastic possesses little insight into the functioning of the unconscious, magic, the various uses of language or conceptual aesthetics.

The magical use of language breaks down into glossolalia, speaking in tongues, inspired, enthusiastic speech, *délire verbal,* the *langage* of voodoo, litanies. (I don't mean that "warbling" (*Zwitschern*) popular among intellectuals – a late bourgeois linguistic softening, which neither has meaning nor communicates.)

The refined and educated assume that everything that lies beneath their university career and salary scale is wild, unrestrained, disorderly, and barbaric.

Magical language use is subtle and finely structured, like the rhyme schemes and metrical forms of baroque poetry.

The language of voodoo is a linguistic alloy, thought to reproduce the African of the ancestors and gods, it has no dictionaries and no grammar, every believer discovers it anew, and it recalls the

---

7. In English in original.

first phonemes described by Roman Jakobson in the language of newborns, or that of Schwitters. Lohenstein, too, reaches so deeply, and at a young age (*Ibrahim Bassa*, 16):
Receive this laughing woe, damned abyss!
Damned abyss! O my legs
Drip with the sweat of terror! Woe of woes!
The *délire verbal* is an emotionally charged, floodlike release, which intercepts aggressive tendencies like a short circuit, dissolves difficulties.
The entrance monologue of the priest of magic, Zoroaster – a singsong hardly foreign to the voodoo priest (*Agrippina*, 104):
Let the king have no cares. The stars follow me.
I write the rules for the very gods.
In a litany one finds certain formal invariants: historical citations, names of ancestors, names of heroes, names of gods, magical objects, ciphers for certain sensations – and in such a jumble, that a union takes place between spectator and priest, drowning out the individual stream of consciousness by combining speech fragments drawn from tradition and the extended family – a type of poisoning of the individual through language, perhaps even a chemical alteration of glandular activity.
Bring the dyed cloth . . .
Bring the incense burner . . .
Bring the herbs . . .
Bring his virgin-wax . . .
Now bring the thorny shrub . . .
And is Osiris present, through whom one
Conjures the pale throng of the dead?
Language is a psychic reality; in voodoo it brings on psychic changes (*Agrippina*, 106):
The eyes that shine in the lynx and in the basilisk,
The herb that one ought never give Diana, and that
When cast into the water blinds the eye
And hawks-herb juices that refresh the face
Shall now be mingled in this temple
To renew again her extinguished light.
Here is the lizard skin that she herself devours so we won't.
The dead shall by these offerings receive new flesh and skin

And fresh brains, stolen from salamanders
On the fecund Nile will fill her empty skull.
And now, the marrow of unborn children.
The *ars combinatoria* of the baroque does exactly that – creating a *Unio Mystica*, a *concordia discors* – through a compilation of learned reference and emotional cipher.
Rhetorical figures are secularized magic formulas.
Even the *concetto,* that late, extremely compressed form of verbal artistry (prior to society's degradation of language to a mere bon mot), is seen in voodoo, in the names of gods, for example:
Ti Jean Pied Fin – the savage, destructive god, "little John with the fine feet" – or the murderous god of the dead Guédé Journaille, the "skeleton journalist," or in a Haitian's expression over the death of a white colonialist:
Blanc vini vert – white turns to green.
In the wake of Lohenstein's juxtapositions – pre-Freudian and, at times, looking beyond the Freudian hermeneutic – one might ask whether Freud and his theories aren't actually a kind of poetics, and poetry, combinatorics, charlatanry, psychological voodoo.
Metaphors limp – just like Oedipus.
Just like Freud, announcing a new method of limping metaphor for the cure of the soul's wounds.
Form and content are completely one – concealing, often, the outcome, unfortunately.
There is the idea of disguise, in language and through language.
There is a baroque irony and a voodooesque irony.
Is it a coincidence that Dr. François, who didn't shy away from working Mao Tse-tung and Rosenberg into his worldview, also mocked the most powerful man in the world – JFK?

II.

It would be nice if the German media and general public possessed the requisite patience, tolerance, and inquisitiveness to work through the corpus, lengthy and artistically polished, of an almost unknown seventeenth-century poet.
But can we count on it?
For three hundred years, the German *literazzia* let slip its chance to take up the critical task offered by Lohenstein's *Agrippina*.

My revision shall above all prove that the play is thoroughly performable, theatrically potent, and one of the most significant tragedies of the German language.

I have made suggestions that are, I hope, both logically consistent in themselves and that will provoke further suggestions.

A decisive falsification will have occurred, I feel, if Nero's voodoo is played like a sex show.

A fuckfest instead of magic.

But I'm no voodoo priest, let alone a baroque poet! Backward and forward, left and right, the crusaders of the New Modesty will most likely enforce their strictures – I'm simply not one of their number.

Why should German season ticket holders have to renounce pleasures that, only a few years ago, were the standard fare of every home movie and Father's Day excursion?

No one lays restrictions upon the depiction of violence and aggression – I call for the release of voodoo, Countess Marizza, and the rubber dick.

Tendernesses, actually – to counterbalance Agrippina's rituals of dismemberment.

Tacitus, Suetonius, and Pliny are on my side – I'm sure I can convince Daniel Casper.

Unfortunately, the play must be shortened. And, since the music for the allegories of the intermezzi is lacking, and since I don't like allegories in general, I wonder whether these lines can't be cut entirely – excepting the dream vision of Agrippina's redemption, which was so important to the poet that he repeated it four times.

My third suggestion is the addition of Monteverdi's *Incoronazione di Poppea*. The delicate revolutionary composed this work about twenty years earlier – a lewd opus magnum, in which, for the last time, the seventy-four-year-old outshines his plagiarizers.

Monteverdi's *Incoronazione* is sharp and perverse, like Lohenstein's *Agrippina*. The slight temporal displacement engenders a tension – a tension highlighted by the refractions undergone by Nero, Nerone, Poppaea, Poppea, Otho, Othone.

The conclusion of Lohenstein's tragedy, even when its allegorical ending is included, is indecisive; the mother's spirit does not appear, Nero and the magician faint.

At this point Monteverdi intervenes with trumpet fanfare, delivering catharsis as an operatic happy ending.
Mnester's line, *From Nero's (eyes) yet blood will flow instead of tears,* gives a direct invitation to compare the emperor's fate with that of Oedipus.
What spectator of the 1970s wouldn't be reminded, viewing Agrippina, of Sophocles and Hölderlin?
Comparing Hölderlin's northern, puritanically seasoned locutions with Lohenstein's Roman-Romanic turns of phrase.
In voodoo as well one distinguishes between Protestant *délire verbal,* in Trinidad, and its Catholic variant in Haiti.
Lastly, I could adduce a historical argument to the fifth act of my Hölderlin-Oedipus collage:
Magical and ecstatic religions, as they existed in early Greece, were secularized into the form of tragedy and satyr plays – part Scala di Milano, part Oberammergau.
(In Trinidad there exist, in the Indian *Mahabharata* plays, a naive form of Greek tragedy – War of the Gods and prayer hymns.)
Sophocles and Hölderlin mark the precise point of connection between voodoo and the Rape of the Sabines.
The problem of directions for the play's mise-en-scène presented itself to me – just as for Lohenstein the problem of a commentary.
For the poet there is no alternative language of evasion outside of the poetic – or else he simply lies.
Proust's newspaper articles are likewise always a form of the search for *un temps perdu.* I can't write:
Hans *(shuts the door, peeved):*
Such things kept me from writing plays, even radio plays, for fifteen long years.
I have now taken George Braque as my model.
Braque was given the task of finishing one of the Louvre's decorative rooms, all in gold, and in rococo style; he painted, on the central medaillon, a large dove, stylized to the point of looking like a coarse white cross, set against a blue background.
Otherwise I wouldn't have written very much.
An Oedipal Orestes ought to be worked in, too, since Nero played the mother-murderer Orestes as well as the blind Oedipus.
Otho is an interesting figure, enlightened even. I wanted to stress that by the sentence: *I want to hope for pleasure.*

Voodoo Bloodbaths – Heroes of Mixed Religion

I have striven to retain alternate spellings of certain words: *purpur* and *purper* [for "purple"], *Freind* and *Freund* [for "friend"], and *itzt* and *jetzt* [for "now"], and in general I would rather that the text be misunderstood than glibly received.[8]

Every interpretation is overinterpretation and remains far behind its object.

If one has an interest in voodoo, and likes to read baroque literature, things become increasingly easy.

It isn't unreasonable to imagine that, with a little skill, one could bring Sappho and Idi Amin into a single essay.

And why not?

I wanted to demonstrate that Afro-American culture is not entirely exotic, bizarre, primitive, and topsy-turvy, and that the culture of Lohenstein isn't at all that of a dismissible, queer, perverse, and elitist man of letters.

Both sides do the work of each other's presentation.

In the aesthetic of the rule-bound disordered system, voodoo has its proper place.

The gestures of magic are like manic gestures are like mannered gestures.

---

8. The use of *contemn* in the translation approximates this degree of archaism.

WOE OF WOES!
Remarks on Daniel Casper von Lohenstein's Turkish Tragedy *Ibrahim Bassa*

Hamburg, 1978

1.

In 1649, one year after the Peace of Westphalia, Lohenstein, at the age of fourteen, begins writing *Ibrahim Bassa*.
The play was performed in 1650, most likely in celebration of carnival season, by the students of the Magdalenäum in Breslau. In 1653 the play is printed, and sent out by its author.
Lohenstein signs his name Daniel Casper von Nimptsch, using, on the return address, a nobleman's title that he is not to receive from the kaiser until 1670,
taking at that time the title von Lohenstein.

Asia is introduced onto the stage in the figure of a woman bound by vices.
Woe, poor me! alas, Asia.
Wretched me! I damn myself!
I who by this melancholy sea
Gaze on my face, tear scarred from bitter woe;
And that I might, among these howling, murderous cries
Condemn myself by righteous judgments!
Take then, profound abyss, this laughing cry of pain!
Profound abyss! Limbs wet

With the sweat of fear! Woe of woes! the tepid flow of my thin veins does surge
The foam of the purple flood!
My misery by bloody foam inscribed in sand!
Oh queen dethroned! Unsceptered ruler of the world!
Fallen Asia! Country, blown from something into nothingness and dust! (16)

An extraordinary piece of poetry, unlike the work of any other fourteen-year-old; the closest comparison would be the *Bateau ivre* of the seventeen-year-old Rimbaud.

But it's true, I've cried too much! Each dawn is an affliction,
Every moon savage, and each sun too harsh:
Caustic love has filled me with a drunken languor.
O that my keel might burst! And that I might plunge into the sea!

Or, written in the same year, *Vowels*:

A noir. E blanc. I rouge. U vert. O bleu: Voyelles.[1]

. . .

Engulfed in shade:
Comparable only to the *Rowley Poems*, by Thomas Chatterton who committed suicide at the age of seventeen – Chatterton's *African Eclogues*:

I'll strew the Beaches with the mighty dead
And tinge the Lily of their features red.

Content.

Ibrahim, a Welsh prince whom Soliman, on account of bravery, promotes from the status of serf to that of a high-ranking vassal is, while fleeing toward Genoa (where he thought to rescue his lover, Isabelle, with whom Soliman has fallen deeply in love during Ibrahim's extended stay in Persia), captured and brought in chains to Constantinople, where, spurred by the disclosures of the empress and others, he is brutally strangled.
The setting is the Fortress of the Seven Towers at Constantinople. The tragedy should begin in the morning and end around midnight.

Well, yes and no.

---

1. Although a straight translation might read: *A black. E white. I red. U green. O blue: Vowels*, the French makes, though not precisely, another kind of sense on the level of sound: *In black. And white. Some red. Open. Oh blue: Vowels.*

Woe of Woes!

There are several possibilities for reading the play – both official and apocryphal; the 1653 edition oscillates between political and intimate spheres of action.

Alberto Girri, the Argentinian lyric poet, summed it up well in 1963:

La poesía es el tema del poema.[2]

The object of Lohenstein's poetry is poetry and the poetic; the most foregrounded and hidden senses of his work consist in allegories, metaphors, similes, citations, words, syllables, and sighs.

O word that lightning-quick
Pierces to the marrow and vein! O word that tears a seam
In the soul! O thunder striker of the heart! (28)
yes, each single word-part
compelled me. (35)
and for the sake of a word, he often put at stake his life and limb,
fortune and possessions. (60)

Labyrinths of feelings, labyrinths of words:
The prince vowed his death, and now he would preserve him.
A promise made destroys what one had only just declared,
And then another oath, in turn, the promise.
The first was never sworn, it seems. It binds with a mere silken thread.
A prince must always give his word. (60)
And that he might be bound by our agreement. (66)

King Soliman the Great is portrayed with respect to the way in which he uses words.

The character of Queen Roxelane is revealed in the way she handles words and oaths.

Allegory is – like the simile – a wholly unpoetic form of expression; it strives to grasp that which lies behind all language, it is explanatory, supplementary, synthetic, ideal.

Just as the effect of my own text is lessened if I have to trouble Lady Verity to clarify some detail.

(And just as, in a particular sentence, the power of my words is weakened if I have to say that they are "like" something else.)

2. Poetry is the theme of the poem.

Poetry is analytic.

It seems, however, that human thought is always accomplished through comparisons, whether in taking recourse to a utopian ideal or intruding upon sensory matter.

Every writer is familiar with the many *likes* and *as it weres* that go into a rough draft and that are only reluctantly edited out of the final version.

Poetry is also contradictory.

It contradicts its principles as soon as these are raised to the status of principles.

Something new occurred to Lohenstein, under the impact and influence of baroque form:

He employs allegorical archetypes not to pad his expressions, but rather to burden them and overburden them to the point of fracture:

Is Soliman absolved from his oath, his word, his loyalty to his friend, by Sleep?

The senses break into a dance and discuss it – like spirits, drunk first thing in the morning.

The *as it weres* fall away like the *likes* in the absolute metaphor of Rimbaud's *Bateau ivre*.

Boldness and Childhood stand side by side, kettledrums and trumpets and the low notes of Black Bile, Mystery stands alongside figures conjured up by the mannerist's objective eye:

What does Desire have to say?

Kidneys are with love enflamed, by me. (41)

Who would not, today, be reminded of an adrenalin release, or of sexual hormones flowing from the adrenal cortex, things that have become clear only today, some three hundred years after the appearance of Daniel Casper's early work? Hans Henry Jahnn, moreover, in his experiments during the late 1950s, proved that desires incite the adrenal glands.

Conflict of the historical time – conflict of the author's preadolescent age – drastic verbal constructions:

Exceptionally long verses followed, in syncopation, by short bursts:

Woe! woe! woe!

Have you, you snake-souled father, you worm on tigers fed,

Bloodhound, viper eater,
Have you brought down such a storm and sea, such a dark wave of grief upon me? (73)
Rustahn:
Onward! There is little enough time as it is, that we should squander it so.
Isabelle:
Farewell! My life!
Ibrahim:
Alas! Farewell!
Isabelle:
My light!
Ibrahim:
My heart!
Isabelle:
My love, my only consolation! Farewell! We must be torn asunder! Alas, good night!
Ibrahim:
Not alone, my love!
Leave me not, my only reason, stay!
Isabelle:
Farewell! The time has come.
Ibrahim:
I will love you though they set flames upon my body!
Isabelle:
And I will love you though I am shattered and die of grief!
Ibrahim:
A last kiss my love!
Isabelle:
A final kiss! Farewell! (28)

Lohenstein, by breaking up his alexandrine lines, lends them the effect of free verse and, in so doing, reveals to us that, behind every conversation, there stand certain rhythmic laws – that behind Proust stands Racine, behind Döblin, Hölderlin and Novalis.

Not simply unbinding the rhythmic corset, however, he also straitens it, vigorously, as well – for instance, when, in a six-

footed alexandrine, he seems to play with the caesura at midverse, displacing and stretching the syllables to the point of almost flawing the line:
You all who look upon me fallen, and it seems . . . (51)
with the ambivalent *and* toward the end of the line, which offers the actor a marvelous medium to express emotion;
And four mute attendants, with dark silken ropes . . . (56)

From the midverse caesura he jumps, then, from foot to foot, both dizzying the ear and reproducing in turn the trembling effect of the death scene; nature as pure form, manneristic mimesis.

Lohenstein crushes the vehicles of his own metaphors.
He stacks ruins upon rubble – often crossing, even for his contemporaries in 1649, the borders of the comprehensible:
He went down the blue path,
His visor down, to the arbor. (58)
The more sharp thorns have pierced one's fingers,
The more one's crowned with blood-milkened roses. (68)
– and the borders of preadolescent madness:
Bloodthirsty bloodhound! Ah! the blood of brave Ibrahim
Rich in innocence that you soak up like a sponge
In its ebb and flow, or a reed, now licked by his tongue
And that writes on the wall and colors the sullied
Shrouds of the dead (74)
a type of clairvoyant-automatic writing, not unlike that of early or late surrealism:
How well they fit, pain and time
Upon these dark limbs and mantle of death! (50)

And yet one should be careful not to dismiss the work of the fourteen-year-old dramatist as somehow merely pathological, ludicrous, an isolated extreme, branding it with any of several dismissive epithets: bombastic, exotic, perverse – and thereby lending credence, moreover, to an impotent narrative of German literary history that attaches to Lohenstein like a pink or yellow star; he never distinguished himself in the manner of his suc-

cessors, marked by their officious scrawling, stale affectations, and ecstatic productivity – this is not to say that his work knows no measure, proportion, repose, or depth of feeling:
These princes are dreamers, like lowly shepherds
Who wear their hair and straw like regal garb. (65)
O Discord between soul and senseless senses! (35)
Heard but not answered, accused but nothing charged,
Condemned! (28)

A school-age author uses a construction that would be strictly forbidden within any school's confines, or according to scholastic doctrine.
The seventeen-year-old Hans Henry Jahnn, in prewar expressionism (1911), uses formulas that recall the conceits of Little Erna jokes.
In the novel fragment *Jesus Christ* he writes:
A more suitable notion occurred to the king much later.
For now, he screamed at him, enraged, calling him a stupid decrepit old man.
Consider, Joseph, that every tree, animal and stone, and every man, is soulless, and apart from God.
. . . but it gave them pleasure that all these things had taken place in such a manly, serene fashion. For this was, all things considered, a rather pleasant way of broadening one's sentiments. . . .
. . . he believed that the entire art of speech lay in nuance, he gurgled, squeaked, he laughed, he cried; but he was not understood.

Is one not reminded of:
Frau Puhmeier, what's wrong? You look so haggard.
My husband is dead.
How unpleasant!

For us present-day readers it's hard to distinguish between what might have been formal speech from schoolboy slang;
yet when Lohenstein writes:
His body hung twitching and the bones, strained and splitting, crackled (27)
he reveals an allegiance to a powerful everyday speech, to which Luther is no stranger, but which German classicism thoroughly

extirpated, with the result that today one can hardly describe a good fuck without sounding clinical or brutish.

The French language, like Latin, never severed its ties to anal or bodily functions, etc., and when, in 1828, Hammer-Purgstall wanted to Germanize the name of the Turkish city Amm göti, which means, quite simply, cunt-ass, he had to write *cunnus anus*, which means the same thing.

The small step from the ridiculous to the sublime, which marks the inception of the tragic, is taken already by Villon:

My name is François, as I well know.
I was born in Paris near Pontoise.
Hung from a cord, at the end of my days,
My neck shall know how much my poor ass weighs.

Jean Genet, as well, mixes rakish slang with the lofty linguistic gestures of the French imperial court:

To break you in, handsome boy
These strapping sailors catch you up beneath their coats.
My love, my love, will you steal the keys
To open that sky where the high mast lightly sways
. . .
From where you scatter majestic white enchantments.

Lohenstein disassembles words and meaning, into matter and phonemes:

. . . you who through me, in smoke
And embers swirling and dread transfigured Persian . . . (51)
Ah! if woe and pain so . . . (26)
What heavy-sighing grief . . . (72)
. . . woe of woes! (16)

Lohenstein lets the whole tragic plot hinge upon this syllable; the friend condemns his friend to death, by hanging – not on the grounds of any rational deliberation, but rather as if from a distance and spurred by recollection of the death of his two sons, the king lets out, again, a sigh. It is this "woe" that brings on the death of Ibrahim. The entire tragic action can be compressed into the difference between a short and a long vowel:

And Ossman, who asks her, has the power to command her. (47)³
A semiofficial, hormonally charged drama finds the light of day through an intentionally misdeployed possessive pronoun:
Was the hand that rocked you into sleep with gentle fingers
Too severe? The Byzantine sun
Too sombre that lent to you, as to his moon, its lustre? (22)
How does Malaparte say it?
In German the sun is feminine.

In 1645 Philipp von Zesen published, in Amsterdam, *The Wondrous Story of Ibrahim, or the Illustrious Bassa, and Steadfast Isabelle: publ. by Phi. Zesen von Fürstenau;* prior to this there had appeared Madeleine de Scudéry's *Ibrahim ou l'illustre Bassa*, in 1641.
Zesen felt such a close connection to this latter work that, in 1663, he complained:
O infernal jealousy! My translation of the Ibrahim story has also been copied in Saarbrücken. There too, not surprisingly, my name is omitted, as well as my preface – even my letters to the highly commendable Palm and Rose Societies.
The fact that he himself dropped Mme. de Scudéry's name doesn't seem to bother him especially – witness to a common, rather contradictory sensitivity often seen in translators and editors.

Zesen's work is a predecessor not only of Lohenstein's *Ibrahim Bassa* – in 1647 (!) Zesen published, as well, a *Sophonisbe,* and it would be very informative to investigate whether the man Lohenstein is as indebted to Zesen as the student Daniel Casper. Does Lohenstein follow Zesen?
The work of Zesen-Scudéry is meticulous and extensive. A good question, whether all who claim to depend on it have actually read it.
But I surely don't want to imply that it is equal to *The Messiah.*
A naive fantasy:
and as a morning gift, he gave her 300,000 sultanas. (60)

3. "Daß Ossman der sie bitt ihr macht hat zu gebitten." Informing Fichte's frame of reference, contemporary orthography now distinguishes the short "i" of *bitten* (to ask) from the long "i" of *gebieten* (to command).

And not sultana raisins, mind you, which would come to about 30 kg – but 300,000 real concubines of King Soliman, along with their daughters – a lubricious Parisian dream-image, at your doorstep.

The book is rich in somewhat withered flowers; the uniform multiplicity of detail often smothers any real meaningful perspective. What does it mean, when Zesen remarks:

He [Soliman] said to him [Ibrahim] with a more heartfelt affection than ever a man conceived for another that he thought himself to be a most unfortunate man, since he must admit to himself that he was unable to make such a one happy, whom he loved, singularly and with such devotion (141).

As soon as he walked into the room, Soliman ordered everyone out in order that once he saw that the two of them were quite alone he might give him a passionate embrace (559).

Lohenstein himself addresses his kindly disposed reader, in 1653, at the age of eighteen, in the following fashion:

However much I have availed myself of Zesen's detailed descriptions, which were taken from his work Ibrahim, *the latter work translated from the French, I have nevertheless broken ranks with the majority of the chroniclers when they report that he was able to come away without being strangled* (13).

Who are these chroniclers?

Lohenstein appended no explanatory remarks to *Ibrahim Bassa*, as he did to all of his other dramatic works.

We don't really know what Lohenstein read as a student.

However, upon looking into the reading list of Daniel Casper the adult, which includes *Augerii Gislenii Busbequii legationis Turciae Epistolae*, or the four Turkish letters sent by Ogier Ghiselin von Busbeck, we find evidence for the fact that the student didn't know these documents in the misplacement of the ghost of Mustafa, since, if he had, he would have placed Mustafa's murder *after* the murder of Ibrahim, instead of, wrongly, before it, a detail in which he follows Zesen-Scudéry.

Nor is it only in the fulfillment of Ibrahim's death sentence that Lohenstein diverges from Zesen's fifth book, fourth chapter, or I should say from his entire thirteen hundred pages, which

Lohenstein knew in detail, as we shall soon see, and which he paraphrased in the oddest ways.

The thrice-repeated condemnation of Ibrahim by his friend the king and the corresponding reprieves are Lohenstein's invention. The funeral banquet and the black mantle are present in Zesen, but in Lohenstein they come to the fore at the play's turning point, along with numerous other details, horrendous for a fourteen-year-old mind to conceive of – fourteen years old, that is, twelve months after the Treaty of Westphalia.

(Recall that Lohenstein has Seneca remark, in the *Epicharis*:
Whoever reads my work
Shall judge: that death was the midpoint
Toward which my thought and work were drawn
From their circle, out of vanity, and were lost.)

Ibrahim, according to Lohenstein's correction of his model, is no nobleman, as in Zesen-Scudéry (in the second book of the first part), but a former slave.

So, quite clearly, selection, transformation, manifold emendation.

Why he insists upon including Isabelle's love affair – a sheer fabrication – is beyond me.

Whether Lohenstein was compelled, consciously or no, to stage the masculine conflict between male friendship and the love of women, he surely had sufficient examples in a number of historically verifiable female figures:

Soliman's sister, the wife of Ibrahim; and Roxelane, the former slave from Russia, the wife of King Soliman.

Oriana Fallaci once remarked, after Pasolini's murder, that the only thing the victim lacked was a woman; so perhaps Mme. de Scudéry must have reasoned as she novelized the numerous inconsistencies of the events surrounding the Turkish court, adding, to the rest of her account, tales of the "steadfast Isabelle."

2.

A straight reading of *Ibrahim Bassa* yields some condemnation of the Turks – Soliman, the insecure, cruel Moslem versus the loyal, self-sacrificing, normal Christian that is the Roman – as if it were lifted from the type of Turkish horror story that circulated during the Ottoman Empire, one hundred years after Soliman, identifiable by its marvels, vagueries, and naïveté.

Ogier, the reactionary Busbeck, whose *Four Turkish Letters* we discovered in Lohenstein's library, paints – though, for the most part, in sharply prejudicial tones – a more varied picture of the developing country than the tempestuous, repressed student Daniel Casper. It is a liberating experience to juxtapose the pristine naïveté of Ogier, the worldly humanist, with the furrowed bookishness of Zesen-Scudéry. In the former, such an endearing aphoristic style; in the latter, such a cramped officiousness.

Ogier combines prejudice with observation, so that myths stand side by side with exact detail, a combination one often meets, still today, in the writing of envoys to the Third World:

(Busbeck, I, 16)

I was astonished, on my way to his house, to observe that the frogs were still croaking in the harsh December chill: the warm sulphur springs that bubbled there allowed such a thing to occur.

(I quote from Wolfram von den Steinen's translation of the Latin original.)

(Busbeck, I, 19)

The janissaries usually came up to me two at a time. If they were allowed into the mess tent, they greeted me with bowed heads, then came up to me quickly, almost running, and grasped the hem of my coat, or my hand, as if to kiss it; I was then presented with a bouquet of hyacinths, or narcissus flowers, after which they again ran, almost as fast, but backward, out the door, that they might not turn their backs to me – an act that they consider discourteous. They then stand silently, their hands folded before their breasts, without pretention, and their eyes fixed upon the ground; in such a state they seem more like monks than soldiers. As soon as one gives them any spare change, however – which is their sole purpose in doing all this – they retreat a final time, with renewed bows, thanks, and blessings.

(Busbeck, I, 42)

A group of mothers, made up of slaves and nobles, arrives from

Brussa. When they hear of the ghastly deed, they become wild with rage and immediately pour out of the city gates, like Bacchantes.

Zesen-Scudéry rely, as well, on archaic notions of the trance state, with expressed reference to the god Pan:
All the priests and priestesses screamed and wailed, in frightening voices . . . in a manner not unlike the ancient Greeks during their triennial religious celebrations, or the Romans, during their festivals held in honor of the god Bacchus (32).

Busbeck writes of taboos on certain foods and their preparations, which are common still today in Africa, and which one would sooner expect to find in Haiti than sixteenth-century Turkey:
(Busbeck, I, 44)
For – to put it succinctly – they would sooner have their tongue ripped out, or their teeth pulled, than eat anything they consider to be unclean, such as frogs, snails, or turtles. The Greeks have the same superstitions. I had taken a young boy into my service, an avowed Greek Orthodox, whom I needed to do my shopping. My other servants could never get him to eat snails. Eventually some snails were set before this one, prepared and seasoned in such a manner that he thought they were some kind of fish, and so he ate them greedily. Once he began to notice the others snickering, however, and some laughing outright, even tossing the empty shells onto his plate, he became livid with anger, withdrew to his room, and proceeded to retch, sob, and generally lament his sorry state, for several hours: not even two months pay would be sufficient to purchase pardon for his sins. For the Greek priests have the following custom: according to the type and magnitude of the sin confessed to them, they determine that a greater or lesser sum is necessary for absolution, which they refuse to grant until the required funds have been given them.
(Busbeck, I, 50)
In this area we also noticed several very large turtles, and in large numbers, which would have made a substantial booty for us, had we not been compelled to honor our Turkish companions. For these would think themselves so unclean, if they touched a turtle, or if they merely saw one on our dinner table, that no amount of water could purify them.

(Busbeck, I, 57)
They find the color black vulgar and wicked. Whoever goes out among them in black dress is held to be either malicious or a bearer of misfortune: once we approached the pashas, in our black clothing, and were greeted with astonishment, our very presence lamented.

One can still encounter such reactions, in Miami, during the Santeria ceremonies performed by exiled Cubans.

In Lohenstein's Roman tragedies – just as in Haiti or New York – one can observe the practice of pillaging.
As Ogier remarks:
(Busbeck, I, 62)
The Turkish soldier is rather fond of torches. Since it is with their aid, as I've mentioned, that one gives oneself greater opportunities for theft. Since the fire can only be stopped by demolishing the adjacent buildings, these too can then be plundered. Because of this the soldiers often secretly torch buildings so that they can plunder more.

(Busbeck, I, 64 f.)
As a rule, the sultan tends to bestow the greatest amount of power on the sons of shepherds or oxen drivers, and these are so far from being ashamed of their parentage as to actually boast of it: they consider it a reflection of their own heightened self-worth, that their fortunes should not depend on any accident of birth. They don't believe, in other words, that one is born with virtue, or that it can be acquired by inheritance, but rather that it is partly given by God and partly attained through education and upbringing, not to mention zeal and effort; and just as no other paternal expertise, whether in music, mathematics, or geometry, can be inherited, so likewise with virtue. Moreover, the soul, they feel, is born not from the paternal seed, which fact, as we know, accounts for the similarity of fathers and sons, but comes rather directly from heaven. As a result all sense of worth, as well as honors and official responsibilities, are held to be rewards based on the degree of virtue displayed, and services rendered. . . .
For us, on the other hand, the custom is quite different: virtue is never given such a free rein, all things being rather entrusted to the position

of birth; and access to the various offices of power is likewise granted according to this same principle.

It is thus the bureaucrat, Busbeck – and not the trio of poets – who clarifies for us the nature of Ibrahim's rise to power on the basis of local norms.

The sixteenth-century Turks had thus already conceived and worked to accomplish that for which even today our instructors are often expelled from their positions.

That is, enlightenment.

And respect for women.

(Busbeck, I, 69)
Also, at that time, he [Soliman] never let himself be seduced by wine, or that disgraceful pederasty that the Turks look upon with so much favor. Thus the malicious have no grounds to slander him, other than a too-fervent attachment to his wife, a tendency that accounts for his forgetfulness, following the death of Mustafa, of the various magical arts and love potions that had been ascribed to her. Once he had taken her as his lawful wife, as is well known, he at no time had contact with any concubine, though no law hindered him from doing so.

No, Soliman seems not to have given in to the practice of pederasty – but, before Roxelane, he did yield to a strong affection for a man, and this with a startling loyalty, even to the point of catastrophe – a loyalty that he then again modulates in his relationship to Roxelane, *une femme impossible* (if one disregards his relationship to Rustahn, his friend's executioner, which relationship seems to mirror, once again, his former friendship).

(Busbeck, III, 116)
Separations are quite common among them, for many reasons, and the man has no trouble finding one. If the woman has not committed some wrong, the dowery gift is generally returned to her. Women, however, have a more difficult time initiating a separation. Among the grounds that the latter may cite include if the husband cheats them out of the support that he is bound by law to provide; or, if he attempts to force her to perform unnatural acts – a misdeed for which

the Turks have no small inclination. She then goes before a judge and declares that she is no longer able to live with her husband; if the judge inquires as to the reason, they do not reply, but rather remove one of their shoes and, holding it out before them, turn it upside down.

Already in Ogier, one finds a description of Soliman's *maquillage*, which we will later witness in more grotesque proportions:
(Busbeck, I, 69)
He sought to improve his poor coloring, which we mentioned above, by the application of purple dyes, both by squeezing out drops, or smearing an oily tincture upon his cheeks, whenever he wished to send off a messenger with a suitably high opinion of his health. He felt that this contributed to his reputation among foreign princes, who might then have more reason to fear him as a thriving, vital adversary. I have myself seen him do this several times.

And what of our own television Turks, Brezhnev, Pompidou, and Nixon?

His time spent at the Turkish court seems to have left Ogier both more tolerant and more ironic:
(Busbeck, I, 76)
Having been officially released, I came on that day to the city of Komorn. After spending several days there, waiting for my fever to subside, I eventually realized that I was free of it, and that the Turkish fever had not dared to occupy a Christian territory.

Achmet, whom we encounter in Lohenstein, also makes an appearance in Ogier:
(Busbeck, III, 89)
Be that as it may, one morning as he walked unawares into the building that houses their offices of government, the divan, he was approached by a man who informed him, in the name of the sultan, that he was to be put to death. This news so little upset Achmet, who was, moreover, in all his affairs a man of the most imperturbable resolve, that it seemed not to concern him at all. He simply refused to let his would-be executioner lay his dirty hands on him – the latter desiring

to carry out his charge right then and there – on the grounds that to do so would be unseemly, Achmet being a man of considerable rank. Thereupon, turning his gaze upon the onlookers, he requested of an honorable man, his friend, in fact, the favor of letting him die by his hands, saying that he would consider this to be a great and final gift. The latter, following several repeated requests, consented. Achmet first informed him, however, to not simply tighten the noose around his neck all at once, but to loosen it at first, so that he might be able to breathe out his last slowly, bit by bit; only then was he to draw the knot to the point of suffocation. His desires are granted. It seems to me that Achmet wished to first sample a taste of death before dying, and to hail the underworld while still alive, rather than die at a single stroke.

Ogier, who suffered wrongs at the hands of the Turks, nonetheless shows them a higher regard than the student Casper, who rarely shows any Turk not in the act of cursing someone:
(Busbeck, III, 113)
And if there happens to be a dog with a litter nearby, they will often go and look for bones, mush, or leftover soup, and they consider it a pious task. I reproached them once on this subject, declaring that they seem more willing to help an unreasoning animal than they would ever be for a creature like themselves, not to mention for a Christian; they replied to the effect that God has given that most splendid instrument, the faculty of reason, to man, but that the latter puts it to poor use, with the result that no misfortune can be said to be entirely fortuitous but rather stems at least in part from some human negligence, and that therefore humans were deserving of a lesser pity. To animals, on the other hand, the creator gave only needs and drives, which they have no choice but to obey, for which reason men have an obligation to give aid and be merciful to them. And therefore they become quite angry if an animal is killed in a cruel way, or if someone takes pleasure in tormenting one.

The Latin-writing Ogier discovers the Latin *miser Sacer* at the Turkish court:
(Busbeck, III, 102)
They [Turkish beggars] are much more rare than ours and are, for the most part, wanderers who take on the pretense of religion, drift-

ing to and fro for the sake of some supposed holiness. Many pretend to have a mental disability; I find the latter cases, in principle, rather charming – that fools and other madcaps, who are doubtless bound for heaven, should be treated as such while still on earth.

Is one not dismayed to find the fourteen-year-old Lohenstein repeatedly using the blunt phrase "Turks get out!" – a variation of the familiar "Jews get out!" that one encounters again today as graffiti on walls and in bathroom stalls?!
Compare Ogier:
(Busbeck, III, 156)
The first thing I noticed was the striking orderliness with which their soldiers conduct themselves . . . everywhere one maintains complete silence and a profound calm, there is no fighting, or even horseplay; one hears no sounds, sees no evidence of mischievousness or drunkenness. On top of this an almost perfect cleanliness reigns: all waste matter is meticulously disposed of, there is nothing offensive to nose or eye – without exception all is either buried or kept from sight. When they do eliminate, each one digs a trench large enough for several men. In this way the entire camp is kept free of filth. And there is also no immoderate use of food or drink and no gambling – the preponderant vice of our own soldiers: the Turks know nothing of playing cards or dice.

Ogier describes filicides and a grandchild's hanging with profound feeling:
(Busbeck, III, 142)
In time Soliman's hatred of Bajazet became increasingly intense. He thus reprimanded him, in a stern letter, reminding him how much leniency he had been shown, as well as the promises the son had made – all the events of the past were dredged up. There is no hint of a conciliatory tone; he is warned to stop provoking his brother by his irresponsible conduct, and to leave off creating difficulties for his father. He goes on to say that he, Soliman, has only a short time left, and that soon thereafter the fate of both sons is to be in God's hands. Until that time he must show some restraint and keep in mind the good of his country and his father's peace of mind.

(Busbeck, IV, 213 f.)
The fate of the father [Bajazet] was also visited upon each of his four children. I mentioned earlier a son whom Bajazet had left behind while still an infant, when he took flight into Amassa, and who was subsequently brought to Brussa by his grandfather, where he was then raised: once the time of Bajazet's death had been fixed, he dispatched a trusted eunuch to Brussa to carry out this son's murder. The eunuch, however, being possessed of a rather mild sensibility, took with him one of the palace guards who was sufficiently hardened to carry out even such a monstrous act as this. As the guard came into the son's chamber, however, and put the rope around his neck, the young boy smiled at him, raised himself up as far as he was able, and with open arms tried to embrace and kiss him. This act so moved the otherwise pitiless man that he was unable to continue, and he fainted. The eunuch, who was standing behind the door and wondering at the delay, entered and found the guard stretched out on the floor, so that he himself was forced to take the child's life, carrying out the official task with which he had been charged.

(Busbeck, III, 117)
Women here frequently desire other women, and the place to make contact is the baths. . . . But only the commoner class is dirtied thereby; the wealthier, as I have mentioned, bathe at home.
Once in one of these baths a highborn woman was overcome with desire for a young girl, the daughter of an unassuming man from Constantinople. And when the noblewoman was unable to attain her wishes by charming and flattering the younger one, she attempted something that, according to our own custom, would be quite outrageous: changing her clothes for those of a man, she rented a house in the vicinity of the father and, claiming to be one of the sultan's servants, a Chaushen, she managed, as neighbors often do, to come into familiar contact with the father. Not long after she broached the subject of marriage to the daughter, and the father seemed not to scorn the proposal. In fact he heartily assented, offering the dower gift he could afford and fixing the day of the wedding. When the handsome bridegroom approached the young bride in their chamber, doffed his turban and began to chat, he was immediately found out: the girl shrieks in fear and runs from the house, crying for her par-

ents. . . . *A few days later she goes before the highest-ranking janissary, who rules the state in the sultan's absence. He inquires in disgust as to how a highborn woman could be so foolish and asks her, in her disgrace, if she is ashamed of her mad plan, which was driven by the basest of lusts. To which she replies: "You clearly know nothing of what love can do – and may you never learn, so help you God."*
The judge cannot suppress his laughter at such a bizarre response; he orders that she be taken away and drowned, this being the outcome of the old witch's little joke.

Ogier isn't above a little moral drum-beating from time to time, nor does he refrain from making cultured cracks about the torture and subsequent death of a subaltern woman.

The commonplace "Turkish torture" makes an appearance in the writing of the diplomat and the student:
(Busbeck, I, 49)
. . . and for his punishment, which was truly dreadful, a metal rod was bored into his anus all the way up to his shoulders, yet he suffered it with the greatest dispassion.

But in any case, Lohenstein's image of the Turks would hardly have suffered if Busbeck's influence had been more pervasive.
It remains noteworthy that the poet, who elsewhere shows himself to be an almost obsessive editor and revisor, never polished up his youthful work after adding Ogier's collection of letters to his library.
Does this suggest that Lohenstein was concerned, in the end, with an altogether different story, if not a different reality?

The magnificent Hammer – also one of the great forgotten writers – who squeezed his history of the Ottoman Empire into more or less Homeric dimensions, had a different take on Soliman and his century:
(Hammer, vol. 3, 2)
Rarely has any age, ancient, medieval, or modern, witnessed such a profusion of excellent, farsighted, and industrious kings as the sixteenth century, all possessing a deep love of science and art, and all

inhabiting the throne during the same period: Henry VIII of England; Francis I of France, glorified both in his native land and abroad; Pope Leo X, overseer of the epoch's dazzling artistic renaissance, and Karl V, under whose rule the great spirits of the Reformation made their deep impressions. All of their names have been duly exalted. What's more, the same period saw the seat of the doge most ably occupied by the worldly wise Andreas Gritti; Russia's future glory firmly established by the conqueror of Astrakhan, Wassili Ivanovich; the welfare of Poland secure, for forty years, under Sigmund I; and lastly, in Asia, two great leaders passed the torch of enlightened rule on to their Eastern brethren – in Persia, Shah Ismail, the founder of the Saffian Empire, and in India Shah Ekber, the greatest of the Grand Moguls. In such illustrious company one can also include, without hesitation, King Soliman.

(Hammer, vol. 3, 3)
Soliman is the name Solomon as it was pronounced by the peoples of Arabia, Persia, and Turkey.
(Hammer, vol. 3, 4)
Just as Timur is recognized as the ruler of the ninth century (or the fourteenth, by our reckoning), so is Soliman the ruler of the tenth (or fifteenth).

And we might extend the parallels still further:
Just as Christopher Marlowe brings Timur – or Tamburlaine – to the sixteenth-century stage, so Lohenstein, in the seventeenth, brings Soliman – Solomon.

(Hammer, vol. 3, 17)
Strong brows, a dark-colored countenance, and a grave expression all gave notice of his fiery temperament, his looks made even more foreboding by his habit of wearing his turban pulled down almost over his eyes.

(Hammer, vol. 3, 454)
In the eyes of his people, Soliman's laws are the most important monument to his greatness, and for this reason they gave him the title Kanuni, that is, the lawgiver, while European writers of history refer to him as the Great, or simply the Magnificent.

(Hammer, vol. 3, 455)
No period of Turkish history, before or since, has shown itself to be so rich in great works of architecture and literature, in scholars of the law, poets, and philologists.

(Hammer, vol. 3, 463)
Soliman's poetry, while not bearing the stamp of genius, is nonetheless marked both by a kingly dignity and the highest ethical principles, and the humane voice that breathes through these works corresponds well to the name Muhibbi, that is, "he who loves in friendship," Soliman's nom de plume.

(Hammer, vol. 3, 471)
Soliman, possessing by nature an open-minded and generous disposition, nevertheless knew the importance of wealth both for war and peacetime projects. At the very beginning of his reign, campaigns in Belgrade and Rhodes necessitated the imposition of an extraordinarily large tax, and immediately prior to his third engagement, at Mohacs, the entire, vast empire was beset with another extraordinarily large wartime collection of revenues – to the tune of fifteen aspers per person, to be collected without regard to means, or religious affiliation. This was the only large taxation under Soliman's reign, there being no need to repeat something that would, moreover, have presented considerable risk, in light of the popular resentment, since the nation's wars had yielded, at great cost, not only new territories, that is, Belgrade and Rhodes, but also repayment for all expenses, both in the form of plunder from the conquered lands, as well as tributes imposed upon the subject peoples.

(Hammer, vol. 3, 485 f.)
The excerpts we have given show that Soliman's moral and policing laws could not help but be popular with the people to whom they were directed, since these were concerned above all with the accessibility of basic needs, that is, food and clothing, and were also lenient, if not indulgent, toward offenses concerning sensual pleasure – were in fact more likely to encourage rather than restrict these latter offenses. If, then, in this regard, Soliman's laws cannot altogether escape the censure of stricter judges of morality, they nonetheless warrant praise both from humanity at large and the statesman.

Soliman was equally lenient with respect to other newly introduced indulgences, concerning which it is unclear whether the Prophet would have condoned or condemned them – such as the use of coffee – and although toward the end of his rule he decreed a ban on the consumption of wine, the fact that wine-drinking establishments were ordered closed attests to the earlier acceptance of this practice as well.

(Hammer, vol. 3, 493)
The treacherous deaths of Ibrahim, a grand vizier, and the pasha Ahmed will forever stain the history of Soliman's great accomplishments, even though the execution of so many other outstanding individuals, talented and powerful men whose deaths must have been carried out, not for reasons of cruelty, but as a necessary safeguard for the maintenance of law and order.

(Hammer, vol. 3, 495)
. . . and so, although on account of his human failings, to include uxoriousness, and a rather harsh strictness toward his sons and grandsons, we may refuse to grant him the title of 'great man,' yet we can hardly fail to call him a great leader; in fact, looking beyond a few lesser crimes and minor failings, he would seem to be more deserving of the title "great" than Constantine, the founder of Constantinople; he, who raised the Ottoman Empire to its highest pinnacle of greatness, power, and splendor, Soliman the lawgiver, the conqueror, the powerful, the magnificent, the Great – the only Ottoman sultan to be given this illustrious epithet, and deservingly so.

A popular scholar adds the following to a modern history text: (Barber, 57)
For several days the sultan's corpse was placed, in his tent, upon the throne. The eyes were left open, the cheeks colored with red and the hair blackened. . . . Once the battle had come to an end and the ruler's tent taken down, the body was placed in a royal coach, in order that his severe, stern countenance might be clearly seen and recognized by his soldiers, who cheered him as he passed.

What does Hammer-Purgstall have to say about the mysterious relationship with Roxelane?

(Hammer, vol. 3, 228)
This one [Soliman], long since under the sway of his most beloved wife, to a greater degree than was fitting for an absolute monarch, became even more so following the death of his friend and protégé Ibrahim – a death most likely orchestrated by Roxelane in the first place. Soon he began, little by little, to turn the reigns of power over to Rustahn, who then ruled not according to his own whims, but after those of the harem.

Hammer-Purgstall has the murder of Mustafa take place on September 21, 1553 – seventeen years after the execution of Ibrahim.

(Hammer, vol. 3, 316)
The prince then mounted a splendidly outfitted horse and, accompanied by several viziers and a host of janissaries, the latter giving him loud applause, made his way to the sultan, who had granted him an audience. But what a shock of horror went through the prince's limbs when he realized that there, inside the tent, was no father, no sultan, and no vizier, but rather the seven mutes, the sultan's bloody henchmen, who had seen to the death of the grand vizier, the protégé, who had strangled the pasha Ibrahim in his sleep. They quickly pounced on him and drew a cord tightly around his throat, the prince calling out in vain upon the sultan, for pity, the father silent behind the thin partition.

(Barber, 54)
Deaf-mutes were often assigned the office of executioner to the king, for which duty they were prepared by having their tongues cut out, and their eardrums bored through. . . .
When everything had been completed and the son whom he had loved lay dead before him, Soliman "gave no evidence of the slightest compassion or remorse."

And later:
(Barber, 54)
A letter was issued from the divan, in white ink on black paper, in which the death of Soliman's son (Mustafa) was acknowledged. Soliman, for his part, cast his turban onto the ground, tore his jewels

from his clothing, and turned over all of the carpets, so that the undersides were visible.

(Hammer, vol. 3, 350)
The sultana Chasseki, the Russian Churrem, i.e., the "merry one," did not long survive . . . the triumph of her son-in-law's reinstatement to the office of grand vizier, following the death of the successor to the throne, and her expectation that one of her own sons would now be next in line; she was entombed at Soliman's site, beneath a dome that bears her name. The burial site of this native Russian who by charm and talent not only raised herself from slavery to become the sultan's wife, but who also, by sheer force of personality, became the sole possessor of his affections long after her youthful beauty had faded; who ruled the state after the dictates of her own will, hearkening to the careful deliberations of her own intelligence and character; who is implicated in the blood-guilty execution of two grand viziers, as well as the filicide that Soliman carried out on Mustafa; and who spread the bloody seeds of mortal conflict between brothers, as a result of which the princes were locked up in the cage of the harem, an event that marked the beginning of the sultan's increasing enervation – this grave site, in the cemetery of Soliman, at the side of the Ottoman Empire's greatest ruler, he whom a woman lorded over as he lorded over the state, with absolute dominion, the grave site of this Russian slave stands in the middle of the imperial city, on the third of Istanbul's seven hills.

Hammer-Purgstall mentions the fairy-tale princess Isabelle only twice, as an aside.
And what of Ibrahim?
(Hammer, vol. 3, 72 f.)
Ibrahim.
The son of a Greek ship's captain from Parga and from the time of his youth a skillful violinist, he was kidnapped at an early age and sold into slavery by Turkish corsairs. Purchased by a widow from near Magnesia, she took upon herself his continuing education, further enhancing his natural gracefulness and talent through dress, ornament, and instruction. Soliman, while still a crown prince, was one day taking a leisurely ride and discovered Ibrahim playing the violin.

He was so taken by the young Greek's liveliness and merry disposition that he immediately made him his constant companion, and when he came to ascend the throne, he selected him to be overseer of the inner pages' chamber, as well as his head falconer.

Ibrahim in Cairo:
(Hammer, vol. 3, 41)
Criers shouted out to the oppressed to make their miseries known; the poor, incarcerated merely because of bad debts, were granted their freedom, and the well-being of the orphans was seen to.

Ibrahim as a general – in comparison to modern war games:
(Hammer, vol. 3, 55)
The march was characterized by the highest orderliness and the strictest discipline; to walk on a freshly sown field, or allow one's horse to trample it, or simply to help oneself to any small item of produce were all offenses punishable by death.

Ibrahim – arrogant:
(Hammer, vol. 3, 134)
If he [Ibrahim] wished it, he could call for a concilium, put Martin Luther on one side of the table, the pope on the other, and compel both to embrace the unity of the Church.

Ibrahim's insolence:
(Hammer, vol. 3, 160 f.)
. . . after the execution of that figure, Ibrahim thought the moment favorable to have himself named sultan and head of the Seraskierate, presumably as the first step on that ladder leading to the highest realms of power. . . .
Twelve years earlier the vizier Ahmed had, while in Egypt, taken on the title of sultan, out of revenge for having had to yield the post of grand vizier to the young protégé Ibrahim; the title, however, did not stick, and Ahmed has instead come to be known, in history, as the Traitor. The fact that at the present time Ibrahim had also assumed the same rank and privilege alarmed Soliman to the possibility that Ibrahim, too, like Ahmed, might become famous for a title other than sultan. In addition to this fear, Soliman was also tormented by a

dream he had had, a nightmare image of intense terror, immediately following the execution of Iskendertschelebi in Bagdad. The wrongly murdered Defterdar appeared to him in an angelic light, hurling reproaches upon him, namely that he had let himself be led by the nose by a faithless, treacherous vizier, to the point of sacrificing an innocent victim. The figure leaped upon Soliman, threatening to strangle him, before he awoke from sleep with a loud cry.

(Hammer, vol. 3, 161)
The impression was deep and lasting, but not, for the moment, so intimidating as to keep him from visiting, with Ibrahim, the graves of the saints, or from praying with him openly at Tebris, or granting him easy access to his palace, or even letting him sleep beneath the same roof. In the course of a year or so, however, the anxiety felt by Soliman in the face of his protégé's growing power and impending betrayal became debilitating, whether this was due to Ibrahim's long-confessed disregard for the Koran and all books of law, or whether as a result of some unknown insult to Soliman's majesty, which the latter wished to keep as secret as Harun Raschid.

Hammer emphasizes the monstrous/unknown factor still further by the following remark:
(Hammer, vol. 3, 161, 690)
Harun Raschid: "If my shirt knew this secret, I would tear it to shreds"; and Philipp II: "If my wig were in on this, I'd burn it."

The playful conflation of sleep and death echoes through the ages:
Bandier reports from Turkey:
You swore that you would not take his life so long as you were alive. So then strangle him in your sleep, since someone sleeping cannot be said to be actually alive, and then you can avenge his disloyalty without breaking your oath.
Scudéry-Zesen flirt with this notion as well, and Sagredo reflects, in 1688:
Che gli insino che se il sonno non e morte effetiva e almeno per il tempo, che se dorme un imagine o una copia tratta da quel originale.

(Hammer, vol. 3, 162)

In any case, one night while in Ramasan, Ibrahim went, as was his custom, to the Serai, to have dinner there with the sultan and afterward sleep in the same chamber with him. The following morning revealed his violently strangled body, and no small evidence of resistance – a century later one could still see traces of the blood he had spilled in the harem.

(Hammer, vol. 3, 162 f.)

Thus ended the life of the powerful, proud Greek, who had raised himself from a violin-playing slave to the lofty rank of imperial statesman, field general, and sultan's primary ally, whose power knew no bounds. First attracting the sultan's attention through his flattery and bold familiarity, his lively spirit and musical talent, he soon proved himself indispensable through brilliant service to the state, both at home and in the field, and finally by force of character and habit he fully subjected the sultan's will to his own. So ended the glorious rise of the grand vizier; the sultan's brother-in-law; beleaguer of Vienna and Güns; conqueror of Tebris and Bagdad; the Seraskierate sultan Ibrahim. He who shared the sultan's table, clothing and bedchamber, and the bed of Soliman's sister; who called Ferdinand his brother; who referred to himself as the cousin of Kaiser Carl and of the sultan; and who, in the end, named himself sultan, a title related to the German Kaiser – like Caesar Augustus wanting to share power with Zeus – and to Julius Caesar, whose history he knew, and with whom he was so presumptuous as to do battle for the glory of historical renown, having had no doubt the same arduous ambitions, the same manner, and even the same day of death – like Julius Caesar, he fell to an assassin's blow on the fifteenth of March (1536). Of the two hundred celebrated viziers of the caliphate, Persian shahs, and Tartar chakanes whose lives are described by the Persian chronicler Chondemir, no fall from power has so echoed down through history as that of Jaser of Barmekid; and of the two hundred viziers that the Ottoman Empire will soon have produced, none has fallen more dramatically and with such force as the protégé Ibrahim.

Reading Soliman's journal, a meager mock-up emerges out of words chosen with a poet's sensitivity:

Woe of Woes!

Severed heads.
Applause.
Kissing of hands.
Graves full of corpses.
Torture.
Reward.
Nothing.
Nothing again.
A march.
Bridges.
Rain.
Cold.
In any case, on July 3, 1535:
The Seraskier [Ibrahim] slept with the kaiser in the palace at Tebris.

Were Soliman and Ibrahim gay?
Can nearness to one another, and a sudden murder, be explained on the basis of erotic motives?
Was Roxelane, the *femme impossible,* another Anna of Edward II, or Proust's Oriane de Guermantes, Cocteau's Coco Chanel, a Sarah Leander of the Turkish court?
Can Lohenstein's often heated language, which recalls the steamier passages of the gay cantor of St. Thomas Rosenmüller, be explained on the basis of a fourteen-year-old's sympathetic bisexuality?
Hammer-Purgstall, the contemporary of Goethe, did not shy away from addressing directly the homosexual conduct of several Turkish sultans. And, at the beginning of Soliman's history, we find the following, deliberate assertion:
(Hammer, vol. 3, 50)
The deposed Wlad received, at Constantinople, a daily pension of fifty aspers – his son, however, a sixteen-year-old, received one hundred; the son's fresh allure had so much more worth than the father's withered dignity. As far as Soliman is concerned, Hammer is expressly undecided:
(Hammer, vol. 3, 40)
The sultan, in an unheard-of gesture, accompanied the fleet in a gal-

ley all the way to the Prince's Islands, where, with much emotion, he took leave of his grand vizier, brother-in-law, and protégé.
(Hammer, vol. 3, 53)
The intimacy of Soliman and Ibrahim with regard to one another was the greatest that any sultan had ever granted his vizier. They not only ate together often – the kaiser thus breaking an old taboo by allowing himself to be observed eating – but often even slept in beds arranged side by side.

Bragadin confirms this assertion:
Ibrahim . . . molto amado dal Sr. dorme spessissimo al Seraio in un letto che si tocca uno ad uno.[4]
Does Hammer forget his own text, or try to forget it?
(vol. 3, 161)
. . . and shared a palace, and bed-chamber . . . with Ibrahim.

With real finesse, the great Hammer describes a historical chain of events from an as-yet-unrevealed psychological perspective:
(vol. 3, 38)
At Constantinople Soliman celebrated the wedding of his sister, in a manner unlike any that city had ever witnessed, to the Grand Vizier Ibrahim Pasha, who in marriage attained the honor of becoming a sultan's relation.
The circumcision of Soliman's sons is likewise described as a wedding.
(vol. 3, 99)
. . . in solemn procession, carrying wedding palms, or so-called circumcision candles.

And finally:
(Hammer, vol. 3, 100 f.)
In an added gesture of good will, Soliman inquired of the grand vizier/protégé:
"Tell me, Ibrahim, which wedding did you find the most magnificent – that of my sister and yourself, or the circumcision of my sons?" To which his favorite immediately replied: "The wedding

---

4. Ibrahim, much enamoured of the sultan, very often slept with him at the Serai, in beds that lay close enough to touch each other.

in which I took part was unlike anything the world has ever seen, nor shall it ever be equaled, so long as the world exists." Soliman, caught somewhat off guard by this unexpected response, asked, "And how is that?" To which Ibrahim answered: "As the host of your wedding, your majesty had no guest that could equal mine – the Padishah of Mecca and Medina, the Solomon of our day, who graced our ceremony by his presence."

Soliman, by drawing a comparison between Ibrahim's marriage and the rite of circumcision, not only elevates the two rituals to a position of archaic equivalence and, in so doing, blurs the distinction between Ibrahim and his own sons – he also hints at the ghostly figure of a marriage *to* Ibrahim.

We will see how the fourteen-year-old Lohenstein takes up this constellation and confirms it, in the example of the loved one's murder.

3.

The students of the Magdelenäum learned little of the historical events of the day from their own little sex pistol Daniel Casper – and of what they did, much was false.

The character of Soliman is misinterpreted – he was hardly plagued by doubt, nor does he repeatedly attempt, waver, leave off, yet still in the end carry out Ibrahim's murder.

The peculiar correspondence between Soliman and Proust's Albertine – the obsessional attachment of a homosexual to a single female – Roxelane – is presupposed in Lohenstein's piece but not developed or represented.

The student suppresses the fact that Soliman allowed his sister to marry his friend Ibrahim.

The marriage with steadfast Isabelle, Soliman's lust, and the sexual jealousy of Ibrahim are all romantic invention.

Rustahn, who became the sultan's favorite after Ibrahim, is killed, within the dramatic machinery, shortly after Ibrahim.

And finally, Soliman's son Mustafa was not murdered before Ibrahim, but seventeen years later, on September 21, 1553.

In the play, however, Mustafa's ghost appears on the stage before Ibrahim's murder.

Asia's entrance onto the stage, accompanied by the vices, is grotesque.
The choir of chained Christians, accompanied by rows of Saracen priests, shows the religious ambivalence surrounding the Turkish court, and of old Byzantium in general.
And yet the play is hardly explained by all this.
The biographical sketches and battle descriptions are more like conventional ornamentation, surprising for a fourteen-year-old's poetic genius – but hardly breathtaking poetry.

Although the play's title is *Ibrahim Bassa*, the main character, at least in terms of stage presence, is Soliman.
Soliman the weakling, that is, who has little in common with Soliman the Great and Magnificent, whose character and accomplishments could have been easily found out by any educated person in the seventeenth century.
What could have driven Lohenstein to credit these falsehoods, or – if he found them in Scudéry-Zesen – what could have motivated him to perpetuate them?

If one removes the political action and brief sketches of local color, there remains a haunting chamber-tragedy.
Its major motif – doubled desire – appears doubly broken and doubly doubled.
Soliman loves two women, Roxelane and Isabelle;
Isabelle is loved by two men;
Ibrahim wavers between adherence to his marital vows and loyalty to his friend;
Soliman between love of women and devotion to men.
And yet:
When Isabelle rebuffs Soliman, he nonetheless pardons his friend and rival Ibrahim.
Once Ibrahim has been slaughtered, and effectively gotten out of the way, Soliman lets the desired Isabelle escape.

There are at least two apocryphal versions of the text, and it would be an impossible task to distill out of the work its formal armature of pubescent attitudes.

Nevertheless a few indications:
How does Isabelle interpret Soliman's advances?
. . . he, who through his affection
elicits my contempt . . . (26).
What does Soliman want with Isabelle?
To dazzle her with majesty's splendor! (37).
Roxelane's statements concerning her relationship to the king are strange enough:
Shaking off her lowly state she charmed her way, artfully, *into the king's bed* (57).
He took me to the altar, instead of into his bed (58).
Soliman, who very likely shared a bed with Ibrahim – at any rate slept in a bed adjacent to him – elevates Roxelane to be his wife, and not his sexual lover; did Lohenstein put his finger on that particularly unfathomable detail – that Soliman's loyalty to the Russian slave had nothing to do with sex and seemed, in fact, to be predicated on its avoidance?
Roxelane says of Ibrahim and Soliman:
Their bond will soon be strengthened (57).
And she speaks of Ibrahim's death as of a redemption.
She weaves the strands of the cabal with a sureness and an ease inexplicable in terms of the play itself (39).

Rustahn has a keen innuendo ready at hand:
Who knows whether Ibrahim lay, faithlessly concealed,
beneath this blanket? (24).

Betrayal as intercourse?
Betrayal through intercourse?
Rustahn denounces Ibrahim before Roxelane:
The king gave kiss upon kiss to Ibrahim. . . .
To which the king's wife replies, straightforwardly:
Ha! Such feminine mercies! (56).

Between Isabelle's remarks on her love relations with Ibrahim, and her feelings of hatred for Soliman, every note on the sadomasochistic scale is sounded.
And, in the end, Isabelle has the same torture fantasies with respect to her husband as she does for the cursed Soliman.

Ibrahim appears in the play as the naive, normal figure whom the sadistic Isabelle has to instruct. He shuns the company of his lenient friend with the following metaphor:
What more could I want, than to kiss the empire's feet
In profound humility and earnest solicitation (54).

It is the metaphor of Poppaea, flirtatiously declining:
(*Agrippina*, 40)
Since now the prince esteems this gold
Of greater worth than it deserves, I praise this most kind affection
And kiss his hands and feet.
Had Ibrahim insisted upon the separate beds, and was Soliman justified in his feelings of neglect?
This would make sense of Ibrahim's remark, to the effect that he hopes to quell the sultan's passion with his blood – since the latter's passion for Isabelle would be intensified by the shedding of Ibrahim's blood.
. . . alas! the sultan's ardor may only
be assuaged by the spilling of my blood (51).

Does Ibrahim mean another passion: a subterranean, underworldly one, as Thomas Mann described it in his novels (– but not in his diaries)?
This might also explain a glaring mistake on the part of the fourteen-year-old (or a printer's canard) – when Soliman, for the last time, condemns his friend to death, Ibrahim is present, in the king's bedchamber, and the young poet does not have him utter a single word.
Did Daniel Casper want to depict him as the normal type, choosing death over the distortion of his hormonal drives?
Soliman, by elevating a woman of the harem, with her claim to a certain level of sexual intercourse, to the rarefied status of sultan's wife, solves the problem in a different fashion.

Soliman's utterances concerning his relationship with Ibrahim are widely divergent. The most innocuous statements lie side by side with contradictory riddles.
The friendship of Ibrahim moves along its old, familiar path

Woe of Woes!

As mists of love give way before the new luster of dynamic reason (52).

In *Sophonisbe*, a work written explicitly on Zesen's model, Scipio, in a similar situation, says to Masanissa:
Once reason's light has driven out the fog (349).

And contradictory:
Who then? that one who drives Soliman, in his rash pursuit, to ruin
And who blows out the flame of our longing?
Can he be living still in whose presence all are bound to perish
And for whom Soliman, so long as he lives, can only slowly die?
(34).
Daniel Casper here fashions a speech alloy: the language of love is imperceptibly blended with the language of rivalry, and the listener is left in the balance – does the kaiser's speech refer to a lover, or a rival?
This thought alone consoles us: that she
Shall never again make love to anyone
Now that Ibrahim is dead (35).
That, however, seems very uncertain.
It is only certain that Ibrahim will not make love ever again.
Who was the object of Soliman's jealousy: Ibrahim or Isabelle? The fourteen-year-old's psychological means leave his characters and his audience in limbo.
And my heart is sorely pained that Ibrahim was more inclined
To heed your wishes than my own. Don't try to dissuade me:
It shall cost him his head (21).

Ibrahim, then, shall lose his life for loving Isabelle more than his friend.
He who held us, heart and mind, in hand and limb,
Knows now our hatred, and the rage of our revenge against him strikes
Like the sea's white crests in their frenzy, dashing on the rocks (38).
And even Ossman speaks on his behalf,
Even Ossman, who shall send him to the scaffold;
Who one moment curses, reviles, and despises

And who at another favors, graces, and crowns,
Now blesses and now condemns (40).

That Ibrahim's fate should be explained as the result of an amorous overture seems clear enough – but was it welcomed or declined?

. . . he, to whom
Our gentle hand now seems too harsh! (40).

Did Ibrahim enjoy it or not?
And was that hand too heavy, which with soothing fingers
Rocked you into gentle sleep? (22).

In spite of the image of the solicitous nurse, Soliman's hand was indeed too heavy, and it is this gently heavy hand that draws Ibrahim not only into mutual masturbation, but – figuratively speaking – draws him into the noose as well.

The ghost of Mustafa's whirl of words draws the entire play into the gay vortex:
Ah! the blood of brave Ibrahim,
Rich in innocence, which you soak up like a sponge
In its ebb and flow, or a reed, now licked by his tongue,
And which writes on the wall and colors the sullied
Shrouds of the dead . . . (74).

The fourteen-year-old's keen awareness of male beauty speaks out quite clearly in the following lines:
O most-cursèd head!
By this panther's claw bereft
Of the charm of its calm brow, and the allure of its
Fair gaze with earnestness admixed!
The noble severity of its eyes' two thrones (76).

The young writer lets Isabelle speak – displaying an authorial cunning already evident in the minnesinger Kaiser Heinrich:

Woe of Woes!

Ride behind me, then, dearest man . . .
as well as Thomas Mann:
O Willo, such arms! – in the *Selected Stories*.

Lohenstein doubtless identifies with his abominable hero: the weakling, but, historically, great and magnificent.
The elephant, the object of a later discourse by the fifteen-year-old, appears at Soliman's court as well.
So we come to the point:
Lohenstein depicts not a weak statesman, but a man torn apart by his passions who is aware of it as it happens.
Like a somnambulist, Lohenstein zeroes in on a problem:
Why does Soliman kill his friend Ibrahim?
And behind this the question:
Was Soliman gay?
And behind this the question of puberty:
Am I gay?
And the question every child ponders:
Why did my friend betray me?
Can we take it this far?
Might a compiler, on the lookout for subterranean materials, conjecture that the *Ibrahim Bassa* is a gay love story, a vehicle for the working out of Lohenstein's own pubescent conflicts?
Is there a baroque sexual outlook?
What took place in the dormitories of the Magdalenäum?
A structural history of the variations of sexual practice is poorly documented.
Just go into any institute for the sexual sciences and try to find something on, say, the laws regarding homosexual conduct in the People's Republic of China.
Let alone the conduct of students in the seventeenth century.
In Grimmelshausen there is a transvestite episode that borders on the lewd.
Gerhard Spellerberg once told me of a student condemned to death in Breslau for getting a girl pregnant.
The townspeople petitioned to save the young man's life.
He was put to death.

And yet a harsh sexual morality doesn't preclude harsh sexual practices.

During the Third Reich, when any same-sex tryst might have meant the concentration camp, the public restrooms and hostels were, during air raids, filled to the brim.

Can we justly compare the comparisons of pricks and pissing contests of our own youth with the conditions of a Breslau boarding school in the period following the Thirty Years War?

Johann Beer, in *Jan Rebu*, writes of the German composer Rosenmüller:

Because I was a German, he was extraordinarily fond of me and would, every week, bring me twenty ducats.

A remark that is usually overlooked.

It becomes still more significant when one considers that Rosenmüller, the cantor of St. Thomas, was forced to give up his post on charges of pederasty, wandered over the face of Europe in a state of dependency, surviving only by the good will of aristocratic benefactors.

In *Ibrahim Bassa* it is a question of an event that takes place between dream and death. So the friendship of Soliman and Ibrahim develops by means of dream images that become images of death and that end in death.

4.

Excursus: on the motif of the severed head.

Not only the preadolescent's longing for death – but also the limb-rending rage of the deceived, psychic anguish and an alarming recognition of the rules of realpolitik; all this can be found not only in the wise Hammer, but also in Meyer's *Encyclopedia* (1876), and the *Encyclopedia Britannica* (1965), under the heading: Soliman.

Lohenstein injects an archaic death-rite into Scudéry-Zesen's florid account;

Lohenstein gives us – multiply refracted in the course of the play – one of the most unwavering accounts of an execution ever written.

One might compare it with Melville's subtle dodge in *Billy Budd*, with Ernst Jünger's gutless preciosity, or Che Guevara's rapturous lies.

Woe of Woes!

The fourteen-year-old adds to this the debilitating rhythm of condemnation/pardon, and condemnation/execution.

One apocryphal reading of the play might see it as the portrayal of a leather fetishist – Isabelle and Soliman's sadistic relationship. The fairy princess becomes transformed, in such a light, into a precursor of Epicharis; Soliman possesses, to an even greater degree, decidedly Neronian characteristics.

Mustafa's ghost says it best:

The murderous palace is a violent lion's den – a lair of leopard men and man-beasts, a theater for plays of sanctification and the fulfillment of blood contracts.

The student selected the proper landscape. His references to milk and breasts, animal husbandry, and violent tenderness all find a natural home in Turkey: eight thousand years ago, in the Anatolian city of Çatal Hüyük, goddesses were often represented with sharp beaks piercing out of their breasts.

One need only read the play in the order in which it was written to observe how pervasive the sadomasochistic component truly is, the teenager's drunken lust for scenes of death and execution. Soliman says of his dearest comrade:

Treacherous! has ever slave or lowly servant
So come to rule the one he should obey?
To trample the head of him at whose feet
He ought to humbly serve? (22).

Nor does Ibrahim show any more restraint:

Ha! Ibrahim won't falter –
With spirit intact I'll gnaw the hard knot
That's soon to choke me; with deep joy
Thrust the blunt dagger into my scarred chest;
Kiss the sharp axe, the sword,
And hangman poised to hack and pierce my flesh.
So constant I'll remain, so true to the tyrant's wish (23).

And Isabelle, the Christian:

Come, slash away;
Carve, sever the limbs from my body;
How lucky for me

That you should do me such a service.
Come, shove hard into my breast
Till my blood and soul gush forth – let me die like Christ (27).

And the Christian slaves:
Will they put us in chains?
Boil us in seething oil? (31).
etc., etc.
The whole catalog of savage cruelties wrought by the savage Turks, which echoes still in Mozart.
Soliman:
She shall have the king himself at her disposal, a mere slave (47).

And, in sharper recognition of the ambivalence of S-M:
Isabelle:
Granting us chains instead of freedom, then, I trust.

Isabelle wishes to be united in death with Ibrahim:
So then! cut me up as well, my body strangled at his side
Then cook and scorch the lungs and heart,
To quench along with me your tongue's bloody craving! (70).

The culinary art is identical with the art of torture. Proust will rerecognize this, as will Marcel's cook Françoise.
In a gesture of nuanced sadistic courtesy, Soliman sends the severed head of Ibrahim to the longed-for Isabelle, the dead man's wife, as a token of her release from prison.
Nor is the sexual accent lost on Isabelle, for she immediately inquires:
Is this then a mark of gratitude, a sweet morning-gift?
So Stendhal ends *Le Rouge et le noir*:
Un grand nombre de prêtres escortaient la bière et, à l'insu de tous, seule dans sa voiture drapée, elle porta sur ses genoux la tête de l'homme qu'elle avait tant aimé.[5]
Theodore Ziolkowski tells me that Goethe kept a plaster cast of the skull of Raphael in his study.

5. A large number of priests accompanied the bier, while, unknown to all, alone in her covered carriage, she carried on her knees the head of the man she had so dearly loved.

Woe of Woes!

Goethe's poem on the skull of Schiller is well known.
Dr. François Duvalier, the former president of Haiti, kept the severed head of a former enemy on ice – so the story goes – which he would display on his writing table when meeting with rivals.
In *The History of the Ottoman Empire*, by Goethe's contemporary Hammer, one finds a severed head on almost every page.
And, since Lohenstein wasn't able to read Hammer, the fact that the severed head is every bit as much of a topos in his play, as in the later chronicle of Turkish history, speaks to the depth of his psychological insights.
If, upon the bloody head of Ibrahim . . .
So the sultan's sturdy heel shall
Soon walk upon your own . . .
Come Carl, come, come, your head will soon bare its teeth
And shriek upon the sun . . .
The head of Zellib, resting on a stake . . .
Soliman's diary also refers to head-hunting, and head games:
July 7, 1521.
Dispatched a hundred-head occupation force.
July 8.
The heads are set on stakes along the side of the road.
July 15.
. . . and sixty severed heads . . .
August 31, 1526.
The kaiser on his golden throne is paid homage by his beys and viziers; two thousand prisoners decapitated, their heads brought into the divan; hard rain.
(Hammer, vol. 3, III)
"*Everyone* (Hammer quotes the Turkish historian Pechevi) *took courage and shouted: I'll take off the fiend's head, or give my own.*"
(Doesn't Goethe's poem on the head of Schiller now take on an uncanny aura?)
And hair, too, has its role in Stendhal, the leatherman's close-cropped cut.
The haughty Mathilde de la Mole has surrendered herself to Julien.
The mother and chambermaid are awakened.
Julien flees and cuts himself in the process.

Il sentit tomber quelque chose sur ses mains, c'était tout un coté des cheveux de Mathilde, qu'elle avait coupé et qu'elle lui jetait.[6]
Busbeck (I, 25) observes, in Serbia:
In like manner, hair was often hung at grave sites, put there by women and young girls following the burial of their loved ones, as a sign of grief.
And Lohenstein:
and Persia's crown, resting on Ottoman's abundant hair . . . (25).
And, I read in Busbeck:
Whatever is above their head does not concern them, they claim, and so they often leave to mice and rats their upper stories (I, 21).
Frazer (whom Freud, following a cursory reading, often cites) declares:
(*Taboo and the Perils of the Soul*, 252)
The head [is] sacred because a spirit resides in it.
Objection to hav(ing) anyone overhead (254).
When the head is sacred, the cutting of the hair becomes a difficult and dangerous operation (258).
Lohenstein has the figure of a rebel take the stage and speak for the rights of the Moors, women, and the citizenry; the poet's sympathies clearly lie with the underground-insurgent Ibrahim, the nonnoble parvenu.
(The nonnoble Daniel Casper signs his *Ibrahim Bassa Daniel Casper von Nimptsch.*)

The Thirty Years War had just come to an end.
We know nothing of what the fourteen-year-old experienced, saw, or heard.
How can I, a human, attempt to thwart what is human? (49)
says Ibrahim.
And yet isn't it astonishing that the young Lohenstein can so quickly incorporate themes of loyalty to authority and belief in justice into his work.
The Christian slaves sing:
And thus God succours the oppressed

6. He felt something touch his hands – it was a large mass of Mathilde's hair, which she had cut off and which she now let fall upon him.

Yet lets the tyrant be,
Though he put a thorn into his eye
And drain and bleed us of our strength
That we might be of use
Until that time when he
Will visit on our many sins
And send You, the slave of his revenge,
The messenger of his wakefulness,
And shed the glowing rage and fury of his ire (32).

The mufti decides that the kaiser, provided he is asleep, may lawfully break his oath and take the life of his friend Ibrahim, since Soliman cannot be said to be alive when sleeping.
The Senses discuss the point of faith with Sleep.
They reach the same conclusion:
The more one, while he lives, gives in to sleep
The less alive he truly is.
One may think so. That wasn't the question.
The teenager is mustier than the mufti – and more diplomatic. And this half-hearted gnomic sentence, thunderously delivered by the figures of the omniscient celestial allegory, implies, of course, the death of Ibrahim, the beloved protagonist.
Lohenstein here becomes something of an armchair culprit, much like Seneca, later, in *Agrippina* and *Epicharis*.
However:
He may have been referring to Al-Ghazali, who wrote the following in the twelfth century:
Even when you are troubled, do not seek to induce sleep by artificial means or make your bed overly soft; for sleep severs our connection to life.
As in the Koran:
Allah takes all souls back to himself at the time of their death, and even those not yet dead, during their sleep (sura XXXIX, 43).
While Heraclitus is of the following opinion:
That which inheres in things is always the same: living and dead, waking and sleeping, young and old. For the one is changed into the other and then changes again back into its former state.

A man lights a candle in the night, during which time he is dead but yet lives. In sleep, while the light of his eyes is extinguished, he comes into contact with the dead; awake he brushes up against those who sleep.

We witness, in the young Daniel, the outbreak of sadistic fixations:
The figure of Isabelle, beside herself:
Let it turn out as it will. He'll gladly suffer it
Rather than see us cut off from one another
Out of service to the king – but no!
What am I saying? Will I carry him
On this my tattered vessel into torture, fear, and death
That thunder cloud brooding black upon him? (48).

Lohenstein again gives expression to psychic strata through verbal means:
The raging lions tear off "heads."
The Voices of Humanity never seem to get a "head."
I fall silent! This head is the cause of my sorrow (76).
O respected head (77).

5.
Excursus: On the ghost of Mustafa

Prior to the death of his beloved Ibrahim, there appears before Soliman the ghost of Mustafa, the son he had had murdered – wrongly: the son he *will have* murdered, since Ibrahim dies on March 15, 1536, and Mustafa on September 21, 1553, some seventeen years later.
In Zesen-Scudéry Ibrahim is pardoned – and therefore no ghost of warning need appear.
Lohenstein distinguishes himself from Zesen by the fact that he is more faithful to the historical truth, by having Ibrahim executed. In the same breath, however – consciously or no – he inserts a new, unsubstantiated, and fabulous tale.
It must have been a matter of some deliberation for the student, then, to insist upon an inconsequential, poetic alteration of the facts at the very point in the story where he had earlier, in the foreword, congratulated himself for reestablishing the true account of events.

Woe of Woes!

Lohenstein, by this distortion of the historical record, anticipates a dramatic and psychological move he will make again, at the age of thirty, in the *Agrippina:*
The ghost of Britannicus appears to Nero before the latter attempts his matricide.
Further parallels between the youthful play and the masterpiece:
The mufti, who reinterprets Soliman's oath for life as a license to kill, has the sultana Roxelane to thank for his priestly office, just as Seneca has Agrippina, for his post as tutor.
Both works contain a world leader's attempt, fraught with deferrals, to carry out the murder of a cherished, close friend.
Each attempted murder is connected with water – the ancient shamanistic means of purification.
Agrippina is ordered on board a death ship;
Ibrahim is apprehended upon his return from a journey by water.
Further correspondences are still more microscopic.
The *Ibrahim Bassa* marks the beginning of a kaleidoscopic playfulness, in which sensations, rituals, and modes of conduct collapse into a sort of rhetorical shorthand and which continues down through Lohenstein's final work, the *Ibrahim Sultan*.

Soliman:
It is custom to leave it
Upon the poor player whether or not to tear up the cards (36).

Paris, in the *Agrippina*:
One laughs when a poor player rips the deck in two.
Soliman:
My son! my Mustafa! my Mustafa! forgive me;
Forgive me! / God help me! What is it? Heaven help us!
Does this ghostly image not alarm you? (74).
Nero:
Woe! mother, no! forgive me! forgive your wicked son!
Wash away in pain and blood the scars of that deed most vile!
Is your curse upon me? Yet forgive! (100).
Is that the intent? is there sense in it? as the Thalian theater patroness Klein Erna would ask.
I think so.

Hammer, the writer of history, leaves us an important observation (before Frazer and Freud), which proves how both murders (of the son Mustafa and the brother Britannicus) are bound up with magical practices:

(Hammer, vol. 3, 383)
Among the Parthians the murder of a father, child, or brother was held to be a solemn kingly prerogative. Among the Romans paternal affection succumbed, under Brutus, to the republican ax, and under Manlius, to blood feuds. Mithridates had more than one of his sons killed, and Philipp of Macedonia poisoned his son Demetrius. The filicide Shah Abbas the Great trod in their footsteps. The violent deaths of the sons of Constantine, of Peter the Great and Philipp II, cover the pages of their annals. Among the Ottomans there was Sultan Murad I and the sad example of the execution of his son, Savedshi. Soliman, however, far outbid this one. Prior to the death of Sultan Mustafa, Sultan Bahezid, and their sons, he twice dipped his hand into receptacles containing the blood of his children and grandchildren.

Through the historically false insertion of the ghost of the murdered Mustafa, the figure of Ibrahim – in comparison with Agrippina – functions within a totally different psychological perspective.
Is Ibrahim like Agrippina?
Are the emperor Nero's incestuous longings similar to those of Soliman?
Is Ibrahim like Mustafa?
What does Hammer say? That the wedding candles were brought, by Soliman, to the circumcision rites of his son Mustafa. Can one see here, vaguely shimmering in the work of Lohenstein and Hammer, a possible explanation for the as yet so insufficiently explained rite of circumcision?
A subterranean antimarriage?
Antilove?
Anti-incest?
A hymen that the father tears, violently, away from the son.
A deadly transaction between father and son – not a castration – transfigured into the rite of circumcision, in order that social life might continue?

In Hammer, too, Soliman brings his son's circumcision into the closest possible relation to his friendship with Ibrahim.

The accounts also state that Soliman was frightened by a dream vision prior to the death of Ibrahim (Hammer, vol. 3, 161).

It was Lohenstein's flash of genius to give this dream the name of Mustafa.

Ogier reports that the mufti was drawn into Mustafa's murder, just as Seneca was drawn into the murder of Agrippina, and the mufti – in the fiction – into the murder of Ibrahim.

The historically misplaced remorse over the murder of Mustafa is a product of Lohenstein's model, Scudéry-Zesen, which Lohenstein then transforms into remorse over the murder of Ibrahim.

In the account of Scudéry-Zesen, the soldiers want to tear out Rustahn's heart following Ibrahim's execution; Lohenstein, too, lets Rustahn's heart be torn out – at Soliman's command, following Ibrahim's execution.

The emperor Nero wants to kill Agrippina when the spirit of Britannicus appears and reminds him of his earlier fratricide; Nero had an incestuous relationship with both.

King Soliman wants to kill Ibrahim, the ghost of Mustafa appears.... Britannicus, like Mustafa, was a pretender to the throne.

Mustafa dies, too, not as a son but as a pretender to the throne, the rival of his brother, the legitimate heir to power – like so many other brothers of the Ottoman king.

Sigmund Freud bequeathed us several intriguing psychic puzzles, as well as a rather baroque attempt at an explanation of the psychogenesis of deviant sexual behavior – the Oedipus complex, a theory that he, unfortunately, like so many religiously inclined scientists, elevated to the status of a dogma.

Freud made plausible, as it were, the way in which the image of the desired mother may insert itself between a man and an unknown female and occasion a neurotic impotence.

There then comes a leap for which Freud's patients paid through their noses, which turned Fliess into a sworn enemy, and which rendered Freud himself powerless before the bust of Oedipus, at the University of Vienna – and which, in the Third World, left many homosexuals subject to amateurish methods of treatment.

Namely, the young boy becomes gay, sick.
(Just when exactly did the Psychoanalytic Institute strike homosexuality from its list of mental disorders?)
The gay patient now gives himself over to the feared image of the Freudian, castrating father.
The image of this father functions as an erection- and ejaculation-enabling signal.
And that is where Freud leaves us in the lurch.
Lohenstein and his ghosts take us further, earlier.
His dramas contain few open representations of homosexuality, the more numerous references – in Greek or Latin – being repressed into the notes.
Consciously or unconsciously, Lohenstein uses metaphors:
Knives tear into intestines *(Agrippina)*; soft fingers rock to sleep *(Ibrahim Bassa)*; Ibrahim chews knots.
He likens the murder of Ibrahim to that of Mustafa, just as Hammer-Purgstall likens the wedding-circumcision of Mustafa and his father to the latter's friendship to Ibrahim.
Thus a homosexual longs after the image of his father – whose could be more near?
Oedipus comes to grief because he yearns for his father, having slain him.
Lohenstein played out, in his dramatic work, the various combinations of the Greek model:
Oedipus's love for his mother in the *Agrippina*; the murder of the stepfather; Orestes' matricide; Medea's murder of her children in *Sophonisbe* and *Cleopatra*; and, once again, the murder of a son in Lohenstein's final work, *Ibrahim Sultan*.

The poetic clarification of the pleasure taken by men in other men, through its transference onto the Turkish relation of son to father, and of father to son, presupposes all the constellations we have noted in *Ibrahim Bassa*, in the fourteen-year-old's tragedy.
I said earlier that Lohenstein surpasses Freud.
What does the student say of dreams and their interpretation?
To strive after the sense and pattern
Of innocuous events
Is a labor without result (59).

And thus Lohenstein raises himself out of a good deal of murky babble that, stemming from the hermetic tradition, found its way into his century, at the same time anticipating the results of more recent research in the study of dreams.

REVOLUTION AS RESTORATION
Jean-Nicholas-Arthur Rimbaud, Ethnologist

Hamburg, August 1979

The right is again predominant.
Is this one of the reasons that Matthes and Seitz are reissuing the works of Rimbaud?
Is Rimbaud a precursor of the so-called Fascist Literature of the First Order, as Walter Heist classified the work of Sartre, Camus, Genet, etc.?
France has never wavered in its admiration for Rimbaud.
There are something like three thousand volumes of secondary literature, Rimbaudian studies, and of course the literary papacy's various coloratures.
Paul Claudel:
Arthur was a mystic in savage dress, a deep spring oozing up through the soaked earth.
Jean Paul Sartre:
Rimbaud's attempt to become his own progenitor . . . etc., etc.
Rimbaud is all but ignored by the powerful West German families who determine the market value of literary works.
Twenty years ago, Rimbaud failed to make Fischer's list of the *100 Exempla Classica*, a judgment upheld by *Die Zeit* only last year, whose list included the *Nibelungenlied*; the Italian *Espresso* put

together a counterlist, in which the *Nibelungenlied* was replaced by Rimbaud.
In the land of poets and thinkers, myths still predominate on the subject of modernity's youngest poet:
Genius.
Flung lice at passersby.
Had a relationship with Verlaine, which the older man played up as a love affair.
Fell silent at eighteen.
Slave trader.
Lost a limb. –
Rumors – always vague.
What holds them together?
In part, the fact that few people take the trouble of familiarizing themselves with the major texts of European literature – let alone those of the Third World, which are rarely even spoken of.
At least three of our more prominent critics of lyric poetry could hardly translate, from the French, more than the exclamatory *rien ne va plus;* which is not to say that the "visionary" attitude isn't practiced here.
I know two German literary critics who claim that they can review a work without reading it. A third lets the popular Rimbaud caricature escape his lips: Looking back, pointing forward.

The new German edition of Rimbaud's work has a bonus attraction:
The poet's account of his experiences in Ogaden, Ethiopia.
How does the revolutionary iconoclast and prominent member of the avant-garde behave himself in the Third World?
Fundamental being meets the most modern of tongues.
What's the outcome?
The Ogadenes are at constant war with their neighbors, and among themselves.
They dress themselves in relatively clean clothing.
An observation that squares with those of Helmut Schmidt in Santo Domingo – and that, in the latest edition, is sharpened to:
The Ogadenes . . . are neatly dressed.
How is this possible?

One of the revolutionary's early wishes is for retirement.
Je ne veux pas de place. Je serai rentier. I don't want any position. I'll be a pensioner, the ten-year-old writes in a school essay.
And yet this expression, too, has been spliced, like so many of the poet's utterances.
Je serai rentier has its source in a sociological daydream. Rimbaud longs for educational instruction as it was administered in the early sixteenth century.
The sixteen-year-old composes, in meticulously patinated French, a letter of the poet Charles d'Orléans to Louis XI, in which he pens archaisms, in the manner of the expressionists, on the poet Villon.
Sixty years later, Paul Zech will attempt something similar, in Germany.

Rimbaud on Villon:
tous ces pauvres enfants secs et noirs comme escouvillons, qui ne voient de pain qu'aux fenêtres, que l'hiver emmitoufle d'onglée, ont choisi maistre François pour mère nourricière (176).[1]

Paul Zech on Villon:
High shelves contained all the weighty volumes, sitting row upon row, far too heavy for the thin little tyke. At seven years old, however, he had already learned to read Greek and Latin and had, with the help of the monastic writer Sabeau, become an accomplished calligraphist, as well as an astonishingly skillful miniaturist. The chaplain was very pleased with the progress of his young protégé, and one fine summer evening he set him down in the calash and brought him to the school of the Faculté des Arts.
Villon was thirteen at the time. He had the look of a fine young man of sixteen, a small moustache was already sprouting above his upper lip, his voice was full and resonant. He was immediately accepted into the choir, learned to play the virginal and effortlessly dispensed with his daily chores. The institute's rector was a man in his mid-

1. . . . . all these poor children, dried and blackened like chimney-sweeps, who see bread only on other people's windows, whom the winter brutalizes until their fingers are swollen from the cold, all these have chosen Master François for a loving mother.

fifties, rather rotund, and, as was not uncommon in those days nor counter to the dictates of the higher authorities, he engaged his entrusted young pupil in a relationship somewhat more than strictly professional.

One expects to find the shrill tones of the nihilist and not, as in the Pléiade edition, the fourteen-year-old's Latin verse.
He was incredibly well read, having read "every" book, and he often leaves his French commentators far behind, as when for instance the latter fail to see the many allusive references to murder and assassination in the hashish poems and their connection to the Assassins, who killed in a state of hashish intoxication; Rimbaud knew these connections, these etymologies.

A little more bookishness and stealthiness would be welcome on the part of commentators in general.
The transition from seed to dust elicits from Rimbaud the most striking stylistic gems, and which reveal the archpoet as a *poeta doctus*.
The line *Ithyphalliques et pioupiesques*[2] in *Le Coeur du Pitre* receives the comment in the Pléiade edition, page 891,
Obscène. Le phallus est dressé.[3]
Sure – anyone who's seen ithyphallic statues in an Egyptian museum knows that; the prefix *ithys*, or *euthys*, meaning "straight, upright" however, can also have the meaning "direct, straightforward," or "just."
Ithyphallic verse is scanned like the rhythm of the bobbing wooden phalloi put on parade during bacchic festivals:
_ ∪ | _ ∪ | _ ∪
in which the final long/short seems to be the decisive foot, in terms of obscenity. (Bayer, Willige *Sophocles: Tragedies and Fragments* [Munich, 1966]; see also Korzeniewski's *Greek Meter*. Intriguingly, Bruno Snell, the progressive, fails to treat ithyphallic verse in his *Greek Meter*. Korzeniewski, however, gives the omission ample attention.)

2. Ithyphallic and "at attention."
3. Obscene. The phallus is erect.

The warlike gestures of young soldiers are transformed by Rimbaud into a classical metre, the ithyphallic, which in classical Greece was modeled precisely on these same gestures.
The connection is insinuated by two other appearances, as in a dance, of the line *Ithyphalliques et pioupiesques* – and at the emphatic end-position, which traditionally determines the meter: The line is lengthened by one long/short, as in several other poems written in this rhythm:
_ ⌣ | _ ⌣ | _ ⌣ | _ ⌣

In four groups of poems Rimbaud summed up the impulses to modern lyric, expanding their limits toward the first inner monologue on pubescent conduct and intellectuality.
The great lyric discoveries had been made:
In 1751 the French *Encyclopedia* began to appear, in which Diderot asserts the coincidence of genius and immorality, in effect granting genius the rights to savagery.
Free rhythms, it is usually agreed, are first mastered by Klopstock.
In 1758, in *Omnipresent*:
That which no eye saw, nor ear heard
Entered no heart, though it vainly struggled
And thirsted after God, after God
And the infinite;
. . .

Earth, from whose dust
The first of men was molded,
Where I lived my first life
And in whose lap I'll be consumed
And rise again.
And in 1759, in *On the Earnest Pleasures of Country Life*, known more widely as *A Spring Celebration*:
Nor into the ocean of the many worlds
Will I go down, drifting suspended
Where the first creatures, the jubilant chorus of the sons of light
Pray on, pray on and in their rapture pass away.
In the 1798 *Fragments*, and the 1801 *Heinrich von Ofterdingen*, Novalis announces that:

The magician is a poet. (1851)
The true poet is omniscient. (1852)
Poets are "prophetic, magical beings."
The poet is pure steel, hard as flint.
In 1827 Victor Hugo writes an introduction to his dramatic work *Cromwell.*
This introduction comes to serve as the manifesto of French romanticism; one can still perceive its effects in Rimbaud:
Dans la pensée des modernes, au contraire, le grotesque a un rôle immense.[4]
The idea for the prose poems *Spleen de Paris* and *Paradis Artificiels* came to Baudelaire in 1855.
Rimbaud will admire them.
With his forty-page *Poëme du Haschisch,* Baudelaire will also have an influence on Lautréamont and his essayistic *Poésies.*
Walt Whitman's *Leaves of Grass* is published, at the author's expense, in 1855, and the *Fleurs du Mal,* containing the poem *Correspondances,* which introduces synaesthesia into modern lyric – a decisive move both for the so-called symbolists as well as the surrealists of the next century – appears in 1857.
Sainte, the almost sense-less, dark, strictly premeditated poem of Stéphane Mallarmé, is written in 1865.
Between 1868 and 1870, Isidore Ducasse proclaims collages, scientific jargon, and essayism to be *Poésies.*
Rimbaud knew all this, or almost all of it, citing and paraphrasing it.
At age fifteen he writes
Les Etrennes des Orphélins:
La chambre est pleine d'ombre. On entend vaguement
De deux enfants le triste et doux chuchotement.
Leur front se penche, encore alourdi par le rêve,
Sous le long rideau blanc qui tremble et se soulève . . .
Au dehors, les oiseaux se rapprochent, frileux;
Leur aile s'engourdit sous le ton gris des cieux;
Et la nouvelle Année, à la suite brumeuse,

---

4. By contrast, the grotesque plays an immense part in the thought of the moderns.

Laissant traînant les plis de sa robe neigeuse,
Sourit avec des pleurs et chante en grelottant. (3)
Walther Küchler translates these lines in the (now out of print)
Lambert Schneider edition of 1946:
The room is full of shadows. One hears, soft and faint,
The sad whispering of two children.
Their heads hang heavy with sleep,
Behind a long white curtain, gently fluttering.
Outside, the birds stay close against the cold,
In the cold sky's gray their wings are stiffened.
The new year, still in the misty veil of the old,
Trailing the folds of its snowy robe,
Laughs between its tears and, trembling, sings.

This mendacity has its tradition, too. It's in Sade, Hugo, Lautréamont.
The beginning:
La chambre est pleine d'ombre
is a citation of a line from Hugo, in Pauvres Gens:
Le logis est plein d'ombres,
in which the plural *shadows* seems kitschier than Rimbaud's more objective, singular *shade*.
The next poem – Sensation – is one of the most perfect poems in all of world literature.

Sensation
Par les soirs bleus d'été, j'irai dans les sentiers,
Picotés par les blés, fouler l'herbe menue:
Rêveur, j'en sentirai la fraîcheur à mes pieds.
Je laisserai le vent baigner ma tête nue.

Je ne parlerai pas, je ne penserai rien:
Mais l'amour infini me montera dans l'âme,
Et j'irai loin, bien loin, comme un bohémien,
Par la nature, – heureux comme avec une femme.[5]

5. On blue summer nights I'll walk down narrow paths,
   Stung by the wheat, trampling the thin grass:

I do not know of an adequate German translation.
Perhaps Büchner had, a half-century prior to Rimbaud, put similar impressions to words:
Open field. Danton.
Open field. Leonce and Valerio.
Open field. Woyzeck: On and on! on and on! Silent music!
Lenz: . . . or he stood still and lay his head upon the moss, half closing his eyes, and it withdrew quite far from him, the earth softened and shrunk until it was as small as a wandering star, then plunged into a thundering stream, where he was sent churning along within the flood.

Rimbaud was sixteen at the time he wrote this, in 1870.
He had also discovered the Parnassians.
In 1866, C. Mendès and Xavier de Richard had published *Le Parnasse Contemporain*.
Rimbaud knew the poems of Coppée.
Vers le passé had been printed in the first issue of *Parnasse*.
Coppée writes:
Quand je vais dans les champs, par les beaux soirs d'été
Au grand air rafraichir mes tempes . . . [6]
Compared to Rimbaud:
Par les soirs bleus d'été, j'irai dans les sentiers,
Picoté par les blés, fouler l'herbe menue.

The blue nights were borrowed from Mérat, yet neither Mérat nor Coppée achieves the classical precision of the young revolutionary. An exemplary alienation combined with a light earnestness, worldly posturing to the tune of beer hall rhythms.

Dreamer, I'll know its soothing coolness at my feet.
I'll let the wind bathe my naked head.

I won't speak, I'll think of nothing:
But a love eternal will well up in my soul,
And I'll wander, far off, like a bohemian
Into nature – and be blissful, as with a woman.

6. When I go out into the fields, refreshing my brow
In the open air, on pleasant summer evenings.

Neither Isidore Ducasse, Verlaine, nor Whitman is able to pull that off; one detects it occasionally in Nietzsche, Wedekind, Morgenstern, Ringelnatz, and their later progeny Olga Rinnebach and T. A. Odemann.
The ancient art of trilling.
Arnaut Daniel began in this way, and Rutebeuf – in Villon it comes from the rendering yard; in folk songs from the occasion of battles:
Le Roi René de guerre revient
Il tient ses tripes à la main.[7]
That proletarian elegance spoken of by Lautréamont and Jean Genet.
Gottfried Benn calls it both simple and refined.
Théodore de Banville thought that the poem should not be published in the second *Parnasse*.

The year 1870 saw the sixteen-year-old crystallizing, in his verse, the various exempla of preadolescent thought:
Anticlericalism and a frisky maliciousness in *Le Châtiment de Tartuffe*;
an anticlericalism that he develops still further in *Un coeur sous une soutane*.
A caricaturish piece of prose, yet nevertheless a precise depiction of pubescent demeanor from the pen of the young teen, a gentle satiric teasing of his own lyrical subject, like Baudelaire's albatross:
Jésus! Joseph! Jésus! Marie!
C'est comme une aile de condor
Assoupissant celui qui prie!
Ça nous pénètre et nous endort!
. . .
La fin est trop intérieure et trop suave; je la conserve dans le tabernacle de mon âme. A la prochaine sortie, je lirai cela à ma divine et odorante Thimothina.
Attendons dans le calme et le receuillement. (199 f.)

7. When King René comes home from the front,
He'll carry his guts in his hand.

Paul Zech translates:
O Jesus, Joseph, Holy Mary:
Like a condor's wing the wind
Swirls about us, when we bend our knee
Before it, dazed by that sweet scent.
. . .

The end seems to me too interior, and too pleasant. I will preserve it in my soul's tabernacle. During my next visit I shall read it aloud to my angelic, fragrant Thimothina.

The cult of youth – in *Soleil et Chair*, which first had the pompous title *Credo in unam*.
Je regrette le temps de l'antique jeunesse.[8]
This becomes, in Wedekind:
I slaughtered my aunt,
She was old and weak,
But you, my judge, you are pursuing
My shining youth, this beautiful youth.

In Brecht:
In the soft light, Jacob Applegoat
Did in his father and his mother.
He hid them both in the linen closet
And stayed at home alone, all by himself.

Clouds drifted lazily across the sky
The summer wind blew mild against the house
Where he himself sat,
Just seven days ago a child.

In Benn, this same motif becomes a "Dorian World":
Above, the white team of horses, and the well-built figures known as demigods: Victory and Might and Force and the names of the Great Sea, below a rattling: chains, slaves . . .

8. I long for the time of antique youth.

Hugo von Hofmannsthal – to roll back the clock again:
Many must die there, below
Where the ships' heavy rudders cleave the deep.

Je regrette les temps de l'antique jeunesse.
I long for the times of antique youth.
Parce qu'il était fort, l'Homme était chaste et doux.
Because he was strong, man was pure and kind.
Et qu'il a rabougri, comme une idole au feu
Son corps Olympien aux servitudes sales.
And now he's bowed, like an idol to the flame
His Olympian body to menial tasks.

In *Venus Anadyomène* he tries out the effect of clinical-cruel shock, in high song:
Belle hideusement d'un ulcère à l'anus.
Repulsively beautiful, an ulcer in her anus.

Le reparties de Nina – the machismo of a Gallic student from a bourgeois family.
Morts de quatre vingt douze – The Dead of (17)92 recalls de Sade's speech on Marat and Le Pelletier, of 1793:
Rimbaud – at sixteen:
O Soldats que la Mort a semés, noble Amante,
Pour les régénérer dans tous les vieux sillons.
Sade the editor – at fifty-three:
Unique déesse des Français, sainte et divine LIBERTE . . . *ce seront des lois, des exemples, des vertus et des hommes que nous donnerons à la terre étonnée.*
Rimbaud:
O soldiers whom death dispersed, illustrious lover,
To bring them back to life in all the old furrows.
Sade:
Sole goddess of the French, sacred and divine liberty . . . it will be the laws, examples, virtues, and men that we give back to the astonished earth.
Nonsense poetry:
Death sows the soldiers as a "lover," to "regenerate" them in all the old furrows.

Who, or what, shall be regenerated?
The furrows or the soldiers?
Sade would like to give men back to the astonished earth.
It should be an image of life:
To give laws, examples, virtues, and men to the astonished world.
To give laws, examples, virtues, and men to the *earth,* would mean to bury them, like corpses.
He means both – and implies both, by a Freudian mechanism.
But what does Rimbaud mean?
The tone is one of patriotic celebration, *Anciens Combattants,* and National Socialism:
And still you prevailed!
The tone of the uprising in Granada, 1979:
Fertilizing our revolution.[9]

Dreaming of winter – a tender frivolity, the sought after insect is also in Sardou – is a topos of elegant, erotic boulevard comedies. The sleeper in the valley – *Le Dormeur du val* – Rimbaud never saw him lying down. The two impressive drops of blood were gotten from a quick read.
He wrote the poem in October 1870. At this point in time there was no Battle of Charleville.
Rimbaud knew the motif from George Sand's *Lélia,* and her Stenio also rests on Cresson bleu.
Leconte de Lisle cites the soon-to-become-famous scene, and the name Stenio, in his *Poèmes antiques,* and Léon Dierx published, in the first *Parnasse,* a poem of the same theme.
Rimbaud probably also knew Hugo's lines:
L'enfant avait reçu deux balles dans la tête.
The child took two shots in the head,
when he wrote:
Il a deux trous rouges au coté droit.
He has two red holes on his right side.
A hanged-man's ball – *Bal des Pendus* – sour kitsch in contrast to the orphans' syrupy kitsch.
Sour kitsch, known to Schiller as well as Heine.
In the German classical author's cadaver fantasy, and in the Romantic-journalist's *Belsazer.*

9. In English in original.

Le Forgeron – the smith – a poem that, like others, deigns to ingratiate itself with the turbulent masses.
A limp-wristed admiration for raw power:
ce maraud de forge aux énormes épaules
this scoundrel of the forge, with enormous shoulders
Le bras sur un marteau gigantesque, effrayant
His arm wielding a massive, terrifying hammer
D'ivresse et de grandeur, le front vaste, riant
In drunkenness and grandeur, his forehead broad, laughing
Which is later transformed into the Reich's Congress, *Kunst am Bau,* and Françoise Sagan.
Nothing is more dangerous than when a decadent gets folksy:
Nous sommes
Pour les grands temps nouveaux . . .
Où l'homme forgera du matin jusqu'au soir
We are for the great new days,
When man will forge, from morning to night.

Good prospects for the workers, shoved down their throats by a lover of workers.
But of course such lofty revolutionary principles are sometimes transformed into operational procedures, as in the Chile of Allende, or the New Jewel Movement.[10]
Even Rudi Dutschke drafted a utopia where the workers, for the sake of the movement, live in factories.

On August 29, 1870, Rimbaud leaves Charleville.
On the 31st, he arrives in Paris, Gare du Nord.
His ticket, however, was good only as far as Saint Quentin.
He is picked up by the police.
He has no place to live, and no job. He is taken to the Dépôt de la Préfecture de Paris.
He lives through the fall of the emperor, on September 4, 1870, behind bars.
His friend, the rhetorician Izambard, gets him off on bail.
Rimbaud accompanies him to Douai, where Izambard has been publishing a republican journal.

10. In English in original.

Rimbaud writes a piece requesting arms for the Nationalgarde, in a tone somewhere between Saint-Just and the Chilean MIR.

He also publishes the minutes of a republican meeting in the Rue d'Esquerchin.

1870 – a year in the life of the sixteen-year-old poet:
Medieval preciosity.
A reader of all books.
Whininess and moderation.
Satiric, anticlerical, and lewd.
Arrogant and ingratiating, machismo and queenishness.
Boulevard humor and republican pomp, sketches of provincial revolutionaries comical by virtue of being exact replications.

Two of the seventeen-year-old's letters have become known in literary history as the "visionary" letters.
The new German Rimbaud edition begins:
First letter of the "visionary," to Georges Izambard
Charleville, May 13, 1871

Cher Monsieur!
You are once again a professor. One is indebted to society, as you put it. Once again you find yourself a member of the instructing body: back on your proper path. – For my part, I, too, hold myself to this principle: I let myself, in cynical fashion, be supported; I disinter the school's old idiots: I give them anything I can think of that is stupid, foul, or nasty, in word and deed: I'm paid for this service in pints and glasses. Stat mater dolorosa, dum pendet filius. – I am obliged to society, it's true; – and I'm in the right. You, too, are in the right, for the moment. At bottom, you see in your principles only subjective poetry: your obstinate determination to be readmitted to the academic trough – pardon the expression! – proves that only too well. But you'll end up merely satisfied, having done nothing, and having had no desire to do anything. Not counting the fact that your subjective poetry will always strike me as terribly insipid. One day, I hope – and many others have the same hope – I shall recognize, in your principles, an objective poetry, and that I shall do so with more earnestness than you would ever be capable of feeling!

I will be a worker: this is the thought that restrains me when mad rage pushes me toward the front lines, in Paris – where so many workers perish even as I write to you! Work now? No, never; I am on strike.
For now I squander my time in as base a manner as possible. Why? I want to be a poet, and I'm striving to become a seer: you wouldn't understand this at all, and I could never explain it to you. It's a matter of attaining to the unknown by the disarrangement of all the senses. The suffering is great, but one must be strong, having been born a poet, which I know myself to be. This isn't at all my fault. It's wrong to say: I think. Better to say: one thinks me. Pardon the play on words. I is an other. So much the worse for the wood that finds itself a violin, and scorn for those sluggish fools who quibble over matters in which they are totally ignorant!
You are no professor to me. I offer you this: is it a satire, as you would say? Or poetry? As always, a piece of fantasy. – But, I beg of you, don't underline it with a pencil, or think too much about it:
The Crucified Heart
My sad heart foams in rage upon the deck
. . .
It isn't meaningless.
Send your reply to: M. Deverrière, for A. R.
Bonjour de coeur,
A. Rimbaud

Je veux être poète, et je travaille à me rendre Voyant.
I want to be a poet, and I'm striving to become a seer.
C'est faux de dire: Je pense: on devrait dire on me pense.
It's wrong to say: I think. Better to say: one thinks me.
Je est un autre.
I is an other.
What's the source of this idea of the poet as visionary, or seer, combined with the notion of an egoless, unself-conscious production?
Should both be explained by reference to the use of hashish and absinthe?
It's possible that Rimbaud traveled a third time to Paris on April 19, 1871, and stayed until May 3.

The first "visionary letter" would then have been composed ten days after this trip – a week before the *semaine sanglante*.[11]
Was it during this period that he familiarized himself with narcotic substances?
Antoine Adam notes:
The idea that the poet is a visionary was hardly discovered by Rimbaud. A progressive journal, Le Mouvement, published an essay by Henri du Cleuzio, on January 1, 1862, which developed this notion: The true poet is a seer.
Nor does du Cleuzio claim to have discovered the idea. He claims that it is originally German, being one of the principles of German romanticism.

He's right. But this doesn't explain the resurgence of the concept ten years later, at the time of the Paris Commune, in the work of Rimbaud the labor supporter.
Many of Rimbaud's texts may be read as descriptions, or sketches, of journeys of initiation, spiritual voyages like those written on Mohammed, or Christ; Quirinus Kuhlmann composed a wholly imaginary trip to Jerusalem, and the ship of the *Bateau Ivre*, the ego-as-vessel, can be understood as the old sacred vehicle of initiation used by shamans for a water journey.
(For Ibsen's Peer Gynt as well, the horse is the vehicle of his mother's death-journey, Selma Lagerlöf's wild geese make a shamanistic air-journey possible for the young Nils Holgersson, and Strindberg envisioned a spiritual journey to Damascus.)
Prophecy, hashish, surrender of the ego, and cursing, are all once again brought together by the poet in the hemp poem *Matinée d'Ivresse* – that is, when he highlights the word *assassins*.
The Assassins, from which our concept is derived, were an Islamic secret society that carried out its murders, for religious reasons, under the influence of hashish.
W. S. Burroughs wrote a piece on it.
In *Voyelles*, too, one can find allusions to Eliphas Lévi's *History of Magic*; Rimbaud will later quote Michelet's *Sorcière*, and in the *Alchimie du verbe* there is a sentence that refers to magical sophisms.

11. I.e., the "bloody week."

All of this proves a close engagement with magical thinking on the part of the young materialist, an involvement that one can also discern in the tropes of Che Guevara, or – in a concrete way – in the embalming rhetoric of Lenin and Mao Tse-tung.

The leftist intellectual's schizophrenic relationship to the workers is most apparent in the letter to Izambard – probably without the young visionary realizing it:

je me fais cyniquement entretenir; je déterre d'anciens imbéciles de collège: tout ce que je puis inventer de bête, de sale, de mauvais, en action et en paroles, je le leur livre: on me paie en bocks et en filles.

I let myself, in cynical fashion, be supported; I disinter the school's old idiots: I give them anything I can think of that is stupid, foul, or nasty, in word and deed: I'm paid for this service in pints and glasses.

Je serai un travailleur: c'est l'idée qui me retient, quand les colères folles me poussent vers la bataille de Paris, – où tant de travailleurs meurent pourtant encore tandis que je vous écris! Travailler maintenant, jamais, jamais; je suis en grève!

I will be a worker: this is the thought that restrains me when the mad fools push me toward the front lines, in Paris – where so many workers perish even as I write to you! Work now? No, never; I am on strike.

To Paul Demeny:
Mais il s'agit de faire âme monstrueuse: à l'instar des comprachicos, quoi! Imaginez un homme s'implantant et se cultivant des verrues sur le visage.

But it is a question of making one's soul into something monstrous: in the manner of a thief of children, what! Imagine a man planting and growing warts on his face.

Antoine Adam's comments:
The comprachicos – a word that in Spanish means one who deals in children – appear in L'Homme qui rit *(The laughing man), by Victor Hugo (1869). These are kidnappers who try to physically deform their victims, in order to make monsters out of them.*

I suspect that these mutilations were carried out in order that the children might be put to use as beggars, a practice that still occurs in the poorest societies.

Imagine a man planting and growing warts on his face.
Mallarmé turns this thought on its head, when he says of Rimbaud:
His was a poetic operation performed on a living body.
The mention of mistreatment of children is also a reference to Lautréamont, specifically to the first *Song of Maldoror,* first published in 1868.
The all-encompassing language of all things, of social progress, visionary experience, and criminality soon gives way to, and is repressed by, a mundane Franco-African terminology of commerce: conversion rates, capital accumulation, and intentions of marriage.
A year earlier, another young French intellectual joined the ranks of the quasi bourgeoisie: Isidore Ducasse, the Count de Lautréamont, who, after penning the hallucinations of Maldoror, published, in two volumes, his views on poetry, *Poésies,* prior to his death at the age of twenty-four.
In these essays Ducasse issues a retraction of his entire work. (Whether this is done playfully or cynically is hard to tell. But why should this radical turn toward classicism and respectability be done in jest? The gesture seems to be a topos in the life of a rebel – we can observe it in the Marquis de Sade as well as in Georg Büchner.)
Rimbaud's visionary letters take up issues that Ducasse had introduced in the songs of Maldoror, and which he then, in the *Poésies,* renounces.
Did Rimbaud know the work of Lautréamont?
It is never mentioned outright.
But Rimbaud also never mentions Aeschylus or Jules Verne, whom he paraphrases nonetheless.
The first *Song of Maldoror* appeared as a book, in Paris (1868), as well as in Bordeaux (1869), in the anthology *Parfums de l'ame.* Songs two through six were printed in 1870, but were not distributed.
A few samples made their way into the literary circles.
The two-volume *Poésies* was published in Paris in 1870.
Did Rimbaud come to know *Maldoror* via Izambard's library, during that period in which he read "every" book?

Did he know Ducasse's *Poésies*, that most vehement renunciation of romanticism, from the *Nouveau Parnasse*, when, in 1871, he composed his own vehement avowal of romanticism in the visionary letters?

Ducasse, in *Poésies* I:

Since Racine, poetry has not progressed one millimeter. In fact it has regressed.

Rimbaud praises Racine too, in his letter to Demeny – but sarcastically:

the great, the powerful, the pure Racine.

. . .

After Racine, French drama becomes mildewed.

Not only Racine, however, but the entire classical tradition, which Ducasse wishes to restore, would be demolished by Rimbaud.

Both refer to the dictionary of the Academy.

Ducasse:

Villemain's introduction to the Dictionaire de l'Académie *will outlive the novels of Walter Scott, Fenimore Cooper, will outlive every possible, every imaginable novel.*

Rimbaud:

Since, besides, every word is an in-sight, one day a universal language shall arise! One must already be an academic – more putrid than a fossil – to make a dictionary.

Rimbaud's conceit is already known to Ducasse:

what! has it not been shown that a tail, which has been cut from a rat and placed on the back of another living rat, can be successfully transplanted?

Rimbaud:

What! Imagine a man planting and growing warts on his face.

The question of the influence of Lautréamont on Rimbaud's work should be followed by the question of the influence of Whitman. Rimbaud writes, in the second visionary letter:

Ineffable torture où il a besoin de toute la foi, de toute la force surhumain, où il devient entre tous le grand malade, le grand criminel, le grand maudit – et le suprême savant!

An unspeakable torture, where he needs complete faith and superhuman power, where he'll be viewed as the great sick man, the great criminal, greatly cursed – and supremely wise!
And Antoine Adam, in the Pléiade edition:
There is a striking resemblance between this statement and that of Walt Whitman:
If you are degraded, criminal, sick – so will I be, out of love for you.
But it seems clear that Rimbaud, in Charleville in May 1871, could not have had any familiarity with the work of Whitman.
Is it so clear? Following the three trips to Paris and having thoroughly surveyed the library of his friend Izambard, the teacher of rhetoric?
Whitman's *Leaves of Grass* was published in 1855. It appeared in England in 1868. In 1872 it was very much in style in France.
Couldn't the young avant-gardists have read him a year earlier?
But perhaps these are merely elective affinities, *correspondances*.
Both Rimbaud and Whitman were decadents with a weakness for the simple man, both were bisexual.
It seems to me quite sure, however, that Rimbaud and Verlaine read Whitman's work, at the latest, during their 1872 trip to England.
What else would they have read, if not the great avant-garde American poet?!

Lautréamont writes:
Judgments of poetry have more worth than poetry.
Rimbaud transforms this opinion into poetry.
Les Poètes de sept ans – a scintillating poem on early puberty and precocious poets.
Ce qu'on dit au poète à propos de fleurs – a treatise on metaphors, and on phainopoieia, as Pound would have called it, in poetic form. In the *Alchimie du verbe* Rimbaud sketches once again – as in the lyrical prose of the *Saison en enfer* – the development of a lyrical subject, whose origins are intimated in the *Poètes de sept ans*.
A se renfermer dans la fraîcheur des latrines . . .
To enclose oneself in the freshness of latrines . . .

Urinary rites and modern literature!
Marcel Proust:
A small room that smelled of irises. It was set aside for a specific and vulgar purpose, and often served me as a place of refuge, it being the only room which I was allowed to lock, and thus offering an imperturbable solitude to my various pursuits: reading, dreaming, tears, and pleasure.
The smell of urine, and reflections on it, find their way into the entire body of Proust's work.
Rimbaud:
Il pensait là tranquille en livrant ses narines.
And there he meditated in peace, with open nostrils.

In the midst of the most bizarre engagements, in the *Orgie Parisienne* – one suddenly finds a synaesthetic moment, Baudelaire's *Correspondances* makes its presence felt, Huysmann's Des Esseintes and Proust's Charlus, both of whom have their model in Lord Montesquiou.

Voyelles

A noir, E blanc, I rouge, U vert, O bleu: voyelles,
Je dirai quelque jour vos naissances latentes:
A, noir corset velu des mouches éclatantes
Qui bombinent autour des puanteurs cruelles,

Golfes d'ombre; E, candeurs des vapeurs et des tentes,
Lances des glaciers fiers, rois blancs, frissons d'ombelles;
I, pourpres, sang craché, rire des lèvres belles
Dans la colère ou les ivresses pénitentes;

U, cycles, vibrements divins des mers virides,
Paix des pâtis semés d'animaux, paix des rides
Que l'alchimie imprime aux grands fronts studieux;

O, suprême Clairon plein des strideurs étranges,
Silences traversés des mondes et des Anges:
– O l'Oméga, rayon violet de Ses Yeux![12]

12. A black, E white, I red, U green, O blue: vowels,

The Gay Critic

German translation by Stefan George:

Vokale

A schwarz E weiss I rot U grün O blau – vokale
Einst werd ich euren dunklen ursprung offenbaren:
A: schwarzer sammtiger panzer dichter mückenscharen
Die über grausem stanke schwirren; Schattentale;

E: helligkeit von dämpfen und gespannten leinen;
Speer stolzer gletscher, blanker fürsten, wehn von dolden;
I: purpurn ausgespienes blut, gelach der Holden
Im zorn und in der trunkenheit der peinen;

U: räder, grünlicher gewässer göttlich kreisen,
Ruh herdenübersäter weiden, ruh der Weisen
Auf deren stirne schwarzkunst drückt das mal;

O: seltsames gezisch erhabener posaunen,
Einöden durch die erd- und himmelsgeister raunen:
Omega – ihrer augen veilchenblauer strahl.

> Someday I will reveal your latent births:
> A, black fuzzy corset of brilliant flies
> Buzzing around nasty stenches,
>
> Gulfs of darkness; E, white innocences of vapors and of tents,
> Lances of proud glaciers, white kings, shudders of umbels;
> I, dark reds, coughed-up blood, laughter of lips beautiful
> In anger or repentant raptures;
>
> U, cycles, divine vibrations of greening seas,
> Peace of pastures sown with animals, peace of the furrows
> Which alchemy draws on large, studious brows;
>
> O, supreme clarion full of alien shrillnesses,
> Silences traversed by worlds and angels:
> O, Omega, deep blue ray of His Eyes!

See also 164 n. 1.

There are, fundamentally, two interpretations:
Either the poet is indulging in a scornful game with the reader; magical obscurity is just a ruse – Rimbaud is merely painting the pretty colors of a primer – or he is seriously attempting to translate mystical experiences, studies of magic and hashish into a new type of language.
Antoine Adam suspects that it is not the sounds of the vowels that led Rimbaud to associate them with the different colors, but rather the forms of the letters on the page, and the things or creatures that their shapes were able to evoke, which in turn suggest the colors: for example, A – fly – black.
This is a distinction – not a fundamentally new reading.

I believe that Rimbaud's interest in magical and mystical connections is undeniable, and with this his interest in a universal language, in the world-as-language.
(Mallarmé expressed this same notion in his idea of the book as world – Mallarmé, whom Rimbaud met for the first time, according to Henri Mondor and G. Jean-Aubry, on June 1, 1872, at a dinner held at the Vilains Bonshommes.)
Rimbaud writes, in the second visionary letter:
Du reste, toute parole étant idée, le temps d'un langage universel viendra . . . Cette langue sera de l'âme pour l'âme, résumant tout, parfums, sons, couleurs, de la pensée accrochant la pensée et tirant.
What's more, all speech being an idea, the day of a universal language shall come . . . This language will be spoken from one soul to another, encompassing all things: perfumes, sounds, colors; a product of thought, latching onto thought and drawing it forth.

And in the *Alchimie du verbe* he formulates his own interpretation of the poem *Voyelles*:
J'inventai la couleur des voyelles! . . .
Je réglai la forme et le mouvement de chaque consonne, et, avec des rhythmes instinctifs, je me flattai d'inventer un verbe poétique accessible, un jour ou l'autre, à tous les sens.[13]

13. I invented the color of vowels! . . .
I fixed the form and the movement of each consonant, and, with instinctive rhythms, I judged myself capable of discovering, one day or another, a poetic word accessible to all the senses. – TRANS.

The impressionists as well, and especially Seurat, wanted to reduce the world to a scheme of colors and ABCs, a scheme that, in the case of pointillism, finds an abstract, mechanical application. Seurat paints with premixed colors, not letting himself be influenced by any momentary effects of light.

No poem is so closely identified with the poet as *Le Bateau ivre* – *The Drunken Boat* – and none has so furthered his literary influence, right down to Brecht:

Comme je descendais des Fleuves impassibles,
Je ne me sentis guidé par les haleurs:
Des Peaux-Rouges criards les avaient pris pour cibles
Les ayant cloués nus aux poteaux de couleurs.[14]

One can well imagine that the poetically revolutionary, the lyrically prophetic element must be accompanied by a flood of images, tonal innovations, and mad verbal gestures:
Marlowe's *Tamburlaine,* Kuhlmann's *Kühlpsalter,* Hölderlin's translation of Sophocles. One must concede, with this, the existence of a complementary moment of calculation, the astounding mastery of rules and topoi. Magic and mathematics, manic vision and cool deliberation always come in pairs.

Rimbaud instructs us further concerning the function of revolution and prophecy, on paper.

Just as revolutions in flesh and blood atrophy into citations of July 14, speeches by Marat, Festivals to the Higher Being, monuments, triumphal arches, and superhighways, so the *Bateau ivre* consists in a metal jacket of citations, in a passion for reading and a literary mastery almost inconceivable for a seventeen-year-old. At the time of writing the poem, Rimbaud had no firsthand knowledge of Africa, America, or even the sea.

Des Peaux-Rouge criards les avaient pris pour cibles
Les ayant cloués nus aux poteaux de couleurs.

Chateaubriand describes a squirrel that some Indians had fastened to colorful stakes.

14. As I descended down impassable rivers,
    I felt myself no longer guided by the boatmen:
    The redskins had taken them for targets
    And nailed them naked to painted poles.

In the *Magasin pittoresque* the rope towers sing, just as in the *Bateau ivre,* and the *péninsules démarrés,* as well, are drawn from the floating promontories and drifting foothills of chapter 23 of the *Magasin pittoresque.*
. . . *où, flottaison blême*
Et ravie, un noyé pensif parfois descend[15]
refers to the pensive dead of Hugo's *Tristesse d'Olympio* and the cadavers floating in the Bay of Bengal, from Jules Verne's *20,000 Leagues under the Sea.*
Et j'ai vu quelquefois ce que l'homme a cru voir.[16]
The fact that Rimbaud was so well versed in the Bible leads Antoine Adam to derive this line from St. Paul. Once again, however, one need look no further than Jules Verne's *20,000 Leagues: I want to gaze upon that which no man has ever seen!*
A sentence that will reappear in Rimbaud's letters from Ethiopia.
The singing fish were the rage of the day.
Rimbaud knew them from Jules Verne and the *Magasin pittoresque.*
The quotations in Rimbaud's emphatic poem come so thick and fast that one might speak of a collage made up of fragments of Chateaubriand, the *Magasin pittoresque,* Victor Hugo, Aeschylus, Poe, Vigny, and the Bible – a collage technique that had been practiced by Lautréamont three years earlier.

The rhetorical procedure of the *Bateau ivre* has been characterized as absolute metaphor.
Rimbaud no longer draws comparisons – I am like a drunken boat.
Nor does he set up a metaphor: I, a drunken boat.
Thus he no longer sets one reality over against another in the course of the poem.
He sets himself up as an absolute, other reality.
(*On me pense.*
One thinks me.
I is an other.

15. where, on the surface, translucent
    And violated, a pensive drowned body often drifts.
16. And I sometimes saw what men before me thought they saw.

Je est un autre.)
That doesn't hinder him from falling back on traditional, manneristic methods, however:
The same within the same – the mirrored in the mirror:
Et dès lors, je me suis baigné dans le Poème
De la mer.
And from that time on, I bathed myself in the poem of the sea.
The poet, who is a drunken boat, or more precisely: a poem with the title *Le Bateau ivre,* a ship poem, bathes *itself* in the poem of the sea. This assertion becomes doubled once more when, toward the end of the work, the drunken boat, which has the entire time spoken as if it were floating, exclaims:
ô que j'aille à la mer!
O, that I might go to the sea!
Concerning which I am unable to judge whether Rimbaud means also to imply some destruction, as is the case in the German phrase *ins Wasser gehen* (to go into water).
The drunken boat sees itself mirrored once again, like a toy boat in a European pond:
Si je désire une eau d'Europe, c'est la flache
Noire et froide où vers le crépuscule embaumé
Un enfant accroupi plein de tristesse, lâche
Un bâteau frêle comme un papillon de mai.[17]
(The closing simile: *like a May butterfly,* I can only guess is some sort of formal joke.)
Cutting loose from reality.
The poet himself more like a poetic form.
Mirrorings.
Mirror inversions.
Panthères a peaux
D'hommes![18]
Leopard men, panther men, black-magic guilds and assassins are as old as mankind.

17. If I long for one of Europe's waters, it would be the pond
    Black and cold where on balmy sunset
    A child kneeling, full of sorrow, sets off
    A boat, frail like a May butterfly.
18. Panthers in human skins!

In *The Three Brothers*, a cave painting approximately twenty thousand years old, a magician is cloaked, like a leatherman, in an animal skin.
Rimbaud inverts this archaic image:
Panthères à peaux d'hommes.

By contrast the *Vers nouveaux et chansons*, with their similarities to Verlaine, have a lesser effect. Sensuality and early fascism.
Qu'est-ce pour nous, mon coeur, que les nappes de sang
What are these lakes of blood to us, my heart.
. . .
Tout à la guerre, à la vengeance, à la terreur,
Mon Esprit . . . Ah! passez,
Républiques de ce monde! Des empereurs,
Des régiments, des colons, des peuples, assez!
. . .
Jamais nous ne travaillerons.
The poem is often explained as the bitter wish of a disappointed revolutionary. The refusal to work, however, and thereby allow whole peoples to be murdered – this was long since the postulate of other classes, and long before the rise of the proletariat.
Rimbaud's lyrics become so obscure that now, one hundred years after their publication, they can hardly be deciphered.
The seer sees, at this point, only for himself.
Many things come to mean anything – a fate he shares with James Joyce.
For me, the *Bonne Pensée du matin* exudes an inexplicable, intimate magic.

Une Saison en enfer is the first of two soul-features, two inner monologues – amazing works, stylistically unequaled, and terrifying.
That which, in the visionary letters, had disguised itself as a refusal to participate in systematic labor –
Je suis en grève
is transformed into a bare hatred of those who do:
J'ai horreur de tous les métiers.
Maîtres et ouvriers, tous paysans, ignobles.

I despise all manner of employment.
Masters and laborers, all farmers, base types.
. . .
La race inférieure a tout couvert.
The inferior race has covered all.
Down to the thoroughly inhumane democracy of the *Illuminations* –
which is lacking in the most recent German edition.
. . . *au service des plus monstrueuses exploitations industrielles et militaires.*[19]
Even though these lines were first written in 1876 and are in some ways a product of Rimbaud's experience in the Dutch Foreign Legion – it is an immoral poem, and sings flirtatiously of brutality and the cynicism of mercenaries.
A few years later, in Ethiopia, Rimbaud will join the same outfit, under no compulsion.
The quotation stems from his lips like a transplanted wart.

These texts are accompanied by letters, a melodrama in Brussels, shots, operations, and legal proceedings.
The eighteen-year-old keeps company with the older Verlaine – not an old man, as one often imagines, he was himself only twenty-eight.

Verlaine to Rimbaud:
Mon frère (brother-plainly),[20] *j'espère bien. Ça va bien. Tu seras content.*
Are these lines written sincerely, in good spirits?
Brother-plainly?
Marriage in the background, and Christianity as a second bad conscience.
Is there not evidence of a professional jealousy that has been converted into high respect?
And a revealing passage:

19. In service to the most monstrous military and industrial exploitations.
20. In the following passages, those sections that are left unitalicized appear in English in the original.

Je suis ton old cunt ever open *ou* opened, *je n'ai pas là mes verbes irreguliers.*
I didn't understand this, but I suspect an important obscenity.
Is *cunt* not an obscene word for "vagina"?
The 1971 Oxford Dictionary has no entry listing, a source that isn't, as a rule, overly squeamish.
Likewise *The New American Webster Dictionary* and the *Encyclopedia Britannica*.
The bourgeois Burcka's pocket dictionary of 1832 makes no such fuss:
Cunt: the female genitalia.
This has implications, moreover – which are in no way supplied us by Antoine Adam, in the Pléiade edition.
Rimbaud was widely addressed as Miss Rimbaud.
I am your old cunt ever open or opened, I don't have my irregular verbs with me –
reverses this perception.

In the next letter there is the threat of a suicide blackmail.
Rimbaud's response of July 4 has been harshly judged, mostly from a misperception of his role as Mademoiselle Rimbaud.

Henri Guillemin:
Rimbaud writes like a prostitute who has been abandoned by one of her patrons, promising to be nice if the wealthy gentleman should take her back.
Verlaine as a wealthy gentleman?
Rimbaud's letter of July 5 isn't any more impressive.

Even the bitter malice of the letter of July 7 – Verlaine has not yet put up bail for him – is exemplary as a love/hate letter, well composed in comparison with Verlaine's listlessness:
So you want to return to London! You have no idea how everyone will receive you there! And the faces that Andrieu and the others would make if they were to see us back together. Still I'll be brave. Only tell me your true intentions. Do you wish to come back on account of me? And on what day?

Rimbaud's *Déclaration à la Police* shows him to be pretty shaken up, but still wary, and lucid – after all, Verlaine had shot him; on

July 17, 1873, a bullet had to be removed from the young man's wrist.

Verlaine, however, begins:

Je suis arrivé a Bruxelles depuis quatre jours, malheureux et désespéré.

The shabby style is the perfect complement to his shabby actions:

I have been in Brussels for four days, miserable and despairing.

A stylistic lapse in Rimbaud's second declaration reveals, it seems to me, his attachment to Verlaine.

He says of his beloved:

Il était fort surexcité.

He was greatly aroused.

Verlaine is imprisoned.
Rimbaud travels.
Brussels, Paris.
In 1874, in London again.
In 1875, Stuttgart, Milan, Paris, Charleville.
He takes piano lessons.
His mother rents a piano.
Vienna, Bavaria, France, Brussels.
In May 1876 he joins the Dutch Foreign Legion.
Rotterdam, Java.
On July 19 he arrives in Batavia.
Samarang, Salitaga.
On August 15 he is proclaimed a deserter.
Queenstown, Cork, Liverpool, Le Havre, Paris, Charleville.
On May 19 Rimbaud is in Bremen.
He wants to enlist in the United States Navy, and writes to the American consulate:
Late a teacher of sciences and languages.
Recently deserted from the 47e Regiment of the French Army.[21]
Stockholm, Copenhagen, Norway, Marseille, Rome, Charleville.
Hamburg, Roche.
On October 20, 1878, he travels to Switzerland.
Lugano, Milan, Genoa, Alexandria, Cyprus.
He supervises work in a stone quarry.

21. In English in original.

Typhoid fever.
Back to Roche.
Marseille. Relapse. Roche.
March 1880, departs for Alexandria.
Cyprus.
Rimbaud seeks employment in Alexandria, in Djedda, Souakim, Massouah, Aden.
On December 13 he arrives in Harar, Abyssinia (modern Ethiopia), where he will remain, with few interruptions, for ten years, until March 1891, working as a trading agent.

Africa is present throughout Rimbaud's oeuvre.
The prose poems were originally titled *Livre païen ou livre Nègre*. (Letter to Delahaye, May 1873.)
In the *Vers nouveaux et chansons* he calls upon the unknown black race:
Oh! mes amis! – mon coeur, c'est sûr, ils sont des frères;
Noirs inconnus, si nous allions! allons! allons!
Oh! my friends! – my heart, it is certain, they are brothers;
Unknown blacks, if we could escape! Away! Away!

In *Jeune Ménage* he sings of an African fairy.
In the *Saison en enfer* he calls himself black and rails against the false blacks of culture.
Oui, j'ai les yeux fermés à votre lumière. Je suis une bête, un nègre. Mais je puis être sauvé. Vous êtes de faux nègres, vous maniaques, féroces, avares.
In the new German edition this reads:
Yes, my eyes are closed to your light. *I* am a *beast*, a negro. But *I* can be saved. *You* are false Negroes, maniacal, savage, greedy.

In the letters from Africa we witness a change in Rimbaud's attitude.
In the *Illuminations*, blacks are still the *Superbes Noires dans la Mousse vert-de-gris* . . .
Superb blacks in the verdigris foam . . .
(The new German edition reads: *mossy-green* foam, building on the text's association of sea and garden imagery.)

In *Villes* we read, for the first time, of rupees, which appear so frequently in the letters from Africa – down to the remark of the aged rebel:
Il s'est produit depuis deux mois une révolution énorme dans le change de la roupie.
In the previous two months there has been a major revolution – in the exchange rate of the rupee.

Rimbaud did not fall silent in Africa.
His letters fill up three hundred narrow-spaced pages.
He writes of money, of profit, of interest and annuities.
He occasionally orders technical books.
Otherwise the talk is of elephant tusks and elephant hunts, of rifles and other firearms, of wolf traps, which he wants to use to hunt leopards, of caravans of covered pottery.
A little bit on the Koran. A little bit on marriage.
The fear of military service runs through all of this correspondence.
He comments on the weather as the mood strikes him.
Now it's unbearable, now excellent (385).
But the climate is hardly considered without a view to business opportunities:
On January 15, 1883, at age twenty-nine, he writes to his family:
Tout l'avantage est que le climat est très sain et qu'on y fait des affaires assez actives.
The major advantage is that the climate is very healthy and allows one to get much work done.

The lust for adventure and longing for the unknown are bought off:
Soyez tranquilles, je ne m'aventure jamais qu'à bon escient. Il y aurait beaucoup à faire et à gagner ici (338).
Rest assured, I will only venture out under careful consideration. One could accomplish a great deal here, and make a lot of money.
. . . où c'est inconnu et où ça me rapportera une petite fortune (351).
. . . where it is still unexplored and where I can amass a small fortune (Sept. 28, 1882).
Even the idea of the *homme de lettres* who takes up an interest in photography – one thinks of the essays of Susan Sontag, the films

Revolution as Restoration

of Robbe-Grillet, or Warhol's snapshots one hundred years later – never occurs without an eye to profits:
. . . *et je rapporterai des vues de ces régions inconnues. C'est une très bonne affaire* (341).
. . . and I will bring back images of these unknown areas. It's a very good business.
Rimbaud the businessman fails to reflect on the transformation from a culture of ideas to a culture of images.
It appears that Rimbaud lured an Ethiopian girl out of her village, and then later chased her off with a few thalers; that he burned thirty-four volumes of notes and records belonging to his companion Labatut, afterward showing remorse only for the stock shares that were inadvertently burned with them (462).
Even in 1891, the year of his death, Rimbaud was compelled to pay back money that he had embezzled – there is no other way to describe it – from the liquidated estate of Labatut (654).
Ilg, the Swiss engineer who, as an adviser to Emperor Menelik, was certainly not a squeamish fellow, complains to Rimbaud:
You never give sufficient travel provisions. Not a single caravan in which the workers don't arrive in a state of starvation; all your servants are in a pitiful condition and complain bitterly of you (591).
I was forced to send several stores to Hawash, since it seemed that the inhabitants there were starving to death (591).
Rimbaud takes these accusations seriously enough; he defends himself repeatedly:
Je suis au contraire connu partout pour ma générosité dans ces cas.
On the contrary, I am known for my generosity in these cases.

Letters are halfhearted witnesses.
What isn't referred to there?!
In what mood were they composed?!
What is exaggerated?!
What are mere lively gestures?!
When the facts are sufficiently clear:
Je vous confirme très sérieusement ma demande d'un très bon mulet et de deux garçons esclaves.
I wish to confirm my sincere request for a good mule and two slave boys (602).

So that Ilg has to answer:
As for the slaves, I beg your pardon, I can't trouble myself about them, since I have never owned any and have no plans to start (638).
Rimbaud to Ilg:
Morale, rester l'allié des nègres, ou ne pas les toucher du tout, si on n'est pas en pouvoir de les écraser complètement au premier moment.
The moral: remain an ally of the Negroes, or don't even deal with them, if you do not possess the means of crushing them in an instant (480).
How frequently even the ethical element here eats its way right into the grammar:
. . . quelques fonds . . . de retour du massacre d'Ensa, et dont je paie d'ailleurs les intérêts!
. . . several sources . . . of revenue, from the massacre at Ensa, and which I'm paying interest on besides! (609).
Il va peut-être y avoir quelque chose à faire à Massouah avec le guerre abyssine.
Perhaps there is something to do in Massouah, in the Abyssinian war (459).
Rimbaud:
. . . perdu au milieu des nègres dont on voudrait améliorer le sort et qui, eux, cherchent à vous exploiter et vous mettent dans l'impossibilité de liquider des affaires à bref délai? Obligé de parler leurs baragouins, de manger de leurs sales mets, de subir mille ennuis provenant de leur paresse, de leur trahison, de leur stupidité! (502).
Does anyone else hear the voice of Claude Lévi-Strauss?
. . . lost in the midst of Negroes whose lot one would like to improve and who, for their part, only try to exploit you, and make it impossible for you to see to your affairs in a timely manner? Forced to speak their gibberish, to eat their dirty food, to undergo a thousand annoyances that stem from their laziness, their untrustworthiness, and their stupidity!
Leading to the outrageous statement:
Je jouis du reste, dans le pays et sur la route, d'une certaine considération due à mes procédés humains. Je n'ai jamais fait de mal à personne.
. . .
Les gens du Harar ne sont ni plus bêtes, ni plus canailles que les

nègres blancs des pays dits civilisés; ce n'est pas du même ordre, voilà tout.

. . .

Il s'agit d'être humain avec eux (612).
I am granted, moreover, both in the country and on the road, a certain consideration due to my humane conduct. I have never harmed a single soul.

. . .

The people of Harar are neither more stupid, nor more vulgar, than the white Negroes of the so-called civilized lands; the two are incomparable, that is all.

. . .

It is a matter of being humane with them.

Goodheartedness is no prerequisite for good literature.
Moral influence often derives from the most corrupt of individuals.
We could dispense with Rimbaud's letters as barren, personal trash – the letter of Ogaden, however, is not so easily dismissed. Rimbaud sent it to a scholarly society, under his own name, as a piece of prose having for its subject a people of the Third World – not as a letter.
Here, then, is the dream scenario – the avant-gardist in black Africa, the revolutionary gives an account of a region in misery.
Voici les renseignements rapportés par notre première expédition dans l'Ogadine.
Ogaden *is the name of an alliance of Somalian families sharing a common ancestry and living space, which is bordered to the north, south, and east by the following Somali tribes:* Habr-Gerhajis, Dulbohantes, Mijertines, *and* Hawiyas. *In the west Ogadine borders on the* Gallas, *the shepherds of* Enniyas, *and the* Wabi, *a river that separates it from a large tribe of the* Orussis, *the* Oromo.

I don't believe that this report was written by Rimbaud's collaborator, Sotiro, as has been conjectured.
The simple man would not have composed something so abnormally dry as the off-duty poet.
Sotiro's letters to Marseille bear witness to this:

c'est la peine que j'aurais eu de trouver le long de la route des personnes mortes de faim. Le sac de riz est monté à 14 th. Moconen a fusillé beaucoup de Gallas Itous qui mangeaient leurs frères et enfants (683).
the pain that I would have felt, to discover starved corpses along the route. A sack of rice now costs fourteen thalers. Moconen has shot many Gallas Itous, who were eating their brothers and children.
Whereas Rimbaud speaks:
Of routes, markets, prairies, the unavailability of silk, the scarcity of waterways, the general aspect, and the tribal ensemble.
The rare comment on human behavior is marked by an unscientific generality unworthy even of the Société de Géographie.
The Ogadenes are at constant war with their neighbors, and among themselves.
They dress themselves in relatively clean clothing.
Their daily occupation consists in squatting down among the trees and brush, weapons in hand, and fighting without end over their various shepherding concerns.
They are completely inactive.

Only one time does Rimbaud interrupt this schoolbook prose:
There are large numbers of ostriches. Hunters, disguised in female ostrich skins, pierce the male with arrows when he approaches.

For European literature the Third World does not exist.
Should not avant-garde writers be judged according to the new accusations they bring to bear against the preconditions of their society?
For Rimbaud's France, these preconditions had long since been the raw materials of the Third World.
That, in fact, is our goal. One of our own traders, or a native with the necessary initiative, will collect, in several weeks, a ton of ivory, and then we can ship it toll-free out of the port of Berbera. Some of the Habr-Awals . . . brought feathers to Boulhar, for which they received several hundred dollars.

One would almost like to believe that he had been stricken with some illness, like the aging Darwin, with malaria, perhaps, which

debilitates the entire sensorium – one hesitates to draw from this any example for European literature.
Would Verlaine or Mallarmé, Pound or Eliot, Kafka or Joyce, Proust or Döblin have done the same?
What a breakdown of language before the presence of Africa!
What a breakdown of language before one's own tongue:
Absurde, ridicule, dégoutant, he remarks, on the publication of his works in France.
Des rinçures, ce n'était que des rinçures.
Dishwater, nothing but dishwater.
Absurd, ridiculous, disgusting.
This is, in fact, a double denial of responsibility: once in respect to his own influential work, and once in regard to his own actions in Africa.
An air of humanity returns only when he refers to his own suffering.
But even the letters written from his sickbed are a correspondence carried on with the powerful, with feudal lords and bourgeois traders.
Why Rimbaud chose to leave his servant the sum of 750 thalers – out of a savings of 37,000 francs – remains a mystery.
(Am I mistaken or would Rimbaud's fortune, judged by the price of the hospital and the wooden leg, amount to around a half million marks?)
All these business letters become yet again, in extremis, chaotically reconfigured, forming a death's harlequinade the likes of which no surrealist has ever produced.
On November 9, 1891 – one day prior to his death – Rimbaud wrote from the hospital at Marseille to the director of the Messagerie Maritime:
Item: a single tooth.
Item: two teeth.
Item: three teeth.
Item: four teeth.
Item: two teeth.

Monsieur le Directeur,
I would like to inquire as to whether I still owe you anything. I wish to leave this service, whose name I do not even know, but in any case

let it be the service of Aphinar. They are everywhere here, and I, impotent, unhappy, can find nothing – the first dog in the street will tell you that.
Send me, then, the list of ticket prices from Aphinar to Suez. I am completely paralyzed: thus I wish to be on board at an early hour. Tell me at what time I am to be carried on board . . .

Par les soirs bleus d'été j'irai dans les sentiers,
Picoté par les blés, fouler l'herbe menue.
Rimbaud began with these lines, written at sixteen, and ends up, at thirty-seven, hoarding ivory and spitting out one tooth after another.
They are, by now, familiar names that we read in Rimbaud's letters:
Ogaden, Mogadishu, Asmara – a land in which another revolution came to no account:
Although the Eritrean revolution against the central power in Addis Ababa was supported, for several years, by the Havana government, today Cuban military advisors fight against this same uprising, and out of Addis Ababa.
A further consequence of the European idea of revolution, and its restorative application in the countries of the Third World.

THE EWE TRIBES OF JAKOB SPIETH

Hamburg, August 1979

The human sciences do not take on poetic dimensions simply because researchers insert little quips, and other material more appropriate to scrapbooks, into their work. Six poems, Gottfried Benn used to remark, must endure from the writings of a lyric poet – and of how few may that be said! – for their work to have poetic significance.
How unnecessary then, for Konrad Lorenz to compete with Wilhelm Busch, or for Claude Lévi-Strauss to rival Kurt Schwitters; the result is a nonsense text, neither scientifically nor poetically relevant.
Poetic ethnology has another source.
(I refer not to those poets who happened to be scholars, not to *Don Carlos,* or the *History of the Revolt of the Netherlands from the Spanish Government,* not to Bourbaki, Lewis Carroll, or Tacitus.)
Could not anthropology, ethology, sociology, ethnology, and psychology, both materially and as disciplines, broaden and rejuvenate poetic practices?
This would also imply moving beyond the separation of form and content – something taken for granted in experimental physics, and the *nouveau roman,* for the past thirty years.
Poetic organization is not so different from scientific organization.
Poetry, too, is human behavior.
The most alien of human activities takes place within a network of verbal – and thus poetic – rituals.
Such crossovers become more clear, I would suggest, in a work like the *History of the Ottoman Empire,* by the great Hammer, Frazer's *Golden Bough,* the treatises of Lydia Cabrera, and to the highest degree in:

The Gay Critic

The Ewe Tribes: Material for the study of the Ewe nation in German Togo, by Jakob Spieth, Missionary of the North German Missionary Society. Berlin, 1906.

FOREWORD

The following book sets out to familiarize the reader with the various tribes of the Ewe nation in Togo, which nation has, since 1890, by agreement with the English government, been brought under German sovereignty. This event, of such lasting significance for the many peoples there, brings them closer to us, and not merely as imperial subjects, but as human beings, to whom we owe certain obligations. However we choose to understand these obligations, whether from the perspective of culture, or that of religion, their beneficial fulfillment cannot be accomplished in the absence of the most precise knowledge of the inhabitants in question. This book provides information not only upon the history and legal fabric, the social and economic life of the Ho, Matse, and Tafiewe tribes, but also furnishes insights into their spiritual life. It is precisely this latter element that has so often been denied to Europeans. The reason for this lies not so much in a lack of linguistic competence, but rather that the African requires time before he is willing to disclose, to a foreigner, the innermost workings of his soul.

During my missionary stay in Eweland, which lasted over two decades, I had ample opportunity, in the course of countless amiable conversations and encounters, to see and hear things that Europeans had hitherto never been allowed to witness. Inasmuch as my time and energy allowed, I strove to immediately record that which I had heard and observed, along with the time and place in which it occurred. I was aided in this endeavor by a few native assistants. The most precious bits of information that I was able to gather I owe to several especially cooperative chieftains, priests, and magicians. The remarks of these latter individuals, even as they spoke, were immediately written down, either by myself or by one of my assistants in their language. . . .

The greater part of the following work is written in the Ewe language, accompanied by the most precise translation possible. The latter work, however, proved itself to be one of surpassing difficulty. If I chose to emphasize formal completion, I often saw the meaning become widely divergent from the original text; on the other hand, when I attempted to faithfully transcribe the original, the end result was, in German, often far too succinct. When the galleys were read by members of the Oriental Seminar in Berlin, the opinion was that a closer relationship to the original Ewe text would be preferable. I then subjected the entire manuscript to a thoroughgoing revision and made many improvements.

. . . In order to guard my informants against possible reproach from the community, I took the precaution of abbreviating their names.

On page vi, Spieth provides a brief table of contents. A detailed listing is given on pages 928–53.

Introduction
  I. The Ho Tribe
    1. The Ho Countryside
    2. Akofiewe
    3. Kpenoé
  II. The Matse Tribe
  III. The Tafiewe Tribe
  IV. The Klewe and Tsiavi Tribes

Thus the missionary made precise ideological and theoretical considerations prior to laying out the organization of his project. He begins with a consideration of the world that he wishes to describe.
He doesn't divide his subject into nations, administrative districts, or races, like a colonialist, but into tribes, as an African would.
On the heels of this, however, an irruption of the European worldview:
XV. Supplement: Barometric and Temperature Measurements

The act of juxtaposing Jakob Spieth and Arthur Rimbaud is done not out of chauvinism, and yet it is, nonetheless, unjust to compare the two:
Rimbaud was no ethnologist;
Spieth no modern, lyrical subject.
And yet:

Both, at about the same time, lived in and described Africa. Rimbaud indulged, consciously, in ethnological speculation; Spieth, unconsciously, in poetic art.

In what kind of linguistic and scientific situation did Spieth begin his work?
In *Meyer's Encyclopedic Lexicon* of 1874, one reads, under the heading *Africa:*
The almost insular, southwest portion of the Old World, long inaccessible to Europeans, who have been denied entrance into its interior by the forbidding effect both of nature and the African people. Since ancient times a land of puzzle and wonder. Few harbors; an inhospitable coastal climate; a people foreign both in manners and language, who have been rendered more savage in the South by centuries of slave trade, and more fanatic in the North by an even older religious conflict against the Christians of southwestern Europe – all these elements have conspired to erect obstructions that have begun to be dismantled only in recent times, due to the combined effect of three of the most powerful levers ever wielded by mankind: mercantile egoism; scientific ambition; and religious devotion. To these we owe our modern, though still incomplete, knowledge of Africa.
Crude, Herr Meyer.
1874:
It is first of all the Arabs, those cultured peoples of the Middle Ages, whom we must thank for the earliest significant foundations in our knowledge of African geography. . . .
In the fifteenth century the Portuguese embarked upon their great voyages of discovery, bolstered in their efforts by the infante Henry the Seafarer (1416–60), who was tirelessly active in promoting his nation's shipping capabilities, and was thus the instigator of Portugal's greatness. . . .
After the end of the religious wars, which had shaken all of Europe to its foundations, new interests arose in trading circles. . . .
In 1788, the African Society of London. . . .
The work of evangelical missionaries begins in Northern Guinea. . . .
the tough and clever German, Burckhardt (1816) . . .

After the murderous climate had claimed Steudner, Schubert, Frau Tinne, and many of their companions, the remainder returned to Europe in 1863. . . .

The efforts of several churches to have a lasting impact on the Nile region, while not yielding any real successes for the churches themselves, led to significant advances in geographical science. . . .

And finally, alone, in heroic defiance, Mungo Park led a group deep into the jungle, near to their goal at Bussa, where he met a glorious but meaningless end. The Germans Hornemann, Seezen, and Röntgen were the next victims. . . .

The German-African Society, founded in Berlin, in 1873. . . .

Great Nimrods like Cumming and Wahlberg, the Swede who was trampled to death by a wounded elephant, made deep incursions, but none so deep as the missionary Livingstone, the son-in-law of Moffat. . . . an enterprising American by the name of Henry Stanley, on assignment for the New York Herald, *completed the great work. Loaded with provisions, he set out from Zanzibar for the interior on March 21, 1871. On November 10, in Ushidshi, he met Stanley Livingstone, just as the latter was returning from Manjumaland.*

Jakob Spieth's procedure can be deduced from his list of illustrations:

Women carrying wood, on the way to the market.
King Hofi of Ho with his primary wife.
View of a plowed field.
Traders crossing a river.
Porters at the river crossing.
Yam house, seen from within.
Yam house, from outside.
A slain leopard, hunter kneeling before it.
Curing palm wine. (vii ff.)
Compared with the pictorial inscriptions in Lévi-Strauss's *Tristes Tropiques:*
Playful diversions . . .
. . . and friendly contests.
Dreaming woman.

The text material of the ethnological presentation consists in:

protocols;
essayistic compilations;
statistics, etc.
These textual strata usually interact freely.
A particular tension results when various responses to a given event follow closely one upon the other:
Agatha Christie uses this trick in *Death on the Nile*, Döblin in *Hamlet; or, The Long Night Is Over*.
One sees it frequently in the Gospels, and in Lydia Cabrera's essays on Afro-Cuban culture.
And in Jakob Spieth:
Ad: Our forefathers came from Notsie, which lies beyond Gava. They left this region on account of the cruelty of their king.
Kw: . . . following the death of that gentle king, a cruel king ruled over them. One day he called all of his chieftains into his house and informed them that there was to be a trial at which they were, with him, called upon to preside. After saying this, he had all of them killed, so that he might more easily do as he wished. He plagued his subjects with burdensome labors, commanding them, for example, to stamp him clay. Before the workers set about their task, however, he had thorns and cacti mixed into the clay, so that those who kneaded it with their feet received painful wounds. They then left in anger. Another time he ordered them to make a cable out of thorns and cacti.
Adyr: At that time the king of Hogbe commanded his subjects to build him a house. At the site where he wished it to be built, he gave instructions that sharp objects be mixed into the earth, which the Ho workers had to stamp down. An old woman heard of this; she told one of the Ho elders, at the same time charging him to tell the workers to bind fragments of wooden plates beneath their feet before stamping the clay. The chieftain did so, and they followed the advice (4).

Spieth's work is, roughly speaking, a compilation essay, mixed in with citations in the original Ewe and in German translation. But Spieth is not always consistent. On page 2 we read: *Chapter 1: History* – and across from this, the translation into Ewe, which I find rather amusing: the word *Ta*, i.e., *head*, the Latin *caput*, to be understood as *chapter*.
Titles and lengthy essayistic passages (for example, p. 638f.) often expand the German text to twice the size of the Ewe.

Spieth thus conceived of his project on the society and religion of Togo not simply as a thousand-page compendium on the Ewe people, which uses their comments for quotes, but as the first reading and lesson book for the Ewes, whom Spieth asks, in turn, to check the veracity of his observations.

He works with a large number of compositional elements.
One title reads:
Transcriptions of court proceedings.

1. *An embezzlement.*
   a. *Its cause.*

One just has to come up with something like this.
Why should legal transactions in Africa be thought less significant than the case of Bovary in France?
Hear, people of Ho, large and small, hear! From this day forth, Dente Komla is barred from close contact with the king; it is forbidden to all to enter his house. He may collect any debts owed him. When his wife takes water from the spring, no one may help her set her jug upon her head. If any lay a hand upon his wife, he need pay no penalty; we forbid it (150).

Spieth takes the trouble of describing necromantic rites and – without a tape recorder – transmits the performance of a priest and his visitors from the beyond: that spirit theater which one encounters, to this day, in Haiti, where the influence of the Ewes is strongly felt:
The conjurer immediately withdraws, taking the money and food into the darkness of his Trō-house, where he first has his dinner. Once refreshed, he calls down the gods' messenger by striking a clear-sounding iron; in a few moments, the messenger is there, and greets the priest in squeaking, nasal tones.
The messenger, upon his arrival: "Beware!"
Priest: "I am here."
Messenger: "Why have you called upon me?"
Priest (answers in a loud voice): "The brothers of the dead N. N. have come and bring water for their dead sister. May she drink it and cool

her breast. Then may she tell them who it was that killed her, whether an evil trō, an evil gbetsi, or a sorcerer. Her relatives have, for this purpose, brought flour water into the room."

Messenger leaves for the land of the dead. Several moments pass, and he returns.

Messenger, upon returning from his journey into the realms of the dead: "Beware!"

Priest: "I am here!"

Messenger: "How do they fare, who were left behind?"

Priest: "They are well! Have you seen her?"

Messenger: "I made my way there, and I saw her."

Priest: "What was the spirit of the departed doing when you arrived?"

Messenger: "She had gone to the spring, and into the bush, to gather wood . . ."

The priest, meanwhile, repeatedly strikes against the iron. He suddenly breaks off, and the spirit makes itself heard.

Spirit: "Take heed!" (He speaks in a high, soft voice, the way someone would sound speaking with a finger in their nose.)

Priest greets the spirit in a loud and deep voice: "Welcome, how are things in the land of the dead?"

Spirit: "The same."

Priest: "How are your brothers doing there?"

Spirit: "Well! But who calls upon me to speak?"

Priest, in the name of the trō: "I have called upon you to speak. I summoned the petitioners; therefore take the flour water and drink it and cool your breast. If there is a word in your mouth, speak it to me, that I might relay it to your brothers (and sisters) who still walk upon the earth, so that these might know the manner of your death."

Spirit: "No one devoured me with sorcery; I had to die, for the sake of my mother and my husband. My mother had given me to a man in Wegbe, then took me back from him and gave me to another for a wife. She then tore me from this one, and gave me to a third. But this one beat me, whereupon my father brought me to the house of my uncle, K. In time my father's anger cooled, and he bid me go back to my husband. The village chieftains also said that I should return. I, however, in the meantime called upon the earth. . . , that I might never have to return to my husband. No one knew of this. In spite of

my oath, however, I returned to my husband, and yet I failed to first assuage the spirits of the earth. My father went to Wegbe and left the trō behind, who was very angry and set a snake upon me, which bit me, and I died. Had I said openly to my father that I had sworn to the earth never to set foot again in my husband's house, death could not have found a way to me. But give my thanks to the white man, whom my death grieved as if I were his own child. Had I not died of a snakebite, I would have died while giving birth."
The spirit withdraws, and the priest eats the food brought for the spirit in the same room in which he has spoken with the spirit. He then gives the calabash back to the deceased's family members, who had listened to the entire conversation just outside the hut. They believe that the spirit itself has consumed the food (500 ff.).

It is immediately clear that Spieth translates the Ewe expressions into fairly learned German, with a liberal use of subjunctive, and a full genitive:
returned into the house of my husband . . .
And the missionary writes, in an ethnological treatise:
Messenger leaves for the land of the dead. Several moments pass, and he returns.
Messenger, upon returning from his journey into the realms of the dead . . .
The faithful Christian knows enough about journeys into the kingdom of the dead from Lazarus and Christ; but how few Christians even tolerate other peoples' references to a similar faith-based reality.
At the close of the passage he splits levels of consciousness:
They believe that the spirit itself has consumed the food.
By not transforming the performance of a few crafty Ewes into an ingratiating, hypocritical primitivism, he achieves two things: On the one side a tact, understanding, and clarity with regard to the ethnological situation that he tries to grasp, on the other a reader doubting everything that much more severely because it is being presented to him in his own jargon; one can immediately be drawn into the story of the dead woman and still question it radically – the text thus stands in a psychoanalytical perspective, without doing violence to the reality or the reader.

He speaks in a high, soft voice, the way someone would sound speaking with a finger in their nose.
Spieth goes so far as to insert adjectives into the Ewe narratives, as if they were his own:
Intoxication by hard liquor is a "sickness," since the one affected suffers for three days under its symptoms. Someone drunk on brandy, for example, will often lie on the ground and is so hot that his family will splash cold water on him until, eventually, he is left lying in a dirty puddle (400).
Spieth analyzes the work of girls, children's games.
He keeps track of the Ewes' remarks on a given scene and adds his own:
The Hiding Game
If the child is unable to find the others quickly, he or she goes through the entire village and says all sorts of strange things, so that those in hiding will be forced to laugh. . . . .
. . . the food that a young girl cooks for her husband-to-be is called atsunu. *After the wedding, however, there is no more cooking* atsunu. *Also, a mistress is said to cook* atsunu *for her lover, which she then sends to his house,* according to the missionary's gloss (212).
He transcribes riddles and offers solutions:
Meto du gome de Asante.
Egome: Alododo.
I came to Asante and walked around the cities.
What is that? Answer: Sleep.
Explanation: Whoever wishes to go to Asante, in a waking state, must pass through the cities along the way. Whoever comes to Asante while sleeping, however, is suddenly there, without having seen any city along the way.
Fofonye wle godoe gāa de nam mede edo ge do kpoe.
Egome: Mowo.
My father bought me a big loincloth. I wanted to put it on, but I couldn't.
What is that? Answer: the way.
Explanation: The loincloth band consists of a long, narrow piece of material. The African way is equally long and narrow, but one cannot cut it up and wrap it around one's loins.
Wudu gbo.

Egome: Ne, ago, adiba.
Falling and whispering.
What is that? Answer: The nut, the fruit of the fan palm and the watermelon.
Explanation: Heavy fruits fall to the ground and make a whooshing sound as they go. The names of the fruits must be specifically stated by the solver of the puzzle (597).
This is how the reader takes part in an analysis of Togo thinking, learns Ewe metaphorics, their style and understatement.[1]
For proverbs, Spieth not only gives a translation and explanation, he also sketches how it is used:
Ayroe medoa golowo dome o.
The ayroe bird does not sleep with the ostrich.
Explanation: The ayroe is very small, and doesn't keep company with ostriches.
Use: A poor man cannot mingle in the society of the rich.
Agata-kese be, wole ye kom, eye wole ye tsola ha kom.
One laughs not only at the monkey in the cage, but also at him who carries it.
Use: A man who befriends a fool is ridiculed along with him.
Nyowola hoa fu.
A charitable man reaps scorn (599 ff.).

Section 4:
Literature.
A. Fables
1. *The fable of the king's son,* Safudu Kwaku
One day, a king lied about his son, saying that he had engaged in some intrigue with his wife. His son, Safudu Kwaku, told his father that he wished to have the gods make the judgment. His father agreed and dispatched men to Ge, to purchase a sword and needles. When they had bought these objects, the king ordered them to be sharpened for seventeen days. He then bid the sharpened machete and needles to be placed upright, in the earth, beneath a high silk-tree. The king then invited all to come and witness the god's judgment. The king, his wife, and his son Safudu Kwaku were all borne to the place where the judgment was supposed to take place. The king then told his son

---

1. In English in the original.

to climb the tree, and to let himself fall upon the sword and needles. His mother began to cry; he himself had no fear, however, since he knew that he was innocent.
Safudu Kwaku *climbed the tree, and sang this song:* Dedende manyimato Safudu Kwaku . . . *after he had finished singing, he plunged from the tree but was not injured. The king, however, said that he had not seen it, since he had at that very moment been bathing himself. His son climbed the tree a second time, sang his song, and fell onto the earth. Thereupon the king said that he had only now just dried off, and that he ought therefore climb the tree a third time:* Safudu Kwaku *climbed the tree again. But the king said that he had been getting a rubdown and was unable to see. He ordered him to climb the tree yet again; this time, though, he did not see him because he was taking a pinch of snuff. And so on. After he had climbed the tree for the sixth time, the king said: "Now for the first time I can come to watch you fall" and ordered him to climb the tree a seventh time. All the spectators were now pulling for* Safudu Kwaku; *he, for the seventh time, climbed the tree. As he fell, heaven,* dzingbe, *bore him aloft and carried him into the sunrise. Now, whenever the sun comes up and one wants to look upon its face, it quickly hides itself and says: "I have been done a sevenfold wrong." And so it happens that one cannot quite make out the face of the sun* (572f.).

In this text, one learns not only of Togolese aggression and its avoidance, of subjection and despotism – the myth relates a tale of incest at the world's origins, one told neither by Frazer, in the *Golden Bough*, nor by Freud, not to mention Ortigues, in the *Oedipe africain*.

Spieth unearths fairy-tale dialogues that recall those of the Grimm brothers:
The Yams appoints a king.
It happened one day that Kasanti, *a breed of Yam, came to* Klewu *and discussed with him the hierarchy of the Yam breeds.* Kasanti *asked whether it were true that he was king of the Yams. To which* Klewu *replied: Is it not said that I have been a king now for many years?* Kasanti: *O,* Klewu, *such a thing you say – you who live today, yet not tomorrow! For you could die then, or the next day, and leave us all orphans.*

The Ewe Tribes of Jakob Spieth

Are we not reminded of the wondrous conviviality of the early children's fairy tale?

For a time a blood sausage and a liverwurst lived together, and the liverwurst invited the blood sausage to dinner.

Spieth further divides his material into parables, and – disregarding, for the moment, the artistic economy of African narrative technique and the problems of translation – I wonder who, if anyone, could differentiate a parable from a tale with such ease as the restless, ecstatic missionary.

Spieth does not give mere statistics, but complete sentences, which help to leave a deeper impression.

With regard to infant mortality, the following facts may be observed. Kdz. had nine brothers, of whom only Kdz., now twenty-five, is still living. Mrs. H., from A., gave birth to twenty children, of whom, as of 1886, only five were still living. Kk. fathered, by three different women, twenty children, eighteen of whom died (218).

Spieth thus sets out to provide a large, unofficial chronicle of the living conditions of the masses of the Third World – a work that neither Brecht nor Marquez ever attempted: *Mrs. H., from A., gave birth to twenty children, of whom, as of 1886, only five were still living.*

Where in modern literature could I find such a remark?

In 1847 the Ewe people first came into lasting contact with Europeans. At that time, the missions of the North German Missionary Society were established in the Pekier nation, west of Ho between Volta and Tsawoé; their objective is described by Spieth (lxxiii ff.), who clarifies as well his sources and methods of research:

It is not surprising that the Ewes, an illiterate people, possess no ancient manuscripts. . . .

Thus the only source is the people itself. . . .

They often know a great deal; in all probability, however, they have combined, in their imagination, various borrowed elements into a unified whole. . . .

Similar patterns are discernible in older teachers and Christians. They may be able to recount many truthful details concerning the history of their race and economic and social relations; ask them of the indigenous religion, however, and their facts are not so straight. For one thing, most of them would like to forget about the old ways. A woman, for example, asked me not to inquire of these things any further, since it always troubled her to think of them. What's more they seem to mix, unconsciously, their pagan and biblical recollections. . . .

Methods of research must, of course, adjust themselves to changing situations. For my part, I suggested the following: as my duties originally brought me into frequent contact with those who were resolved to renounce paganism and embrace Christianity, I sought to elicit from them an account of their religious experiences. Although the content of that which they told me is not a part of the following work, nevertheless it has exercised a determining influence upon its shape, since it was from them that I first learned what the practice of paganism in Eweland actually involved. And certain questions arose that concerned me deeply, in that I wished to know the quality of the spiritual atmosphere, the intellectual sustenance that the Christians had had in pagan times. For it is only with a view to this context that one can rightly understand certain events that transpired within the early Christian community. But even the pagan priest cannot make do without a clear vision on the past and present of his listeners. I will never forget with what a worldly air of superiority an elder chieftain once informed me that I knew nothing at all of the pagan customs. This comment made me determined to seek out those individuals within the specific tribes who, according to the judgment of their own people, were thought to know a great deal of tribal lore. I befriended these, took them with me as porters and hammock bearers on various trips and heard, in the lonely savanna, or by the hearth fire of some far-off lodging, the most engaging stories. I also had sent to the station, at my own cost, those knowledgeable ones whom I was unable to meet in my official ventures, where they were even more open than usual, away from the watchful eyes of their brothers and sisters. . . .

Here, too, it was soon clear that too many questions only fatigued my informants, and that it would be more useful to let them simply tell their stories, interjecting questions only intermittently. . . .

I myself spent many late nights, both on journeys and at home, and my own free time, transcribing and collecting information. If this is

The Ewe Tribes of Jakob Spieth

continued, at a steady pace, for several decades, one gradually amasses a handsome amount of material.

In what circumstances did this book arise?
It would take too long to map out the maneuvers of the German merchants, and of the *Sophia*, which bore the kidnapped royal family from Anecho to Germany.
The *Möve* takes them home. Nachtigal, who was at that time the German consul in Tunisia, boards the ship at Lisbon and accompanies the hostages back to Anecho, a voyage that will assure Germany of a West African empire.
On July 4, 1884, Nachtigal disembarks near the village of Bagida, makes his way to Togo, and finds himself in the company of one of Chief Mlapa's adjuncts (the former had only recently died). Nachtigal dispenses gin, rum, and tobacco and has the natives sign, with a simple *X*, a treaty drawn up in English, this being the sole European language understood in this region. Robert Cornevin writes:
On the next day Nachtigal traveled back to Petit-Popo and, before going on to Cameroon, named Henry Randad, a German industrial agent, to the post of executive consul. With inexhaustible energy, the latter worked to expand this small, German protectorate.
Viering writes:
The Germans name a king and begin to administer their strict occupational government. The Kabyé are drawn into forced labor. An old man recalls this period:
"At first we thought that we would have to work in the fields, but in fact we were sent to haul iron for a bridge-building project. The work was so hard that all who took part in it were possessed of the same thought: to flee, given the slightest opportunity. The burden was too great and the guards stood by, constantly beating with their whips. Of every ten men who left from Atakpame, *no more than three or four made it to* Lama-Kara." . . .
In order to strike a decisive blow to the military capabilities of the inhabitants of Kabyé, the Germans force the residents of those areas that had been especially active in the previous war to leave their homes, and to settle in the South. Lacking sufficient provisions, they are driven on foot upon a three-hundred-kilometer forced march.

Many cannot hold up and die along the way. The remainder arrive, totally exhausted, in the northern part of Nuatya, where they are allowed to make their homes near a river that flows into the Mono. They name the river Ahala, which, in their language, means "pain." To the Germans this becomes Kra; later the settlement will become known as Chra.
Today Chra has only two inhabitants, both of whom, as children, underwent this torturous exile.

Can Spieth assign blame for all of this, with a Christian hand?
Page xii:
Granted that the greatest riches of a colony lie in its people, Togo is not only the most productive, but also the richest German colony in Africa. We ought not to regret, then, the work and capital that we have put into Togo.
Page xxxv:
The most important city is Lomé, formerly a fishing village, and now the seat of the German government in Togo. In 1884, when it was placed under German sovereignty, the once small marketplace quickly blossomed.
Robert Cornevin mitigates:
Of course, the Hanged-Man's Tree, near the tavern, or which rises next to every administrative building, may evoke for certain people god knows what sort of Teutonic sadism, but in fact punishment by hanging was executed only upon those who had been condemned to death for murder, this sentence seeming to the Africans themselves more fair and just than the traditional system, or in contrast to the endless French legalities. Thirty years after the German withdrawal, the Togolese said of them that they were "hard but fair."

Colonialism gives rise to the most varied linguistic posturings. Spieth resists these, for the most part.
When his logic becomes, in Enlightenment fashion, reductive, it is without condescension or contempt:
Let us add to these accounts, however, several well-attested proofs of such magical effects.
The effects of the type of war magic known as ankui *consist in the following: the man who bathes in the* ankui *potion becomes bul-*

letproof at nine paces. A bottle of the magical substance is purchased, and a test is made of its authenticity, in the presence of several witnesses. The dealer counts off nine steps from his location, gives two guns, each loaded with three bullets, to his two assistants, and gives them orders to shoot. He stands before them, resting his hands in a basin filled with water and sacred leaves. The two aim their rifles at him and shoot, and behold! the magician picks up the bullets and shows them to the spectators gathered around. They marvel at him, take him home, and load him down with gifts. The secret of his power lay in the fact that the bullets with which he was shot had been made from goat manure, which was then wrapped in fine tinfoil. Beneath the sacred leaves, in the basin where he put his hands, he had hidden two of the same type of bullets, which he afterward presented to his credulous audience (530).

Spieth-the-missionary's lack of sexual prejudice is considerable – and lets him make even the following observation:
Ahali is a man with large sexual organs.
One must search in the large opus to find traces of a missionary's jargon.
It is limited to the expressions *idol, heathen, morally reverted,* and *often cruelly tortured to death.*
At one point, he lets slip a really stupid remark:
Having learned the Gospels, they showed themselves equally adept at other cultural acquisitions, taking up carpentry, masonry, and joinery (47).

Spieth's appraisals are, for the most part, finely nuanced:
On moonlit nights the Hoans play freely in the open street. The character of these nightly games, however, is usually repulsive (242).
(233): *The cleanliness of beds and mats leaves something to be desired*
is preceded by:
(230): *Cleanliness of personal attire is a trait common to almost all the Hoans.*
Already in the introduction, the German Spieth remarks:
The Hoans are industrious farmers and weavers, and among them the word "lazy" is one of the most insulting things which can ever be said of another person (45).

A tender missionary:
They speak in such a manner, because they are afraid of the forest, which they think is a trō. They believe that the woods are angry with them (396).
Spieth often refers not to Negro music, or Negro pottery, but to African music, African pottery, revealing a diplomatic tact and, indeed, a self-evident truth, yet most of our modern, enlightened writers choose not to follow him, a full one hundred years after the work of the Bremer missionary.
Page lv, though, threatens the *contenance* of the entire work:
From the materials presented thus far, it may be deduced that the Ewes have attained to a certain level of cultural development in the areas of farming, cattle breeding, and crafts, but that they have remained at this point for a considerable length of time. Their hoe and loom are exactly the same as they were a hundred years ago.
An unchristian expression, spoken by one caught up in the exuberance of the early years of the second German empire.
What author, living in this difficult climate, never once felt fatigued?
Bombast and a synthetic, crabbed style are rare in these thousand pages:
and before he knew it, the enemy's bullet had laid him low. Having pierced him in the middle of his breast, it put a sudden end to his young life. Soon after, two black soldiers, badly wounded and dripping blood, came up to the Ho station, and several minutes later the brave young Scot was also brought there, dead, and borne on a hammock. On Sunday evening, May 12, he was buried in our graveyard (66).

Such a style is so rare that I can almost detect a tone of mockery. It also seems to me incorrect when (at p. 213) he uses [the variant form] *erratet* instead of *errät*. But perhaps this was the preferred usage in 1906, and if not, it's a good example for a history of German professorial style in the twentieth century.
Otherwise, Spieth's German shows little sign of mold from his lengthy stay in the primeval forest.
Only one interpretation struck me as a bit hasty:

The Ewe Tribes of Jakob Spieth

And underneath his long fingernails he had hidden bits of pepper. The owners of Aka *let their nails grow very long for the same reason* (678).

Letting a single fingernail grow long is a practice seen around the world, and those who do so give the most varied explanations. There's even a study on it.

Unfortunately, as is often the case with scientific summaries, which tend to shed the least amount of light on precisely those areas one knows something about, I find little in Spieth on the subject of mental illness and its treatment, nothing on shock rituals, on Togolese psychoanalysis – which does exist – nothing on the botanical system, the Kpele harvest, geomancy, and nothing on the sadistic initiation rites practiced by the Bush school, by the secret sects and priests that are so divisive of the Togolese youth.

Spieth puts a brief, half-page table of contents at the beginning of the work and, at the end, another over thirty pages long. European categories, and a rage for order, driven to an extreme:

I. *The Ho tribe*
1. *The Ho countryside*
1. *Chapter: History*
1. *Subsection: Universal Tribal History*
I. *The Oldest Hoan Traditions*
A. *The Ancestral Home*
1. Dahome *and* Adadam

I'm not exaggerating; this is how it's set up.

2.
B.
C.
1.
2.
3.
II.
A.
1.
a.

Scientific rituals, which have their source, perhaps, in earlier rituals, not unlike those of the Ho and their magical systems.

At any rate, one comes away with a sense of alienation.
What Wilhelmine, Victorian, Napoleonic, and Umbertonic bandages were laid upon the Africans and their reality.
And yet the book's thousand pages, encapsulated into a thirty-page table of contents, have quite an effect – the wildest inscriptions follow upon so many small and capital *A*s, after the Roman and Arabic numerals:
The Material Culture
The Spiritual Culture
The Use of Magic in Legal Matters
The Hoans among the Ruins of Their Cities
Premature Certainty of Victory and the Latest Allied Defeat
Adultery in Relation to Theft
Hair of the Godslaves
Death of the Murderers

In what other ethnological treatise could I find a chapter on that topic so crucial for farmers, *The Various Types of Soil*? Or on a topic of such evolutionary relevance as *Distribution of the Game Animal*? Like no other, this book gives the impression of truly covering all, or at least the most important, aspects of a people's existence.
How does he do it?
The secret lies, first of all, in the methods of research.
Jakob Spieth collected his material in twenty years of missionary work.
What other ethnologist can write:
I myself was a witness, in Have *and* Wodze, *as well as in the village of* Dzake *and in* Peki, *to the practice whereby all of the women of a village band together and, on a predetermined day, leave their husbands. The women of* Have *gave themselves to the king of* Nyagbo *in* Avatime, *and those of* Dzake, *to King* Kwadzo De *of* Peki. *In both cases the men were punished and forced to plead with their wives to return, and afterward to accompany them home* (lxv).
In the year 1881, I was an eyewitness to the execution of a man found guilty by the judgment of the god. He was first dragged to the edge of an open grave, in the bush. There, two men offered him a mixture of palm wine and brandy poured into a human skull. Then they threw a

white cloth over him; two men armed with clubs fell upon him and bludgeoned his head and body, until he fell, dead, into the grave. A chieftain then shot his rifle above the grave. The grave was filled, and the people returned home. On the way, all the participants washed their feet in a stream (542–43).

In the second place:
An astounding mastery of languages:
The indigo plants, which grow on the plain and in the hills, have for the Ewes the greatest significance. From its leaves and blossoms one extracts that indelible blue which, for them, is the color of eternity. In Agu the expression tso ama me yi ama me, *"from indigo blue to indigo blue," means "from eternity to eternity"* (xxvii).
In light of the fact that the Ewes possess no writings and can neither read nor write, one is unprepared for the fervor with which individual Ewes treat their language as a cultural object. That this is in fact the case was made clear to me when, on one occasion, a speaker in Anlo, while delivering a public address, misplaced a part of speech, and so offended the aesthetic sense of his listeners that the latter quickly gave him to understand their intense displeasure (lvi).
Now the language takes us a step further still. It says that God is dressed in "white," and "bright colors," and that "he hides his face in darkness." During the rainy season, for example, a friend may call out to another: Mawu gadze adanu wo nu bubu, va kpoe da: *today God shows us a different face – come and see!* (424).
All of Eweland, trees, stones, and people, all have been sent by God. How this happened, though, is not for men to know. "Just as the son does not ask his own father how he created him, so humans cannot ask of the origin of all things" (550–51).

And lastly:
The visible heavens are called *dziwo, dzingbe, dzimenyi, dzingoli,* and *dzingo*.
In addition, Spieth has a knowledge of the surrounding regions, of their agriculture, for example, which keeps him from making certain mistakes, to which a socialistically engaged aesthete like Thomas Mann, and even an anthropologist like Lévi-Strauss, often fall prey.

The very stony soil of Ho has little mineral content and would have to be thoroughly fertilized. But since cows cannot be maintained in Ho, and with the tsetse fly in abundance, they will not be able to survive there at any time in the near future, there is no possibility to add their manure to fertilize the fields. Whatever lands are cultivated, then, must lie fallow for several years before they are able to support a new crop (298).
Planting corn is done by making a small hole and tossing in three or four seeds, in any way one likes. If one has a large field, hands are hired for assistance. One digs the holes, and the other plants. If the seeds have been properly soaked beforehand, it only takes three or four days for the stalks to appear. Unsoaked, the seeds take seven days to sprout (320).

The long duration of fieldwork, the knowledge of language and related fields leads to assertions of humbling exactitude:
The ashes of burned fruit are an important ingredient in the local production of soap (xxiv).
An inscription on page 65 reads:
Enemy skulls, out of which those who have been condemned to death are forced to drink.
Chieftains, too, sometimes drink from them.
Soot is rubbed into a fresh wound to stay the flow of blood. If the markings are to be very pronounced, a salve made from ground gunpowder and cactus milk is applied (227).

From this, the possibility of comparing structures within the historical process emerges – beyond the bombastic adoration:
In former times, a groom had to give a young girl the following: seven hoka *of snail shells, two armlengths of cloth, seven* hoka *worth of soap, a calabash full of limes, and a native chair. Nowadays this has become: a native dress, two armlengths of European fabric, a breastband of two armlengths; three headbands, a European comb, a mirror, a mug, a wooden plate with yams and one with bananas* (738).

Even Spieth's generalizations are, for the most part, offered in a spirit of modest restraint.
It is a known fact that the Ewes are lovers of music (61).

The Ewe Tribes of Jakob Spieth

The strange and the mysterious have always made a deep impression upon the Ewes (418).
As already remarked, most of the heathens practice magic and provide it to their relatives as well. This takes the place of a medicine cabinet for them (lxix).
Why one becomes a magician:
It is fear that drives the Ewes to practice magic and to enchant others (722).
The Hoans have no love for their fatherland, but an intense love for their homeland (568).

One can observe in the text the way in which a differentiated relationship with the world expresses itself in nuances of speech. *A man who was possessed by him behaved like a madman every evening.*

A half-century later the trance, an element of the voodoo religion of Haiti, that resembles certain Togolese rites – is perhaps an actual descendant of them – is treated as a neurosis, a hysterical phenomenon. Only recently has the African and Afro-American trance begun to be understood as a means of therapy for neuroses and psychoses – an interpretation foreshadowed by Spieth.
A man possessed . . . behaves like a madman (855).[2]
A question of style:
The Hoan feels the need, whenever possible, to greet his friends and family members on a daily basis (238).
In former times the opinion would have held . . . (555).
Spieth coins bold new phrases that succeed on the literal level:
The changeringer
Coign de vengeance
The grave kings
The Knotty-headed – recalls Hamlet and Schlegel:
Yet who, O grief!
Has seen the shaky queen –
Like one barefoot she raced about
Drenching the flames with her tears;
A cloth on her head, where once

2. The German edition indicates that this page reference is incorrect.

The diadem stood.
Stealing is base . . .
We beg of you . . .
He moaned and cried upon his chains . . .

Alongside this refined simplicity stand formal exclamations, repetitions, which lend the scientific text an air of the magical oaths and litanies that are its subject:
Whoever is shot in the bush has "fallen in battle" (756).
Whoever is struck by lightning has "fallen in battle."
If someone falls down and dies, he is said to have "died in battle."
Whoever has been swept away by the river or drowned, whoever burned to death is said to have "died in battle."
This ability lets Spieth come up with beautiful turns:
They buried the child; for the mother and father, it is lost, but the murderer was sold off, is (ist) still alive and eats (iβt) salt (176).
Sisters . . . of the deceased put food in the dead man's mouth, and say that this is his last meal (294).
The raffia palm's tough bast is put to various cultural uses, and in Matse, if one throws its leaves into a particular stream, the stream takes away that person's sorrows and the sorrows of men in general (xxvii).
Spieth falls, now and then, into conscious archaisms, into an almost biblical, Old Testament language that seems quite fitting to the Ewe sense of religiosity.
The Hoans took grandfather Letsa himself to Kpevi, to a small plantation village in the area of Klewe. When grandfather Letsa saw that all of the village's inhabitants were in the field and that only the children were still at home, he called the children to him and slew them, then threw them into a stone mortar and ground them up like yams (16).
Are we not reminded of the passage on David?:
And he brought forth the people that were therein, and put them under saws, and under harrows of iron, and under axes of iron, and made them pass through the brick-kiln.
(2 Sam. 12:31)
O Mawu Sodza, *may he stand by mankind, you ship full of yams and full of* wle! *Give to me, so I give to you; overlook me, and I overlook*

you. Here is your yam, which I have unearthed for you. When I harvest mine, give forth, that I might receive the fullness and add other yams from other places (344).

And reaching back to the prebiblical, to the beginning of time and sounds:
One day the sea began to pound and sang many songs (96).

But not only the dark mist of magic – concise pithiness as well, to the point of a terrifyingly classical:
When someone has hanged himself near a city, he is pierced through the breast with a rod and dragged like a pig and buried in the bush (274).
Couldn't Kleist have written:
In anger he stuck the knife into her breast and hanged himself next to her (243).

Spieth's work establishes new parameters, new criteria for both poet and scientist.
What sort of theoretical thoughts does he stimulate?
The text gives a ready example on the concept of magic:
A second class of gods, much closer to humans, are the any-imawuwo, *earth gods who in Eweland are also called* trowo *and which we wrongly call fetishes* (lxvii).
I also find material for a study of voodoo, and its hitherto unrevealed sources in Togo.
On the genesis of rituals:
Only after a long time did they discover stock yams (manioc) in the bush (94).
They thought them edible but were quite afraid, so they cooked them first and fed them to the dogs. When they saw that these suffered no ill effects, humans also began to eat them.

Spieth's repeated descriptions of animal torture and the quasi-religious stipulations concerning the preparation of food show us, twenty years before Proust, that the art of cooking is a form of torture and that the culinary arts are perhaps implicated, in terms of human evolution, with the development of various forms of torture.

In Spieth it is not only language that describes behavior – it is made clear that language is a type of behavior:
This being the language of subjection, and devotion . . . (469).
And lastly, it must not be forgotten that this highly significant, comprehensive book on the people and culture of Africa was written by a Bremer missionary, who was sent by the German empire during the earlier period of its revival under Bismarck.
The European governments were presented with the task of pacifying the Ewe people, and of instructing them in the peaceful development of their land, under the assistance of the German mission (lv).

Seldom have such insights been made into the life of an African people, as by Spieth – but they are made to "pacify," to "instruct," and for the glory of the Lord. The perversion that results when a missionary so affectionately describes a religion that he wishes to destroy, shines, on Spieth's formulations, the light of a recaptured innocence.
I am almost inclined to believe that Spieth's research into the Ewe rites was not done simply as a preliminary to their conversion to Christianity, but rather that his being a missionary was a precondition that allowed him to empathize with a foreign people's system of beliefs.

THE LAND OF LAUGHTER
Polemical Remarks on
The *Tristes tropiques* of
Claude Lévi-Strauss

Grenada, May 1979 / Hamburg, August 1979

Titles can be grouped into several categories:
Lucien Leuwen – you will read about someone named Lucien Leuwen.
Ulysses.
Nora.
The Ewe Tribes.
L'Education sentimentale – you will read of a process involving the development of the sensible faculties, of a struggle in *combattimento di Tancredi et Clorinda*.
There are titles that play with words:
The Shade of the Coachman's Body.
And with meaning:
As You Like It.
And finally:
A Cheating Heart.
A language of allusion, of double meanings, false severity and false playfulness – a spinsterish atmosphere.
Les Fleurs du mal stands at the beginning of modern literature.
There follows:
Une Saison en enfer.
Frühlingserwachen.
Thus Spoke Zarathustra.
Si le grain ne meurt.

Eight in the Morning and All Is Well with the World.
The book series with the bright red band on the cover.
As well as:
À la Recherche du temps perdu, with:
À l'Ombre des jeunes filles en fleurs.
And with this, symbolisms like *Les Faux Monnayeurs* are again reduced to *Recherche.*
But lost time does not have to be made into kitsch.
Proust's work is an essay on the passing of time.
Perdu – sure, but what would have been better? *Passé? Écoulé?*
À l'Ombre des jeunes filles en fleurs is a title that, like no other, strikes one as enervated, sweetly perfumed, and slightly redundant, but which on closer examination seems clear, concise, and simple:
I think of women as blossoming trees and write of things that took place beneath their shade.
The comparison of women to trees is a very old one, and since Proust is concerned with the analysis of the unconscious, when he refers to an ancient mythic idea he simply reveals his poetic means.

Tristes tropiques is a book whose author thinks of himself as a sociologist, an ethnologist, but most of all as an ethnographer – as a scientist, therefore, who described the ways of peoples without the theoretical corset of anthropology, sociology, and ethnology.
Et voici que je m'apprête à raconter mes expeditions – and now I shall begin to tell of my expeditions, Lévi-Strauss announces in the first chapter of the French edition of 1955.
It is a statement of intention that is lacking in the German edition of 1970, which was decisive for the reception of its author in the Federal Republic.
The German version, as well as the English and American one, underwent abridgment, with the author's approval.
Mme. de Scudéry's *L'Illustre Bassa* also makes use of a qualifying adjective to hint at the work's theme within its title.
Yet *illustre* here is less qualifying than delimiting – the story is of the *famous* Bassa, and not any other. *Nils Holgerssons underbara*

resa genom Sverige uses *wondrous voyage* like a colorless phrase, and throughout the many unexpected turns of events encountered in this journey through the airy realms and early childhood dreams, *wondrous* strikes us as merely conventional.

Tristes in combination with *tropics* is less so – if one disregards the fashionable wink at the *nouveau roman* (Nathalie Sarraute's *Tropismes* appeared in 1939; *Les Gommes*, by Alain Robbe-Grillet, in 1953): *unclean, starving, overpopulated, devastated,* or *barren* "tropics" would all attempt to describe a factual state of affairs; *dreadful, terrifying,* etc. "tropics" would describe the author's own opinion.

Tristes, however, refers to an unfavorable prejudice – it is less "sad" than disparaging.

Strauss thus reports to us on the conditions of a downtrodden reality, unable to stir up, in himself or his reader, any feelings of revolt, but which does elicit disdain, some small, begrudging sympathy, and finally, with a shrug of the shoulders, acceptance.

1955 – one year earlier Mendès-France put an end to the war in Indochina – and the *grande nation* (de Gaulle is not yet Président de la République Française, endowed with special powers) condescends to notice a deplorable situation.

In 1952, Jean-Paul Clébert, the Parisian mendicant, argued, in *Paris insolite* (in spite of the nasty undertone: dishonorable, insolent Paris) for a quite different dialectic:

The book depicts the sad tropisms of the Paris housing market: In the winter of 1954 the homeless laid the bodies of people who had died of hypothermia on the boulevards of the Ville de la Lumière, to force a reaction in public opinion.

In 1952 as well, *The Géopolitique de la faim* appeared in France, a study of world hunger written by the Brazilian agronomist Josué de Castro – Strauss didn't know of it, when he happened upon the teary, consolatory title for his own Brazil book.

Just as with *Africa addio,* so too behind this title there stands a second, implied verbal posture, and a further ideological conception:

The tropics were surely not always so sad.

They must have become so.

People who were either given their independence too soon, or who never received a proper education, manage the tropics so poorly that something sad must inevitably result.

Structuralism has been accused of having a restorative tendency – I'm less concerned with evaluating the philosophy itself than with examining its linguistic gestures, the transmission of facts.

Tristes tropiques makes use, just as *Gods, Graves, and Great Minds, Rolls Royce,* or *Rowohlts Rotations Romane,* of the poetic technique of alliteration – or at any rate that which is commonly understood by this term.

We recognize the source of this poetic device and its outgrowths – right down to the Germanomania of the symbolists.

I don't know what would possess an ethnographer, in 1955, to use such a device, nor a translator, in 1970, to dare preserve it in the German.[1]

But even if we suppose that an ethnographic sterility has been pollinated in the shade of blossoming young females – is it then, even in a restorative sense, impressive, poetic, attractive:

Tr—— Tr——?

Claude Lévi-Strauss's book, published in 1955 by Plon, without genre designation, under the series Terre Humaine, is a combination of travelogue, ethnological investigation, autobiography, lyrical appeal, whose component parts overlap arbitrarily. Novel, though, the attempt: to expand the account of a journey among South American Indians by drawing Asian parallels, and thus to lay claim to substantial knowledge of the tropics in general, as well as to a quasi-poetic license.

A second peculiarity are the many dichotomies and contradictions – some intentional, some forced.

Since that time, the book has been held up as the beacon of a science that has turned away from the natural world toward the mind of man, and belongs, along with Freud, Artaud, Sartre, Bataille, Leiris, Lacan, Foucault, to the repertoire of a more fantasy-laden Left – it was chosen for *Die Zeit*'s all-time top 100; George Bataille praised it as *un livre humain, un grand livre. Peu*

---

1. And in the English – the version of 1961 (Hutchinson of London) is entitled *A World on the Wane*.

The Land of Laughter

d'ouvrages soulèvent des problèmes aussi vastes, aussi fondamentaux.[2]

Tristes tropiques – *the title of the following book refers to a mass extinction taking place in the rain forests of Brazil. It is the story of a hazardous journey among the sad remnants of what were once the great cultures of Mato Grosso, experienced and related with poetic skill* – this from a blurb on the German edition.

Am I justified in accusing Lévi-Strauss of vulgarity and sentimentality on the basis of his title?

Perhaps he was really touched and wished to express nothing more than a desire to relate things and events in Brazil that brought him sorrow?

On page 1 of the French edition:
mais cette scorie de la mémoire: "A 5 h 30 du matin nous entrions en rade de Recife tandisque piaillaient les mouettes et qu'une flotille de marchands de fruits exotiques se pressait le long de la coque," un si pauvre souvenir mérite-t-il que je lève la plume pour la fixer?
but this, from the dregs of memory: "At 5:30 A.M. we entered the port at Recife while the gulls screeched and a flotilla of merchant boats full of exotic fruits pressed off along the length of the shore," such a pitiful memory, does it merit my raising the plume to preserve it?

The ethnographer raises his plume to preserve pitiful memories! The faculty of memory itself may be impoverished.

As well as that which Claude Lévi-Strauss remembers.

But is the port of Recife a poor object of remembrance? The statements that Josué de Castro had published, three years earlier, in French, on hunger in Recife, were anything but impoverished; they provoked the first reflections on hunger in the Third World. Josué de Castro probably didn't raise his quill – in the heat of Pernambuco he would more likely have reached for his ballpoint pen.

What objects and forms of memory did seem important enough to Strauss to preserve, in his 169-page introduction?

19: *I wish today that I had known how to appreciate, twenty years ago, the unheard-of luxury and almost royal privilege that consists in*

---

2. A human book, a great book. Few works raise issues so vast, so fundamental.

having exclusive access, with eight or ten other passengers, to the deck, cabins, smoking room, and dining room of a ship built for a hundred to a hundred and fifty people.
Strauss finds this memory so important that he uses it at the beginning of the abridged edition.
Maybe in 1970 such a statement could be smeared with enough rouge to pass for agitprop.
The next statement, however, which was left out of the German edition, can hardly be so benignly construed:
The other [cabin] was shared by four men, of whom I was one – a tremendous favor that I owe to M.B., to whom I would like now to extend my gratitude, since he found it quite unacceptable that I, one of his former first-class passengers, should be herded like a domestic beast.
Only three persons were allowed to disembark . . . myself among them, as a favor long owed me by the commander from the Contrôle Naval – for we had recognized each other as old acquaintances (27).
Fortunately, at this period, in the heart of every Brazilian official there lay a slumbering anarchist, surviving on the remains of Voltaire and Anatole France and who, even in the deepest bush, maintained, in his free-floating state, a contact with the culture of the nation. ("Ah, good sirs, you are Frenchmen! Ah, France! Anatole, Anatole!" exclaimed an agitated old man in a village of the interior, as he took me into his embrace; he had never before met any of my countrymen) (30).
my situation at Martinique improved following the intervention of a high official of the Ponts et Chaussées (32).
I was able to explore the island under the friendly guidance of Christian Belle, at that time a general consul (35).
Célestin Bouglé, at that time director of the Ecole Normale Supérieure . . . (50).
I heard it from the mouth of the Brazilian ambassador in Paris (51).
At about seventeen I was initiated into Marxism by a young Belgian socialist, who today works abroad as his country's ambassador (62).
Finesses, all of which are lacking in the German edition.
The following, though, is in both editions (88):
In these woods, which lie on either side of the Rio Tibagy, approximately one thousand meters above the water's surface, as I accom-

panied an officer of the Bureau of Native Preservation on one of his official journeys, I had my first encounter with Indians.
The original, though, reads *sauvages* – "savages," in place of Indians (174).
As Lévi-Strauss himself remarks, on page 66:
These are tedious and useless considerations!
Nor is this name-dropping indulged in without a lyrical, expressionistic air:
The chapter entitled *La Fin des voyages*, which can mean both the end and the goal of the voyages – begins:
I detest journeys and researchers, and yet I now find myself ready to tell you of my expeditions.
Campers, camp in Parana. Or better, no; stay away altogether (173), is in the original but not in the German edition.
Strauss summons entire classes, whole societies, and then orders them back:
It should be required of society as a whole to confess to the superiority of the mountains, and then to recognize my rights to sole ownership (391), is judged worthy of an appearance in the abridged version.

Adventures have no place in the ethnographer's occupation, page 13 – yet no other grammalogue is used more frequently, in Strauss's shorthand, than that for "adventure":
30: *a similar adventure befell me*
92: *the end of the adventure*
182: *I was prepared for real adventures.*
301: *Following this, the adventure was to begin.*
305: *There is nothing comparable to these adventures.*
383: *this adventure, begun with enthusiasm, left me with a feeling of emptiness.*
455: *My adventurous life . . .*
To what end?
To what end such flighty ignorance:
16: *I no longer know if it's a Thursday or a Sunday morning.* – A Frenchman who can't tell the difference between Thursday and a Sunday morning?
23: *The ship transported who knows what sort of contraband.*

32: *Monks, of what order I couldn't say.*
45: *Oblivion, rolling my memories in its flux, has more than merely used and buried these. The lofty edifice that it has constructed out of these fragments offers a more stable equilibrium to my methods, a more clear design to my vision.*
Oblivion – if I sum up the original – offers to Lévi-Strauss's methods a secure equilibrium and his vision a clear plan.

Twenty years of forgetting have been necessary to bring me face-to-face with an ancient experience in pursuit of which I have traveled the world over, yet whose meaning has always been refused me, its intimacy harshly denied.
The highly placed official of the Ponts et Chaussées?
The director of the Ecole Normale Supérieure?
The Belgian ambassador?
The official of the Bureau of Native Preservation?
How can one, after Proust and Freud, be such a dilettante of forgetting?
Or, mon esprit présente cette particularité, qui est sans doute une infirmité, qu'il m'est difficile de le fixer deux fois sur le même objet (56).
Now, my mind has this particularity, which is doubtless a weakness, that it is difficult for me to focus more than once on the same object.
This statement on thinking is followed, on the next page, by an insult leveled against the Stone Age:
57: *J'ai l'intelligence néolithique.*
Meant to be lively and cute, if not poetic.
In fact – as Lévi-Strauss is very much aware – by allegedly not turning his thought upon the same object twice, he simply wants to show off.
And pad his text.
How much time and money the French intellectual had to have at his disposal, in 1955.
Text and time that Lévi-Strauss can't afford to give to his description of the Indian tribes – or to the study of their languages.
The German text lacks the chapter introduction of page 161:
Sans que j'en ai formé le dessein, une sorte de travelling mental m'a conduit du Brésil central à l'Asie du Sud.

The Land of Laughter

Though I never planned it, a kind of mental traveling led me from Central Brazil to South Asia.

Claude Lévi-Strauss was entrusted with youths, workers, and funds – I wonder how Kafka would have fared with the bank executives, had he written such things about his own mental state.

Lévi-Strauss can't stand to leave anything out – not the fact that he hums Chopin to himself, nor that he loves to climb mountains, makes surrealistic sketches, draws up an outline for a Roman tragedy. He writes pamphlets en route, composes poems for the carnival newspaper.
A poetry penned with pipe in mouth:
Plus haut encores dans le ciel, des diaprures blondes se dénouaient en sinuousités nonchalantes qui semblaient sans matière et d'une texture purement lumineuse (70).
Since Lévi-Strauss was smart enough not to insist on these lines for the 1970 edition, I'll try to translate them without rancor:
Higher still in the sky, pale variegations unraveled in careless unwindings that seemed without substance and of a purely luminous texture.
un fragment de lune rougeâtre qui passe et repasse et disparaît comme une lanterne errante et angoissé (98).
is embellished in the German edition to:
a piece of redding moon . . . that again vanished like a frightened will-o'-the-wisp.
when it actually says:
a fragment of reddish moon that comes and goes and disappears like a wandering, anguished lantern.
This at a time when, in France, one could read the prose of an Alain Robbe-Grillet.
Les bananeries qui la couvrent sont du vert le plus jeune et le plus tendre qu'on puisse concevoir; plus aigu que l'or vert des champs de jute dans le delta du Brahmapoutre avec quoi mon souvenir aime à les réunir; mais cette minceur même de la nuance, sa gracilité inquiète comparée à la paisible somptuosité de l'autre, contribuent à créer une ambience primordiale (101).

Even the translators of the Kiepenheuer Verlag couldn't defuse this passage:
45: The banana trees that cover the plain are colored with the freshest, softest green that one can imagine; lighter than the gold-green of the jute fields in the delta of the Brahmaputra, which they mingle with in my memory.
Memory?!
A harmless self-invention.
Harmless?
Une race plus sage et plus puissante que la nôtre (173), reads, in the German edition: *a race that was wiser and more powerful than our own.*
In the book's final passage, for
adieu sauvages! adieu voyages! one finds:
Adieu savages! Adieu journeys!
Is the animal fondly addressed, in the French, merely for the sake of a rhyme?
Yet we also witness such embarrassing outbursts in Heisenberg and Lorenz. Lévi-Strauss doesn't name himself St. John Perse, and the *Tristes tropiques* shouldn't be read like the *Anabasis*.
It became the book that brought structuralism into fashion. What does Lévi-Strauss say about his method?
Page 50: *J'ai appris que la vérité d'une situation ne se trouve pas dans son observation journalière, mais dans cette distillation patiente et fractionée que l'équivoque du parfum m'invitait peut-être déjà à mettre en pratique, sous la forme d'un calembour spontané, véhicule d'une leçon symbolique que je n'étais pas à même de formuler clairement.*
The German translator was smart enough to delete this passage. I have learned that the truth of a situation is not found in its journalistic observation, but in this patient and fragmented distillation that the ambiguity of the vaporous release was already inviting me to put into practice, in the form of a spontaneous pun, the vehicle of a symbolic reading that I was not yet able to formulate clearly.
Page 62: *Comprendre consiste à réduire un type de réalité à un autre.*
Understanding consists in reducing one type of reality to another.
I don't feel that this statement should have been kept out of the German edition, offering, as it does – in 1955 – not only a justifi-

cation of French colonialism and by extension of the tortures in Algeria – it also provides an epistemological foundation for colonialism in general, a stroke of genius waiting to be woven into the album of poetry, presenting even torture as part of the struggle for understanding.
The torture of the French system of higher learning.
The torture of ethnology.
And of colonialism, of every stripe.
Was Lévi-Strauss unaware of this?
Surely not.
On the very next page, one finds:
Elle [l'ethnographie] tranquillise cet appétit inquiet et destructeur dont j'ai parlé, en garantissant à mes réflexions une matière pratiquement inépuisable fournie par le diversité des moeurs, des coutumes et des institutions.
Ethnography stills that restless, destructive appetite of which I spoke, in that my reflection is guaranteed a practically inexhaustible content, furnished by the diversity of manners, customs, and institutions.
How did George Bataille characterize this book?
Human.
If I disregard, for the moment, the fact that Lévi-Strauss mistakes ethnography for ethnology, and that his thinking is so base as to bind this ethnography to such a fascistic model – to include the work of Spieth, Frazer, and Malinowski – there remains his assertion, ten years after the end of the Second World War, that other nations, made up of human beings, offer a guaranteed supply of practically inexhaustible material.
A restless and destructive appetite.
What are the qualities that make up an ethnographer?
Even the German reader finds out, on page 199:
One year after my stay among the Bororo, I had finally completed the conditions that were to make me into an ethnographer. I had received the blessing of Lévy-Bruhl, Mauss, and Rivet, had displayed my collection in a gallery of the Faubourg Saint-Honoré, I had delivered lectures and published articles.
Never has the relationship of the most intelligent nation in the world to the world at large been so clearly revealed as here, in the remark of its most tactful scholar.

On page 350 the German edition fumbles:
Yet before this culture was to become forever silent, a last surprise awaited me.
The French reads:
415: *Pourtant, vers la fin de cette liquidation mélancholique de l'actif d'une culture mourante, une surprise m'était réservé.*
Nevertheless, toward the end of this sad liquidation of the assets of a dying culture, a surprise awaited me.
The corpse plunderer wants to be entertained.
Humans as cultural assets are sadly liquidated.
To liquidate, let us not forget, means both to make liquid and to execute – it is a term that was frequently used during the twelve years of national socialist fascism, and in the same double sense that Lévi-Strauss reactivates.
Could the gold teeth of Auschwitz mean nothing to him, in 1955?

And yet perhaps one cannot get a real insight into the workings of Straussian structuralism from a few brief quotes on ethnography, copied down after a few readings of the *Tristes tropiques*. But then where is this procedure, which falls between the *Feuilles de Route* and the *Parties de Corps*, integrated, whether poetically, scientifically, or privately?
Perhaps on page 61, where he claims that his intellectual development was colored by his geological interests:
Que le miracle se produise, comme il arrive parfois; que, de part et d'autre de la secrète fêlure, surgissent côté à côté deux vertes plantes d'espèce différentes, dont chacune a choisi le sol le plus propice; et qu'au même moment se devinent dans la roche deux ammonites aux involutions inégalement compliquées, attestant à leur manière un écart de quelques dizaines de millénaires: soudain l'espace et le temps se confondent: la diversité vivante de l'instant juxtapose et perpétue les âges.
La pensée et la sensibilité accèdent à une dimension nouvelle où chaque goutte de sueur, chaque flexion musculaire, chaque halètement deviennent autant de symboles d'une histoire dont mon corps reproduit le mouvement propre, en même temps que ma pensée en embrasse la signification. Je me sens baigné par une intelligibilité plus dense, au sein de laquelle les siècles et les lieues se répondent et parlent des langages enfin réconciliés.

The Land of Laughter

I don't understand why the German text fails to include this concise text on diachrony and synchrony, this integrated statement on the new method of structuralism, this example of a poetic anthropology – or why Claude Lévi-Strauss himself finds this unworthy of appearing in the abridged edition:

And the miracle happens, as it sometimes does; on either side of the secret crevice, there rise, side by side, two green plants of different species, each of whom has chosen the most favorable soil. And, in the same moment, two ammonites, unequally complex in their involutions, are revealed in the rock, bearing witness in their own way to the gap of several millennia between them. Suddenly, space and time are confounded. The vital diversity of the moment juxtaposes and perpetuates the two ages. Thought and sensibility attain to a new dimension, where every drop of sweat, each flex of a muscle, and each gasp becomes the symbol of a story whose particular movement is reproduced by my body, and whose meaning is at the same time grasped by my thinking. I feel immersed in a more dense understanding, at whose source the centuries and locales speak out to one another, in languages at last reconciled.

It seems to me a pretty fair quote.
Yet it reveals the writer as much as it justifies him.
Even this axiom, however, is empty prior to its scientific application, and in this regard it is not unlike a mathematical or logical axiom.
Their worth is first revealed in praxis.
In the praxis of this book by Lévi-Strauss, it means that he introduces the living conditions of Asians into the structural representation of events in Brazil – that, in order to lend intelligibility to the cultural structures of the Bororos of South America, he must first render Asiatic history reasonable.
That, at any rate, would constitute an *intelligibilité nouvelle,* and *plus dense.*
The danger: that the double vision might leave him, and us, cross-eyed, that ethnographic empiricism might degenerate into one of Dr. Tigge's study trips, and that precise historical research could give way to panoramic visions, à la Malraux.

Claude Lévi-Strauss's book opens up, in its final pages, into statements in which breadth no longer stands in any relationship to substance:

463: *One senses here, again, Islam's difficulty in grasping the idea of loneliness.*

466: *The all-embracing goodness of Buddhism, a Christian desire for communication, and Moslem intolerance.*

Written in 1955!

472: *Man accomplishes truly great things only at the beginning.*

473: *At that time the West lost its chance to remain female.*

Summaries from 1955 that, without exception, are absent from the German edition.

As always, such conclusions are usually based on doubtful premises.

Vagaries make their way onto every page.

Here are several examples:

On page 35:

Bertrand Goldschmidt . . . explained to me one evening the principles of the atomic bomb and informed me that, in May 1941, the most highly developed nations had begun a sort of scientific race in which victory was guaranteed to whoever viewed himself as number one.

In which case Strauss knew more than Bohr or Einstein.

For it was not until November of 1941 that Niels Bohr took the famous bottle of heavy water from Copenhagen to America, to warn Roosevelt of the Germans' atomic bomb.

Heisenberg's boasting, while in occupied Denmark, had falsely convinced Bohr that the Germans were on the threshold of using atomic weaponry.

The atomic race began only after Bohr had warned the United States.

The accounts of Haiti that Strauss, on page 81, disseminates are plucked out of thin air – and tendentious. They are uncritically repeated in the German edition of 1970:

Although . . . in 1492 (when it was discovered by Columbus) the island of Hispaniola had a population of approximately one hundred thousand people, one hundred years later there were only about two hundred.

The "about" is inserted into the German edition.

It is generally agreed that the number 3 million, which Las Casas estimated the Indian population to have been at the time of their discovery, should be reduced to 1 million.
And yet, in the latest and most thorough treatment of the history of Haiti, by Heinl, the author writes:
Probably exaggerating, Bishop Bartolomé de las Casas put the Indian population at 3 million when Columbus came. . . . In 1550 only 150 Caribs could be found.
Strauss reduces the number of native inhabitants to one-thirtieth of the number arrived at by Las Casas, who was in the service of the Spanish crown – in fifty years more than one million Indians were slaughtered, and not, as Lévi-Strauss fudges, less than one hundred thousand, over the period of a century.
Is this a sound scientific method for the writer of a book on Indians?
On page 97, Strauss applies structuralist principles to the layout of cities:
in the year 1935, an individual's social standing could be measured, as it were, by altitude – the higher the residence, the lower the status.
An elegant reading – if it could only be grounded in fact.
Yet in Rio, for example, one can visit the colonial, bourgeois quarter of Santa Teresa, the Largo do Boticario, or the Alto da Boa Vista – all at a high altitude – and just outside of Rio, at a three-hundred-meter elevation, the luxurious mountain village of Petropolis, where Pedro II had his summer residence.
Vagaries and ignorance, mixed with condescension:
58: *In Brazil, which has yielded few, but nonetheless brilliant, men of learning* (Gelehrte), *like Euclides da Cunha, Oswaldo Cruz, Chagas, and Villa-Lobos, education and knowledge were, until very recently, the playthings of the wealthy.*
The French text reads *réussites individuelles,* which the German edition translates with *Gelehrte,* "men of learning" – few?
Strauss omits the names Nina Rodrigues, Arthur Ramos, Gilberto Freire, Guimarães Rosa, Jorge Amado, Edison Carneiro, etc. *La culture* – "learning and knowledge" – a plaything of the very wealthy?
Are the *escolas de samba* not a culture, Carnival, *Candomblé,* religious architecture, Brazilian music – does folk, or popular, culture mean nothing to Professor Strauss?

Page 62: *I hope that all of my delightful former students – now my colleagues – who read my book, will not be angry with me. When I think of them, I hear again, in my mind, the astonishing variety of their given names, which it is their custom to use, and that quaint baroque resonance so foreign to European ears, in which is reflected the father's right to choose from a long, rich, and revered tradition – Anita, Corina, Zenaide, Lavinia, Thais, Gioconda, Gilda, Oneide, Lucilia, Zenith, Cecilia, Egon, Mario-Wagner, Nicanor, Ruy, Livio, James, Azor, Achilles, Decio, Euclides, Milton. I look back without irony on these tentative beginnings.*

What gives Strauss the right to cite these names with irony?

And, in doing so, is he documenting anything other than his own provinciality, if not illiteracy?

Quaintly baroque? Anita? Egon? Ruy, James?

Isn't he familiar with Proust's *Temps retrouvé*, written after the First World War?

The names of M. de Charlus's friends and relatives:

Hannibal de Bréauté.

Boson de Talleyrand.

Sosthène de Doudeauville.

And Charlus himself: *Palamedes.*

64: *in a country where an abundance of different races and – at least until very recently – an almost total lack of prejudice have led to a variety of racial combinations.*

That's the official line.

Did Strauss never fill out a hotel registration with a section marked *Cor – color?*

Has he never looked through a newspaper and noticed the requests, in the want ads, for *boa aparencia* – light-skinned appearance?

When was divorce legalized in Brazil?

Page 79: *The winter rainfall would transform the tree trunks into rich topsoil.*

Perhaps an anthropologist can't be expected to have a precise knowledge of farming methods – the author Thomas Mann often made incorrect observations on agriculture – but then the anthropologist should refrain from commenting on topsoil.

The creation of topsoil is a very complicated microbiological process, which is dependent on the existence of so-called friable conditions.

There are several distinct factors involved in the production of topsoil: the friability of shade, heat, frost, and manure – there is no such thing as friability of rainwater; rain of any kind not only hinders the creation of topsoil, it often washes away substantial amounts.

And perhaps the completion of a simple rule of three, on page 166, is too much to ask of a professor in the humanities – yet from someone so thoroughly trained in scientific method?

On page 163 Strauss introduces issues of very complex, closed systems – in which he has no firsthand experience:

It is possible to infer all that one needs to know of an Asian bazaar, without ever having visited one, apart from two factors: the density of the crowd and the dirt. Neither of these are imaginable and must be directly experienced.

The nonsense blends into mendacity, and from there into racism. Lévi-Strauss does not like gays, as he documents on pages 27 and 52.

Page 300 shows him not above making cracks to make his point:
Besides, the bishop of Cuiaba had insisted upon providing me with one of his servants, for a cook; after several days we remarked that we were dealing with a veado branco, or "white roe," that is, a homosexual, who, what's more, had such a bad case of hemorrhoids that he could hardly ride (218).

A human book.

It sounds correct, if not novel, when Strauss exclaims:
Whoever says "human" says "language," and whoever says "language" says "society" (450). His comments on Brazil rest upon a knowledge of Portuguese poorly tested by his colleagues in France, and the spelling mistakes that run through the Plon edition find their way into the German as well.

An individualized orthography is something creative; when the structuralist writes *gallinha*, *assucar*, and *favella*, however, it merely reveals that the structure of the Portuguese language remains closed off to him.

In contrast to other Romance languages, Portuguese consonants are not doubled after a short vowel.

155: *In this way I became familiar with the picturesque language of Sertão, which, for example, in the place of our pronoun* one, *offers several possibilities –* homem, *"human" or "man,"* camarada, *"comrade,"* collega [sic! for colega in the German edition as well] *"colleague,"* negro, *"black,"* tal, *"this" or "that,"* fulano, *"anyone," and so forth.*

These expressions are hardly specific to the language of Sertão. Rather, they are used by every Brazilian, indeed by all Portuguese. Possessing such a mastery of Portuguese, Strauss lets the various Indian tongues be interpreted by other Indians, who usually know even less Portuguese than he.

III: *During the time of our brief stay, it was naturally not possible to learn the language (Caduveo), even though our hosts' Portuguese was fairly weak.*

159: *With the help of signs we explained to them that we wished to visit their village.*

237: The German edition embellishes: *I then set myself to the task of learning Nambicuara.*

In the original, Strauss admits that he didn't get very far in this tongue either:

318: *J'apprenais donc un Nambikwara rudimentaire.*

And Tupi-Kawahib?

Page 299: *Knowing nothing of the language and having no access to an interpreter, I nevertheless was able to grasp certain social and intellectual aspects of the group's daily life.*

The failings of ethnographers are their virtues!

Page 300: *The Indians,* translates Suzanne Heintz in 1970, *were ready to explain their customs and ideas to me, but I did not understand their language.*

One of the few genuine admissions by Lévi-Strauss – which he nevertheless tries to defuse, poetically, twenty lines later:

And so, for want of men willing to converse, I let the ground itself speak.

The Indians unwilling? Lévi-Strauss was too lazy to learn their language.

Suzanne Heintz sensed this and, with a nod to the sales division of Kiepenheuer Publishing, wrote:

Thus, in the absence of men whom I was able to understand, *I let the ground itself speak.*

The Land of Laughter

In spite of this state of affairs Lévi-Strauss can say, on page 329:
The women think of themselves as a collectivity.
I would like to know the method whereby one, without knowing a language, is able to form meaningful statements on thoughts that have their only place within this language.
It is the same method that lets young structuralists and psychologists in Senegal assume a position from which to utter judgments on the Oedipus complex, without understanding a single African language. This misunderstanding enables other structuralists and psychologists, further, to perform hundreds of shock treatments every day, all the while failing to observe the most primitive medical precautionary measures, in the corridors of hospitals.

The disturbed relationship of man to language, and language to society, penetrates the French as well:
I'm not referring to the pretentious *passé simple:*
Nous fûmes reduits.
Nous roulâmes, which even in 1955 must not have been any less insipid – or the manner in which Lévi-Strauss splices activities into speech:
sauterelles, qu'ils avaient passé la journée entière à recolter.
. . . grasshoppers, which they had spent the entire day in collecting.
This is a ceremonial French, of which there are countless examples. What I'm referring to, though, are logical problems:
314: *paraît à peine croyable . . .*
Something seems *(paraît)* this way or that, and something is hardly believable *(peine croyable).* But the phrase "something that seems hardly believable" is quasi-syntactic, a semantic scarecrow.
The repeated mix-up between *sociologique* and *social* – parallel to the frequent confusion, in Germany, between "psychic" and "psychological" – leads, in Lévi-Strauss, to an interesting assertion:
Page 261 of the German text rightly corrects the author:
They, the Nambicuara, had taken over the symbols without under-

standing their meaning, and this more with a view to a social *than an intellectual purpose.*

The original, however, states:

– *and this more with a view to a* sociological *purpose.*

This leads, in the original, to an outrageous admission:

They had taken over the symbols without understanding their meaning, and this more with a view to a sociological than an intellectual purpose. Thus it is clearly not a question of knowing, retaining, and understanding, but rather of increasing the prestige and authority of an individual or function.

Who is taking over words – that is, symbols – without understanding their meaning?

Where has sociology ever declared itself more clearly, and in such a grotesque fashion, with the aid of Freudian analysis?

Ill-chosen, meaningless adjectives fill the entire book:
The body is *robust,*
the voice *harsh* or *melodious,*
a letter *attentive* or *discreet,*
advice *deferential* or *frigid,*
a gesture *distressing,*
a posture *charming,*
a posture *discreet* and *obliging,*
a glance *friendly,*
students are *delightful,*
a resolution is *virile,*
a *charming* severity,
discreet fraternity,
a *remarkable* conservatism,
a *characteristic* aspect,
spirits *seductive* and *poetic,*
a *laughing* river,
the week *pleasant,*
the natives *gracious,*
the passage *exultant* . . .
and likewise on every page.

And this nonsignificative speech prepares the way for another type of linguistic posture:

The Land of Laughter

The tropics are supposed to be *triste*, yet throughout the entire work they are never subjected to an analysis in terms of misery, the mechanism of the author's melancholy is never revealed – rather the *tristesse* is implied, hinted at by means of verbal fetishes:

Memories are impoverished (14).

The natives are dirty and poorly groomed (54).

A tribe has been reduced to a handful of poor and uprooted individuals (39).

The most wretched of all retreat to the tops of the morros, *in the* favellas [sic!], *where the black population, dressed in tattered but always freshly cleaned clothing, play on the guitar those enchanting melodies that rain their joyous rhythms down upon the city during carnival season.*

The German translation cleverly whitewashes the paternalistic racism of this picture:

Strauss writes:

Miséreux – poor devil.

Noirs – blacks.

Lessiver – to wash in lye, instead of *laver* – to bathe.

He never set foot in a *favela* and yet observed the stunning elegance in which the Afro-Americans of Rio were always dressed! And yet Lévi-Strauss sees only dying populations, forever afflicted with malaria or hookworms (128).

Wretched farmers (129).

Threadbare living (159).

Fishing methods that are stingily imitated by the whites (197).

Miserable hamlets (197).

Wretched farmers (202).

No real cheerfulness (241).

Deplorable objects (335).

Ridiculous means (354).

Piteous personalities (421).

And meanwhile I wandered through the wilderness, on the lookout for vestiges of foreign peoples (347), translates Suzanne Heintz, a line that in the original reads: *to search out among the refuse of humanity.*

From time to time the disturbances that lead to such a rigidity of expression become clear.
Whoever says "bee" says "honey" (216).
And what did Claude Lévi-Strauss think of the many varieties of rain-forest honey?
J'en ai recensé treize (307) – He never ate it, never tasted it.
Honey is, the wake of Marcel Mauss, "reviewed."
Parfums s'analysent en plusieurs temps (307) – Fragrances are not inhaled, but rather analyzed, in several phases.
When he eats meat, it's never brisket or a leg – *chacun en devora une bonne livre* – he devours a good pound (370).
Perroquet rôti et flambé au whisky – roast parrot with whiskey flambé, is simply another facet of the same insensitivity.
Lévi-Strauss remains a professor, a representative of the *grande nation*, even in the jungle.
My chauffeur (235).
Only twelve head of cattle remained to me (371).
My company cook.
I distanced myself from a section of my company (388).
A half-century of Brazilian history, too short to be of service to the judgment of our millennial societies (107).
Extravagances of style in 1890 are partly excusable due to the sheer bulk and density of the material (108).
Architectural modes are forgiven by Lévi-Strauss.
The painters of Florence are reproached for having made with precision that which ought not to have been made (472).

Yet the brutality is not always hidden behind pity, condescension, and conceit:
Page 179: *Quelle difficulté pour se procurer ces pauvres objets! La distribution préalable . . . de nos bagues, colliers et broches de verroterie est parfois insuffisante pour établir l'indispensable contact amical.* – Suzanne Heintz translates, in order to make the book marketable in 1970: *What difficulties arise in purchasing one of these meager objects! The distribution of all our glassware among the members of the families in question, all our rings, necklaces, and brooches, was often far from sufficient in securing the friendly contact so indispensable to our work.*

The Land of Laughter

The *all*, *far*, and *so* have been inserted by the translator.
The original reads, with more severity:
The preliminary distribution of our rings, necklaces, and glass brooches to the entire family is sometimes insufficient in securing the indispensable friendly contact.
On the same page:
On se sent honteux d'arracher à ces hommes si dépourvus un petit outil dont la perte sera une irréparable diminution.
In the German free adaptation:
One felt, deep down, ashamed to coax from these poor people a thing that they might perhaps never be able to replace.
This is far from the original, however:
One felt ashamed to wrest from these wretched people a small tool whose loss would be an irreparable diminution.

Lévi-Strauss is as coquettish as he is cynical.
What won't he do for the sake of a scientific experiment?
96: *A feverish Indian, whom we encountered alone in an abandoned village, seemed to us an easy catch. We would put a pickax in his hands, shove and shake him up a bit. Unfortunately none of this had any effect, for he seemed not to understand what we wanted of him. Were we once again not to attain our goal!? We resolved, finally, to play our last card and declared to him that we wanted to eat koro. This at last was met with success, as we managed to drag our victim over to a nearby tree trunk.*
The original lacks all conditionality, and the Indian is not just a bit shaken up.
The ax was put into his hands, he was shaken, he was shoved.
Such methods recall the Nazi occupation of France, a period that Strauss avoided by staying in New York.

On page 256 a somewhat lengthier story begins:
At least I succeeded in convincing my friends from Utiarity to take me with them to their village, where I could arrange some sort of meeting with other related, or allied, groups. . . .
. . . he insisted on one condition, however: that we leave a part of the baggage behind, taking only four oxen to carry the gifts.
This journey, in fact quite dangerous, remains a grotesque episode in my memory. We had hardly left Juruena when my Brazilian col-

league pointed out to me that there were no women or children traveling with us – only men, and that these were all armed with bows and arrows. According to travel literature, *such circumstances suggested that an attack was imminent. We made our way forward, then, with mixed feelings, making sure from time to time that our Smith & Wessons – what the natives called Semeet Veshton – as well as our carbines, were ready at hand.*

Like a friend among friends.
The anthropologist's shocking behavior is supposedly minimized by the friendly poke at the natives' poor pronunciation of English.
Later, there is nothing to eat:
The Indios – Frau Heintz translates the neutral *les indiens* with the racist *Indios* – *the Indios had counted on our finding wild game along the way, and thus had no provisions; for our part, we resorted to our emergency rations, which naturally could not feed everyone.*
Compared to the original:
It was impossible to divide it among everyone.
Page 62: *and seldom do I attempt to solve any sociological, or ethnological, problem, without first sharpening my reflections on a few passages from Marx's 18th Brumaire, or the* Critique of Political Economy.
The leader of the Indian tribe has a different socialist consciousness:
This one then disappeared, in the company of one of his wives; around evening the two returned, their large basket filled to the brim with grasshoppers, which they had spent the entire day in collecting. Although grasshoppers don't seem like much of a delicacy, everyone fell vigorously upon the basket of food and refreshed their spirits.
The story ends with a list:
The list of objects that I was to exchange for the Indians' gifts. –
Evil Indians.
Tristes tropiques.
Lévi-Strauss loads four oxen with gifts, the Indians only make a show of giving. In reality, they simply await the gifts of the generous European.
Suzanne Heintz recognized the extent of this hypocrisy and softens it in her translation:

The Land of Laughter

the list of objects . . . that I wished to exchange for the Indios' gifts.
On page 200 one can observe Lévi-Strauss on his Parisian shopping spree:
Since the Indios like to dye their twine with urucú, I selected a red, roughly twisted fiber, which had a handmade appearance.
With his gift of artificially primitive-looking yarn, Lévi-Strauss tries to cheat the Indians out of valuable objects, working to cheapen their sense of style. In his account, however, he describes the Indians as materialistic.
It is the same procedure he uses when he deplores their seeming unwillingness to rebel, or when he transforms his own inability to learn their language into a vice on the part of the Indians.
On page 21:
je me sentais déjà gibier de camp de concentration.
There is an expression in France, *gibier de potence* that, while often translated as *gallows bird*, actually means *gallows game*, that is, as in wild animal.
Gibier de potence would be used in a casual, seigneurial situation; it has a you-know-what-I-mean air about it.
Gibier de camp de concentration.
A concentration camp bird.
Pauvre gibier, pris aux pièges de la civilisation mécanique, sauvages de la forêt amazonienne, tendres et impuissantes victimes, je peux me résigner à comprendre le destin qui vous anéantit.
Poor beast, caught in the traps of mechanized civilization, savages of the Amazonian forest, tender and helpless victims, I can resign myself to comprehending the destiny that destroys you.
More rhetorical doubt cast upon the inhumanity that is ruining the Indian cultures, then back to insight into "the way things are," the right of the stronger, etc.
The designation *pauvre gibier*, poor beast, poor little chick, both damns and redeems the Indians from the very beginning of the paragraph.
Never, without a doubt – except in the concentration camps – has man so mistreated other men, like cattle (144).
as in India:
as in the bitter sales exhibition, in which the religious life of the Indian peoples runs its course.

Not colonialism or its consequences in India, mind you, recall the death camps, but Indian folk religions! They take men for cattle.

Il suffit d'une balle dans leurs troupes bondissants (de singes) pour abattre à coup presque sûr une pièce de ce gibier; rôtie elle devient une momie d'enfant aux mains crispées, et offre en ragoût la saveur de l'oie (377).

One need only send a bullet into these leaping bands of monkeys to kill, with relative ease, one of this type of game; roasted, it becomes an infant mummy, with clenched fists, while in a ragout, it is pleasantly reminiscent of goose.

One of this type of game *(gibier)*.

Gibier of a concentration camp.

Indians, poor beasts *(gibiers)*.

Infant mummy.

The Indian folk religions take men for cattle, just like in the death camps!

Or, if a band of natives passes by, another routine goes into effect, new methods of counting, names of parts of the body, kinship designations, genealogies, inventories, etc. (370).

It is the routine of a camp leader.

Our friends were not actually people, but functions (112).
Comment donc ne pas emporter . . . ne pas les traiter en bêtes, puisqu'il vous contraignent à les considérer tels par cette déraison qui est le leur? (152).
Lévi-Strauss is speaking of the *rickshaw boys*:[3]
How can one not lose patience . . . and not treat them like animals, since they force you to think of them as such, by their inherent madness?

Not he who invokes inhumanity is guilty of it, but those who suffer it:
And, though I am somewhat ashamed at the thought, I cannot resist comparing these refugees – whom I hear from the window of my

3. In English in the original.

palace as they sigh and whine all day at the gate of the prime minister, rather than chase us from these rooms where several families would be able to live – with the gray-faced black raven who would ceaselessly crow in the trees of Karachi (135).

An incendiary, self-incriminating air!
And with this the grossest of vulgarities as one, speaking from an impregnable position, reproaches the incapacitated victims: *you are so bad off that you can't even rise up against me.*
And is even this insight sincere: *if things were arranged more reasonably, more families would be living in my palatial room*?!
Page 455 can be read as revealing how Lévi-Strauss would react if the Indians did insist upon their rights.
He thrusts himself – *officiel et urgent* – into the first-class compartment, forcing a family to be separated.

Many of the passages cited seem to have been composed in a kind of trance, in a singsong voice that we can also observe in Sartre, Malraux, Claudel, Jünger, and many others.
I find his intimate, succinct, and humorous passages more disturbing, as in the work of Lorenz; in a less excited state it might be more reasonable to take him at his word:
Je suis tout occupé à photographer des détails d'architecture, poursuivi de place en place par une bande de négrillons à demi nus qui me supplient: tira o retrato! tira o retrato! ("Fais-nous une photo!") A la fin, touché par une mendicité si gracieuse – une photo qu'ils ne verraient jamais plutôt que quelques sous – j'accepte d'exposer un cliché pour contenter les enfants (29).
The ethnographer is *completely* engaged in photographing some architectural *details* – thus dabbling in a fairly difficult, specialized activity (an attitude that comes out in his touristic shutterbugging, as one can judge from the subtitles that accompany the photos in the French edition: *Playful jostling and friendly contests; The Dreamer*), when he is *pursued* by a *mob* of small Afro-Americans, Strauss uses the slave trader's term, *négrillons*. They are *half-naked* and *beg* him: take our picture. Nor would they have incorrectly said *tira o retrato*, but rather, more logically, *tira um retrato,* take a picture *for us.* They were not thinking of it as a

possession. No black youth of Bahia is so stupid as to think, before anyone knew of the discovery of Polaroid, that he could have had this photo.
They probably only wanted to be thought worthy of representing their city.
Finally, the diligently working European scholar is *touched* by such gracious begging.
Gracious in that they could only hold a few pieces of money in their hands. Black children beg from an early age. In general they can only conceive of that which they can grasp with their hands. He thus shows himself quite ready to expose a *cliché*, to *satisfy* the children.
Did the thought never occur to Lévi-Strauss as to what might actually satisfy a child in Bahia, living under the dictatorship of Getulio Vargas?

The inhumanity of such conduct and language is outdone only by the strategic silences – in the 1955 version as well as the 1970 German translation.
Gontram de Veiga Jardim, who in 1968 published a series of articles on the Indians of the Brazilian Correio de Manha, claims the following:
In the past thirty years an unprecedented genocide has been waged against the Indian people.
They are hunted with bloodhounds, shot from airplanes, their food is poisoned with arsenic, their clothing infested, they are left to starve, strafed with napalm, injected, not with vaccine, but smallpox, and cut into pieces with machetes.
Today, the Nambicuara have been exterminated. The Bororo work as slaves on the fazendas.
Perhaps, in the end, I am too severely critical of the theoretician Lévi-Strauss, perhaps his abstract writings are more humane, precise, substantial. I would not try to hide the fact that much of that work, after a single reading, seemed to me like puffed-up nonsense.

Is it not shameless, when an author is so abusive of one of his fellows?

Sure.
What did Claude Lévi-Strauss ever do to me?
Still, what did Claude Lévi-Strauss ever do to modify his statements on the Brazilian Indians?
And so the *Tristes tropiques* became a point of departure for a new tumescence, a plaintive and brutal voice that had a formative impact on both the poetry and the science of the 1970s.

THE SEMBLANCE OF A CURE
De Instauranda Aethiopum Salute by Pater Alonso de Sandoval, Society of Jesus, 1627

Hamburg, June 1980

In 1627, when the Thirty Years War had been raging for nine years, there appeared, in Seville, the first part of a planned two-volume work, whose second part, however, was never published. Its title:
De Instauranda Aethiopum Salute,
which, translated favorably, might read:
How to Bring Salvation to the Ethiopians – and unfavorably:
On Instituting Salvation for Blacks.
Sandoval was born on December 7, 1576, in Seville, the son of Tristán Sanchez of Toledo.
The king of Spain ordered the father to Lima, Peru, one year later, as Contador de las Cajas Reales.
Tristán Sanchez took his son along.
On July 30, 1593, after completing his studies at the Seminary of San Martin de Lima, at the age of seventeen, Alonso became a member of the Society of Jesus.
Several years later, the order declared New Grenada a Jesuit diocese.
In 1605 Sandoval traveled to Cartagena, and in 1606, as a missionary, into the Urabá region.

A companion writes:
Upon seeing a black man he was immediately overcome and, whenever possible, would stay a moment and speak with him and also instruct him in matters of faith and religion.
Sandoval settled again in Cartagena and immediately went searching for blacks.
In 1612, Padre Gonzalo de Lira relates the following of the thirty-six-year-old:
He had a great inclination for this work, of such importance, and was so determined to carry out this labor for the conversion of souls, going without sleep for days and nights on end, that his superiors were forced to restrain him, eventually convincing him to moderate his efforts.

From the introductory essay to the new edition, by Angel Valtierra, SJ, one can conclude that Sandoval advanced to the position of rector of the Jesuit College of Cartagena.
He befriended Pedro Claver.
Sandoval was called before the Court of Inquisition, and the General of the Jesuit Order instructed him to *address the Inquisition's representatives with the proper respect.*
Valtierra gives the following account, though it is left undated:
Being, perhaps, short on funds, Father Sandoval may have thought that the solution to his problems lay in sending a trusted monk into the region of Cabo Verde, to sell linens and salves; the economic mission was unsuccessful, and, on its return, the boat was attacked by the Dutch, the monk lost everything, and was able even to survive only with great difficulty.
Father Vitelleschi, the Jesuit General, first ordered that the facts be investigated and, if found true, that the rector be relieved of his duties. What's more, he would be subject to a second, severe punishment.
We are given to understand that God intended to punish the greed of Father Sandoval.
Was he relieved of his duties?
Valtierra's account is coyly reticent.
De Instauranda Aethiopum Salute was probably written in Lima, between 1617 and 1619; the work's citations are drawn from a list of books larger than that of the Jesuit College in Cartagena.

The Semblance of a Cure

In 1619, Sandoval published, in Seville, the translation of a Portuguese biography of St. Francis Xavier.
In 1651, a fierce epidemic broke out in Cartagena.
The Jesuit College lost nine monks.
Alonso de Sandoval fell ill.
A festering tumor covered his body.
He died on the first day of Christmas, 1652, at the age of seventy-six.
By 1627, the affairs of Ethiopia had become routine.
Scarcely 200 years after the beginnings of African colonization, not 150 years since the discovery of the New World – and yet still, under the biblical aegis, and with the blessing of several popes, a program of genocide, death camps, and forced migrations was imposed, openly and without resistance, upon the people of Africa.
Sandoval's book offers little new.
Sandoval's compilations on the subject of Africa, now openly tolerant, now reproducing the resentment of other writers, are seldom based on his own field research – rather, he quotes from already published works; even the notion of an instauration of salvation had already been formulated by Pater Joseph de Acosta, in the *De Procuranda Indorum Salute,* which Sandoval quotes, in two places.
Bartolomé de las Casas's *The Sole Means for Bringing All Men into the Proper Faith* (1537) is not mentioned by Sandoval.
Today, the work is acute due to its republication, due to the popularized celebration in Colombia of the four hundredth birthday of Pedro Claver, a student of Sandoval, and above all due to its schizophrenia, its contradictions, its transcriptions of prejudices and modes of conduct that continue undiminished, to this day, in connection with Afro-American culture.
The text is not without its artistic merits:
Concerning several unique and miraculous events . . . in the kingdoms of these Ethiopians (164).
Among the other, excellent qualities that the story reflects, two are present in extraordinary measure: truth and pleasure.
Full of rare and memorable things.
Not less marvelous or, to put it another way, monstrous (166).

Sandoval was a contemporary of Góngora.

We find a description of hermaphrodites – astounding for a Jesuit steeped in Aristotelianism and who, perhaps, retained a deep affinity for it:

Hermaphrodites, by nature both male and female, sometimes function as a man and sometimes as a woman, like androgynes, of whom Aristotle says that they have the right breast of a man and the left of a woman (29).

Since the female principle, like the male, is, for the sake of reproduction, active, she acquires a real similarity to his principle, yet remains essentially feminine.

And therefore it is more reasonable to say that the monster is nothing other than a mistake, an error (pecado) *of nature* (29).

Entrails fascinate him:

In its bowels this earth produces minerals and many rich metals (135).

It seems that we can discover the most important reason from the very bowels of the matter (29).

And the Jesuit father Sandoval successfully works Jesus Christ into an African sacred rite:

Dressing ourselves in the bowels of our Lord Jesus Christ, and in His infinite Mercy . . . (466).

The Serere in Senegal, in the psychiatric rite known as *n'doep*, tie up an initiate with the intestines of a sacrificial animal.

In a clever turn Sandoval hints, in 1627:

I now believe that such animal forms are possible in the world, above all in Ethiopia . . . endowed not with a rational faculty, but with a natural instinct so highly developed that one is convinced of its free employment; observing this, one can almost believe that they are human, since these creatures bear a marked resemblance to men. This is also clearly the case in certain apes who, with respect to their body parts, recall the forms of men, and who as a result of their highly developed instincts seem almost rational.

Darwin's *On the Origin of Species by Means of Natural Selection* did not appear until two hundred years later, in 1859.

In 1865, the Jesuit priest Mendel published *Experiments on Some Hybrids of Plants*, which, along with the Mendelian rules of inherited characteristics, was more or less ignored prior to 1900; are these principles foreshadowed in the work of Sandoval?

The Semblance of a Cure

And the treatment of such ideas as instinct – *instinto* – and reason – *entendimento* – does this not presuppose our more modern, ethological notions?

On page 67, Sandoval seems pretty far-out, for a priest, yet he still remains lucid:

and, in order to strike fear and terror into an enemy, no one (of the African Gallas) was ever without a foot, or hand, or some other part of the human body, which they would, in a dire situation, carry in their mouths – this and their wild behavior being sufficient to put whole armies to flight, even if the latter were gathered expressly for an attack upon them.

From which we can imagine, if these barbarians are able to rout their enemies by the mere sight of human flesh in their mouths, how much a humble Christian, son of the Church and soldier of the militia of Christ, our Lord, could do by carrying himself the flesh of God in his mouth.

He reveals, in this remark, a religious-historical context that had hitherto been camouflaged.

No matter how poetic, bold, and naive in style, method, and expression –

Valtierra: *He uses index cards and translators.*

Sandoval: *I myself witnessed all of these events.*

Sandoval: *As the drawings attest.*

Valtierra: *In Cartagena, Sandoval's great sociological experiment was carried out.*

– the Jesuit priest never lets the Catholic Church, nor the order, nor its founder, Iñigo, slip from his memory:

Praise for the Society of Jesus – or, that which Sandoval understands as praise for the Society of Jesus – pervades the entire work.

Page 48, in the Philippines:

Conversion and the establishment of native "reductions," or doctrinas, . . . are the perennial task of the Compañia de Jesús.

Page 63, in Africa:

Wherever the great commercial transactions of the Portuguese take place, there the priests of our faith are never lacking.

Page 108, in Cartagena, as the inhabitants gather round to observe the arrival of new African slaves:

And, among them, the priests of our Compañia.
Sandoval has a parasitic manner of exploiting his various topoi and motifs – the image of the moon, for example, is drawn out into an ideological and verbal apotheosis of Ignatius Loyola, in a place, moreover, of great importance, in any literary work – shortly before the end, at the high point, just before the great tome comes to a close:
The most beautiful moon of our Holy Father Francis Xavier derives its divine light from our sun and our patriarch, St. Ignatius.
Sandoval's discreet loyalty to the Order extends, quietly, to his bibliography.
Taking the trouble to follow up on his citations, one soon finds that almost all the important works on the subject of African discovery and development have been left out of consideration: Herodotus is cited only once, and incorrectly:
The Ethiopian queen is not mentioned in the second chapter of the first book, but at I, 185, and II, 100; also, her name is not Nitrotes, but Νίτωκρις – Sandoval cites from memory, which suggests that he did not make use of the extensive library at Lima. The classics, above all Aristotle and Pliny the Elder, are well represented, even Homer and Diodorus Siculus.
But beyond Marco Polo and Mendez Pinto, one finds neither Arab accounts, nor Idrisi, nor Ibn Batuta, or the descriptions of Jewish traders employed by the Arabs.
The Portuguese explorer Azurara is passed over, as are Ramusio's works, Jasper Thompson, and Boccara.
In their place one finds Brother Juan de los Santos, Father Guerrero, Father Guelino, etc., etc.
The explanation for this is given on page 493:
Como refieren nuestros autores – Sandoval gives precedence to the accounts of the Jesuit Fathers.

In his renunciation of the African slave trade his sentences often take on a Büchnerian acuity:
It is a known fact – even though the men of honor about whom we will write do not believe so – that, at the beginning of the world, God did not people the earth with masters and slaves.
A sentiment in which Sandoval, unwittingly or no, opposes the example of Scripture:

The Semblance of a Cure

The poor man as well as the king, says Solomon, the emperor and the humble shepherd, are born into the same fate. They are subject to laws . . . nature has not given the noble born more eyes than the sinner, nor more hands and feet.
Great and small, we all are born, and must die (105).
I know of no text, in all of world literature, that exposes the reality of the slave trade to such an extent as the *De Instauranda Aethiopum Salute* of the Jesuit priest Alonso de Sandoval, and in all its brutal phases:
On page 100 he shows how the Europeans conspired to support two rivaling African princes, in order that, after the war, a greater number of slaves might fall into their hands. The captains of the slave ships themselves acknowledge, to the priest:
– that there wouldn't be half as many wars among the Negroes, if they thought for a minute that no Spaniards would afterward come and buy up the slaves (102).
Once the Negroes are captured, under god knows what legal title, they are immediately put into harsh captivity and are not allowed to exit before they arrive in Cartagena. . . .
In the area surrounding the rivers of Guinea, they (the slave hunters) secure their catch and cargo with long chains known as corrientes. . . .
And on the island of Loanda, they suffer such hardship, deprivation, and ill treatment, being bound with iron chains and insufficiently fed, that the days pass in misery; they are stricken with dejection and melancholy, as well as the certain conviction that their captors will, upon their arrival, either use them for fuel or eat them. As a result of this fear – exacerbated by the conditions of their captivity – during the journey, which lasts over two months, about a third of them die. Those who transport them have themselves told me that they (the Negroes) are forced to make the journey in cramped, unspeakably squalid conditions, that they are bound with chains by the neck, six to a single iron bar, as well as by the feet, two to a chain. . . .
Under the deck, where no light of the sun or moon ever shines, and which no Spaniard could ever inspect, however briefly, without vomiting, let alone linger for an hour, without risking exposure to serious disease . . .
One is also told, as a pretext, that everyone is fed once a day, though this consists only of a half bowl of cornmeal, or millet, a grain simi-

lar to our rice, uncooked, with a small cup of water, and nothing else,
only countless beatings, whippings, curses, ill treatment, shackles,
chains, abuse, iron maidens, stocks, fetlocks, neck irons, and other
inventions with which to punish and abuse their charges – who could
count them all?! (194).

And then the priest approached the ship, carrying a small container
of water, no larger than the palm of your hand, and sprinkled the
heads of all, before they had a chance to be washed. . . . And I was
told that there were so many Negroes to baptize on that day, that the
priest in charge had become fatigued, finally sitting down, yet still
baptizing so many more that his arms became tired.

Sandoval helps him in the following way: *As each Negro came up,
Father, and kneeled before the holy water, I took him by the nape of
the neck and plunged his head into the water, after which he stood up
and the priest laid his hand upon his head* (355).

Sandoval contrasts this harsh caricature of baptismal practice in
Africa with his own zealous methods in Cartagena, which I will
later treat in some detail:

*Before anything else, when a ship arrived and the Negroes had been
unloaded, we had to quickly see to the needs of each one individually,
a count was taken, and their point of origin determined, as well as
the original, native land of each one; we checked them for disease,
separating out those who were seriously ill, attempting to find out
what specific disease was afflicting them, and taking a count of the
children in this latter, sick group. We had to treat them with precise
haste, all the while signaling to each other as to which ones had no
more water, giving drinks to these and others who were dying of
thirst or were simply dying. These latter were the majority. I experienced a profound pity.*

*For they did not know how to ask for what they needed. The hopeless
mothers did not dare to point out even the most extreme needs of their
sons. They simply poured forth their cries. Countless times I have
seen a young man, crying at catechism, only to be given two or three
whole pitchers of water to drink* (378).

– *The water would run down from the head of each initiate into a
small basin, and, wondering where it could have gone, I realized that
this one had drunk it all, to the last drop.*

*So great is the thirst and need that these pitiable creatures suffer, as a
matter of course* (381).

The Semblance of a Cure

Whatever healthy ones have managed not to become sick . . . are ordered to be fattened, that they might bring a higher price on the market.

However much these suffer from a general deprivation, it cannot be avoided that many others will become sick upon their arrival, from abundance, following upon the heels of that ravenous hunger which had, until recently, afflicted all like a plague. One beneficial effect of this, however, is that it teaches the slave owners a measure of patience – who, when they are poorer, treat their slaves more kindly and give them small presents; when they are wealthy, turn them over to cruel and faithless domestic servants, since the masters themselves have more important matters to attend to, with the result that, several days later, the entire estate has become a sick house, a world of the dead. Some die of dysentery, cramps, and fever, others from the pox, typhoid, or scarlet fever, and a disease they refer to as Luanda, *which is untreatable, and whose symptoms include a swelling of the entire body and a rotting of the gums* (108).

One feels great pity and compassion to see such suffering, so many sick and helpless people, and so little encouragement or assistance on the part of the masters, who usually leave them lying, naked, on the ground, without shelter or cover, dying miserably on all sides, with no one to trouble themselves over their bodies or their souls, so that one often wonders whether the cause of their death is disease or simply neglect and abandonment.

My proof shall be that I have seen with my own eyes and wept: in several of the ship owners' houses, the lodgings consisted of planks, or crates, which were used to separate the men and women while sleeping. . . .

and there, finally, tormented by flies, some lying on planks, others below, they died. . . .

and this only after the owners had taken measures to ease their situation: earlier, they were left, naked, on outside porches, in the cattle runs and other out-of-the-way places where heavy sickness all the more easily struck them down (109).

And the punishments to which their masters subject them, often for very minor offenses, consist in the following: tar and feathers; burning the skin to the point of flaying and killing them; severe whippings and the worst forms of torture. They often died of fear, gangrenous and full of worms . . . and who would not cringe with horror to learn that a noblewoman killed her slave, as a form of punishment, along with two others.

The first she hanged from a beam in her house, later claiming that the dead woman had hanged herself. She then put her in a box, weighted and secured it with stones, and ordered another of her Negroes to throw it into the sea, that none might know of her sins, but the body was retrieved and the wounds bore witness to her unheard-of brutality (194).

Turning our attention to the nourishment that is usually given them, it is, for the most part, so small as to be hardly deserving of the name. And when, after so many beatings and harsh words, such inadequate care and ill treatment, the masters finally let them sleep, it seems as if they rest for half of their lives only to suffer, miserably, through the other half. But this is hardly the case, for if a Negro works in the mines, say, he does so from sunrise to sunset, and often for a good part of the night, and if he wishes to rest, he must first of all find a place where this is possible – where the fierce and pitiless mosquitoes will leave him in peace. At 3:00 A.M. it is off to work again.

If a Negro works on a plantation, it is more or less the same (195).
Christians punish their slaves more often, in one week, than the Moors do in an entire year (195).
Many slave owners will, as a rule, free their slaves if they are sick, so as not to have to care for them, with the understanding that these will return to work as soon as they are recovered (197).
They let them perish in their own excrement (196).
When the mass had ended, we went up to him, only to find him with his mouth upturned and spewing forth some liquid matter, his eyes bulging, his hands clutching his temples (578).

But one could also cite different sentences:
St. Ambrosius remarked that the reason Abraham was so concerned that his son not marry a woman of Canaan lay not in the fact that the Canaanites were worshipers of idols, but that they were the descendants of a dishonorable father; Noah had cursed his son Ham, on account of the shamelessness with which he had conducted himself before his father, showing him so little deference. Ham lost not only his birthright, but his freedom as well, and became a slave, as did his entire line (26).

The Semblance of a Cure

How did the blacks come into slavery?
The crimes are usually adultery, murder, and theft, and when any of these has been committed, all the elders of the (black) republic come together at the center of the city; the guilty party is brought forth and the elders decide upon a fit sentence, which could be as extreme as death or serfdom. The king disposes over the criminal's descendants as well, who, like him, may be either sold or put to work as the king saw fit.

Slaves, Sandoval implies, were thus criminals – Africans who, in any case, did not have very long to live, facing either an immediate, cruel death or the prospect of harsh servitude in the king's employ, and who were thus granted a reprieve by being sold as slaves for the New World.

How does Sandoval characterize the captains of the slave ships?
. . . several Portuguese captains (were) men of such quality that one could not have asked for any better (9).

An exception?

Did Sandoval, as a Spaniard, want to transcend his own chauvinism with respect to the Portuguese?

During the period in which the Jesuit priest's writings were composed, almost every European ship carried slaves to the great slave emporia of the New World. Sandoval's that's-the-way-of-the-world attitude is hardly unique.

. . . a Portuguese captain, a knightly, trustworthy man . . .

Knightly, sure, but the remark isn't meant as a critique of the idea of knighthood.

Nor is the trust that the slave dealer evokes subjected to any further analysis.

On page 60 the friend of man lets slip the following remark:
Negroes, and other things . . .

And this is no mere rustling of verbal fetishes, no grinding of semantic gears but is rather supported by an entire stratum of muddled, contradictory notions.

. . . bony Negroes, healthy and capable of a great deal of work, and therefore more highly regarded than all the other African peoples (91).

. . . harder to manage, and of a lesser worth . . . for laborious tasks, resist disease more effectively, not as sensitive and less inclined to flee (94).

And the role of divine grace?

But rather, the divine Goodness desired that these slaves be given a lesser understanding, in order that their sensitivity be not so acute, since sensitivity is based upon subtlety of understanding and temperament (193).

And what says *prudencia*, the prudent foresight of the Jesuit who had wanted to sell linens and salve to the Negroes?

Our greatest glory is that God so loved and redeemed us, all men, without exception, by the blood of his Son (106).

Blood like money.

Slave trade *in excelsis*.

Slave trade with Africans.

Africans as commodities:

I know a powerful merchant whose wish is to collect the most precious pearls from the East and the West – souls that have been redeemed by his blood – from the crude and hideous shells of black and Indian bodies (587).

The church has rarely so openly declared itself the vicar of bloody imperialism.

A world of goods:

God, our Lord, wished to broaden the market for his wares in the New World, and therefore he sent countless kinds of precious material, golden brocades, displays of velvet, satin, damask, along with rich and important men (587).

If one believes in God, this would be hard to deny.

And if children ought to serve their masters as God himself, whose person the masters embody, and because God himself wills it that they should thus serve and obey, it is only right that the masters should prevail and lord over children (206).

And just as a child should neither disrespect his master nor break God's law, so the master must not disrespect the child, nor break God's law. . . .

Servants are children, and like children I raised them and freed them from the servitude of sin.

Thus begins an insidious conceptual maneuver.

Since Sandoval knows how to present his material in a concrete, convincing manner, he is able to win the goodwill of his reader to follow his extrapolations.

The Semblance of a Cure

"God himself," "God's law," and "masters" are detached from their social and moralistic landscape and presented as manneristic, descriptive terminology. "Africans," "Negro slaves," "bondsman," and "child" are ponderously interchanged. The father can cover his weak spot with the mantle of a liberator, because of his contribution that the prisoners of the death camps may be "freed from the servitude of sin."

And still more lurks behind the following phrases:

"Child," "servant," "slave," "African" – "animal-like," "not treated like an animal, lacking any higher sense," "chattel," "Siglo de Oro's goods," "raw materials":

Where is the noble animal for which you bear responsibility? And call it noble with good reason, for it was purchased by the most holy humanity of Christ (206).

Diego de Torres was a missionary in Africa. Sandoval says:

He discovered, for God, a large and rich mine, where he now labors (353).

Sandoval is not alone in such sentiments. He follows a tradition. The general attitude toward the enslaved masses has always been the same – from Moses to Angel Valtierra:

The Spanish king guaranteed freedom and independence to Domingo Bioho – but the governor of Cartagena de Indias did not honor the agreement and wiped out the Zimaron settlements, thank God!

says Valtierra, but still writes:

The work of Father Sandoval comprises, on the whole, a vast apology for the Catholic Church. She was never in solidarity with oppression.

Similar self-congratulatory, sleight-of-hand gestures can be seen in Holy Scripture; Sandoval, too, knows his Bible, referring to it often in his compendium on salvation:

In the first book of Moses, one finds:

Cursed be Canaan;
a servant of servants shall he be unto his brethren.
And he said,
*Blessed be the L*ORD *God of Shem;*
and Canaan shall be his servant.
God shall enlarge Japheth,

and he shall dwell in the tents of Shem;
and Canaan shall be his servant.
(Gen. 9:25–28).
Both Moses and his translator Luther refer to humans as money:
When a man strikes his slave, male or female, with a rod and the slave dies under his hand, he shall be punished. But if the slave survives a day or two, he is not to be punished; for the slave is his money (Exod. 21:20–21).
As for your male and female slaves whom you may have: you may buy male and female slaves from among the nations that are round about you. You may also buy from among the strangers who sojourn with you and their families that are with you, who have been born in your land; and they may be your property. You may bequeath them to your sons after you, to inherit as a possession for ever; you may make slaves of them, but over your brethren the people of Israel you shall not rule, one over another, with harshness (Lev. 25:44–46).
The apocryphal Jesus of Sirach is hardly less forward:
Fodder and a stick and burdens for an ass;
bread and discipline and work for a servant.
Set your slave to work, and you will find rest;
leave his hands idle, and he will seek liberty.
Yoke and thong will bow the neck,
and for a wicked servant there are racks and tortures.
Put him to work, that he may not be idle,
for idleness teaches much evil.
Set him to work, as is fitting for him,
and if he does not obey, make his fetters heavy.
Do not act immoderately toward anybody,
and do nothing without discretion (33:24–29).
One may object that that is all old, atavistic testament; or: these are recommendations, not commands; or: examples, ethnological, not ethical.
Yet even in the Gospel of Love, Matthew 25:24–30, one can find a harsh example on the subject of surplus value:
He also who had received the one talent came forward, saying, "Master, I knew you to be a hard man, reaping where you did not sow, and gathering where you did not winnow; so I was afraid, and I went and hid your talent in the ground. Here you have what is yours." But his

The Semblance of a Cure

master answered him, "You wicked and slothful servant! You knew that I reap where I have not sowed, and gather where I have not winnowed? Then you ought to have invested my money with the bankers, and at my coming I should have received what was my own with interest. So take the talent from him, and give it to him who has the ten talents. For to every one who has will more be given, and he will have abundance; but from him who has not, even what he has will be taken away. And cast the worthless servant into the outer darkness; there men will weep and gnash their teeth."
Christ seldom speaks in such terms.
But he does.
The Apostles assume this ideology as well:
Paul, in the Letter to the Romans:
Let every person be subject to the governing authorities. For there is no authority except from God, and those that exist have been instituted by God.
Paul to the Ephesians:
Slaves, be obedient to your earthly masters, with fear and trembling, in singleness of heart, as to Christ.
To Titus:
Bid slaves to be submissive to their masters and to give satisfaction in every respect; they are not to be refractory.
Peter, in the First Epistle:
Servants, be submissive to your masters with all respect, not only to the kind and gentle, but also to the overbearing. For one is approved if, mindful of God, he endures pain while suffering unjustly.

Here, too, one preaches a gospel of masochism, that exploitation might run more smoothly.
White is changed into black.
Injustice as grace – grace as injustice.
A straight line, a crooked deal.
In the second epistle one observes the ever-present conflation of man and animal, which also implies that one may be cruel to animals, and that one can help push the poor toward their irredeemable predestination:
Those who don't hesitate to malign kingly authority:
But they are like irrational beasts, by nature born to be hunted and killed, who slander what they know naught of, and who will perish in

their ruinous nature, and bring down upon themselves the reward for injustice.

Just as later, in the work of Lévi-Strauss: The victim is unjust, not the slave driver!

Thus it is hardly unorthodox when Angel Valtierra, SJ, author of a biography of St. Pedro Claver, writes – in a gesture of naïveté and self-evident truth:

The churches and monasteries had slaves, as did the popes and saints.

In 1488, the Catholic kings sent one hundred Moorish slaves to Pope Innocence, who received them with pleasure; Pope Nicolas V, in a famous bull, granted the Portuguese a monopoly in the commerce of African slaves.

Sandoval writes:

God showed them a way, that they might bear the trophy of the Holy Cross into the lands of barbarian, unknown peoples, a famous undertaking that would bring them eternal glory.

The first who began this work, to the glory of God and country, was the outstanding infante of Portugal, Don Enrique (54).

. . . when Cristóbal de Gama liberated the Moors (Abyssinians) (127).

The reality is less embellished by professions of faith:

In 1441, the first twelve Africans were hauled to Lisbon by Antam Gonzalvez and Nuno Tristão.

Henry the Seafarer sends an ambassador to the pope, setting out for him his plan for a more extensive plundering of the African continent.

Pope Eugene IV welcomes such campaigns, promising all who took part in them the total absolution of their sins in advance.

On May 3, 1493 – three weeks before, Columbus had returned from his journey of discovery – Pope Alexander VI, in the papal bull entitled *Inter Cetera*, concedes the entire New World to the kingdom of Spain.

Overnight, pressed by the intervention of the Portuguese, the pope changes his decision and, in the bull entitled *Inter Cetera II*, grants the west coast of Africa to Portugal.

A decision that puts the Spanish in the role of slave purchasers – and the Portuguese, of slave suppliers.

The Semblance of a Cure

In 1517, the Hieronymites of Haiti request more African slaves. The priest Las Casas receives his import license – a detail that he leaves out of his melancholy confessional memoirs.
Each Spaniard was allowed twelve Negro slaves.
In 1518, Pope Leo X, Giovanni Medici, is given an imprisoned Moor, Leo Africanus, as a gift.
In May 1520 again, the king grants, to the priest Bartolomé de las Casas and fifty other colonialists, the right to ship slaves into the New World.
On January 20, 1531, Las Casas writes the Spanish court, requesting more slaves.
The best expedient for the Christians is surely this: if your Majesty could be so kind as to lend each of these islands five or six hundred Negroes.
Not only did the archbishop of Cartagena de Indias dispose over Negro slaves, who had been "stripped of all rights"; the heads of the Inquisition employed black workers, and the Christian orders were known, in the slave markets, as good customers.
In 1540 Ignatius Loyola founded the Society of Jesus.
In 1540, fifty years after the discovery of the New World, slave imports were already at ten thousand per year.
In 1540, Las Casas's work, *A Brief Account of the Devastation of the West Indies*, was published.
In 1540, cattle were introduced into Cartagena from Santo Domingo. This marks the beginning of a cattle farming whose final effects are being felt today, by the disenfranchised descendants of the slaves.
The cattle farmers hire hit men, who get the labor representatives out of the way.
In 1547, Jesuit missionaries reach the Congo.
1548, Morocco.
In 1549, a Jesuit college is established in Brazil.
1557, one in Ethiopia.
Angel Valtierra writes, from the Jesuit college in Cartagena:
One found oneself forced to hire slaves as translators.
That may seem paradoxical.
Pedro Claver, the slave-dealing defender of slaves (212).
How does one get out of it?

Angel Valtierra:
The Church, profoundly moved, pursued an excellent tactic: Rather than embitter the hearts of the slaves by hatred, she dedicated herself to the task of softening the hearts of the oppressors (181).
And when Valtierra describes the saint Claver, how he lashed his way into Afro-American rites, he refers – rightly so – to St. Paul:
He teaches in a spirit of mildness!
But:
His punishment is severe!
The Jesuit Alonso Rodriguez who, along with Sandoval, was a teacher of the saint Pedro Claver, alone expresses dissatisfaction with the inexorable rules of the order's founder, Iñigo:
All the other things on the face of the earth have been made for humans. It follows, then, that man should use them insofar as they aid his development, and, insofar as they hinder it, they should be left alone. Therefore it is necessary that we should become indifferent to all created things.
San Alonso Rodriguez adds:
Humble yourself before all creatures, for the sake of God.

The Bible and the climate, profit and askesis, infections and sensitivities drive Sandoval, his student Pedro Claver, and a group of colleagues made up of monks and slaves into an insane undertaking.
Baptism and baptismal discussion invade the priests like an epidemic:
Sandoval devotes hundreds of pages to this question:
Do the hasty mass baptisms of African slaves possess any lasting validity?
How were they baptized?
Did the water touch the scalp?
Did the Negroes realize the significance of the act?
Did they give their consent? How should baptism, here in Cartagena de Indias, be performed?
How does one baptize *sub conditione?*
And *sine conditione?*
And in extremis, that the dying not fall into Hell?
If he hasn't assimilated the necessary knowledge of the sacraments?

The Semblance of a Cure

If he can no longer give his consent?
The idea never seems to occur to Sandoval that such considerations draw him into a religious materialism, helping to establish that which he allegedly opposes – namely, magic.
A magic broadened, moreover, by tears, strokes of the whip, cloths for wiping blood, and the sadomasochism of a bureaucracy drunk with Jesus, which has only scorn for humans.
Surely, it is this baptism fetish that triggers such successes in the conversion of slaves.
Angel Valtierra is liberal with the numbers:
Pedro Claver baptized three hundred thousand Negroes.
That would mean seventy-five hundred per year, by himself, or twenty per day, 365 days a year, for forty years.
And yet, according to the Congregación of 1627, Sandoval, in the first twenty years of his stay in Cartagena, had baptized seventy thousand Africans.
At the Congregación of 1642, however, this number is reduced to forty thousand, over a thirty-year period.
That's still twenty per day, every day.
Sandoval himself notes the following:
This is how we examine in Cartagena, how we conduct the catechism, as well as how we baptized six thousand people each year, in such a manner that no impropriety could be observed.
The Africans knew of similar, alogical machinations from their own religions; magic joined to magic, intolerance to intolerance, forming a continuous chain.
Since, for the intellectual priests, it was not reason and insight that guaranteed the functioning of the system of faith – irregardless of how insistently this was maintained by Christian doctrine – but beatings and bonbons:
The ones that must be baptized sine conditione come ten at a time, first the men, and then women; they are set down, roughly, onto their knees, following the custom of the Holy Father St. Francis Xavier . . . their hands are, with much devotion and tranquility, set over a spring, or a basin, if nothing more suitable is available, to catch the baptismal water; the priest of the Compañia wraps himself in a stole and puts the same questions to each individual, along with a brief exhortation, whose details we listed above, and which is immediately

translated, to insure that they have the will to be baptized, as well as the necessary faith, hope, charity, and contrition, or at least remorse, for their sins.
Once the father is convinced that they have been sufficiently prepared, they are given, always ten at a time, the most common name that they can pronounce, and which they are told to repeat, so as not to forget it . . . after this they are instructed that they must henceforth be known and addressed only by this name, as a Christian, and that they must forget their previous Moorish name, the latter suitable only for heathens and the son of the devil (402).

The sacred bureaucracy of the concentration camp, which recalls the song of the soldiers of the swamp.[1]

A chapter is entitled: *On the Excellence of this Task, and the Great Benefit to Those Who Accomplish It* (270).

Following upon this lie, which is supposed to contribute to salvation, is the moment of condescension and easy familiarity:

Tell me, children, Sandoval asks those who come ten at a time, seeing that I have taught you so many things and have, as you can see, labored so strenuously to make you into Christians – do you not love me? Do you not love me deeply?
All reply "yes" (396).
They heard, all lifted their hands and, looking upward, pointed toward God (391).

Is such mass brainwashing still the goal of the Society of Jesus?

A respect for Ethiopians, Africans, blacks, and Negroes is frequently announced in Sandoval's work:

Of the great respect that the Lord our God Lord has made evident with respect to these Negroes and their conversion . . . (211).

Forever schizoid, two pages later prattling away with renewed vigor in the most blunt, racist language:

For God never disdains a skin color, but rather the soul itself (213).

A statement that implies that a skin color may be contemptible.

---

1. The *Moorsoldarhenlied* (Song of the Soldiers of the Swamp) refers to a song by prisoners of the early concentration camps who had to work draining swamps in northwest Germany. See Wolfgang Langhoff's account *Die Moorsoldaten: Dreizehn Monate im Konzentrationslager* (Zurich: Schweizer Spiegel-Verlag, 1935).

Of the respect that the most Holy Virgin, our Queen, has made evident with respect to these peoples . . . (219).
Appallingly touching arguments!
Of the great respect that the Holy Apostles maintained with respect to the spiritual fulfillment of these Negroes . . . (224).
He knew how to juggle with words.
Of the high estimation and great respect that the Compañia de Jesús had with regard to the salvation of the Ethiopians (490).
With regard to the salvation of the Ethiopians – sure.
Is one not reminded of a desperate intellectual solidarity with workers, oppressed peoples, and noble savages?
Only the brief sentence on page 543 is of any importance:
Estos negros no son bestias como he oido decir.
These Negroes are not animals, as I have heard said.

He didn't have to listen around very much.
He need only have leafed through his own manuscript.
For as if in a state of *délire verbal*, an ecstatic chatter that is not overcome even today, on almost every page the tried-and-true soldier of Jesus lets slip numerous insults concerning those he is supposed to love, whom he claims to love, indeed whom he loves to the point of revulsion:
Page 11: *Uneducated Negroes . . .*
Page 14: *Without laws, without a single human trait . . .*
Page 16: *Barbarians . . .*
Page 18: *Detached from all human activity . . .*
Page 23: *Soulless . . . detestable . . .*
Page 35: *Soulless . . .*
Page 41: *Wretched . . .*
Page 47: *Like animals . . .*
Page 56: *Barbarian and black, with frizzy hair . . .*
Page 89: *Unhygienic . . .*
Page 115: *Bestial . . .*
Page 116: *Comparable to animals . . .*
Page 118: *Like cats . . .*
Page 118: *Like sullen animals . . .*
Page 119: *Like savages, or beasts . . .*
Page 119: *Not human . . .*

Page 166: *Ethiopians, or beasts . . .*
Page 269: *With such a foul smell . . .*
Page 323: *Awful smelling . . .*
Page 355: *Greasy, dirty hair . . .*
In the third book, chapter 18, there are sixteen similar, offensive statements, on six pages.
Page 558: *O race of Kaffirs! No less dark and loathsome in their bodies than their bodies!*
The penitential practices to which they subject themselves are no less bestial (38).
Only a Jesuit could make such a remark!
At the Jesuit College of Cartagena, flagellations were often so severe that a cloth was kept handy to wipe up the blood.
At his worst, however:
The Negroes, tyrannical and cruel, make others their slaves (50).
The respect of God for Negroes, respect of the Virgin Mary, the Apostles, the Society of Jesus:
The fate of the blacks, sad and dark – he babbles, tipping his hand.
A colleague writes him, from Africa:
And therefore Negroes were born . . . we could also say, "slaves" (27).
And though they are black in appearance, they too can attain to that white spotlessness which Christ bestows upon those who wash themselves in his blood (5).
To be black is thus not only an earthly misfortune; the skin color also expresses a state of sin and spiritual damnation.
These are prejudices that outlive St. Pedro Claver, who, whip in hand, took part in African rites, and who once demanded a fine from an African man and woman whom he heard talking in the marketplace, down to our day, down to Father Angel Valtierra, at the same Jesuit college:
Negroes – so crude (XV).

This was the mind-set of Father Sandoval, and later, of St. Pedro Claver. They went head-to-head with slavery (XXVI), says their brother Angel Valtierra. In a more extensive publication, he will claim:
St. Pedro Claver – liberator of a race.

The Semblance of a Cure

It is not a question, as Peter Michel Ladiges has asserted, of pointing out an individual's contradictions, but rather of revealing a contradictory individual.

Cynicism could hardly have been completely foreign to a well-traveled intellectual like Alonso de Sandoval; and yet perhaps he bled out this resistance as well, under the blows of the lash – in any case, he neither writes nor acts like a cynic.

That which he writes, he means to be taken "sincerely," his contradictions are "genuine" – which neither explains their occurrence, nor excuses their consequences; the ideologue's baptismal fervor all but extinguished the Afro-American culture in Colombia.

Nor is it possible to line up all the ugly quotes from the *De Instauranda Aethiopum Salute* on one side, and all the finer quotes on the other, and reach a sort of summary, final judgment.

Is it praiseworthy, when he writes:

Although it is true that the great controversies that have arisen among our learned scholars, from the need to justify this laborious and massive undertaking, have for some time left me quite perplexed. . . .

Still, I am resolved to write about it, and to leave the justification to the doctors who have written so learnedly on this point, above all our Dr. Molina (97).

He cites the letter of Father Luis Brendon, SJ:

There have always been priests of our Order, highly learned men, who have consistently held that there was nothing immoral in this affair, and in Brazil, myself and other priests often bought slaves for our services without the slightest scruple.

For the traders, who transport these Negroes, transport them in good faith, and you can buy them from them without any misgivings, just as they may sell them, without misgivings, for it is generally accepted that the bona fide owner of a thing is allowed to sell it, and that the thing itself may be purchased (98).

Is it reprehensible when Sandoval, in response to a confession, replies with an accusation:

Father, I am going to Angola, to pick up Negroes. On the way I shall undergo many hardships, much expense, and I will encounter many dangers; eventually I shall return with my cargo of enslaved –

whether justly or unjustly – Negroes. I ask you: is their captivity at all justified by the hardships, expense, and dangers that I will take on, both on the way there and during the return journey, in order that I might then sell them, in Christian lands, where they will remain heathens their entire lives?
I responded to him:
Go, your Grace, from here to the Church of San Francisco, which is quite far, and when you arrive, cut the cord from which a large lamp hangs and take it to your house. You will be placed under arrest and sentenced to death (just as a someone was recently hanged for stealing from the Church of Santo Domingo), but they will let you go when you tell them that you did not steal the lamp, but rather only took it as a token, and a reimbursement, for the hardships you had incurred in making the journey. If then, the judge accepts this justification for your efforts and spares you all punishment, I would say to you that you can go and transport your Negroes in good faith, and that the ground of your reasoning is secure.
Upon which his companion turned to him and replied, in great anger:
For God's sake . . . didn't I tell you not to ask these priests about anything?!

Was Sandoval enlightened or a reactionary?
Did he dissemble when he spoke for the slaves, or when he acted on behalf of the church?
Did he follow the command of the founder Ignatius?
In all things we must endeavor to prove that, even though I may behold something to be white, I will believe that it is black, if the hierarchy of the church has so determined it (365. Spiritual Training).
Was his dissemblance genuine and Jesuitical, or private, unpracticed, helpless?
Did he lose his head in the face of the African genocide, because he had one in the first place?
From what stratum does the revulsion break forth, in its effect like a twisted love?
From book to book, from page to page, and phrase to phrase, such questions must be addressed differently.

The Semblance of a Cure

The book is above all a document of a total contradiction; it shows how an experienced, clever Christian conducted himself vis-à-vis the Africans.

And that is why the work is still so important today.

It reveals certain reflexes, which only some Greeks, like Homer and Herodotus, were able to avoid, and which were already operative when the Egyptians cut from the porphyrite the inscriptions of their black Nubian kings, reflexes to which Sartre and Adorno still succumbed – like Sandoval, in 1627.

MY FRIEND HERODOTUS

New York, November 1980

I pick up a Sunday *New York Times* at the corner of Christopher Street and Seventh Avenue, Sunday night, about eleven o'clock.
It isn't easy to carry.
The ink gets all over everything.
I would guess it weighs about two and a half pounds.
I take the subway.
At least every other person heading in the direction of Times Square has a copy of the *Times* on their knees and reads attentively, greedily, skeptically, and with a touch of subservience, a black woman, a leather type, teacher, tourist, policeman.
The *New York Times* of Sunday, November 9, 1980, has nine sections – *Arts and Leisure, Business,* etc.
Herodotus' nine books were named after the nine Muses – 632 pages of Greek text.
630 pages – advertisements, a magazine, the *Books Review:* the *New York Times*.
On the average, about thirty-five hundred words per page, approaching 2.2 million words in the Sunday edition.
In Herodotus there are about nine words per line, and thirty-seven lines per page, yielding a total of 210,456 words.
He spent his entire life working on it.
He was born in Halicarnassus, an Ionian city of Asia Minor, in 480 B.C.
His father is thought to have come from Caria.
Herodotus took part in a revolt against the tyrant Lygdamis and was forced to flee to Samos.
He journeyed over a large part of the known world.
He is said to have been friends with Sophocles and to have read from his works at an Olympiad.

He died around 424 B.C., perhaps in Thurii, in greater Greece.
Three separate locales claim his burial site.
The *New York Times* edition of Sunday, November 9, contains ten times as many words as the entire extant work of Herodotus, which represented, in its day, the sum total of knowledge of the world, the sum of the life and researches of Herodotus, and an entire epoch's highest expression of artful perfection.
The written statements published every weekend by the *New York Times*, and other two-and-a-half-pounders like the *Estado* of São Paolo, or the *Miami Herald,* with circulations in the millions, fifty-two times per year, or about three thousand times in the lifetime of a Herodotus – it would be impossible for one person to even read through this wall of printed matter, on a weekly basis, if only to check for errors.

The written image of the world, which in Herodotus' day lagged insufficiently, and humanly, far behind its object, surpasses, in the *New York Times*, the world itself; the individual is no more able to assimilate the world's written image than Herodotus could assimilate the world.

Herodotus – still my friend, and maybe because of it?
Right from his very first sentence:
Ἡροδότου Ἁλικαρνησσέος ἱστορίης ἀπόδεξις ἥδε.
The researches of Herodotus of Halicarnassus are here set forth.
I am always reminded that so many trees have been felled for each Sunday edition of the *New York Times,* since by the third page I'm choking on an overabundance of information – nevertheless I buy it, at the corner of Christopher Street and Seventh Avenue. Like every writer, I have to do my research, like Herodotus, like Hecataeus, his Ionian predecessor:
τάδε γράφω ὥς μοι δοκεῖ ἀληθέα εἶναι.
I have written that which seems to me to be true.
οἱ γὰρ Ἑλλήνων λόγοι πολλοί τε καί γελοῖοι ὥς ἐμοὶ φαίνονται εἰσίν.
To me too, the words of the imperialists seem redundant and ludicrous.

My Friend Herodotus

Research.
Discovery.
It's a destructive reflex.
Without it I would cease to exist.
I recognize it in Herodotus – the contradiction between theory and praxis, love and knowledge, enlightenment and magic.
θωμάζω δέ προσθήκας γὰρ δή μοι ὁ λόγος ἐξ ἀρχῆς ἐδίζητο . . .
I am astonished – but since my work has, from the start, pursued the trivial, and matters of secondary importance . . .
(IV, 30).
Astonishment – this can also mean doubt.
In spite of this statement, asserting once and for all the supremacy of an empirical, scientific method, Herodotus has often been accused of falsification and flightiness.
Herodotus separates, as a modern would, between report and commentary and supplies, for a single event, the testimony of several eyewitnesses, leaving the conclusion up to the judgment of his readers.
His procedure is journalistic and poetic.
Herodotus moves within a peculiar, fairly secularized cosmos, which he shows to be dependent, in a precise manner, upon various mystifications; with an investigator's zeal he will enter, for example, into the logic of the magi, only to break off suddenly, remarking that the overall plan of his work compels him to do so.
Herodotus, my friend.
His wanderlust, his inability to sit still.
What's behind that corner?
What's beyond that ridge?
Not: knowledge is power! – but rather: travel is knowledge.
Sex.
The first prose author also writes the first *psychopathologia sexualis* – with more felicity than Freud, Herodotus's work implies that one travels on account of sex, that travel is a sexual need – writing and discovery!

I am convinced of one thing: Herodotus would hate hotels!
The most important chapters were written in semiretirement, in the company of a chambermaid.

The Gay Critic

The priests in Egypt exercised a formative influence upon him.
He liked oysters and visited gay bathhouses!
But how did he deal with lice?
It bothers me that he financed his journeys by selling off some of his belongings.
I can hear the editors, Dr. Thucydides and his contemporaries, upon his return: *Our readers aren't concerned with such things – blacks, difficulties of farming, Scythians. I beg of you . . .*
One can hardly know what he thought.
The word *beauty* escapes his lips, from time to time.

Reports on journeys of discovery are as old as journeys of discovery themselves.
Even today, no one can venture into the city, for the summer clearances, without remarking on the construction, the detours, the colors of the fabrics, and the outrageous coifs of their greedy neighbors.
On clay, in stone, in wax or on papyrus, the little black dwarfs are noted, the chimpanzees, gold, Phiops, Salomon, and the Punic Hanno.
Litanies of goods.
Tables of laws.
Fragments of text.
Hecataeus had produced the first superbook – a giant, world-embracing thing, uncannily unsummarizable, like the world itself.
This work has come down to us only in fragments.
The entire world as a book – in Mallarmé, somewhat later: only the book can be a world – becomes clear for the first time in Herodotus' nine books of researches – ἱστοριῶν – which is unfairly translated as "histories."

Language is – more than numbers, bone fragments, or artifacts – history itself; from language one can read how events were understood and planned – and in Herodotus, how thinking and action functioned, twenty-five hundred years ago.
The Heimeran (German) edition begins in the following way: *Herodotus of Halicarnassus hereby publishes his researches . . .*

My Friend Herodotus

Whereas the original reads:
Ἡροδότου Ἁλικαρνησσέος ἱστορίης ἀπόδεξις ἥδε . . .
the thrust of which might be rendered more faithfully as:
Herodotus of Halicarnassus' research lay out this [is] . . .
The modern editions of Heimeran and Kröner spare us, for the most part, the "either . . . or," the "just as . . . so also," "neither . . . nor," and "whereas . . . still": unnecessary terms that only contribute to the academic flatulence of so much restorative historical writing, semantic scarecrows that have little to do with real thinking, in German minds or Greek.
That's for sure!
In Herodotus, however, one finds a stampede of particles:
μέν, μήτε . . . μήτε, τε καί, δέ are used with extreme liberality. How can one remain sensitive to them, how imitate their nuanced subtleties?
Or are these simply the naturalistic mutterings of an archaic chatterbox?

There are two basic theories concerning the historical relationship between language and music:
The first: *The Birth of Tragedy from the Spirit of Music.*
The second: vice versa.
Music is something relatively late, derived from natural, mimetic expressions; grunts and cries must first develop into sense-conveying phonemes, which are eventually woven into verse, where they undergo musical intensification.
Or:
Differentiated, songlike sounds are secularized into a speechlike ensemble, extremely complex musical phrases simplify into a Sapphic hendecasyllabic line, a tragedy, or a string quartet, and finally into the grunts, cries, and particle stampedes of the weekly tabloids.
Herodotus stands between magic and naturalism.
The tragedies of his friend Sophocles were no longer the pure voodoo of an Aeschylus, nor yet the doubt-ravished melodramas of a Euripides.
Thus Herodotus' prose – following upon the cultic songs of his ancestors and prior to his descendants' naturalistic chitchat –

may preserve a linguistic stratum that is still songlike but has all the powers of a prose litany.

Does not the frequency of particles in Herodotus suggest, then, not the naturalistic, "natural" babble of an emcee, but rather the material remnant of an archaic music, related to the strictly modulated squeaks of primates, or the solemn trances of the Stone Age?

The study of particles in Herodotus might then yield us information on the situation in Greece during the period of the great tragedians, of the first great scholars, and on their concepts of the imagination, the *contenu mental* of an age in which the first and greatest prose that has come down to us was written – and whose subject was the world itself.

(Jorge Luis Borges once hinted at a countertendency – unfortunately, he was interrupted by a truly idiotic television reporter – which doesn't contradict my own hypothesis, however:

Borges remarked:

Free rhythms are more difficult than verse, prose is more difficult than free rhythms.)

It is, perhaps, too much to ask that the origin of prose itself be exemplified by this first piece of extant prose, the gigantic work of Herodotus.

Too many things concerning the preprosaic texts remain unclear. Were the royal cartouches of the Egyptians notations of an imagistic music? Imagistic lyrics?

Were the mercantile lists and early, dreadful law tables a form of litany? Read aloud, like an overly fastidious *délire verbal?*

How did one actually scan Sappho?

The pre-Socratic Empedocles still wrote in verse.

Was the work of Hecataeus organized rhythmically?

How might one translate into modern speech the graffiti scrawled on the *colossoi* at Abu Simbel? *I said to itself, that men who write graffiti treat words like beings able to speak for themselves.*

Can one understand prose as an expression of secularization? Therefore as a demythologizing process? As enlightenment?

As a diminishing of magical power and trance-inducing consonance, the identification of word and world?

My Friend Herodotus

The poor Greek Leo is sacrificed by the Persians – Leo the lion, chosen, perhaps, on account of his name, writes Herodotus, in book VII (VII, 180).

Τήλεφος μ' ἔγραφε . . .

Telephos wrote me, me the word, one can read on the statues of the Gods in Nubia.

The poetic word was an oracular word, a word of power and the world, from Homer to Rimbaud and Kafka, interjected, and calculated for effect; secularization – a distancing from the magical, and a movement toward the science of nature, from Homer to Thales, from Hesiod to Hecataeus and Herodotus, from Aeschylus to Sophocles – involves spurning the obscure, Pythian, spectral utterance, and a rejection of force and identification.

Apodeixis, layout, demonstration – and not of history, since this is a darker, more ominous concept, but of researches – ἱστορίη, as Herodotus refers to it in the Ionian.

In Herodotus this process of secularization is clearly modeled after the influence, and creators, of language.

In book IV (IV, 13), he describes Aristeias as ποιέων ἔπεα, *making an epic*, and φοιβόλαμπτος, *possessed by Apollo*, as if he were writing in a trance.

Hecataeus, on the other hand, whose γράφω ὥς μοι δοκεῖ ἀληθέα εἶναι, *I write what seems to me to be the truth*, shows up in a later phrase: τῇ γέ μοι φαίνεται εἶναι ἀληθές (VII, 139) – Hecataeus is, as Herodotus stresses, in three different passages, a λογοποιός, a word that is translated as "chronicler" but literally suggests "*word maker*" (II, 143; V, 36, 125).

In the German translation the word *historian* is often used, and a historiocentric *Altertumswissenschaft* (the collective study of the ancient world) may have very valid reasons for using this term. (Apropos of translation: I wonder how the 1977 Heimeran "revised" edition, which is also distributed by the Wissenschaftliche Buchgesellschaft, could keep the following phrase: *as befits a master race* (p. 1265), for the Greek:

οἰκὸς δὲ ἄνδρας ἄρχοντας τοιαῦτα ποιέειν [IX, 122].)

But, if we have to have a Father of History, everything must be referred to the idea of history, and, as is apparent in the German text, to a specific kind of historical scheme.

Plan and Organization of the Work. The editions of Tusculum and Kröner cram the unwieldy text into an absurd historical system: I. A. I. II. 1. B. I. 1.
Thus:
Book I.
Introduction:
1. *Purpose of the Work*
2. *Greeks and Barbarians in Mythic Times*
I. *The Greek Colonies and the Barbarians*
A. *The Greeks of Asia Minor and the Lydians*
I. *The Oldest Historical Accounts of the Lydians*
II. *Croesus*
1. *Croesus and Solon*
B. *The Greeks Abroad and the Persians*
I. *The Rise of the Persian Empire and Cyrus*
1. *Cyrus' Youth . . .*

The vast fields traversed by Herodotus in his prose are not so strictly measured – certainly not the mythical conflicts, or the structures of female abduction, which he considers already in book I.

If we believe that Herodotus divided his nine books into the thousands of chapters that we have today, the eccentricity of his juxtaposing such large and small chapters is striking.

The rhythmic organization of the textual groupings is syncopated, non-European, Asiatic, jazzlike.

Sophocles' friend does not observe the laws of classical harmony and balance.

The narrative runs from the mythic age to the Battle of Salamis and the rout of the Persians but is hardly straightforward and jumps convulsively backward and forward – is especially fond of flashbacks.

The first part's rifflike interplay of aggression and female abduction interrupts history: Croesus is introduced (at I, 6–7) only to yield the stage to his predecessors Gyges and Candaules – and the analysis of a sexual pathology:

Exhibitionism, voyeurism, possibly as an expression of repressed homosexuality or of impotence.

VII, 130 ff. anticipates what VII, 138 will acknowledge openly:

This, however, occurred many years after the king's [Xerxes'] campaign, and I must return to my earlier story.

The difficulties of presenting simultaneous events in a diachronic medium are already negotiated by Herodotus, as after him by Heissenbüttel and, in a certain sense, by Döblin and Marinetti. Herodotus is able to situate entire epics in a single sentence:

They (the Phoenicians) came to this sea from the one that is called "red," and, settling the land which they now inhabit, they immediately undertook great shipping ventures (I, 1).

He overlays two parallel narrative lines with such brief remarks that the reader can almost take them in at a single glance; a simple "and" suffices to let the army of Cambyses be drawn in one direction, and – synchronically – the army of the Lacedaemonians in the other (III, 39).

What do Herodotus' researches produce?

Geography and geology, ethnology, psychology, sagas, gossip, dialogues, small dramatic pieces, educational radio programs, history, religion, short stories, novellas, or "novelettes" if you prefer, novels, structural analyses, biology, zoology, architecture, the plastic arts, botany, medicine, agricultural theory, and a diplomatic handbook.

The prose is imagistic and makes pictures superfluous, weighty, sparing of adjectives, occasionally using similes – but never metaphors.

Irony, humor, contempt, hatred, and ethics arise not from ironic, well-meaning, or hateful writing, but from the text's jagged, blunt quality and the constraining effect of seemingly contradictory assertions; these lend the text its witty, deprecatory, anecdotal air. It is poetic, but not by reason of its poetry as much as its materialism.

Herodotus doesn't shy away from dramatic effects:

Croesus, burning at the stake, will cry out into the stillness, three times, the name of Solon, as every student knows.

He does so in the first book, chapter 86, recalling, some fifty chapters earlier (I, 32), Solon's advice to the king: no one may be called truly happy before his death.

Herodotus likes to build these kinds of arches, and he must have expected his readers and listeners to be able to reconstruct them.

The Gay Critic

In book VII he combines various poetic strata and branches of knowledge with impressive ease, in a manner that recalls the modern feature:

VII, 34: Historical, yet fabulous – the bridges over the Hellespont are destroyed by a storm.

Chapter 35:

Psychopathology – or a study in religion:

Xerxes orders the river to be given three hundred lashes of the whip.

Herodotus' careful observation is evidenced in the details he preserves, which are generally lost in the popular accounts:

Xerxes casts a pair of fetters into the sea and commands that the river be burned with branding irons and pierced with spikes.

He also instructed the men to speak while doing so.

Only now there follows a word of commentary:

Barbarian, blasphemous, and unseemly words.

Since Herodotus still understands the violated sanctity of the river, he can at the same time understand the sacred-blasphemous act of the Persian king.

Xerxes' utterance is given by Herodotus in direct speech, like the grandfather of tragedy Aeschylus, who had done the same in *The Persians* – today one finds the same sort of thing in historical novels.

Chapter 35 ends abruptly, and clearly, with the decapitation of the bridge builders.

Chapter 36 begins with three humanistic reflections.

Then follows a page on the construction of bridges.

A restless researcher, moving between maenads and ruins, magic and enlightenment – but not the author of a historical compilation, conceived and composed at the writing table.

In the second book:

πυνθανόμενος περί τῶν πτερωτῶν ὀφίων . . . (II, 75).

Inquiring into the existence of winged snakes – everything interests him:

In chapter 54 of book VII the subject is again Xerxes and the Hellespont. Prior to entering Europe, Xerxes tosses a cup and a Persian sword into the sea.

ταῦτα οὐκ ἔχω ἀτρεκέως διακρῖναι.

My Friend Herodotus

I don't know how to judge this matter accurately, Herodotus writes. Namely, whether Xerxes' gifts were part of a votive offering, or whether he regretted having whipped the sea.

Thus Herodotus has recourse to two sound explanatory possibilities, one magic and extrapersonal, the other magic as well, but individualistic and colored by a psychopathology.

In the seventh book (VII, 125), he describes lions that attack a caravan at night but harm neither the men nor the cattle, only the beasts of burden, the camels.

θωμάζω δὲ τὸ αἴτιον . . . *I am amazed, and wonder at the cause.*

Again the search for a ground, the original cause.

The lions had never before seen or tasted camels.

The student of human behavior wonders about hereditary customs and conditioning.

τε καὶ προεθυμέετο κατά τε τὸ ἔχθος τὸ Λακεδαιμονίων καὶ κατὰ τὸ κέρδος (IX, 38).

Hegesistratus performed sacrifices, both out of hatred for the Lacedaemonians, and for profit.

Not only the gray goose of Lorenz – but Adler and Freud as well. In any case, no models for historical instruction.

His interests and empirical methods are so exact that, in book III, he distinguishes – just as traditional Togolese psychiatrists do – between epilepsy and the mental disorders:

Cambyses' sickness:

τὴν ἱρὴν ὀνομάζουσί τινες . . . *which some call holy.*

οὔ νύν τοι ἀεικὲς οὐδὲν ἦν τοῦ σώματος νοῦσον μεγάλην νοσέοντος μηδὲ τὰς φρένας ὑγιαίνειν (III, 33).

It isn't unlikely that, in suffering from a great physical illness, he was also harmed in his mental capacities.

Here too, he is close to the Togolese, who feel that epileptic seizures of a certain strength and duration can adversely affect the mind as well.

Words.
Truth.
Demaratus asks Xerxes how he should speak:
What shall I tell you – the truth, or something to make you happy? (VII, 101).

The Gay Critic

The Thebans:
λέγοντες τὸν ἀληθέστατον τῶν λόγων . . . (VII, 233)
speaking the truest of words.
Words that Herodotus claims to have heard
τὸν . . . ἤκουον λόγον . . . λέξω (IV, 14)
in contrast to the divinely inspired epics.
He refuses to relate, at any great length, things that seem to him incredible (IV, 36).
He knows the difficulties of trying to write the truth:
I don't know how to judge this matter accurately (VII, 54).
Words unto death – and a loss for words:
ἦν δὲ λόγος οὐδεὶς τοῦ ἀπολλυμένου (VII, 223)
does not mean: *no one expressed grief for the dead.*
But rather: *there was no word from the dead man.*
(If not: *He died in silence.*)
The inhuman silence of battle with regard to the individual fate – which Herodotus rehumanizes and poeticizes by his emphatically brief remark.

Nor does he always show such restraint.
His selection of episodes, lengthenings, and shortenings constitutes of themselves, of course, a kind of commentary.
He can always reassure us:
ταῦτα μὲν ἀτρεκέως ἔχω περὶ αὐτῶν εἰδὼς εἰπεῖν (I, 135–40).
He knows this well, since he saw it with his own eyes.
What?
Persian customs.
A whole one and a half pages.
He says outright that he doesn't like how the Egyptians prevaricate:
ἔμοιγε οὐκ ἀρεστά (II, 64).
He doesn't believe, as the pharaoh Rhampsinitus does, that there is sufficient evidence to convict someone of stealing a corpse.
ἐμοὶ μὲν οὐ πιστά (II, 121).
Herodotus condemns Cheops for sending his daughter into a brothel:
Χέοπα κακότητος (II, 126).
In chapter 146 of book II, he pulls off a brief integration of commentary and objectification:

He presents different versions of a story and adds his own opinion – let my readers judge for themselves!
He laughs at some amateurish competitors:
γελῶ δὲ ὁρῶν γῆς περιόδους γράψαντας πολλοὺς ἤδη . . . ἐν ὀλίγοισι γὰρ ἐγὼ δηλώσω μέγαθός τε ἑκάστης αὐτέων (IV, 36).
I laugh when I see how many mapmakers there are. . . . In a few (words) I will make clear the size of each of these (i.e., Europe and Asia).
Scholarly arrogance is hardly unique to our century.
Σάτραι . . . ὅσον ἡμεῖς ἴδμεν . . . (VII, III)
The Satrae . . . as far as we know . . .
The "we" – modest or grandiose?
A chapter consisting of nine lines on the Satrae, and then:
καὶ οὐδὲν ποικιλώτερον.
nothing more very colorful, artful, interesting.
The world as a circle turning before the curious eyes of the Ionian Greek.
In an eccentric, almost syncopated mass of tales, repeated formulas, stiff gestures, clumps of participles, conceptual knots, floods of particles:
λόγον λέγοντες
οὐκ πιστὰ
punctuated by powerful phrases:
Ἀθηναῖοι μέν νυν ηὔξηντο (V, 78).
The Athenians had, during this time, become a great power.
We find poetological reflections on Homer (II, 116) and on farts, though *euphemistically* (II, 162).
One seldom reads such a series of dense reports in the *New York Times*:
τὸν δὲ θυμωθέντα ἐμπηδῆσαι αὐτῇ ἐχούσῃ ἐν γαστρί, καί μιν ἐκτρώσασαν ἀποθανεῖν (III, 32).
He [Cambyses] became enraged and trampled upon her, though she was pregnant. She later died while giving birth prematurely.
The effect is like a cold slap in the face when the reader realizes that the skeptic, agnostic, and analytic Herodotus erases, in the act of writing, his own opinions – before the overwhelming specter of the Big Time:

The Sigynnae claim to be descendants of the Medes. Herodotus cannot explain how this could be:
ἐγὼ μὲν οὐκ ἔχω ἐπιφράσασθαι, γένοιτο δ'ἄν πᾶν ἐν τῷ μακρῷ χρόνῳ (V, 9).
I cannot imagine how this could be true, but anything can happen in the greater span of time.

If this work is something more than a collection of exemplary models for historical instruction, more than a first attempt to analyze behavior and aggression, if it truly may be said to have a poetic dimension, and not just in the sense of having an "original maker," but rather, offering insights with regard to a late, urban, lyrical subject, where then is the tragic reversal – which Hölderlin demands of all tragedy – the reversal that distinguishes poetry from mere compendia, where does Herodotus, the poet, say "I" to himself, like the graffiti on the colossoi at Abu Simbel, where does the image of Herodotus become clear other than in marginal reflections?

Ἡσίοδον γὰρ καὶ Ὅμηρον ἡλικίην τετρακοσίοισι ἔτεσι δοκέω μευ πρεσβυτέρους γενέσθαι καὶ οὐ πλέοσι (II, 53).
I believe that Hesiod and Homer preceded me by four hundred years, and no more.

Herodotus thus names himself in the same breath with the ancient, lofty figures of the past, just as Thomas Mann likens himself to Goethe, or Grass to Döblin, Rühmkorf to Walther von der Vogelweide – a less absurd, surely, and a rather bold stroke, no doubt in his role as the literary ethnologist of his culture.

At the end of the chapter he brings these three names together again, but more modestly, wishing only now to comment on Homer and Hesiod; following upon his far-reaching previous statement, however, Herodotus' qualification of the chapter's end seems only to raise the stakes.

. . . τὰ δὲ ὕστερα τὰ ἐς Ἡσίοδόν τε καὶ Ὅμηρον ἔχοντα ἐγὼ λέγω.

Apart from his self-assuredness, Herodotus' curiosity is well documented, that encyclopedic curiosity which recoils at nothing and embraces all, ties things together, and at the same time projects them back onto a human scale.

My Friend Herodotus

It remains inconceivable that such an uncurious Europe could have arisen from such a curious origin, for whom knowledge became something seldom distinct from power; European colonial history is the history of an insensitivity, European philosophy an uncurious idealism, Scholasticism, a prayer mill without windows. Thales already stumbled into a well before the eyes of a maid, and the errors of practical perception fill volumes – the mistakes of an Aristotle, Sartre, or Lévi-Strauss.

Several topoi recur in Herodotus' work:

Death; human sacrifice; various images of war; rivers: dried up, and drunk dry; hunger; a son dying before his father's eyes – this latter so often as to seem transfixed in horror, a memory from childhood, perhaps.

Herodotus – up close and personal: never more so than in questions of sex:

Curiosity, a passion for intrigue, and an occasional prudishness. Herodotus paints a counterworld of sensuality, not one of tender mildness.

The disclosure of his researches begins with the question concerning the source of tensions between Europe and Asia Minor – δι' ἥν αἰτίην ἐπολέμησαν ἀλλήλοισι – female abduction.

He opens with a rifflike interplay of stories about rape. The structures of female abduction, one might call it today. On the third page the striking, puzzling story of Candaules and Gyges.

His is the *ur*pornography – if one disregards the pornographic comics of the hieroglyphs – for what is porno except the representation of private nakedness, a lustful participation in the intercourse of others? The wife of Candaules now coerces the reluctant voyeur, Gyges, to accede to her vengeful wishes, and Candaules, on cuckold's row, pays for his little peep show with his life, something that rarely happens on Forty-second Street, or the Reeperbahn, even after midnight.[1]

οὗτος δὴ ὦν ὁ Κανδαύλης ἤρασθη τῆς ἑωυτοῦ γυναικός (I, 8).

Thus Candaules loved his wife with great pleasure and much desire – ἐρᾶν – the verb has to do with ἔρως, Eros, the god of love

---

1. Fichte alludes to the title of a song popularized by Hans Albers about Hamburg's red-light district, the Reeperbahn.

himself – whose place of origin is never revealed and who simply "shows up."

Candaules believes that his wife is the most beautiful in the world. He has to show her off; in Herodotus, a need for recognition and a desire to please go hand in hand with erotic pleasure right from the start.

To whom, then, does he then choose to reveal her, of all people? Gyges, the son of Daskylus, his αἰχμοφόρος, one of his bodyguards, a trabant, or spearman (ironically, αἰχμή means "lance"), whom he is quite fond of.

It seems almost as if Herodotus wished to use a more endearing word to express Candaules' feelings for his guard than for his wife, who, as the most beautiful woman in the world, feels the lance's point directly.

In ἀρέσκω, ἀραρίσκω, there is contained an idea of fitting, or joining – in Thomas Mann's *Joseph* the phrase *underworld humor* is used in relation to the same epoch.

Candaules must have been somewhat in awe of his wife's beauty and had to see how Gyges, the spearman, would long for her in vain, perhaps to induce a state of arousal in him; or indeed, as similar scenes in Casanova attest, to arouse himself, and to let himself be penetrated by the guard's spear – which actually happens: Candaules dies, in the bed of the most beautiful and longed-for woman, having been stabbed by the lance of Gyges – in a double play on love and death.

Herodotus begins this passage with something quite rare in the body of his work as a whole: an impenetrable oracular formula: χρῆν γὰρ Κανδαύλῃ γενέσθαι κακῶς – *Candaules was fated to suffer an ill.*

Gyges is thus positioned to watch the queen undress, having been convinced by Candaules' lewd remarks.

She removes her garments and sets them, one after the other, upon a chair.

Candaules' wife sees Gyges, as he attempts to slip away unnoticed.

Did Gyges let himself be caught?

As a means of getting even with the queer Candaules?

καὶ ἡ γυνὴ ἐπορᾷ μιν ἐξιόντα.

And the woman saw him, as he left gives no indication, simply lies on the page.

We have seen how cruel incidents in Herodotus usually appear briefly.

The queen presents Gyges, the next day, with a choice: he can either kill himself or kill Candaules, and from the very same place where he watched her undress.

ὑπνωμένῳ δὲ ἡ ἐπιχείρησις ἔσται (I, 11).

The attack will take place while he is asleep.

Herodotus has earlier told us that, for the Lydians, it is considered dishonorable to see a man naked.

This primal origin of repressed homosexuality, of homosexuality as deadly eros – origin, as well, of the peep show and striptease – struck Herodotus as so obscene that, six chapters later, as if excusing himself, he drily remarks:

Gyges claimed the kingdom and the woman.

Γύγης τοῦ καὶ Ἀρχίλοχος ὁ Πάριος κατὰ τὸν αὐτὸν χρόνον γενόμενος ἐν ἰάμβῳ τριμέτρῳ ἐπεμνήσθη.

Gyges, whom Archilochus of Paros, a contemporary, mentions in an iambic trimeter (I, 12).

Following this beginning there is scarcely a mention of sexual matters that Herodotus fails to underline:

I, 61: Contraception.

Pisistratus shuns normal sex and lies with his wife in an unlawful way.

ἐμίσγετό οἱ οὐ κατὰ νόμον.

I, 94: *The Lydians mark their daughters for prostitution.*

καταπορνεύουσι.

II, 121: Herodotus censures the temple prostitution of the daughter of Pharaoh Rhampsinitus, as well as Cheops, who does the same with his daughter, out of greed.

I, 196: The wisest custom of the Illyrians, he notes, is the auction of marriageable females.

IV, 176: The women of the Gindanes put a leather band around their ankle every time they make love with a different man, and that one is most respected who collects the highest number of bands.

The Gay Critic

Pederasty, female and male homosexuality are rarely given unambiguous mention (I, 135, 155; IX, 20).

In book V a group of transvestites become murderous avengers (V, 20).

Some tribes in the Caucasus engage in sexual intercourse openly, like animals (I, 203).

The Massagetae may sleep with any woman they choose. A man simply hangs his quiver, as a sign, outside of the wagon (I, 216).

To this day, if a woman and a young warrior of the Masai want to make love, they plant a spear before their tent, so that the husband knows not to disturb them.

II, 46: Herodotus witnesses, untroubled, the open copulation of an Egyptian woman with a goat.

II, 48: The Egyptians' celebratory use of phallic puppets is related to the Greek festivals of Dionysus.

II, 89: He reports on the disfigurement of a corpse.

II, 131: On the incest of Mycerinus with his daughter.

Nervous impotence (II, 181) interests him as much as venereal diseases (III, 149), mother fixation and rape (IV, 43), hermaphrodites (IV, 67), and oedipal fatherhood and "loss" of the mother – as in *Hamlet* (VI, 68).

Xerxes eventually resorts to a type of parasitism (IX, 108), as Lotte alleges of Goethe.

He falls in love with his brother's wife.

He arranges the wedding of his son Darius to the daughter of the beloved sister-in-law and hopes – absurdly! – to thereby increase his chances of success. Instead, he seduces his niece, now his daughter-in-law – like Schiller's Philip II, who likewise seduces his son's lover.

Twisted relations in the work of the sociable Ionian.

Lots of sex.

Not much tenderness.

Why would anyone venture out in search of such hard core?[2]

From his own compulsions, destructions?

Occasional prudery:

II, 30: In the most risqué story, an Egyptian takes out his thing, shows it to Pharaoh Psammetichus, and says:

2. *Hard core* in English in original.

My Friend Herodotus

Wherever this is, there you will find plenty of women and children.
What does he take out?
His αἰδοῖον, his pudenda, from αἰδώς, meaning "shame," or "reverence, fear of god," as well as "scandal."

It is unpleasant for Herodotus to explain why the Egyptians represent the god Pan with goatlike attributes.
What is unpleasant?
Does he even say?
Is it a question perhaps of a vow of silence, of secret sects into which Herodotus may have been initiated, which might have given him the incentive, in the first place, to travel, to study the various forms of religion and, finally, to write? It is also unpleasant for him to speak of the wooden phalloi.
Did they remind him of the severed member of Osiris?
Was he touristically initiated by the Egyptians into the mysteries of Osiris, just as, today, Afro-Americans are often quickly initiated into the ancient religions of Nigeria, where wooden phalloi still play a role?

A single formula for the corporeal runs, like a nostalgic longing, through the entire work:
The country of Ethiopia produces tall, long-lived, very good looking men.
III, 114: ἄνδρας μεγίστους καὶ καλλίστους καὶ μακροβιωτάτους.
VII, 12: ἄνδρα οἱ ἐπιστάντα μέγαν τε καὶ εὐειδέα εἰπεῖν.
A large and well-built man appears to Xerxes in a dream.
VII, 187: *None could compare with Xerxes in beauty and stature.*
At VII, 180, the Persians sacrifice a first Greek, happy that he is also the most attractive.
IX, 72: Callicrates – "he who rules by beauty" – was the best looking of all – ἀνὴρ κάλλιστος.
And at IX, 96, near the end, Tigranes, who outshone the Persians in beauty and stature.
Do the sure narrator's hands here start to shake?
Does he uncover, formulaically, an intimate motive, the drive behind his urge to travel, stronger than normal by contemporary standards, the source of his curiosity, the force behind his research and analyses – also the sexual ones?

The Gay Critic

An interest in unusual sexual constellations doesn't make Herodotus a modern author.

There is a tendency on the part of avant-gardists to attach themselves to Blood and Soil movements: Susan Sontag's hastily qualified enthusiasm for Leni Riefenstahl in the *New York Review of Books;* the quasi-religious devotion to Mao Tse-tung; Castro's *patria o muerte,* banners, hymns, and the lockstep that so infuriated the Auschwitz-drunk Genet that he refused to visit Cuba; Hans Werner Henze and Françoise Sagan feeling so at ease in Cuba, in spite of the prison camps for homosexuals; David's drawings that use the guillotine as a backdrop; Julius K. Nyerere's prudishness – all waver between magic and enlightenment and, in the worst cases, distort enlightenment formulas into a regressive hocus-pocus; and, in the most painful cases, comes the recognition that a free person can only exist within a labyrinth of rites, like a crab in its shell; if the old is destroyed, a new one takes its place, a secondary one, like software.

Herodotus is avant-garde, an enlightener.

A true empiricist who gives a precise report on an as yet unknown subject.

Herodotus' subject was the world.

He is the first avant-garde author.

Magic and religion appear in his work as an object of study – it's hardly his fault if his critics fail to discriminate between his object and its artistic rendering.

He works his way toward the origins of the gods' names – not through piety, but etymology.

πυνθανόμενος – *inquiring* (II, 50).

He mentions that the stories that Phoenix has told him are incredible, before relating them to us.

τοῦτον δὲ λέγουσι μηχανᾶσθαι τάδε, ἐμοὶ μὲν οὐ πιστὰ λέγοντες (II, 73).

At IV, 66, his portrait of the high priestess at Delphi makes her appear venal, a bold statement that neither Gore Vidal nor Norman Mailer would ever dare to make in the *New York Times* if the subject were the pope.

At VII, 12–17, Herodotus describes, in detail, the war council of Xerxes, as well as the Persian king's recurring dream vision.

The reader is left in the dark as to whether or not Herodotus believes that the dream, which pushes Xerxes into war, has a divine origin.
Artabanus, of the war council, offers a dream interpretation that seems close to the modern, scientific, post-Freudian model.
But Artabanus, too, believes that a frequent recurrence of the same dream image suggests a divine source.
The handsome dream figure returns again and again.
Xerxes follows his admonitions.
He is drawn into war.
Herodotus' work ends with the defeat of the Persians.

Such cross-traits of secularization, critique, and analysis stem, logically, from *historia* and *apodeixis*.
More exciting are the remarks that express doubt, oscillation, or hesitation.
Poised between the logic of the magical worldview and the logical worldview of the sciences of nature.
We saw how he expressed an interest in the study of winged snakes.
He inquires where the genealogy of his predecessor, Hecataeus, merged with that of gods.
He believes in the existence of general, divine-moral influences, in the same way that the former president of the Federal Republic, Carstens, expressed these at the Church of St. Paul, or when President Carter said grace on television – neither one seeming foolish in the eyes of the world for doing so – remarks that were reproduced in the *New York Times* without any qualifying commentary.
For Herodotus all this had become so far from self-evident that he makes them appear wholly powerless by doubly emphasizing them.
VII, 191: the magi attempt to appease the storm – that is, Thetis and the Nereids, that it might be calmed. This takes place on the fourth day.
ἢ ἄλλως κως αὐτὸς ἐθέλων ἐκόπασε.
or perhaps it grew tired, of itself.
Doubt, clearly, of the Nereids and Thetis, with a final animistic wavering.

At IV, 105, Greeks and Scythians claim that the Neuri turn into wolves for several days of each year.
Herodotus does not indicate the untrustworthiness of this tale, the way he does in so many other instances.
ἐμὲ μέν νυν ταῦτα λέγοντες οὐ πείθουσι.
I am not persuaded by these reports, however.
Can one hear a childlike trembling in his words?

One is, time and again, astonished at the ridiculous reasonings that are able to satisfy otherwise intelligent people.
For Herodotus, too, it is often difficult to insist on verification, hard to keep from falling back into a naive credulity.
In the third book Herodotus tells us that the Persian skulls are very thin – so thin that one could easily pierce them with a small stone.
The Egyptians' skulls, on the other hand, are hardened by the sun.
VIII, 104: North of Halicarnassus, Herodotus' birthplace, the priestess of Athena of Pedasa grows a long beard when ill luck threatens.
This is not said in the subjunctive.
A live report from Turkey. And this just in:
At VIII, 37: Omens, lightning flashes, voices, and cries of war from the Temple of Athena. Details at eleven.
He will not deny the truth of all oracular utterance (VIII, 77):
ἐς τοιαῦτα μὲν καὶ οὕτω ἐναργέως λέγοντι Βάκιδι ἀντιλογίας χρησμῶν πέρι οὔτε αὐτὸς λέγειν τολμέω οὔτε παρ' ἄλλων ἐνδέκομαι.
In light of this unambiguous oracle of Bacis, I don't dare to speak on the contradictions of prophecies, nor will I listen to such things from others.
A good example for those who lapse into chauvinism, reaction, and fearful intolerance: to admit to fear, allow for contradiction, and exist in the ritual void of intellectual freedom.
The cause of a storm tide is said to lie in an outrage against the statue and temple of Poseidon – and rightly so, agrees Herodotus (VIII, 129).
IX, 65: A goddess's revenge, Herodotus conjectures, explains the

My Friend Herodotus

fact that all the Persians fell upon unconsecrated ground – and then puts this same assumption into question, if rather modestly:
δοκέω δέ, εἴ τι περὶ τῶν θείων πρηγμάτων δοκέειν δεῖ . . . (IX, 65)
I suspect – if it is proper to form opinions on divine matters . . .
This skepticism as to propriety can be read in either of two ways: as a reluctance to commit an offense against sacred matters, or as an impatience with matters of faith in general, indicative of an inclination toward natural science and secularization.

Just as secularization accompanies consciousness, the dwindling and ossification of ritual practices, we are able to see both intellectual processes overlapping, as they often do, in Herodotus. The magical reflexes of the student of human behavior, the discoverer and enlightener, are more than superficial:
τὸν δὲ τύπτονται, οὔ μοι ὅσιόν ἔστι λέγειν (II, 61).
Why they do this, I may not say.
ὅσιόν – "am forbidden to say, by divine interdiction," a subtlety lost in the German translation.
How and Wells make the following observation:
τόν *(The god in question being) Osiris, whom (as usual, cf. 86, 2; 130, 2) H. does not name.*
Did the priests of Osiris give him any reason as to why tens of thousands would come to Busiris and beat their breasts during the festival of Osiris – threatening him with the wrath of the gods if he blabbed about it in the *New York Times*?
Was he initiated into secret ceremonies?
Did he join in the self-flagellation?
Did he possess the sensitivity of the modern author and refuse to betray the secrets of that which others regard as holy?
How did he find the leathermen's rites? Painful? Pleasurable?
Did he wish to avoid bringing them into contact with himself, with god, with enlightenment?
II, 86: For religious reasons and due to a divine injunction, he declines to name the god in whose honor the festival is held – namely, Osiris.
οὐκ ὅσιον ποιεῦμαι τὸ οὔνομα . . . ὀνομάζειν.
οὐκ ὅσιον ποιεῦμαι . . . ἐξαγορεύειν τοὔνομα in chapter 170, in a similar allusion to Osiris, in a formula very much the same.

The Gay Critic

A chapter later, he also holds his tongue on the details of a celebration in honor of Demeter, which he compares with the rites of Osiris, saying that he will reveal only so much as the divine command allows.

A double imperative thus limits Herodotus' utterances.

In any case, he is far more eloquent on the subject of his own reticence than Pierre Verger, the religious historian who, in his descriptions of a religion whose mysteries he was allowed to witness, says nothing on the subject of initiation or oaths of secrecy.

At II, 3, Herodotus issues a precise statement that is, once again, Janus-faced and can be interpreted in one of two ways:

τὰ μέν νυν θεῖα τῶν ἀπηγημάτων οἷα ἤκουον, οὐκ εἰμὶ πρόθυμος ἐξηγέεσθαι, ἔξω ἢ τὰ οὐνόματα αὐτῶν μοῦνον, νομίζων πάντας ἀνθρώπους ἴσον περὶ αὐτῶν ἐπίστασθαι, τὰ δ' ἂν ἐπιμνησθέω αὐτῶν, ὑπὸ τοῦ λόγου ἐξαναγκαζόμενος ἐπιμνησθήσομαι.

I am not inclined to expound on the divine aspect of those stories that I heard, other than to reveal the names of their gods, since I am of the opinion that all men know more or less the same things concerning these matters. I will mention only those details that are necessary to my story.

Neither the humble citizen nor the enlightened intellectual is privileged by such an avowal. The possibility of an initiation is neither broached nor precluded.

Nothing conceals so effectively as openness.

Does the enlightener here cloak something, with a wink at those in the know?

Did he prefer to betray ἀπόδεξις and ἱστορίη rather than divulge the initiatory secrets of the phallic god of the dead, whose severed member, in the form of a wooden phallus, was borne in processions, just as today in Haiti?

We cannot decide.

If I were, to use Herodotus' method, not simply to suggest, but reveal openly, my opinion, I would say:

I think so.

Such an inner divisiveness probably marks all knowledge and enlightenment.

I find it in every modern author whose concerns run closest to my own.

In Proust, Cocteau, Artaud, Genet, Borges, Burroughs, and Henry James. In the politically progressive Herodotus, as seen in the speech of Artabanus; in the waverer and skeptic; in his scorn and contempt for the powerful; his tolerance, compassion, and steady, inquiring eye – like Pasolini's eye – when he writes of flaying or the son's castration before his father's eyes.

In Herodotus I see the gray-haired youth, who buys the *New York Times* at the corner of Christopher Street and Seventh Avenue, and who then cautiously, yet with daring, leather-clad, takes the subway to Times Square, bowed skeptically over the news, a hopeless humanist.

The German edition's table of contents reads *Book IX: Characteristics of the Persians*.

This title hardly prepares us for the death of Artaÿctes, who is nailed to a cross and hanged, whose son is stoned before his eyes. Herodotus' work ends in cruelty, in sadistic rites, wholly pessimistic.

And yet – this too must be said – there is no defense of racism, he never takes the side of those who would try to influence the sexual practices of others, he offers no apologies for abduction or slavery, like the Bible, the elegant Aristotle, or the *New York Times*.

Herodotus, the first author, issues an unyielding protest against inhumanity, like those other aged youths who sue the *Times* on account of its racism.

EXCURSUS
THE MEDITERRANEAN AND THE GULF OF BENIN
The Description of African and Afro-American Rites in Herodotus

New York, November 1980

Is Afro-American culture the brainchild of a few refugees who, no longer able to sustain a dialogue with the native culture, took flight into an exotic, impoverished alternative?
Are Afro-American rites a patchwork, a remainder, faded and stale, on the margins of the United States – or do archaic, originary moments surface within the Afro-American syncretism, constants of human behavior and consciousness, just as in Greek tragedies, or the works of Monteverdi, Artaud, Hitchcock?
Was Yahweh, who created Adam and Eve and Zeus, from whose head Athena sprang, black?
Or at least Afro-European?
A voodoo Oedipus?
The thundergod Zeus Zagreus, or Labdacus, has a beard.
He wears a multibreasted cuirass, in which he recalls the Ephesian Demeter.
Like the thundergod Xango – in Brazil, Haiti, and Grenada – Zeus wields a double ax, a sign of bisexuality.[1]

1. Marie Delcourt, *Hermaphrodite* (Paris, 1958), above all 30; Hubert

The Togolese, many of whose customs managed to survive in the New World, claim descendancy from Egypt.[2]

The Togolese have a keen awareness of their own history and genealogy. Their Sacred Seat, the seat of the ancestors, seems to me to preserve, in its form, the design of the pharaohs' headrest.[3]

Coincidence?

Smuggled in via the big screen, TV, and Neckermann?

Or indices of an early contact between the cultures of the Mediterranean and those of the Gulf of Benin: Yoruba, Fon, and Ewe – and detectable as well in the syncretism of black America, the New World on the far side of the Atlantic?

Still, there is no reason to fall into a unitarian two-step, ingratiating and exploitative, adding to the drivel about like structures, slapping the African Oedipus good-naturedly on the shoulder, and giving the Haitian Aphrodite a lascivious pinch.

That is not my intention.

I would rather like to point out, with reference to the detailed descriptions of African rites in Herodotus, that several of these, which one can still observe in the Afro-American religions, have since the classical period found their place in European culture and further that they don't represent some degenerate version of the original, a mere atavistic relic.

Herodotus and the trance.

Nor to once again prove the superiority of the Western tradition over the so-called primitive peoples, but the other way around: to suggest an interdependence between Nubian, Libyan, Ethiopian trends and their Carian, Ionian, and Attic counterparts.

The seductive theory[4] that states that all of human existence, all religious development, can be traced back to black culture, developing, in the course of time, out of its African and East Afri-

---

Fichte, *La Lame de rasoir et l'hermaphrodite: Psychopathologie africaine* (Dakar, 1975), 395–406; Pierre Verger, *Notes sur le culte des Orisa et Vodun* (Dakar, 1957), 305 ff. (Notes in this chapter are by Fichte. – TRANS.)

2. Hubert Fichte, *Gott ist ein Mathematiker,* radio manuscript, NDR (Hamburg, 1980).

3. Ibid.

4. Richard E. Leakey, *Origins* (London, 1979).

Excursus: The Mediterranean and the Gulf of Benin

can sources, into those forms that hard-nosed scholars of the human sciences still refer to as the major religions – such an Afrocentric model will no doubt be repeatedly proved and disproved in the coming years.

The experts rewrite the history of early man every few months. In 1977, Richard Leakey deduced from some bone fragments that Eve was black, but since 1979 it seems that she came from Burma and that she is not three million years young, but rather thirteen million years old.[5]

Herodotus has a poor reputation.
Greek scholarly envy accused the first ethnologist and student of human behavior of faulty observation and sloppy citation – already the worst charges one could level against an intellectual. The opposite is true – says *Der Spiegel*.

Herodotus reveals his sources like few other modern empiricists, sharply juxtaposes complementary, or contradictory, versions of the same event, and consistently labels what he considers to be commentary and extrapolation.

Herodotus often recedes from his own text in such a way that, presenting a fact or behavior he is unable to explain, the context is, for us, twenty-five hundred years later, still eminently clear, as in the case of the small black men of book II (II, 32), which I will return to below.

His position between magic and secularization – comparable to that of his friend Sophocles, between the mystery play and naturalism, or between Aeschylus and Euripides – could, in an author less devoted to research and demonstration – in Ionian, ἱστορίη and ἀπόδεξις – produce a blurred, streaky effect; in Herodotus such an intermediate status only yields a more intense analysis. The treasures in Herodotus' text stem from his ambivalence.

For the modern reader, who becomes impatient when forced to search out textual fragments and hold them up to the light, Herodotus is the first writer, his book, the first product of a professionalized writing.

5. According to D. C. Johanson, Cleveland Museum of Natural History, and T. White, University of California at Berkeley, *Newsweek*, 29 January 1979.

Yet when Herodotus, toward the middle of the fifth century, made his way to Egypt and collected data on the Αἰθίοπες, the burned-faces, when he, like Allen Ginsberg in the Berlin Congress Hall, read his work at an Olympiad, constructing and obstructing the world with words, he moved within a universe hardly imaginable to us and made up entirely of words, both tentative and more specific.

The verbal (mis)representation of the world is as old as sound, the mimicked sound of the eagle or the snake, as old as cave paintings, hieroglyphs, the alphabet, as old as litanies, commodity lists, law tables.

The world is already covered in signs in the caves of the Stone Age, just as the *New York Times,* in our day, covers the world with its photos, covers the photos with advertising images, and covers Susan Sontag's *On Photography* with an article in the *Review of Books.*

The Cameroon historian Ki-Zerbo writes, not without pride, that the Sahara, up to historical times – thus up to the age of spelling – was inhabited by blacks; *during the Paleolithic era, the black population spread to Europe . . . and beyond.*[6] Ten thousand years before Christ, the black Dravidians occupied a large portion of India.

And Diodorus Siculus, one of the last classical travelers to Egypt, writes of the Nubians, in the first century before Christ:

They add that the Egyptians received a good deal of their laws from their [the Nubians'] *leaders and ancestors. From them they learned to honor their kings like gods and to bury their dead in great splendor.*[7]

The Ethiopians discovered the arts of sculpture and writing.[8]

Up to the Ptolemaic period, the priest in charge of burning incense before the Philopater was a black man, dressed in the skin of a lion.[9]

We can see this from the reliefs on the Temple at Edfu.

Diodorus:

The Negroes seem to have discovered all the cults through which men generally honor the gods.

6. *Die Geschichte Schwarz-Afrikas* (Wuppertal, 1979), 74.
7. According to Ki-Zerbo, *Die Geschichte Schwarz-Afrikas,* 75.
8. Ibid., 76.
9. Ibid., n. 10.

Excursus: The Mediterranean and the Gulf of Benin

This is the reason why their prayers and offerings are generally considered to be most pleasing of all to the immortals.[10]

Of the first dynasties, around 3000 B.C., William Y. Adams writes: *The Nubians are unique among all the people of inner Africa in that their place in history is almost as old as history itself.*[11]

Adams dates the first military expeditions of the pharaonian Egyptians against Nubia at around the same period.

The pharaoh Horen Dyer follows.

Pharaoh Snefru, about 2600, leads a punitive expedition on the Nubian stone quarries. He takes seven thousand into captivity, and a large number of cattle.

Egypt maintains a prosperous trade with Nubia, Kush, and Punt. Forty years later, Vezerkef carves his royal cartouche into the rocks of the first cataract – which is to say, he orders it to be carved.

When Sahura sends a fleet of ships across the Red Sea into Punt, a report of the trip is documented, which is still extant.

Raids.

Uprisings.

A black dwarf at the Egyptian court.

A letter of thanks written by the young Neferkara, later Phiops II, covers his gravestone in Elephantine.

Herkhuf writes, in 2340, that he sailed down the Nile, with *three thousand asses, balsam oil, ebony, ivory and grain.*[12]

Aid as trade.

Military treaties.

Distribution markets.

The Hyksos invade Egypt in 1560 and try to form an alliance with the Nubians against Egypt.

Queen Hatshepsut (1501–1480) attains to stony glory through a renewed invasion.

With Thutmose II there begins – just as in Europe, some three thousand years later – the lust for gold, bound up, as in Europe, with a trafficking in Negro slaves. In one year, 134 female and male blacks are sold and forcibly displaced.[13]

10. Ibid.
11. *Africa in Antiquity* (Brooklyn, N.Y., 1978), 22.
12. Basil Davidson, *Afrika* (Frankfurt am Main, 1966).
13. Basil Davidson, *Urzeit und Geschichte Afrikas* (Reinbeck, 1961), 36.

The Sabaeans arrive in the eleventh century, settling in Ethiopia.[14]

Sandalwood grows, at this time, on Kilimanjaro.

It is shipped through the harbor at Gedi, or Gedeira.

Since 1085, the black viceroy of Kush has, as the vizier of Thebes, ruled over a large part of Egypt.

Approximately one thousand years before Christ, King David had amassed, with a greed comparable only to the Spanish royal house or the Catholic monasteries of the New World, one hundred thousand talents of gold, as is reported in 1 Chronicles 23. His son, the wise Solomon, journeyed to Ophir (the modern Zimbabwe, it is assumed), to rake in more gold.

The Song of Solomon is sung over the 120 talents of gold that Solomon had received from the queen of Sheba.

The modern languages are not alone in reserving a bitter term for such a state of affairs.

Thus, the Bible continues, *King Solomon was more blessed with riches and wisdom than all the kings of the earth.*

The songs of the Homeric rhapsodes, of the second half of the eighth century, anticipated what Diodorus Siculus will recapitulate, seven hundred years later:

Zeus and the Olympians journey over the sea, to the blameless Ethiopians, who offer them such excellent food, in their sacrifices, that the immortals rarely miss the chance to attend them (*Iliad*, I, 423).

The Ethiopians were, for Voß, *divided in two* – διχθὰ δεδαίαται (*Odyssey*, I, 23).

. . . *the most far-off of men, some near the setting of Hyperion, and some near his rising.*

Circumnavigations of Africa, then, must already have been accomplished at the time of Homer, reports of which he wove into his work; and, following the biblical discoveries in East Africa, there must have been similar ones in the West, we can assume. Six hundred years before Christ, the Phoenicians, by order of the pharaoh, sailed around Africa from the Red Sea and returning, three years later, through the Pillars of Hercules at Gibraltar.

---

14. Ibid., 37, 204 ff.

Excursus: The Mediterranean and the Gulf of Benin

Herodotus mentions it in the second and fourth books (II, 158 ff.; IV, 42) and also mentions the campaign of Psammetichus II, at II, 29–33.

Herodotus' countrymen, the Carians and Ionians, who as mercenaries in the service of the pharaoh, around 591, carved graffiti into the colossoi at Abu Simbel, escape his notice. Thus Herodotus seems not to have made it as far as Abu Simbel; the linguistic-theoretical meaning of this graffiti was either forgotten, or so obvious as to be undeserving of mention:

ἔγραφε δ ἀμὲ ῎Αρχον – *Archon wrote us.*[15]

Τήλεφος μ᾽ ἔγραφε – *Telephos wrote me.*

... καὶ Κρῖθις ἔγραφον ἐμέ. – *Krithis wrote me as well.*

Linguistic (mis)representation of the world: the word says *I* to itself.

Thales of Miletus (624–545), like Herodotus of Carian descent, and from an Ionian colony, the first philosopher, is thought to have stayed in Egypt.

Nothing in the way of ethnological or ethological reports have come down to us from his hand.

Hecataeus of Miletus, a sixth-century Ionian, left several revealing fragments.

Enigmatic observations on the Africans:

χειρογάστορες.

Literally, *the hand-to-mouthers.*

Did the Greeks, by contrast, already use eating utensils?[16]

Women wear towels on their heads.[17]

The large, distinctive head towels worn by African and Afro-American women still strike the modern visitor to Lomé, Lagos, Cotonou, and across the sea in Bahia, Port-au-Prince, St. George. The Haitian women also put rolled up towels upon their heads, to serve as a cushion beneath their vegetable baskets.

Finally, Hecataeus remarks, in the first fragment:

For my part, I write what seems to me to be the truth. The words of the Greeks seem to me both numerous and laughable.[18]

15. *Griechische Inschriften* (Munich, n.d.), 85.
16. F. Jacobi, *Fragmente der griechischen Historiker* (Berlin, 1929). See the chapter *Hecataeus.*
17. Ibid.
18. Ibid.

During Herodotus' lifetime, the elder Hanno sailed as far as Sierra Leone. He keeps a journal, in Punic, of this adventure. The Greek translation lets us accompany him.[19]
He takes a chimpanzee as plunder.

Herodotus devotes a good share of his researches to the burned-faces:
In book II we find an ethnography of "Libya" and Psammetichus (II, 29–33).
In the third book (III, 17–26), the mythic longevity of the Ethiopians; a little further (III, 101) Herodotus is taken in by fabulous accounts of the "black semen" of Indians and Africans – black to match their skin – an opinion that Aristotle refutes, in reference to Herodotus, by calling attention to the whiteness of their teeth (*De gen. anim.* III, 2 and 522a).
In the fourth book Herodotus writes of an African circumnavigation carried out by order of the pharaoh Necus (IV, 42):
And they claimed – although I don't believe it, perhaps others will – that in sailing around Libya the sun was on their right side.
The Tusculum and Oxford commentaries have nothing to say on this passage.
The *Liber Chronicarum* of Hartmut Schedel refers to Diego Cão and his African voyage of 1485:
As they turned east, their shadows fell to the south, on the right side.
The next African circumnavigation introduced by Herodotus is the failed voyage of Sataspes (IV, 43).
Sataspes had raped the daughter of Zosyrus and was sentenced by Xerxes to be burned at the stake.
The mother of the condemned man pleaded with the king for a still greater punishment: let the son sail around Libya.
Sataspes departs, sails some distance, and quits, telling Xerxes that he could make no further progress. Xerxes doesn't buy it and, enforcing his earlier judgment, has him impaled.
Such an entanglement of the Oedipal and the anal, a compulsion to travel and the death drive.
The point here is not to prove (again) that Herodotus was an attentive student of African customs (IV, 168–99; VII, 70; IX, 32).

19. C. Müller, ed., *Geographi Graeci Minores,* 1:1–14.

Excursus: The Mediterranean and the Gulf of Benin

I would like to liberate Afro-American culture from its exotic isolation.
I will restrict myself to five examples.
Sleep, and marriage to a god – I, 182.
Intercourse between a goat and a woman – II, 46.
The wooden phalloi – II, 48.
Aphrodite and the androgynous seer – IV, 67.
The snake of the gods and the pastry – VIII, 41.

I would not want to compare the fate of Lampião, a thief and revolutionary whose severed head was carried through northeastern Brazil in a metal canister full of Lysol and put on display at Bahia, with the "embalmed" head of Histiaios (IV, 30), as an example of a fetish common to the Mediterranean countries and the Gulf of Benin; rites of decapitation, the solemn preparation and transporting of heads extend from Japanese seppuku to Stendhal's *Le Rouge et le noir.*
Yet when I read, in book II (32), of the Nasamonians, who after crossing the desert, found some trees and, about to pick their fruits, were espied by some small black men, I am reminded not only of the third book of the *Iliad* (III, 1–7), not only of Adam and Eve, but also of the Sacred Hain of Dahomey and Haiti, referred to by Jakob Spieth.[20]
The penalty for touching the trees was death.
Herodotus brings "plucking" and "apprehending" into a precise and astonishing proximity.
Would it be an intolerable extrapolation if I were to suggest that the Pygmies had probably followed the Nasamonians for some time, remaining hidden only until the foreigners tried to eat of the forbidden fruits?

In the first book Herodotus passes on the report of Chaldean priests, who claim that the god Belos not only appears in their temple, but that he even spends the night there, sleeping on a bed with the priestess – our author, though, doesn't believe it.
The Egyptians in Thebes tell him of a similar incident:
The Theban Zeus sleeps in the temple with a priestess.

20. Jakob Spieth, *Die Ewe-Stämme* (Berlin, 1906), 396, 846, etc.

In Lycia as well, whenever the god appears, a priestess is locked up with him, overnight, in the temple.

Not far from Port-au-Prince, the capital of Haiti, one finds, nestled between residences and small religious huts, a house built specifically for a goddess or god, complete with a freshly made bed, slippers, altars, and candles.

The god sleeps here on the night of his holy day.

He spends the night with a trusted priest.

I know of two such bedrooms – one for the beautiful and vain "goddess of love," Erzulie Freda, the other for the snake god Damballah Ouedo. (I have never heard of bedrooms for married gods.)

Just as in Herodotus, sexual relations, or marriage, between gods is something out of the ordinary; men may be wed to the snake god Damballah Ouedo – though the latter seems amphibious with respect to gender – and women may be married to Erzulie Freda: *massissi* and *madevinaise* – male and female gays, respectively – are hardly foreign to Haitian religious beliefs.

Those who do marry gods are not bound to remain chaste their entire lives; they must rather refrain from intercourse with mortals only on the god's holy day.

In the fourth book one reads:

The androgynous Enarees say that Aphrodite has given them the gift of prophecy.

Herodotus here touches upon the theme of shamanism and homosexuality, a recurrent motif in the development of religions and religious thought – from the breasted Tiresias to Mircea Eliade.[21]

One encounters bisexuality in all the Afro-American religions.[22] *Pessoalidade forte* (i.e., *strong personality*) is a synonym for "female shaman" in Brazilian Candomblé, and the priest is often *entendido*, he hears, he understands – *entendido* is also, in Brazil, a euphemism for a male homosexual.

---

21. Mircea Eliade, *Le Chamanisme* (Paris, 1968).
22. Hubert Fichte, *Die Geschichte der Zärtlichkeit,* manuscript, vols. 7, 9. (The German edition notes that the preceding was the original title of *Die Geschichte der Empfindlichkeit.* – TRANS.)

Excursus: The Mediterranean and the Gulf of Benin

Cuban homosexuals may pray to the Afro-American god Inle,[23] those of Haiti to the gods of the dead, to Guédé Nibo Massissi; their patron goddess is the same Erzulie Freda who – though I would hesitate to call Athena a Greek Erzulie – might be thought of as a Haitian Aphrodite.

In the second book Herodotus also deals with Pan.

Painters and sculptors of Egypt usually portray the god Mendes as the Greeks do Pan: with the face and legs of a goat.

It would be unpleasant for Herodotus to say why they paint him in this manner.

The Mendesians worship all goats, the males more than the females.

During my stay I saw a wondrous sign: a goat copulating, out in the open, with a female. Everyone came to know of it.

How and Wells remark that this animal was revered as an incarnation of Osiris and that Herodotus incorrectly identifies it with the Greek Pan.

Osiris was also known as the lord of young women, the coupling ox (How and Wells, *Commentary*, I, 189).

How to account for Herodotus' holy dread?

Sacred oaths of silence are more clearly spoken of in the second book (II, 61, 65, 86). These appear consistently in reference to Osiris, the "blooming sycamore."

Was Herodotus' lapse an attempt to protect initiatory secrets?

Or did Herodotus, too (IV, 370), like the abridged Pauly-Wissowa encyclopedia, see Osiris as phallic, a god of fertility and the dead?

(At this point I might make a brief reference to Marthe de Chambrun Ruspoli, who in an impressive and ecstatic book, *L'Epervier divin*, remarks:

La terreur causée par ce meurtre – of Osiris – *fut si grande que, même de nos jours, son écho prolonge encore, car les premiers à répondre la nouvelle furent des bergers appelés pans, et depuis lors, une terreur soudaine se nomme "panique"* [12].

Thus Marthe de Chambrun brings Pan and Osiris into the same context.)[24]

---

23. Hubert Fichte, *Petersilie* (Frankfurt am Main, 1980), 392.
24. Marthe de Chambrun Ruspoli, *L'Epervier divin* (Paris, 1969).

The gods of the dead, Guédés in Haitian, are, like Osiris, phallic. On or around November 2, groups of Haitian women run through the countryside and cities bearing a large, wooden phallus, their faces painted white, dressed in purple, and wearing dark sunglasses.
The men, the priests, and the remaining faithful sport top hats and tails, like the ethnologist and dictator Dr. François Duvalier.[25]
Joe, a Cuban emigrant who has maintained a temple, both famous and infamous, named Kaye Joe, for about twenty years, claims to be an ordained priest of the dead.
He established ceremonies in their honor, held toward the end of October and beginning of November, which can last as long as fourteen days.[26]
He leads out a large black goat that, prior to sacrificing, he mounts.
Herodotus describes wooden phalloi two chapters later (II, 48):
The Egyptians celebrate the festival of Dionysus in a manner very much like the Greeks, but instead of phalloi they carry puppets, about eighteen inches high, which are manipulated by strings. During the procession the women move each puppet's genitals – αἰδοῖον, *the pudenda, which are almost as large as its entire body.*
The reason for the large member and why it is the only part that moves is the subject of a sacred tale.
Although he most likely heard it, Herodotus' lips are again sealed, out of holy reverence.
How and Wells likewise have nothing to offer on the topic.
Does this large wooden phallus recall the bound-up corpse of Osiris, the holy sycamore that washed ashore in West Africa, or more precisely, Morocco?
Death and the phallus in Egypt, associated with Osiris, and feared by Herodotus, just as in Dahomey and Togo, and in Haiti, where women carry these wooden phalloi beneath their dresses.[27]
His researches have proven, writes Herodotus, that the Greeks

25. Leonore Mau, *Xango* (Frankfurt am Main, 1976), 82, 102.
26. Hubert Fichte, *Xango* (Frankfurt am Main, 1976), 163 ff.
27. Ibid., 170.

received all of their names for the gods from the Egyptians (II, 50). Poseidon stems directly from Libya, Africa.[28]

Near Thebes there are holy snakes, which do no harm to humans. These are buried, when they die, in the shrine of Zeus (II, 74). They are said to be holy to this god.

In Dahomey, in Ouidah, there is a shrine of the holy python.

A believing citizen of Dahomey or Togo will bury any python that he or she finds dead.

If they are responsible for the snake's death, they must perform a purification ritual. If there is insufficient time for burial, the offending person covers the snake with leaves and says:

I didn't see you.[29]

As late as the beginning of this century, snakes are thought to have been kept in the temples of North Haiti, as embodiments of the god Damballah Ouedo.

Sacrifices to the snake god Damballah are costly and complicated: Food free of salt, drinks, Coca-Cola, and above all, *gnoun grand gateau*.

The priest repeats, in Haitian:

Gnoun grand gateau – a large pastry.

In the eighth book of Herodotus one finds (VIII, 41):

The Athenians say that a large snake, a guardian of the Acropolis, lives in a large temple.

Each month it is given, as an offering, a pastry.

The linguistic (mis)representation of the world.

Magic and tragedy.

Magic formulas and professional writing.

Herodotus' contradictory field of research is never more clear than in the story and sacrifice of the lion – the sacrifice, that is, of Leo, in book 7 (VII, 180).

Male beauty is one of the predominant motifs weaving its way through the entire nine books of this gigantic work, this being perhaps the allure that drew him over the face of the earth in the first place and that later led him to the writing table.

28. See also How and Wells, *Commentary on Herodotus* (Oxford, 1975), I, 188, 364.
29. Hubert Fichte, *Dahomey*, manuscript, 1975.

A longing for the beautiful black male.
The country of Ethiopia produces tall, long-lived and the most handsome of men – ἄνδρας . . . καλλίστους (III, 114), which scholarly temperament flattens out into *very handsome*.[30]
Xerxes' fleet captures a ship from Troezen. The Persians take one of the Greek prisoners, murder him, and consider it a good sign that the first Greek to be killed was also the best-looking.
The victim's name is Leon.
Chosen, perhaps, on account of his name.
Herodotus, at any rate, derives his fate from his name.
Lions and African lion-sacrifices.
Lion men, and traces of a magical rite, in the work of the first modern writer.

---

30. Herodotus, *Historien* (Munich, 1977), 463.

A PETRIFIED MAGIC CITY
Reflections on the Popular Edition of the Monographs of Paul Wunderlich, Edited by Jens Christian Jensen

New York, November 1980

In a society that angrily refuses any consideration of its material bases, in which, behind a duplicitous facade, the realms of ethics and aesthetics have long since ceased to have any real function, large numbers of individuals are drawn to various sorts of alluring fetishes, if only to keep from suffocating in the sickening atmosphere of hatred.

It is easy to understand, in such an environment, the mass appeal of art nouveau, or art deco, the popularity of a Käthe Kollwitz; and so perhaps might be explained the decision of Volker Huber to publish the first of five volumes of the monographs of Paul Wunderlich, in a first run of one hundred thousand copies, produced in Hong Kong, at a price of DM 28, with essays by Max Bense and Philippe Roberts-Jones.

What a coup!
A young publisher searches out the best and cheapest means of production, acquires financing for a special edition, and distributes the generous remainder so skillfully that all are satis-

fied with the profits: Herr Huber himself, the artist, his academic commentator Professor Jensen, and the reading public.

Volker Huber did not even follow the rule of charging six times the price of production, which would have sharply cut into everyone's take – what good would it have done him to print a volume priced at DM 280, in a run of two thousand copies, with a hypothetical yield of DM 140 per copy – if no one were to buy it!

It is very handsomely printed, says Paul Wunderlich.

Even the greens, which, as Richard Avedon tells me, can be printed in the United States only with difficulty, are sharp enough.

The yellow of Schöne Ursula *is too loud, I know. But we can't bother the printer over such details, or else the whole reproduction will come to a halt. One mustn't only consider the original, you know; the reproduction too must harmonize with itself.*

Yet when it comes to making copies of oil paintings, Paul Wunderlich speaks from the vantage point of a lithographer, and one who, early in his career, was fascinated by the possibilities of print reproduction, by tinged and yellowed tones.

On the jacket, a watercolor from 1980:
Couple with Dog.
A portrait of Paul Wunderlich and Karin Székessy.
Elegant people!
She with a small mink cap, before a portiere, he in a stylishly cut suit.

In the middle ground, and responding to the lines of the male figure, a bull terrier.

Elegant, as Jean Genet would say – splashes of green, some cystic yellow, a little pink, but mostly gray; and elegant in form – clearly detailed bodies, almost white, the walls and fabric more hazed, and several cuts left by a razor blade, as if scratched in stone.

This image, at first glance, strikes me as unmistakably the work of Wunderlich himself; stylistically, it is incomparable.

Yet upon repeated consideration, I am struck by an effect similar to that of rereading Proust:

One believes one is viewing a chic and intimate tea visit – which suddenly becomes transformed into a shorthand for the evolu-

A Petrified Magic City

tion of human conduct and artistic representation, whereupon layer after layer, citation after citation become clear, all without the illusion of the work's originality being sundered by explicit reference to Racine, Anatole France, or George Grosz.

The "ugly" faces recall the figures of the Berlin caricaturist – in Grosz, however, the moral drive is complicated by the fact that he actually despises the poor, whom he claims to defend, and envies the luxury he paints in such contemptible colors; Wunderlich, on the other hand, gives us an unironic self-exposure drawn in the soft light of admiration.

The spray technique of this watercolor – in contrast to the effect of brushstrokes – is able to give the background extremely small points of color; using a water pistol, the pointillist technique is refined and pushed to its limits.

The stiffness of both forms would likewise seem to be a citation of Seurat, who has inspired more than one painter to draw figures that strike us as rigid, stilted puppets; the Bauhaus too appears, in Wunderlich's picture, in the guise of an implacable chest of drawers.

The colors are not those of the Frenchman.

In general, though, colors do not have the historical significance of forms. It is impossible to cite another work by color alone, without inserting it into the form of the work alluded to – but one can quote Grosz's figures without even using his colors.

Wunderlich's gray may be the gray of Vuillard, Corot, Chardin, Goya, and Vermeer, yet in the absence of Vermeer's forms one need only add a touch of pink, some yellow around the woman's cloaca, as a zoologist might call it, and the ground for a narrative history of color is quickly withdrawn, the work impossible to date on the basis of its chromatic components.

The figures are also given a different twist than in the work of Seurat or Schlemmer.

Piero?

I'm not confident to judge.

One can't miss the reference to a fragment from the Amarna period.

The radiance surrounding the divine pharaoh is here secularized into a gray portiere.

The cranial disfiguration of Ms. Székessy invokes early African headwraps, the elongated style of the heretical, sun-addicted Akhenaton.

And yet beneath the serpentine, jeweled band of the mink cap, one sees not only the shimmering profile of the pharaoh, but also the primitive ear and the death's-head; the plump man-about-town resembles not only our primitive ancestors from Dordogne – the cranial sutures lie open.

Or more precisely:

The lines of the sutures pass over a material that is collected and tied off behind the head – like a stocking mask drawn over one's face, and changing its shape – except for the fact that the head itself is this material; the impression is that of an executioner's mask, or the mask of a latex fetishist.

An anthropological register, recalling Proust's method in the *Recherche,* specifically: the introduction, on sleep and dreams; the botanical sketches drawn up on the occasion of the scene in the porter's lodge; the religiohistorical remarks on the beauty of slaughter – a detailed pursuit of pictorial expression and human demeanor, achieved with nothing more than colored water and pencil, a pursuit of the Cro-Magnon man, through Amarna, torture, and the torturous mise-en-scène.

This watercolor, which Professor Jensen rightly insists on using as a title piece, is Wunderlich's richest, and yet most sparing, image.

I am familiar with the many objections to Wunderlich's work. Nor do I want to repeat here all the insipid trifles, the banal and arrogant charges that have been leveled against him, for stupidity is not overcome by censure – rather, one only disseminates such ignorance all the more effectively by lending it an air of credibility, in the process only satisfying one's own sadistic impulses.

The director of the Kieler Museum, Jensen succeeds by means of an almost incriminating text and a skillful organization of materials, in documenting Wunderlich as one of the greatest painters of the second half of the twentieth century.

It mustn't be denied, however, that the German professorial mentality can sometimes lead him into error. The art historian often

A Petrified Magic City

ventures out onto the weakest of limbs, driven by some supposed dialectic of pigment and psyche – and in a language that tends to erase the very object of its inquiry:
Sensibility and the perfection of craft.
Nor is he alone in this, by any means.
In the critical appraisal of the so-called fine arts, to include "high" literary productions, critics in general seem to expect artists to present only that which they are capable of comprehending, at the moment, as avant-garde.
Thus we don't read of Van Gogh in Gide, in 1890, but in Artaud, in 1947, nor of Artaud in Gide, in 1947, but in Susan Sontag in 1970, and compared with Leni Riefenstahl.
That gives rise, in Jensen, to the following:
Wunderlich *must*, or *must have* (7).
Here, then, was the filter discovered (80).
This meshing of line and washed-color surfaces is the goal (29).
It *recalls* and is *suggestive of*; and, on page 44, something is *achieved with difficulty*.
. . . an informal element, retaining the imponderables that, in the midst of the dominating presence of the figures, attach, dreamlike, to the image as a whole (13).
Thus Lévi-Straussian jargon made its way to Kiel as well.
Jensen can't always avoid that eclectic pro- and con-fusion of thoughts that the various media bombard us with these days:
antimilitaristic, antinationalistic, anti-ideological, in which the crimes of the Nazi regime make up the moral *background to this stance* (3).
Caviling, to be sure.
Women are repeatedly *females*.
On homosexuality:
Yet rarely has a plastic artist of our time . . . dared to linger in that impugnable *and much-maligned realm of sexuality* (77).
This is the squeamish vocabulary of the German academic bourgeoisie, which doesn't shrink from embracing the benefits of sickness or burning brain cells.
Jensen is right when he speaks of Wunderlich the enlightener.
And just how relevant and unstale the art scholar's formulas can be is seen, for example, when he compares the masculine, English-looking Wunderlich with the *Beautiful Helen*:

Much admired, and much abused, I come –
Helen, from the shore . . .
Witty and malicious.
Jensen's strengths are integration, the analysis of practical methods and their relations to style and content.
Like a detective, he searches out culture-historical combinations; he even digs up Dante and the couple Paolo and Francesca.
And he is able to prove that such a reference is not overly subtle. On page 125, his conclusion is convincing:
Here [Wunderlich] accomplishes what Ingres himself would have done, who never cared for the paintings of Manet.
And page 152, on the knife's edge:
The privacy of his work carries with it the drive toward self-knowledge.
I know of no one who can cite in support of his themes as cleverly as Jensen:
I said that I was very much aware of the disruptive effect that consciousness has on human gracefulness.
Kleist's *Marionettentheater.*
And, mirror-inverted:
Nature is a petrified magic city.
Novalis and finally Hofmansthal:
Depth lies – where? on the surface.
Surely Gottfried Benn, when he wrote *The Problems of Lyric,* in 1951, envied the Kieler scholar his academic stature.
Jensen's book leads us to conclude that Paul Wunderlich's oil paintings, gouaches, and watercolors should not be treated as the secondary production of a significant lithographer, but as works worthy of being classed with those of a Dali, a Dubuffet, Bacon, Botero, Hockney, or Lindner.
His oeuvre attests that Wunderlich, at that time when the trend hinged upon *valeurs, matière et tâche,* saw beyond July 20 and the disastrous *engagement* of *Qui s'explique.*
When the mode turned political, following an event that is, in the painter's biography, only perceivable by the very painful seam in the body of his work, Wunderlich withdrew – the movements of the offended offenders henceforth take place in luxurious cages, beneath thin, supposedly protective latex skins.

A Petrified Magic City

Now, when the evening breeze is redolent of rococo and sweets, he pares down his means to a barrenness, which contains a strong reproach.

The intensity has not been lost – just all the more successfully concealed.

THE OBJECTIVE AND THE SUBJECTIVE AUTHOR
Remarks on Henry James's *Washington Square*

Agadir, March 1981

He's an American standing on tiptoe, behind a wall, trying to eavesdrop on a British conversation.
— Somerset Maugham

1.

Washington Square is the title of a rather sentimental tale of heterosexual love, written by an author who was gay.
The term *sentimental* is not arbitrarily chosen: the novel is based upon the various stock motivations of bourgeois passion:
A rich, cold, and intelligent father.
A handsome dowry hunter, stalking a legacy.
A ridiculous *intrigante* of an aunt.
And innocent, unswerving, pitiful Catherine, whom James repeatedly designates as his heroine.
The reference to homosexuality results in part from the reading itself – the story of Catherine Sloper and the seemingly casual choice of a title allow James to depict several atypical strata of bourgeois existence in the New York of the nineteenth century – a melodrama that seeks to destroy the basis of its own emotional impact, an analysis that lays bare the author's complicity in a sentimental travesty.

During a portion of the first half of the present [19th] century, and more particularly during the latter part of it, there flourished and practised in the city of New York a physician who enjoyed perhaps an exceptional share of the consideration which, in the United States, has always been bestowed upon distinguished members of the medical profession. This profession in America has constantly been held in honor, and more successfully than elsewhere has put forward a claim to the epithet of "liberal." In a country in which, to play a social part, you must either earn your income or make believe that you earn it, the healing art has appeared in high degree to combine two recognized sources of credit. It belongs to the realm of the practical, which in the United States is a great recommendation; and it is touched by the light of science – a merit appreciated in a community in which the love of knowledge has not always been accompanied by leisure and opportunity.

It was an element in Dr. Sloper's reputation that his learning and his skill were very evenly balanced; he was what you might call a scholarly doctor, and yet there was nothing abstract in his remedies – he always ordered you to take something. Though he was felt to be extremely thorough, he was not uncomfortably theoretic; and if he sometimes explained matters more minutely than might seem of use to the patient, he never went so far (like some practitioners one had heard of) as to trust to the explanation alone, but always left behind him an inscrutable prescription. There were some doctors that left the prescription without offering any explanation at all; and he did not belong to that class either, which was after all the most vulgar. It will be seen that I am describing a clever man; and this is really the reason why Doctor Sloper had become a local celebrity.

The trenchant wit of this passage rests upon a pun: the name of the honorable gentleman – Dr. Sloper – has to do with something sloped, oblique, indirect, slippery, if not sloppy; a literary means that Thomas Mann uses to good effect with names like Grünlich [greenish], Naphta, and Professor Kukuck [cuckoo].

The portrait of Dr. Sloper reads breezily enough, unless one takes the time to examine it a bit more closely.

He was very witty.

We will later see what James understands by wit.

He passed in the best society of New York for a man of the world.

Henry James fled this best society.

The Objective and the Subjective Author

. . . which indeed he was, in a very sufficient degree.
This meant next to nothing to James.
I hasten to add, to anticipate possible misconception, that he was not the least of a charlatan.
One had to have been a charlatan then, we can infer, to pass for a man of the world in the best society of New York.
And the haste with which James denies it, the misconceptions against which he innoculates the reader, and the distinction within a society that James despised make the author's implied meaning clear by the second page of the book:
Charlatan, scatter-brained Dr. Slippery Slope!
On the third page we see the proof, or better the definitive insinuation:
The physician has lost a son, as well as his wife, without being able to help them medically; nor did his failure, in such a society, harm his renown in any way. Nevertheless:
he escaped all criticism but his own, which was much the most competent and most formidable. He walked under the weight of this very private censure for the rest of his days, and bore forever the scars of a castigation to which the strongest hand he knew had treated him on the night that followed his wife's death.

We don't understand a single word.
Is the tremolo sincere?
Whose "strongest hand" castigated him?
Was Dr. Slippery a flagellant?
Is there evidence of such an affliction in the later conduct of Dr. Sloper?
Not in the slightest!
Anything but a superficial table of contents would compete, in the most absurd way, with the 174 pages (in the paperback edition) of this condensed and shrewd text.
And now, the minimum essential information for an understanding of the following remarks:
Dr. Sloper, who has lost a son and, during the birth of his daughter, his wife as well, raises, with the help of his sister – Mrs. Penniman – his healthy, charmless, chubby daughter, whom he despises.

Dr. Sloper is a man of some means and has no other heir than this dull, gluttonous girl, who will also receive a considerable sum from her mother's side.

At a cousin's wedding an especially good-looking, intelligent young man – Morris Townsend – takes an interest in Catherine. Mrs. Penniman, the aunt, does everything in her power to nourish and foster the relationship. But Dr. Sloper opposes the marriage of his daughter to Morris, for he suspects the young man of being a dowry hunter, with no occupation, who has already squandered his own paltry means on wild adventures and is now supported by his sister.

Dr. Sloper receives every proof of his suspicions.

Catherine will sooner renounce her father's inheritance than Morris.

The lover presses for an immediate wedding. Catherine hesitates, so as not to anger her father.

Soon Morris begins to waver as well, in the hopes that he might win the doctor over himself and come into a still greater fortune. The father takes Catherine on a trip to Europe, coerces her, appealing to her filial affections, but she does not give in.

She discovers that her father hates her.

Morris Townsend, upon their return, abandons her.

The father dies, and precisely according to the diagnosis he had made of his own condition; for a final time, he constrains his daughter to accede to his wishes, by threatening to withhold her inheritance.

Catherine will still not exclude the possibility of marrying Morris – the father disinherits her, and she receives one-fifth of her father's estate.

Catherine settles down in a house on Washington Square, with Mrs. Penniman, and becomes a respectable old maid.

After twenty-five years, Morris Townsend – still a good-looking guy – tries again to win her hand.

Catherine remains resolved, "dry."

Henry James is an author concerned with time, with history: *During a portion of the first half of the present century* (5) begins the first chapter.

Page 15 speaks of Catherine's red satin dress:
It is a point on which history has not been explicit.
Even the silly Catherine is history – not with a capital *H*, perhaps, but still history – and after he has inserted her life into the book of the world, he writes in conclusion:
This life had, however, a secret history as well as a public one (160).
Time, then, though not in the Bergsonian, Proustian sense, not as the half-chewed madeleine, but rather as a *portion*, as a portion of the cake of ideas.
Already in the opening line one sees – in the temporal determination – the fall of a subjective author into an all-knowing one, as if by the gravitational force of the latter's word. Thus the abstracted time-segment is perhaps only a pretense, an attitude – just as later, when Catherine is seen by her beloved as an object, among other objects, in Dr. Sloper's living room (30). *What she saw was her father's still grey eye and his clear-cut, definite smile. She contemplated these objects for a moment, and then she looked back at the fire; it was much warmer* (54). The objective and the affected author both claim, then, that Catherine looks upon her father's eyes and smile as "objects" – and subsequently the artist lets slip a revealing tautology:
The fire became much warmer.
Clearly warmer than the 98.6 Fahrenheit degrees of Dr. Sloper. And yet in the process James reveals, magically and subconsciously, a mode of perception different from the normal and purposeful – the fire becomes, for him, as it was for the pre-Socratics, a primal element, which actuates the life and the objects, as well as the father himself, from their previous torpor.
The physician's temperature makes manifest, for the daughter, the deadly entropy of the bourgeois era in the New World, an entropy that pervades entire lifetimes, living beings, and emotions themselves, a climate within which these can only be grasped as portions, objects, fragments:
Morris is
a gentleman of fine parts (77),
and this may have been, in the English of the nineteenth century, an idiomatic expression – he is, all the same, a man of fine parts, an appraisal that not only borders on the inorganic but also hints at a more murderous-sexual intent;

a gentleman of fine private parts would be a man with attractive genitalia.
106: *readers disposed to judge harshly of a young man who may have struck them as making but an indifferently successful use of fine natural parts.*

Which one must, of course, in German, translate with *natürlichen Anlagen* – "natural abilities."
Yet at bottom – what is being described?
Or what kind of custom?
125: *Catherine's temper, an article . . .*
that is, an object . . .
125: *this beautiful young man was her own exclusive property*
thinks the pure, suffering, unswerving, not-for-sale Catherine.

Portion of the century – page 5.
Catherine – object – page 30.
Father's eye, his clear-cut smile – objects – page 54.
Morris, a gentleman of fine parts – page 106.
Morris, her own exclusive property – page 125.
One "acquires holdings."
Are such comments repeatedly written without intention, or does the author pursue, objectively or subjectively, a subterranean – or as Thomas Mann would call it, a more underworldly – notion?

Henry James knows the mechanics of rhetorical device.
What doesn't he manage to imply around the concept of "saying"!
I say [when in fact he writes!] *"such as she was," because to tell the truth – But this is a truth of which I will defer the telling* (8).

"He's more like a foreigner," Catherine suggested.
And lest the avoidance of the word "say" become flat, the next line reads:
"Well, I never knew a foreigner," said young Townsend (26).
"I am very sorry," Catherine permitted herself to observe (27),
a sublimatory gesture that doubles the primary act of saying.

The Objective and the Subjective Author

... *these two young persons might confabulate, as the Doctor phrased it to himself.*
As an example of Dr. Sloper's wit and manner of living, James provides us with a conversation he has with Morris Townsend, where the doctor has the final "say":
"Even if [Catherine] were not weak, however, you would still be a penniless man."
"Ah, yes; that is my weakness! And therefore, you mean, I am mercenary – I only want your daughter's money."
"I don't say that. I am not obliged to say it; and to say it, save under stress of compulsion, would be very bad taste. I say simply that you belong to the wrong category" (59).

Not only saying, but (story)telling, James problematizes the narrative position itself.
The omniscient, vague author is, from the beginning, checked by his subjective, fastidious counterpart – one is reminded of the early pages of Mann's *Selected Stories*; not simply a formal concern, however, we see the thought as well, the inner monologue, the *contenu mental* that, during the same period, occupied the Russian W. M. Garshin in *Four Days*, the Frenchman E. Dujardin in *Les Lauriers sont coupés*, and, as it is reflected upon by James: *as the doctor phrased it to himself* (44), we noted above; just prior to this, there is another passage in which the inner conflict of all thought is played out;
What transpires in the small space of my brain, that such various, transitory flights of fancy become molded into a single, precise utterance?
The self-conflict of every novel:
How to stylize so much unfathomable material, which takes place in the minds of the characters, into a single text?
He has abilities, said Catherine's father. . . .
The Doctor, however, kept his reflections to himself and talked to his visitors about foreign lands.
James the author – which one? – tricks the reader for an instant and presents the inner world of Dr. Sloper as if it were actual reality: Catherine's father "would like to say," he is "on the verge of saying"; the split language-existence of Dr. Sloper is, for an

entire sentence, given the status of a real event, by means of the novelist's contradictory utterances, for while Sloper really speaks of foreign lands, he thinks about the statement concerning Morris's talent.

A split familiar to all, which James elevates, as an artistic means, to highlight the subtleties of the fluctuating narrative position – the linguistic situation of the bourgeois epoch itself, a language of psychosis and psychoanalysis.

Henry James's narrative mode is oblique.
His sentences express, indirectly, what malice can only say in words; the father to his daughter:
You are an honest, amiable girl, and an intelligent young man might easily find it out (56).
No – we are a long way from Balzac, from the plaintive Père Goriot and the tottering *coulisses* of Eugénie Grandet – as the author and his figure are well aware:
I am not a father in an old-fashioned novel (62).
The law of this book and its society is taste – to say that something is in *very bad taste* expresses a very harsh censure.
Dr. Sloper would excuse himself for showing very bad taste only in the most extreme circumstances – *under stress of compulsion* – i.e., as regards his daughter's handsome, detested suitor, whom he would like to kill but doesn't, and not out of any sense of morality – *I am not a very good man* (116) – but simply because it would not be in good taste.
Very bad taste, he scolds his daughter, whose life he chokes off. *Very bad taste* is the expression that so offends Catherine that she breaks off all ties (109).
The phrase recurs in the brief work – which is not always so sparing of repetitions – only three times:
that speech about bad taste made her ears burn for three days.

James makes use of hyperbole, quotation marks, parentheses, italics and, on page 81, even makes a joke about italics.
The authors from whom he distinguishes himself are, for the most part, ironic authors, and, as irony is a type of hyperbole, of disingenuous speech or writing, irony is to a high degree the preeminent bourgeois stylistic virtue:

The Objective and the Subjective Author

A class of arrivistes, being of one mind with respect to the truth – or reality – is aided by lies; James, with the help of false statements, hints at the truth.
It will be seen, that I am describing a clever man, will lead the reader, like the epithet *liberal,* down a wrong path.
At the time we are chiefly concerned with him.
The modern era's most fastidious literary taste pretends, in the modest *we,* to draw the reader into the process of creation – in reality it is the "we" of an authoritarian attitude, of solitude, the "we" of a psychoanalyzing, doubled persona.

Time and again, James counterposes this disingenuous, indirect mode – manneristically – with the square, straight-edged statement, almost blunt repetitions, and archaic turns of phrase.
The book's first sentence is six lines long. It ends with:
. . . *distinguished members of the medical profession. The profession* starts off the next sentence; a technique that the author repeats on page 30.
Morris Townsend, the hypocrite *décadent,* states his impression of the party, and of Catherine, in a naively straightforward manner;
What a delightful party!
What a charming house!
What an interesting family!
What a pretty girl your cousin is! – with the musically lengthened closing phrase.
James is quite clearly a keen observer: the rapturous tone is squarely *décadent;* the litany of exclamations forms not only a delightful counterpoint but is also manneristically precise.
Brief, key sentences are used by James for heightened dramatic effect:
"I feel very old – and very wise," said Catherine smiling faintly.
"I'm afraid that before long you will feel older and wiser yet. I don't like your engagement" (55), the father says, and gives an example of his dubious wit.

The crafty writer shows us, on page 74, how to describe two quite different things with the same expression:

The letter, at least, was long for her; and it may be added, that it was long for Morris.
Catherine had written Morris a long letter.
These notes were dispatched on the Friday and Saturday; but Saturday and Sunday passed . . .
Archaic and fastidious:
The Friday, the morrow, Morris's – behind the slowly spun snares, a blunt, bare murder:
"Would you like to have killed him?" asks Mrs. Almond.
"Yes. Very much," the doctor answered.
And again the pleasure in puns:
The doctor's friendly sister is named Mrs. Almond; the poor charity case humbly accepting the doctor's bread is called Mrs. Penniman; and the dowry hunter: Morris Outskirts. I've already mentioned the various associations conjured up by the name Sloper. On page 8 one finds a curiously ornate utterance on truth:
She grew up a very robust and healthy child, and her father, as he looked at her, often said to himself that, such as she was, he at least need have no fear of losing her. I say "such as she was," because, to tell the truth – But this is a truth of which I will defer the telling.

A gesture of coitus interruptus, of asthmatic constriction – for which we owe thanks to another great novel of the modern era; this *defer the telling*, the displacement of truth, is the novel itself.

2.

Behind the trees of Washington Park, behind its sentimentality and decorousness, there lurk Attic vipers and all the violent repressions of the age of Freud:
Dr. Sloper wishes to revenge himself on Catherine, since she has deprived him of his beloved wife and – much worse – ruined him, in his own eyes, as a physician.
The father will deny her all happiness and is prepared, if necessary, to murder her beloved, even to leave her starving and abandoned in the Alps.
Nor does Morris Townsend appear in a better light.
He's clearly after Catherine's money.
And, after hesitating, he leaves her, once it has become clear that he can't get access to her inheritance.

The Objective and the Subjective Author

Mrs. Penniman pretends to help the young couple – in reality she only wants to sponge off of them, and once she sees that the engagement with Morris has miscarried, she repeatedly thwarts her niece's plans, all the while seeming, superficially, to act in her interest.
The melodramatic narrative is hardly concerned with love – much more with hatred, ruin, lust for power.
The author misleads his reader, fundamentally, in the very beginning of the novel, in his description of Dr. Sloper.
On page ii we read of Catherine:
in her younger years she was a good deal of a romp, and, though it is an awkward confession to make about one's heroine, I must add that she was something of a glutton.

So many superimposed layers: of prudishness, baseness, good taste, precision, and false precision – and to such an extent that one continually thinks, wrongly, to have wrested the meaning of a given passage – yet the analysis of specific linguistic posturings remains difficult:
Catherine is a glutton.
This is an uncultured and clumsy, awkward confession – at least according to my Tauchnitz dictionary from the period contemporary to James.
An admission that an author ought not to make – or so James says.
Surely an author ought to reveal such facts – as James knows.
Surely he does so with pleasure, and not out of folly, but careful calculation.

And really – what's such a big deal about a girl who likes to eat? Is it an offense against good taste?
Could James really have been so one-dimensional as not to have ever questioned his ideal, or the supposed ideal, of good taste?
Be that as it may. To make such a confession of one's heroine may have been considered artless, during an age in which Proust was asked:
Vos héroïnes préférées dans la vie réelle?
Vos héroïnes préférées dans la fiction?

And which for James? Heroines, or humans, made of flesh and blood, following André Gide's distinction?
He seemed to want very much to come (26).
Heroes and heroines seem to want very much to come.
(Or perhaps a pornographic subtext: more to "come.") The subjective author distorts, the objective author exhibits.
The young man, within a few days, had made her listen to things for which she had not supposed that she was prepared (50).
Though this is a fad of the author's day, a decidedly English mode, is James's preference for it motivated only by the snobbism of the overseas provincial?
It seems to me that I ought to be very much offended with you (72), as an expression of profound humiliation and anger, is reflective not only of a time and a dialect – it says something as well about the person who would assume such an affected manner.
In the midst of so much masquerade and sublimation, there appears an aside of such apparent insignificance that one almost misses it entirely.
Is this a trick?
Does he want to make this comment early on, like an alibi, but in such a way as to escape the reader's notice?
Her deepest desire was to please him, and her conception of happiness was to know that she had succeeded in pleasing him (12).
Votre idée du malheur, Antoinette Faure asks the young Marcel Proust.
To be separated from maman.
The reader, the attentive reader, dazed by the text's constant teasing, hyperbole, and quotation marks, suspects a ruse.
Deepest desire, conception of happiness – empty phrases, used to characterize the vapidness of the poorly attired, lumpy daughter.
And, at the same time, code words for the entire novel.
Thus it only becomes clear how much Catherine admires her father when the latter starts to denigrate her boyfriend.
Clear that, in the heat of a love affair with one of the most exciting men in New York, she feels
great excitement in trying to be a good daughter (74).
And finally that she hesitates, when Morris abruptly asks to marry him, even without the lure of a great sum of money.

Love for the father.
Devotion for the father.
The ill-fated attachment to people whom one can never please, never win over.
She realizes it.
She experiences it in the novel, metaphorically.
When her father accuses her of *bad taste*, she feels rejected, her ears burn for three days (108–10).
His scorn, a response to her alleged bad taste, drives her from her father, but not because he's destroyed her lover's bliss, in any normal sense of the term – something she never had in the first place. Her knowledge of his contempt is revealed to Morris in words more appropriately spoken with regard to a lover than a father: *He is not very fond of me* (127).
Tauchnitz would translate this as *he is not so keen on me*, or simply *he doesn't like me very much*, whereas today one would probably say *he's not too crazy about me*.
This sentiment renders her incapable of attaching herself to another man.
She spurns all thought of marriage and Morris Townsend, for a second time, following the death of her father and lives out her days with the despicable, malicious Mrs. Penniman. The tasteless creature falls into an existential entanglement, becomes trapped – like Henry James himself – in the vagaries of the prevailing taste and morality of her day.

3.

Henry James's artistic mastery often consists in the illusion of precision, subtlety, and sensitivity evoked by his language – the same qualities said to distinguish Dr. Sloper. It is noteworthy, moreover, with what ease such a reputation can be maintained. *The world, which, as I have said, appreciated him, pitied him too much to be ironical; his misfortune made him more interesting, and even helped him to be the fashion.*
In practice a very precise and polished ironic statement, but one that contains a false knowledge, or a pretended false knowledge, of the nature of irony.
The truth is, every best-seller has to have something stupid about it.

What nonsense often follows upon carefully calculated untruths: *his private opinion of the more complicated sex* (9) – is supposed to undercut, delicately, the idea of the "fair sex":
Women as the more complicated sex?!
Does the author really buy this?
How innocently, or perhaps hypocritically, he takes the reader into his confidence.
It has been noted that the doctor was a philosopher, but I would not have answered for his philosophy if the poor girl had proved a sickly and suffering person (13).
Really?
Much more a question of power, wounded vanity, and occupational status. Had Dr. Sloper been able to simply support his daughter, things may have turned out more fortunately and philosophically for all concerned.
Catherine, though she felt tongue-tied, was conscious of no embarrassment (19) – how tongue-tied but not troubled?
Such fine people!
And yet Mr. Townsend was not like an actor; he seemed so sincere, so natural (20).
And yet Mr. Townsend was not like an actor, writes – objectively – the artist-author of *Washington Square* – yet how could he not have reflected on the fact that the actor's talent, like the writer's, consists above all in seeming sincere and natural?
Nature, and its distorted appearances, is the theme of the brief novel.
She was not at all jealous of Aunt Lavinia, but she was a little envious (25).
Ah, we're so refined, so dreadfully refined we can hardly stand it – writes Gustaf Gründgens.
I have no idea how it's possible, psychologically, to be envious without being jealous – though according to Tauchnitz *jealousy* is a wider concept, suggesting a more profound emotion, often mixed with suspicion, while *envy* is a more petty, superficial "begrudging."
The twilit intimacy is not to the cynic's liking, so he goes *to the window, where the dusk had deepened to darkness* (29).
Not simply to the window, but to where he can be both inside and outside, at the same time.

The Objective and the Subjective Author

On page 37 the scheming dowry hunter Morris Townsend, while talking to his prospective and untrusting father-in-law, drinks a whole bottle of madeira and one and a half bottles of claret.
That seems unlikely, even in New York.
And on page 112 we witness an unironic bit of crudeness, a lapse of good taste:
Mrs. Penniman is wild about kissing people's foreheads; her action is an unintentional expression of sympathy with the intellectual part (of the body).
Perhaps all the irony in this chiseled work ought to be seen as crude, a momentary lapse of good taste.
With respect to his heroine James commits the most inexplicable errors.
This happy certitude had come sooner than Catherine expected (50).
Maybe.
Four lines later, he remarks, on the same topic:
She took, what was given her, from day to day.
Following one of her father's most malicious attacks upon her (57), Catherine marvels at the clarity and nobility of his eloquence.
Dr. Sloper (32):
. . . was never eager, never impatient or nervous.
What does it mean to make such a comment of a living person?
And what does it mean to say this of Sloper, who throughout the entire work is portrayed as a greedy, impatient, nervous, and even psychopathic individual?
Catherine is an oddly puppetlike heroine:
She was the softest creature in the world (15).
Does James really believe in such a mythic being?
And even if he does, does he expect us to believe it would look anything like the obstinate, gluttonous Catherine?
Catherine masks her feelings, for the first time in her life, at the age of twenty-one (21); later, as an old maid (84), she becomes, for the first time in her life, embittered.
Does James exploit such topoi in order to show himself a cosmopolitan New Yorker, or does this unmasking occur spontaneously, without any special prompting?
The frivolity of a writer who repeatedly asserts his own conscientiousness is not compensated for by frequent gestures of inclu-

sion – "taking the reader into his confidence." An exquisite, learned, competent, and ironic style is, in the end, condescending – the author relates to his reader as Dr. Sloper to his daughter.
The girl was very happy (39).
Silly little thing, so thoroughly hoodwinked!
James forgets, when he describes the meetings of Catherine and Morris, "soon to be the most important part of her life," that, twenty-seven pages earlier, he had described quite different things as the "most important."
This is all that need be recorded of their conversation (53) is a condescending turn, the author foolishly leaning on some hack's device.
It seemed a proof that she was strong and solid and dense, and would live to be a great age – longer than might generally be convenient.
Dr. Sloper himself couldn't have said it any better.
That life or death questions be decided on the basis of taste – James burdens his narrator with such a posture.
The puffed-up author often fails to note the import of his own statements:
Catherine begs:
And Morris, Morris, you must never despise me (128).
How contemptible James must have thought himself, to then write:
This was an easy promise to make.
James's condescension is the condescension of Dr. Sloper.
The conscious or unconscious similarities of linguistic manner point toward something like complicity.
Already on page 7:
He walked under the weight of this very private censure for the rest of his days, and bore forever the scars of a castigation to which the strongest hand he knew had treated him on the night that followed his wife's death.
This very private censure, the type of scar, and what hand chastised him – whether god's, his father's, or his own – only Sloper and the author know for certain, as this information is never divulged; the events, their rites and etiology, are kept secret from the public, though clearly they possess a sadomasochistic air.

At any rate scars, psychic or bodily – as in Proust, who covers Charlus with bruises and chains.

Dr. Sloper's . . . opinion of the more complicated sex was not exalted (9),

an assertion the author makes of a – supposedly philosophical and highly cultured – physician.

His wife had been a . . . bright exception.

An assertion that makes James look like an idiot.

The father tortures his daughter; he is on the point of ruining her life:

I know not, whether he had hoped for a little more resistance for the sake of a little more entertainment (74).

I – Henry James – know not, etc.

Once again, one needs some sort of scalpel to cut through and separate the various layers of linguistic ritual.

Outwardly, the author distances himself, in his *concetto*, from such a base action.

I don't know.

The posture of naive innocence.

He knows – and would say so – if he weren't his character's accomplice – if, for example, he were under oath and preparing a deposition.

Yet all transpires, here, in the realm of fiction.

The objective and the subjective author know, of course, as Henry James, that which they present as unknowable, but rather than disclose this, they play out their various attitudinal postures for the greater benefit and pleasure of the reader –

for the pedagogical benefit of the reader, for the one they imagine, condescendingly, to be their reader.

After James has distanced himself, rhetorically and in tasteful self-assuredness, from such a spectacle of baseness, he carries out the defamation of poor Dr. Sloper from above, by putting the blame on the industrious doctor for a specific sadistic inclination – the prolonging of torture for purposes of entertainment – like Proust's episode with the rats.

Prolonging the throes of literary figures by intensifying their resistance: the source of the thrill in reading works of world literature.

Without it we would have neither Kafka nor Dante.
James gave lucid definition to the idea of reading as the application of thumbscrews – just as Agatha Christie: the idea of reading as murder – in *The Turn of the Screw*.
Complicitous:
Both the father and James want Morris to be seen as wicked – this becomes clear in their shabby discourse on the depravity of spontaneous marriage.
Dr. Sloper has earlier remarked:
I don't want to believe in you (60).
And, in appearance moved by paternal solicitude, Dr. Sloper commits the exact same crime against his daughter that he feared Morris Townsend would:
He ruins her life.
That is:
James paints the father in the same light as the father does the beloved.
It's a great pleasure to be in the right, says the doctor, on page 147.
To claim to be right, and with pleasure, is the lever of irony.
Irony cannot function without upsetting a state of affairs generally perceived to be true.
Your pleasures make one shudder, responds the doctor's clever sister, Mrs. Almond.
Nowhere is the author's complicity with the "philosophical and cultured" Dr. Slippery, and with the stupid, coarse, and retrograde Dr. Sloper, more apparent than in the sloppy use of the word *poor*:
The semantic range of the word extends beyond mere condescension:
A peculiar, tragic irritation results when Testanière speaks, in the Provence, of *ma pauvre mère,* as a way of saying:
Here I stand, a poor fool.
The raw, tactless *poor* is, in the plush language of the novel, usually reserved for the heroine, Catherine.
Henry James became familiar with the work of Flaubert during his stay in Paris.
Flaubert was known to rewrite several pages simply because he had noticed the repetition of a single adjective.

The Objective and the Subjective Author

Henry James is untroubled by using his dumb *poor* twice on the same page (57), both in reference to Catherine.
On page 73, it appears again to describe the clever, strong girl, rich in feelings and response – and above all in endowment.
On page 126 even Morris uses it of her, as if to prop up the author in his disparaging opinion.
Poor, poor, on page 57, and aimed at Catherine;
Poor, poor, on 67, spoken by Father Gigot and, sadly, on page 131, James the rhetorician lets it slip out yet again – this time through the mouth of Mrs. Penniman.
Irony. This uninspired, bourgeois artistic device presupposes decisions that are made, of necessity, outside of the work and, as such, are never represented but rather proffered – like chocolate or coffee.
In the end, it's the ridiculous, hyperbolic Mrs. Penniman – a character possessing no awareness of her own absurdity – whom James and Dr. Sloper take "at her word" – thus James himself would seem to take one of his own linguistic manners more literally than others:
that odious, ironical tone (129),
a statement that can hardly be made without its own ironical condescension.
James has her add:
. . . with which you treat the most sacred subjects.
Subjects – people – objects . . .
Don't undervalue irony, James defends himself through the mouth of his doctor.
. . . it is often of great use. It is not, however, always necessary.
Useful.
These sentences stand between Catherine's dramatic outburst condemning her father's contempt for love and the father's realization that his daughter has given up on him.
Irony is contempt.
The usefulness of which James and Dr. Sloper speak precludes all moral and aesthetic necessity.
This, too, is insinuated.
However vulgarly one triumphs over the struggling figures of *Tristan,* or Mrs. Penniman's *ruins of the Pantheon* – it's clear that James was too broken down to get along without her.

4.

There are few traces of love in this love story.

Catherine is more or less paralyzed in admiration of her father. The father, like the villain in a medieval drama, shows no amiable qualities.

Catherine is wounded not by his coldness, but his hatred.

But no sign of sweat, or semen – only once is there a reference to ejaculation, and then only in a figurative sense.

When people, bodies, and actions are seen as objects, when irony is examined with a regard to its possible applications, does it not seem as if the melodrama and its accompanying social critique are merely a pretense for a radically different project?

Is the one the (quite different) other?

And which one is that?

Catherine is repeatedly designated the *heroine* – thus as the heroic figure in a work of fiction.

When Morris says –

It was the way a young man might talk in a novel; or, better still, in a play, on the stage, close before the footlights, looking at the audience, and with everyone looking at him, so that you wondered at his presence of mind (20)

– followed by the false, self-contradictory declaration:

And yet Mr. Townsend was not like an actor; he seemed so sincere, so natural

the latter agrees with the former, in a roundabout way.

He was not *like* an actor – he was a born actor: appearance is his nature, the only mode in which he is able to seem sincere.

To play the love-smitten fool, for money, is his calling.

The false costume is the only genuine one he has.

On page 68 we read of Dr. Sloper's *most professional laugh*, later his *professional smile*.

Are the flighty Morris and his flagellant denouncer blood brothers – like Sloper and James – does the doctor's deadly hatred of Morris conceal a theatrical affinity?

The playlike unreality of the events is signaled in Mrs. Penniman's wish:

She, too, expected to figure in the performance – to be the confidante, the Chorus, to speak the epilogue (50).

The Objective and the Subjective Author

The reader cannot know whether the author makes this "learned error" intentionally or not – James who likewise has Mrs. Penniman constantly refer to the *ruins of the Pantheon,* with no indication that it's a mere lapse of snobbery (– I admit that this would bother me less, if the American author didn't know that the grave of Raphael is not housed in ruins, but in a totally intact structure); in any case the chorus, as one knows since Hölderlin and Nietzsche, whose *Birth of Tragedy* appeared eleven years before *Washington Square,* is hardly the confidante of tragic heroes; the epilogue, though, does belong to Mrs. Penniman, in a strange way.

Page 102, toward the end of the book's third part, a new motif is taken up.
Mrs. Almond says:
I don't see why it should be such a joke that your daughter adores you.
It is to the point where the adoration stops that I find it interesting to fix, the physician answers.
It stops where the other sentiment begins, responds his more human sister.
Not at all; that would be simple enough. The two things are extremely mixed up, and the mixture is extremely odd. It will produce some third element, and that's what I'm waiting to see.
A question of budding sexuality and the disassociation from one's parents.
Like in *Oedipus.*
Or *Hamlet.*
Or *Les Enfants terribles.*
The third element.
Twelve pages later, the resourceful Mrs. Almond remarks:
It's a pity Catherine can't marry her.
It's a pity that Catherine can't marry Morris Townsend's sister, who gets along well with the doctor.
On page 120 the theme of female homosexuality is more openly introduced:
Catherine . . . had often longed for the company of some intelligent person of her own sex. To tell her story to some kind woman – at

moments it seemed to her that this would give her comfort, and she had more than once been on the point of taking the landlady, or the nice young person from the dressmaker's, into her confidence. If a woman had been near her, she would on certain occasions have treated such a companion to a fit of weeping; and she had an apprehension that, on her return, this would form her response to Aunt Lavinia's first embrace. In fact, however, the two ladies had met, in Washington Square, without tears; and when they found themselves together a certain dryness fell upon the girl's emotion.

I don't want to overinterpret the word *dryness* – two pages later James hides the word *ejaculations*, which in the 1870s suggested, primarily, an interjection or a deep sigh.

To Mrs. Penniman she had been lavishly generous, and Aunt Lavinia spent half an hour in unfolding and folding again, with little ejaculations of gratitude and taste.

The object that she folds and unfolds is kept concealed by a grammatical sleight of hand.

Taste appears here not in the sense of judgment, but of pleasure. Let's look for a moment at the "ejaculations." A rather ornate term, it conjures up sexuality as well as clinical observation; neither heterosexual women nor lesbians have "ejaculations," however.

Only men ejaculate.

Is James mirroring, in his novel, his own dependency upon an older parent?

Upon his mother?

Is the impossible marriage of Catherine Sloper his own?

Is Catherine stubbornly, and wrongly, devoted to her father, like the homosexual author, obsessed with a man who despises him?

Is it a man with whom James wished to spend his life, just as Catherine hopes to happily spend the rest of hers (165), with Mrs. Penniman?

If there is such a thing as a homosexual style, can we distinguish between homosexual novelists and writers with homosexual inclinations?

Henry James teases Mrs. Penniman, italicizes her comments.

Henry James qualifies his own comments – with italics, quotation marks, and parentheses.

The Objective and the Subjective Author

Queer speech is vague, indirect speech.
Nowhere are there more quotation marks than on the fliers tacked up in gay bars, during carnival season.
But if understatement, alienation, hyperbole, irony, and travesty are more frequent in Henry James than in, say, Maupassant or Henry Miller – I don't mean to imply any qualitative judgment by my choice of examples – this only demonstrates the difficulty one has in isolating declared heterosexual writers.
To speak of homosexual authors, and a homosexual style, presupposes that there is such a thing as a heterosexual literary style and heterosexual standards of judgment.
And:
Can it be the task of literary criticism to canonize biologistical criteria, when the biologists switch them around every season?

5.

Washington Square is the book's title – the action of the entire story takes place in and around the small, parklike plaza.
Mrs. Penniman dreams of stormy evenings for a farewell visit – and Henry James ironizes the melodramatic effect of natural events, their seeming correspondence to psychic states (147). This irony, too, is a trap, an alibi – one of the decisive arguments between father and daughter takes place before a gloomy Alpen panorama – a view, moreover, which has been carefully sought out by the father.
If there's a metaphor, a utopia in this caustic melodrama, a space of untainted nature, it would have to be Washington Square.
The sloppiness, the inconsistency – the slackness, even, with which James distributes his adjectives and reflections, marks also his treatment of the *locus amoenus*, the "pleasant space," the park that lends the novel its name.
Sometimes Washington Park is the viper's nest of the House of Sloper, an address – and sometimes it is the square in front of it, one of the Baudelairean Isles of the Blest.
The ideal of quiet and genteel retirement, in 1835, was found in Washington Square (15).
1835: Goethe was already dead, and Hölderlin, though still alive, was mentally deranged, as the saying goes . . .

The Gay Critic

. . . the park contained a considerable quantity of inexpensive vegetation, enclosed by a wooden paling, which increased its rural and accessible appearance (16).

I know not, writes James, *whether it is owing to the tenderness of early associations, but this portion of New York appears to many persons the most delectable. It has a kind of established repose which is not of frequent occurrence in other quarters of the long, shrill city; it has a riper, richer, more honorable look than any of the upper ramifications of the great longitudinal thoroughfare – the look of having had something of a social history. It was here, as you might have been informed on good authority, that you had come into a world which appeared to offer a variety of sources of interest; it was here that your grandmother lived in venerable solitude, and dispensed a hospitality which commended itself alike to the infant imagination and the infant palate; it was here that you took your first walks abroad, following the nursery-maid with unequal step, and sniffing up the strange odor of the ailanthus-trees which at that time formed the principal umbrage of the Square, and diffused an aroma that you were not yet critical enough to dislike as it deserved; it was here, finally, that your first school, kept by a broad-bosomed, broad-based old lady with a ferule, who was always having tea in a blue cup, with a saucer that didn't match, enlarged the circle both of your observations and your sensations. It was here, at any rate, that my heroine spent many years of her life; which is my excuse for this topographical parenthesis.*

One of the crucial encounters between the chubby, soon-to-be-wealthy heroine and Morris the dashing legacy-hunter – where shall it take place?
Do you want to meet in the [Washington] park at noon? Morris suggested.
Catherine answers a page later:
You must come to the house (49).
Morris Townsend tells the romantic aunt, Mrs. Penniman
that her niece preferred, unromantically, an interview in a chintz-covered parlor to a sentimental tryst beside a fountain sheeted with dead leaves, and she . . .
It's unclear who – Catherine herself, or her aunt.

. . . was lost in wonderment at the oddity – almost the perversity – of the choice.
The perversity of the choice.
But four pages later, we find out that what he's really referring to, in his double-tongued way, is the condition prior to the result of the choice: for Mrs. Penniman, as she reflects on the *oddity – almost the perversity – of the choice,* makes it very clear that it isn't the chintz that is perverse – in fact she finds it very appropriate that the meeting not take place next to a fountain in Washington Square, but rather in a residence of the same address – which is to say: it's the landscape, nature itself that, in this society, seems odd, almost perverse – that same nature that is affixed to the living room's chintz wallpaper in the form of autumnal scenes.
And the severe, levelheaded Catherine is also relieved not to have to admit to her father that their engagement had been arranged outside, underneath the "naked" trees – of course it isn't the trees that are naked, but Catherine, who would have felt exposed, like a perverse exhibitionist.

(Mrs. Penniman considers a locale to meet with her niece's sweetheart – she seeks "neutral ground."
Her first thought is the Greenwood Cemetery – James had earlier spoken of the *dead leaves* of Washington Square; and after this, the Battery – but here it would be too cold and windy – and besides, it was often filled with Irish immigrants.
James himself was of Irish descent; still, he doesn't hesitate here to insult his own ethnic group, through the reflections of his hated character.
James opposes the park, which the gently teased Mrs. Penniman had called *perverse,* full of dead leaves, to the kitschy, blossoming cemetery.
Mrs. Penniman finally decides upon an oyster saloon on Seventh Avenue, which is run by a black man.
A concealed racist sentiment on the part of the author?
On page 83 James writes that Mrs. Penniman made her way home, through crowded streets, to the preserve of Washington Square – and on page 104, she experiences a moment of terror at the thought of being banished from the respectable address, of

The Gay Critic

being forced to survive on the streets – like the bag women, today, on the same Washington Square.)

Following that most cruel of insults with which the father wounds his daughter, accusing her of having bad taste – we witness the most extreme gesture of defiance on the part of the daughter:
She will write to her lover and arrange a rendezvous in the park, in Washington Square (111). After the passage in which Henry James, as a lesbian's kindred spirit, describes Catherine as a homosexual, the heroine and Mrs. Penniman meet "in" Washington Square for a first embrace (120).
In fact without tears, in fact, however, in Washington Square – the writer's hand trembles at the sensitive juncture.
The residence on Washington Square even has an effect on the venal, legacy-hunting Morris: he becomes domesticated, he consorts, giddily, with Mrs. Penniman, he calms her fears, just as he would have done for his own mother (132).
The disordered indecision in which the author elaborates the figurations of Washington Square becomes clear on page 164, where the address of the slanted Sloper house and the *locus amoenus* appear in the same paragraph:
She [Catherine] preferred Washington Square to any other habitation whatever.
The middle of August found her still in the heated solitude of Washington Square.
. . . she appeared quite content with such rural impressions as she could gather at the parlor-window from the ailanthus trees behind the wooden paling. The peculiar fragrance of this vegetation . . .
Catherine looks out into the *warm darkness* of the park, and, like a ghost, the handsome lover returns, after a twenty-five year absence. And once again she rejects him.
. . . with her confused, petty, dry manner, as Townsend then says to Mrs. Penniman.
Here, too, a fragment of the author's self-portrait?
It was here, at any rate, that my heroine spent many years of her life; which is my excuse for this topographical parenthesis.

This statement is, of course, not true.

As any of James's friends or family must have known.
He lived in Washington Square as a young boy.
Washington Park seemed to him, in the midst of the busy, shrill world of Manhattan, with its long, broad thoroughfares, as a haven of untamed nature, a place of corruption, as well as a preserve of the European tradition – like the "pleasant space" itself, the *locus amoenus* that is a commonplace of the classical tradition.
Why does the author write this lie?
To lay stress on the truth – the truth of his own childhood?
A lie which poses not only the problem of Jamesian sincerity – which is, admittedly, not a problem for everyone – but also the more pervasive and destabilizing dilemma of the Jamesian assertion.
Such an attitude brings James nearer to the tradition of manneristic and baroque distortion, of European "courtesy," in the literal sense – a distortion that is refracted in the one-liner I heard recently in New York:
Always be sincere whether you mean it or not.
(And, I might add, this joke was told to me by the emigrée Helen Wolff.)
Washington Square is no topographical parenthesis – it's the title of the book, for God's sake.
The phrase *topographical parenthesis,* moreover, is a doubly false designation.
The digression has little to do with topography, but with the psychology of the early, formative years of childhood, the psychology of memory – a doubly false nomination that – just as in mathematics – turns back on itself and bites truth on the tail.
Topos is also the term, in the study of rhetoric, for "commonplace" – the topos as a flat and empty phrase, which is transformed, in the novel, into the truth of the writer's childhood.
And perhaps the indecision that marks James's treatment of this space – now a nest of vipers, now a pleasant park – is carefully calculated?
The object of his discourse may be history itself.
The buildings on Washington Park have *something of a social history.*

Of all the characters in the novel, only Catherine is vouchsafed history, private and public, and with a capital H.

Catherine looks out from her dwelling onto Washington Park. The heroine and the utopian space converge so radically, via the concept of history, as to be almost indistinguishable, in the same way that the figure of Dr. Sloper blurs with the subjective and objective author.

The history of a mode of living, of manners and mannerisms in the New York of the mid–nineteenth century.

Madame Bovary c'est moi.

The poet as the space of utopia.

The heroine of the book is James himself, whose childhood on Washington Square conditioned the future Henry James.

The psychotic self-exposure "masked" in effusive language, this "hiding out in the open" is reminiscent of other kinds of relations – economic ones; in applying his overly subtle version of European social topoi to the reality of New York, James becomes their critic and sworn enemy.

6.

The stuff of this love story is above all money, and hatred:

The most honorable and socially acclaimed father and doctor is concerned, from the beginning, with money, but not in the immediate sense: rather with his holdings, the prospective size of Catherine's inheritance. By means of money he tries to coerce her; by money he tries to absolve himself of all responsibility (72).

The suitor is, from the outset, a money-grubbing dowry hunter. On two occasions this scoundrel is prepared to forgo Catherine's paternal inheritance, to marry her only for mother's money – still a sizable sum – and on two occasions she rejects his calculated show of emotion; pension-not-passion is the bottom line in both instances; for Morris Townsend – as Sloper and either author have long since concluded – is, and remains, essentially venal.

Mrs. Penniman's financial flaw is built into her name, as it is into Morris Townsend's – Mr. Outskirts – as well.

Catherine can't be bought, as she proves a final time – the stakes raised, in quasi-abstract fashion – when her father tries to wrest an assurance from her, in exchange for her entire inheritance, that she won't marry Morris Townsend.

The Objective and the Subjective Author

If James did indeed identify with his heroine, this scene would suggest that he, too, was emphatically not for sale.

At least not in the realm of the sentimental.

Anyone who attends 107 dinner receptions in the space of two years (1878–79), as James did, is clearly a socialite, someone who spiced the soup of his society – a society that scorned and harassed homosexuals; nor is it likely that he made so many entrances wearing the same suit from Savile Row.

Early in the novel, James writes:

"You are sumptuous, opulent, expensive!" her father rejoined. "You look as if you had eighty thousand a year!"

"Well, so long as I haven't," said Catherine illogically.

That's not true. Catherine does not speak illogically – something the objective author wishes to reveal, through the chatter of the subjective author.

She follows an inexorable logic:

Not having the kind of money her outfit suggests, she can wear expensive clothing without feeling guilty.

Money, for Catherine, is associated with guilt and sin.

Later, as Morris presses her to marry him and she holds him off, that she might not sever the paternal bond, her thoughts are driven by a reflection on the word *disinheritance*:

The terrible word disinheritance, with all its impressive moral reprobation, was still ringing there – seemed, indeed, to gather force as it lingered. The mortal chill of her situation struck more deeply into her childlike heart, and she was overwhelmed by a feeling of loneliness and danger.

Catherine can't be bought – but, like any well-bred woman, she buys, without shame.

She is desired by the most seductive man in New York – Catherine, James, and both authors add:

it was some time before she could believe again that this beautiful young man was her own exclusive property.

Here the open, hard gaze of the young and inexorably logical heroine veils what is, essentially, an ownership relation – for as James says, she could have had him for herself through her maternal inheritance alone; only her father's money is, from the outset, off limits.

What possibilities for happiness were available to a homosexually inclined writer in the early heyday of New York, in the England of Wilde and Casement?
The examples of Melville and Whitman are also illuminating.
The archives of the Institute for the Sexual Sciences have nothing to say on the subject of this underworld.
There must have been some form of prostitution.
The master, bloodless, on the one side – the rich customer, yielding, on the other.
And is this how Catherine imagined it – did the poor, dull, insipid, charmless girl expect to get laid for free by the hottest gigolo in town, a man with a flair for lively banter and a wild, mysterious past?!
The operatic father and both authors know that Morris Townsend must be interested in one thing only: money.
And James thereby expresses the hope that he, too, might be able to win a Morris Outskirts for himself – by granting him such an authorial honor.
Or can we be so sure?
Must we endure the salon sarcasm of the father, the almost total lack of response on the part of the artificially insipid daughter, the shadow affair of the idiotic Mrs. Penniman with her beau from the country, an affair in which the master caricatures himself, in a gesture of self-debasement driven by a longing after justice? We all know the many reincarnations of Mrs. Penniman, as far off as parts 1 and 2 of *La Cage aux folles,* and no longer need them so artfully rendered – to the point of making us want to puke.
We can't hope to summarize, in a few lines, the cognitive content of this remarkable Penguin paperback:
In the presence of a strong paternal bond, it's difficult for a woman to enter into a marriage.
Love and sexuality only seem to exercise such an influence on the psychosocial – our actions are rather more determined by power, vanity, egoistic self-validation, and lucre.
James translates these kinds of considerations in order to paraphrase his own homosexuality and to shed light on the economic position of the wealthy author – similar to that of a prostitute's client.

The Objective and the Subjective Author

I'm being unfair.

It isn't that the 174 pages of *Washington Square* are redundant, but rather that the mode in which its events are portrayed is such that the language – as in the case of the much-used adjective *good* – seems to control the author, rather than vice versa.

It would interest me to know how Henry James worked, how he planned, composed, outlined, and revised.

He liked to dine out, he was a talkative sort, like Humboldt, who visited three salons a day in Paris.

Henry James pursued the virtues of rhetorical cunning, the subtle point, the still inexhausted postromantic irony, and the short, brilliant enunciation.

Who else, ancient or modern, has written prose of such a dense vibrancy?

Who else has attained to James's complexity?

Borges and Genet, among the living.

And the dead?

The Deceived?

Les Enfants terribles?

Le Petit ami?

Perhaps Billy Budd as well, and the *Marquise of O*.

Reproach Henry James for his irony?

What would lively speech be without irony, without this pleasure of the happy few and the melancholiac.

There is reason enough to forgive James a few twisted adjectives – if the poet had only not tampered with them, after writing his text, to spare his work the barren perfection of *La Double méprise*.